RHAPSODY IN QUEBEC

AKOS VERBOCZY

RHAPSODY IN QUEBEC

ON THE PATH OF AN IMMIGRANT CHILD

Translated by Casey Roberts

Baraka
Books

Montréal

Translation © Baraka Books 2017

© Éditions du Boréal, Montréal, Québec 2016

ISBN 978-1-77186-102-1 pbk; 978-1-77186-103-8 epub; 978-1-77186-104-5 pdf; 978-1-77186-105 -2 mobi/pocket

Book Design and Cover by Folio infographie
Cover illustration: Bruce Roberts
Editing and proofreading: Robin Philpot

Legal Deposit, 2nd quarter 2017
Bibliothèque et Archives nationales du Québec
Library and Archives Canada

Published by Baraka Books of Montreal
6977, rue Lacroix
Montréal, Québec H4E 2V4
Telephone: 514 808-8504
info@barakabooks.com
www.barakabooks.com

Printed and bound in Quebec

Société
de développement
des entreprises
culturelles
Québec

We acknowledge the support from the Société de développement des entreprises culturelles (SODEC) and the Government of Quebec tax credit for book publishing administered by SODEC.

Financé par le gouvernement du Canada
Funded by the Government of Canada | Canada

Trade Distribution & Returns
Canada and the United States
Independent Publishers Group
1-800-888-4741 (IPG1);
orders@ipgbook.com

CONTENTS

Foreword   9

Where I'm from   19

STEP ONE: START BY ARRIVING
Wartburg Blues   27
The Boys of Kárpát Street   31
The dreams of my mother   34
All Quiet on the Western Front   39
Farewell my country   43
Living in America   47
Back to the future   52
The languages we are   56
An American Epic   60
For better and for worse   64
Mr. Nicolas's class   67
The trial   70
"Nigger Black"   72
The Half-Jew   78
Workers of all countries…   82
The Man Who Failed   85

STEP TWO: FIND YOUR WAY
Everyone needs a soul mate   91
God, Woody Allen and me   96
The Gazette   100
Frenchement better!   103

The enigma of the return   108
The Musketeers   112
On Queen Mary   117
The Not-So-Nice Dance   120
1990   124
The "Québécois"   128
Madagascar Power   133
The Apprenticeship of Duddy Kravitz   137
Sneedronningen   143
Hungarian Rhapsodies   146

STEP THREE: ARRIVE AT THE BEGINNING
The life before us   153
A day in the life of a deputy returning officer   157
The words of a man of his word   162
Money and ethnic votes   167
The time of the buffoons   175
The human zoo   181
Land of others   186
Multiculturalization   190
The Perfect Foreigner   193
Montreal Tango   197
Nous   202
Rusalka   206
The shit rains down on my head   211
The Grand Seduction   217
The banality of evil   223
Mon pays (My country)   229
Where are we headed?   234

FOREWORD

"There are as many ways to be a Quebecer as there
are ways to love this place"

One might think there would be something off-setting
and discombobulating about writing a foreword for a book
I thoroughly enjoyed reading, yet didn't wholeheartedly
agree with, but that wasn't the case at all.

Reading Akos Verboczy's book left me entertained,
moved, on my toes, occasionally aggravated, and more than
once questioning and reassessing a few things I previously
took for granted. In other words, it felt exactly like living
in Quebec.

His journey as a young Hungarian Jew who emigrates to
Montreal with his family at the age of eleven, his linguistic
and educational trajectory as a child of Bill 101, and his
gradual transformation into a full-blown, proud, and committed Quebecer is one that I identified with – often
intensely, and occasionally not at all.

Anyone born into an immigrant family, wrestling with
the constant push and pull of what has been left behind and
what needs to be firmly established anew, understands the
unique challenges of navigating the "otherness" while bat-
tling it out with the "same" – both in one's own cultural
and linguistic community and within Quebec overall.

Unlike Verboczy, I was born here to first-generation Greek immigrant parents, and a few years later I returned to their homeland. My formative years were spent abroad. I am not a child of Bill 101. I didn't learn to speak French because I was mandated to. I learned it because to live in a place and not understand or speak the language of the majority would have been absurd to me. Not speaking French would have condemned me to a life in a linguistic and cultural ghetto, to life as an outsider, forever looking in. And I wanted in.

The overwhelming majority of immigrants do, as well.

While the author and I may disagree on our partisan politics, our definitions of what constitutes integration, and the PQ's ill-fated Charter of Values, we both consider this place home. We both agree that the survival and the celebration of the French culture and language are essential and primordial, and we both identify as Quebecers more than we will ever identify as Canadian.

Despite constant linguistic insecurity in this province (some justified, some questionable) my impression is that Bill 101 has succeeded in what it set out to do; ensuring that the French language remains dominant and the public language, face, and voice of Quebec. Contrary to popular belief, you will find few Quebecers (regardless of background) who disagree with that.

The recurring problem we have here is that we don't often make room for the moderates to be heard, while we allow the voices of division (on either side of the linguistic fence) to speak way too loudly. By doing so, we continue to allow ourselves to be defined by our stereotypes and clichés, which, in turn, allows politicians of all colours to manipulate us as they see fit. It's frustrating to watch play out.

When, the day after Jacques Parizeau's death, I wrote a column urging Anglophones and Allophones to get over his dreaded "money and ethnic vote" line, uttered in frustration after the '95 referendum defeat, arguing that one sentence (as unfortunate as it was) couldn't possibly define someone's entire political legacy, I was praised by French media. I was subsequently invited on to the French-language TV program *"125, Marie-Anne"* where I was – very politely – treated as a slight oddity. I came home that night to three hundred more followers on Twitter and messages from francophone Quebecers who seemed so grateful that an Allophone understood their point of view. In sharp contrast, I was treated as either naïve or a traitor by most Anglophones and Allophones.

The following week I wrote an op-ed for the *National Post*, defending Montreal actor Jay Baruchel's move to Toronto and the comments he made about life there being "easier," which were seen by most French media as a personal affront and a betrayal of Quebec. My role and image were suddenly reversed, as Anglophones and Allophones rushed to share it, ex-pats called to commiserate, and Francophones, once again, saw me as just another Anglophone who didn't get it.

The above scenarios have been repeated ad nauseum in my professional life as a columnist and pundit, as I often find myself defending Quebec's point of view to the rest of Canada, while pointing out the often-opportunistic identity politics and blame game I see play out in our local media. It's an often slightly schizophrenic existence, but I like it.

Verboczy writes with a clear-eyed, caustic, tongue-in-cheek tone when he discusses the "quid pro quo" nature of immigration. He makes no qualms about the "why's." A perilously low birth rate and an aging population make it necessary for Canada (and by extent, Quebec) to open their doors to people who are seeking better opportunities here.

In a tone devoid of any sentimentality he describes his slow but steady transformation into a French-speaking,

PQ-card-carrying, separatist Quebecer. While sharing his story he also challenges traditional notions of plurality and diversity being automatic virtues when we discuss immigrants, and he does so with wry wit and fair observations.

He has fun pointing out the discrepancies, the biases, and the hypocrisy inherent in social and political movements – even when he's occasionally guilty of a few of his own. He justifiably mocks Quebec's cultural communities' tendency to vote in predictable Liberal patterns, yet often fails to turn that critical finger inward and question why that is.

Living in a place where two linguistic minorities (French-speaking Quebecers within Canada, English-speaking people in Quebec) feel they constantly need to have their backs up against the wall can be exhausting.

This perpetual sense of victimhood, of survival, of needing to constantly reassert ourselves or risk being assimilated into the hodgepodge of a multicultural stew of a country that continues to struggle to define exactly what it is and what it stands for, often creates unease, tension, anger, frustration, and animosity on all fronts. In our struggle for self-respect and self-determination we become more focused on defining ourselves by what we reject, instead of what we embrace. It needn't be so.

Everything that takes place in Quebec has always fascinated me. This energy that is both clash and coaction, both collision and cooperation, creates something palpable that, if properly nourished and cared for, produces magic.

Unlike Verboczy who sees downsides in the politics of diversity and the celebration of multiculturalism, I revel in it. I believe it's our largest strength if harnessed properly. I've come to accept that there is no one universal "right" experience of being an immigrant and becoming part of this place. There is no one size fits all.

I also recognize it often takes more than one generation for an immigrant to identify with another culture. Patience is a virtue when it comes to both the person knocking on a new reality and the person opening that door. It's something we all should keep in mind as attitudes towards immigration (both in Quebec and in the rest of Canada) seem to be hardening.

Quebec can be just as susceptible to opportunistic identity politics as the rest of the world. Anti-immigrant tensions fuelled by ignorance and fear of the "other" remain a contentious issue that politicians easily and maliciously manipulate on their determined quest for easy votes. The irrefutable fact, however, remains that bilingualism rates have increased with each generation and a French Quebec continues to remain a forceful political, linguistic, and cultural presence – both within Canada, and perhaps as a separate entity down the road.

It seems that French Quebecers continue to underestimate the love and loyalty Allophones and Anglophones have for Quebec, while Allophones and Anglophones continue to underestimate Francophones' openness and desire to be embraced.

One doesn't need to reject the "other" to be part of the "us." Diversity, multilingualism, and multiculturalism are attributes, not albatrosses around our collective necks. Younger Quebecers, raised in a post Bill 101 era, comfortable in their bilingual duality and often-trilingual existence have access to the world in a way that previous generations did not.

While I don't fear sovereignty and, unlike many Allophones and Anglophones, don't consider it as a betrayal of Canada but a very legitimate conversation to have, I'm also not emotionally attached to the idea. Quebec is home to me in a way Canada will never be, but, unlike the author, I hope for a day that Canada will be truly bilingual and bi-national, fully cognisant of its history, fully respectful of Quebec's role in it.

In the meantime, I applaud and welcome the book's translation into English. More conversations like these are needed and more books on what it means to be a Quebecer need to be written in both languages and read by us all.

Racial and gender equality, and respect of real diversity and inclusiveness will be the challenges of the future – and they will affect all of us, regardless of background. Static and stale notions of what a "real" Quebecer is supposed to look like, act like, speak like, vote like, feel archaic to me.

Acceptance means finding common ground, evolving and moving forward together, and ultimately, understanding that – in so much as we ensure the French language and culture continue to thrive – there are as many ways to be a Quebecer as there are ways to love this place. Akos Verboczy's story provides one fascinating example.

Toula Drimonis, February 2017

To my mother, who at my age, left her country to come to mine.

"Where am I from?" recited Kornél to himself, intoxicated by the espresso and lack of sleep. "Where everybody's from. The purple cavern of a mother's womb. I too started out from there on an uncertain journey, and neither destiny nor destination are stated in the passport."

Dezső Kosztolányi, Adventures Of Kornél Esti*

---

* Dezső Kosztolányi, Adventures Of Kornél Esti, translated by Bernard Adams. New Directions Publishing, 2011.

WHERE I'M FROM

Where'm I from? I thought you might want to ask, you seem like that kind of person. You should know that I've been ok with it for a long time now. When you come to a foreign country, with a foreign name, and a foreign accent, you naturally become an object of curiosity. True, you could have waited until we had at least taken our seats and glanced at the menu, but don't worry about it, I'd be glad to try to give you an answer.

I usually start wondering if something's wrong when people don't ask. Your discretion is admirable, but really, don't hesitate, I see that you're dying to know. It's only in the third-person that I resent being asked, as in: "Where's this guy think he comes from?" There's plenty of room at our table, so please, come join us.

Feelings of vulnerability or impatience can be boulders in the path of a foreigner wanting to make something of his life in his adopted country. Being asked about your origins can start to feel imposing, but you might as well just get used to it. I even think it's a good way to launch a conversation. I bought myself a remote starter. Where'm I from? Click! I push the button, and my answer is sent before I even think about it. It may seem like a long time and maybe unnecessary to have to wait five minutes while the car warms up, but it runs better if you do.

Well, good guess, but my family name isn't Polish, it's Hungarian. My first name has a *"sh"* sound at the end:

"Akosh." (What? You're already playing word games? You're so original!) People pronounce my last name however they want. No, no, I haven't forgotten my mother tongue, I still speak it, but not that often: only with my family and on the increasingly infrequent trips back home.

So, yeah, I was eleven when I came to Montreal, and that's when I first started learning French. Nice of you to congratulate me, but I didn't really have any say in the matter. My religion? Umm, let's see, how should I say this? I'm pretty Jewish, but that doesn't mean I can't wait to talk about the Israeli-Palestinian conflict. And I too found it hard to believe that a simple wire stretched around Outremont – I think the word you're looking for is "*eruv*" – could have changed much in the eyes of God. And, I'm sorry, but I don't know your high school music teacher who fled Hungary in 1956. But I'm sure he was great; it's a common cultural characteristic where I come from.

There you have it. Now you know where I'm *from*, but that doesn't necessarily mean you know where I'm *coming from*. Don't be too quick to jump to conclusions (because that, on the other hand, *would* probably irritate me).

I'm an immigrant, true. The term doesn't bother me; the word describes a reality that happens to be mine. Just accept it that *being* an immigrant hasn't really been something that's been on my mind 24/7 over the years. And that coming from somewhere else, just like being from here, is neither a virtue or a sin, nor an interesting fact, nor irrelevant, in and of itself. The immigrant is not – by nature – a victim to be pitied nor a hero to worship, nor a person to be afraid of. But neither is he *the same as everybody else;* he's not *like you and me.* Like you, I mean.

If they examined my DNA under a multicultural microscope, the genome would be a mix at once unstable and dissonant (think Elvis Gratton in a Pierre Falardeau film):

Hungarian-Quebecois, judeo-christian, French-speaking, Eastern European – North American.

This formula is more practical than it might seem. It more than satisfies the criteria for equal opportunity programs and lets me cut ahead of you in the line waiting for the social status elevator while you deal with your guilt over how you have oppressed your (Hungarian) minorities over the years. It also gained me more than a few invitations to social events, forums and conferences, maybe even some jobs and scholarships. While you... don't make me laugh with all the privileges you enjoy as a member of the majority...

I'm like other immigrants, but not like every other immigrant. I'm one among the million who have come to Quebec over the three decades since I came, attracted by the promise of a better life. The majority were *chosen* by Quebec as "economic immigrants," others *admitted* as refugees or *reunified* with their families by the federal government. Some came as children, most of them were adults; some came by themselves, others as part of a couple or family. Some came with pockets full, others were destitute and counting on getting help from their families, the community or the government. Some spoke French, others not a word. Some came to embrace Quebec's uniqueness, others came in spite of it, and still others could have cared less. Some were adventurers, others had a thoughtfully crafted game plan. Some stayed only long enough to obtain their passports, others *never left*. People ended up here by chance or by plan; often, a little bit of both. And they were all supposedly destined to enrich Quebec, financially and culturally, according to official propaganda and general consensus.

I'm no doubt one of the "Saviours" welcomed to Quebec to help solve your problems: your economy, the balance of political power in your dealings with Canada, your debt, your aging, your labour shortage and, of course, the fact that you're closed to the world. That's a lot of weight on my shoulders (and on others like me), and also represents a lot of promises made to the *Québécois de souche.** There will be more than enough legitimate disappointments to go around later on down the road.

You certainly can't blame that on me! I think that so far, I've done my part for the integration of immigrants in general and of myself in particular. And it seems to me that, quite frankly, you have too. But the line outside the American Dream boutique is stretching longer by the day, and it's no surprise that for every person intrigued by identity and cultural politics, there is another who is troubled by how these politics play out on the ground.

The problems of alienation and increasing social, ethnic and religious tensions that confront countries that accept large numbers of immigrants aren't going to go away by ignoring them, through magical thinking, or victimization.

I'm not one to cast the first stone, nor to turn the other cheek. I'm not a bird of ill omen, an ostrich with my head in the sand, a caribou ready to charge down a ravine. But I'm foolish enough to want to tackle the challenge of the integration of immigrants in Quebec without engaging in flights of fancy, bureaucratic double speak, or giving too much credence to taboos: in my mind, that's the only way to be able to look at where we are and *where we're headed.*

I no longer hesitate to claim the heritage of the Quebec that adopted me and that I ended up adopting as my own; to describe myself as a "child" of the political will to make Quebec a French-speaking state; and to want to pass along

---

* Could be translated as "old-stock Quebecers.".

this same determination so that there might one day be "grandchildren" of Bill 101.*

If I have to be labelled, "Child of Bill 101" works for me. A smiley-face sticker kindly stuck on the immigrant children who were forced by the Charter of the French Language to attend French schools from 1977 on, and who then chose to integrate into the French-speaking majority. These children are welcomed into the extended family in varying degrees, but they mostly feel – or believe – that their future is first and foremost tied to the people of Quebec.

This formula isn't perfect; I'd rather talk about what unites us. Our epoch is obsessed with differences; every person wants to stand out, people want to be recognized for their uniqueness. That's not my way. We don't tend to describe ourselves – and others don't describe us – on the basis of our achievements, our ideas, our passions or our interests, but instead insist on what sets us biologically or culturally apart. Collective projects aren't accomplished by fragmenting into various different identity groups or by dividing communities, but rather through finding our greatest commonality.

The point of departure of any collective project for Quebec, as for any nation, is that everyone feel that it's their home, including the descendants of its first peoples, descendants of the people who colonized it and the people who conquered it; and more recently, people who have come here as immigrants. This is obviously not in everybody's interest, especially the advocates of Canadian unity, who seek a Quebec that is fragmented and weak.

I don't deny that I still believe that to the extent that Quebec is autonomous and strong, it will be easier for it to integrate and accept the new immigrants.

---

* More accurately, the Charter of the French Language—trans.

It's hard to know what the future holds in store for Quebec. However, I'm positive that it won't look like the Quebec village from long ago in *Les Filles de Caleb*, nor the trendy Plateau-Mont-Royal neighbourhood I live in. And it certainly won't be through idealizing one and rejecting (or even worse, mocking or scorning) the other that we will arrive at what I think should be our collective goal: to safeguard and develop Quebec, building on what distinguishes it and what is best about it.

The advent of a Quebec where everyone feels at home and where no person will be foreign to the other will not come about by denying people's search for their identities or by turning all Quebecers into immigrants, whether they landed at Pierre Elliot Trudeau International a couple of days ago or the Île d'Orléans four hundred years ago. And certainly not by denying – whether out of shame or disrespect – Quebec's own identity, beginning with its most natural affinity: French. Neither will we get there by integrating immigrants into the economy without encouraging them to integrate culturally, for fear that their rights will be violated.

I want a Quebec where more immigrants can feel at home. Which is a feeling that I've been gradually acquiring, through happenstance and effort, without even realizing it. Today I call myself Québécois, with a few minor qualifications that persist even after being here for thirty years. But don't be too quick to wrap us up in the *Fleur-de-Lys*; it'd be better to start the story of this voyage at its beginning.

Please stay for a while, I'll treat you to dinner. I'm certain that we can come to understand each other.

STEP ONE:
START BY ARRIVING

WARTBURG BLUES

He waved until the VW had disappeared, and as he entered the terminal, alone, he smiled in spite of everything at the thought that there was, somewhere in the vastness of America, a secret place where the gods of the Indians and the other gods gathered and held council in order to watch over him and illuminate his path.

Jacques Poulin, *Volkswagen Blues**

We left in János's car, a gray Wartburg 353 Break Tourist dating, like me, from 1975. János was a friend of my mother's.

As for János, he dated from after the war, like almost all Hungarian adults around me. He was the only man I knew "who lived as a family" with women and children under the same roof, although the child wasn't actually his, but a stranger's, while his biological child was living with his ex-wife. More significantly, he was the only person in our entourage who owned a car, making him the designated driver of our escapes from the ordinary, out to the country for weekend getaways and, on the morning of March 1986, the most extraordinary of our adventures, to the Budapest Airport where we would fly away forever to Quebec.

Back in the day, the Wartburg was made by BMW, but that wasn't indicated anywhere on the car which, after the

---

* Translated by Casey Roberts.

split up of its country of origin, was a cheap castoff of German industrial engineering made in the East. In contrast to the cars made by its sister company, which had ended up in the West, it was noisy and polluting, even in comparison to Trabants, Ladas, Dacias, Škodas, Volkswagens and Polski Fiats, the only other kinds of cars that rolled down our streets. But we didn't put too much emphasis on the details; the important thing was that the Wartburg could carry as many adults and children as needed, with its wide polyester seats and its roomy hatchback trunk.

Being the littlest, I usually was the last to climb in, sandwiched in between the feet of the passengers in the front, seated on the thighs of the occupants in the rear, or if I was lucky, in the trunk.

I didn't have any such luck the morning of our flight, because a place in the back was freed up at the last minute, between a small suitcase and a big sister. It had been reserved for my grandmother, who was so distressed she couldn't handle coming with us to the airport, crowded as we were among the innumerable suitcases and jam-packed bags containing most of the essentials from our old life and the necessities of the new.

Born under the Austro-Hungarian Empire, she had survived two world wars and a sufficient number of civil wars and revolutions for her to have lost count. She had lived under the monarchy, the Republic, bolshevism, fascism, Nazism, Stalinism, socialism. She had lived under Romanian, German and Soviet occupation. She had lost her mother to illness at twelve, her job as a typist-stenographer at twenty-five because of anti-Jewish laws, her family at thirty because of the war and the Holocaust, her home and her shop at thirty-five because of collectivization, her husband at forty-seven, and her health and most of her sight after fifty years of work.

That morning in March 1986, at the age of seventy-five, she would lose what was left of her family: her only daughter, whom she had raised alone, and two grandchildren whom she had cared for tirelessly, as much out of necessity as out of love. This woman, who had faced so many trials with resilience and optimism and without ever complaining, feeling sorry for herself or casting herself as a victim of the twentieth century, forever lost her unforgettable smile that morning.

Standing in the winter dawn at the door of her building, leaning against the stone wall, her vision blurred by cataracts and gray goulash-communism, my grandmother couldn't track the silhouette of the Wartburg 353 Break Tourist as it drove away into the distance.

Nor could she see our hands, waving behind the windows in farewell, nor my mother, weeping at the thought of the tears in her mother's tired old eyes.

THE BOYS OF KÁRPÁT STREET

It was in this same Wartburg, seated in the back seat going the other direction when my mother came home from Canada, that I had found out four months earlier that I would be living in that country for the rest of my days.

My sister and I were asking questions in no particular order about her trip, whose true objectives we didn't know, while at the same time competing with each other to tell her about the beginning of the 1985 school year – for me fifth grade and for her, eighth – that my mother had just missed in order to visit friends in Toronto.

The most important event of my young life had just taken place: I had been nominated by my peers to be vice president of my class's Pioneers group. The Pioneers movement had defined my childhood despite its compulsory nature. To be precise, I became vice president of the movement's most basic unit, the club, which was comprised of the twelve boys in my class. I kind of inherited the position following the quick decision of a people's court to downgrade a comrade who, I assure you, wasn't worthy of holding such a position.

My best friend was the leader of the group, which was named after a nineteenth-century Hungarian poet. Not especially pleased with that old school choice, but without wanting to contradict anything official, we informally called ourselves "The Boys of Kárpát Street," a parody of the title of a popular novel from the turn of century we had all read. The novel represented for us an ideal of solidarity, of dedicating yourself to the group and of frank camaraderie, that truly inspired us (not so much for the disgraced boy whose position I had assumed, I swear). A kind of *Dog Who Stopped the War*, but where the kids fight each other with sticks instead of snow, and where it's not the dog who dies in the end, but the diminutive Ernő Nemecsek, the novel's hero.

"Kárpát" was for Carpates Street, where apartment buildings emerged from the dust of the precast concrete panels which housed the toiling post-war masses between the Berlin Wall and North Korea, including the students and staff of our school, located across the street.

The high-rises looked down on the Danube on one side, and on the other, the school's back yard, the exact spot where I solemnly promised – during our Pioneers swearing-in ceremony – in front of all the boys of Kárpát Street, to be loyal to the homeland and to work responsibly to build the people's republic.

A laudable goal, we all agreed, but in the short term, the group's priority was to make money. This seemed more useful than learning how to tie knots and build campfires, those not insignificant skills whose mastery occupied our fellow scouts in capitalist countries.

We didn't actually need much money, just enough to buy stuff that we couldn't get or things we needed or wanted at school or home. A cake for a birthday; boat tickets for a ride on the Danube; paint to fix up a classroom bookshelf; a hamster, its cage and funeral expenses; a bottle of wine to bribe the janitor when we wanted him to let us into the school on the weekend to play ping pong.

Our treasury was essentially derived from selling food at the annual fair and the collection of paper, fabric, glass and scrap metal sponsored by the sorting center. Nothing too complicated, but it required constant and collaborative work for which I always volunteered, a level of commitment that had just been officially recognized by my nomination.

"Mom, I've just been named VP of the Boys of Kárpát Street."

She didn't take the time to congratulate me. Without much of an introduction, my mother turned to face the back and pronounced my fate in words the sound of which I still clearly remember:

"Before you hear it from someone else, you should know that I've gotten married, and we're going to move to Canada."

My sister remembers my initial reaction. Years later, she still liked to recall my tearful response: "But... what's going to happen to the Boys?"

> *He felt for the first time, in his child's soul, the birth of an obscure feeling of what this life, taken as a whole, was all about; while sometimes joyful and sometimes sad, we are only humble servants, in constant struggle.*
>
> Ferenc Molnár, *The Boys of Paul Street*

---

* Translated from the French by Casey Roberts.

THE DREAMS OF MY MOTHER

M y mother decided to emigrate to Quebec when she found out the price for a full leg wax job in Canadian beauty salons.

"Wasn't it because she wanted a better life for you, her children?"

My mother thought her idea was sensible and felt it was in our best interest, just like she would have if she had decided to stay. And had she decided to stay, she couldn't have been accused of not taking good care of us. (My playmate from back then still lives at the same address and was no less loved by his parents, even if he was a bit of a brat.) Besides, my mother had thought about leaving Hungary in her twenties before having the intimate pleasure of knowing us, my sister and me, but my grandmother had vetoed the idea. The aim of the undertaking being to improve her lot, her fate was naturally linked to that of her family's. So, yes, if it makes you feel better to hear that the needs of her children were central to the most important decision of her life. But what finally convinced her, trust me, was the price of hair removal.

"It was also to escape an oppressive political system, right?"

To my knowledge, she wasn't exactly a dissident. She had no interest in opposing a system that was only dangerous to people who openly expressed their desire for change. During this period, the regime did open up and retired from the business of listening in to beauty salon gossip; what the women said to each from behind their skin conditioner face masks proved to be pretty unsubversive.

We lived a decent life, despite – or thanks to – the regime. We had a small but nice apartment in a central district of the capital. We could rely on free, quality health services and education. For a couple of *forints* (fifty cents) we could go to the theater or to a museum, and we had season passes to the opera, an important legacy that my mother insisted be passed on to us, since the pleasure of going to the theater was pretty much all that was left of our previous family fortune.

That said, the country's generosity was limited when it came to one sole member of the working class, far from the corridors of power. The red pin in the shape of a five-pointed star that was given to my mother in her capacity as "Exemplary Worker of the Northern Budapest Hairdressers and Beauticians Cooperative" simply wasn't enough. She toiled for minimum wage and received zero child support from my father.

Remnants of the dreams of her early twenties lingered, to which were added the new dreams of a forty-year-old woman. The dreams of a single mother, with no effective support, who was tired of her daily routine and her life, both of which were often difficult. Especially since they delivered at best a monotonous existence, set in concrete, a life of working to absurdity without the possibility of any change, towards a pension that wouldn't be adequate. A future even more unsatisfactory when constantly compared to that in store for others, people who always seemed to have whatever they wanted.

And suddenly the horizon cleared: the lure of being paid twenty dollars for leg hair removal as a beautician in Canada was enough to convince her she could leave her world behind. In Hungary, she had no hope for an inherit-ance, no chance of winning the lottery, no way to get rich quick as she had always hoped she might, convinced that it happened sooner or later to everyone except of course to her, even though her daily horoscope promised the opposite.

I'm not making this up. My mother really did decide to emigrate upon discovering that in Montreal, women were willing to pay an astronomical sum to have hot wax poured on their legs before having their hair brutally yanked out. For my mother it was as if she had found out she had a great-uncle who, not content with having survived the war, had gone on to become a millionaire in America.

As she pondered the meaning of the twenty dollars, she began to realize that she was free to move, that she had choices. "The advantage of my profession," she frequently said after deciding to emigrate, "is that there's no place on the planet where hair doesn't grow on women's legs."

She never offered any evidence in support of this hypoth-esis, but she was right. My mother practiced a profession for which no college equivalence or license was demanded. She didn't need advanced language proficiency and she could get a job anywhere in the world and possibly even open her own business. A worker as experienced as she could adapt to local practices without too much trouble while offering innovations interesting to her new clients, and at competitive prices. That last point being one of the most tangible benefits from immigration experienced by average citizen-consumers, justifying their conviction that immigration enriches their lives.

Except for refugees, who have entirely run out of options, the choice of whether people thinking about emigrating stay or go, like the choice of their final destination, is pri-marily an accounting exercise. Prospective immigrants subtract their future expenses (rent, food, school, health, transportation) from their potential income (wages, business profits, parental subsidies, social assistance) and compare the balance line to their current situation. Only university chairs in immigration studies in search of federal grants or people searching for discrimination would think to compare the result to the average income in the host country. Prospective immigrants don't (initially) have any such ambition. They are seeking to improve their situation. Period.

And once the cost-benefit analysis has been conducted, the calculation made that the balance is positive, the decision to leave taken, it would take clever persuasion to bend their will. Lost in their dreams, they don't hear the foghorn's warning.

Warning! it isn't easy to learn a new language; it'll take years, even more to learn two. You may never find a paying job that lives up to your expectations. Your resume, whether populated by truths or lies, won't open all doors. You will find the process of integration tedious; friends, a home in another culture and in another country, are not made easily. Don't think that it will automatically be easier for your children. The native-born aren't waiting to invite you over as soon as you arrive, and people in your community will often seem uninteresting. There is unemployment, long waits in emergency rooms, bed bugs, really stupid TV shows, buses that decide not to show up at twenty below and policy debates that you can't understand a word of.

Information about the challenges of integrating into the culture and local life can seem like insignificant data when put up against the possibility of living a better and more comfortable life. Plans are drawn up – quarterly projections, first month forecasts, and first and subsequent year balance sheets – with the unshakable optimism of an inventor who, once his prototype has been assembled, remains steadfast in the face of critics who point out the flaws, or even the total uselessness, of his invention. For the prospective immigrant, the engine of ambition is hope, its fuel optimism. Realism: the stick in the gears.

"With five waxings, I can buy a week's worth of groceries for my two children and me; with twenty others, I can pay the rent; ten more, pay the bills. For twenty years, I've worked a lot harder to make a lot less." Thus, FLW for "full leg waxing" became our official exchange currency in the months before our arrival in Montreal.

"And a remote controlled electric car is worth how many FLWs, Mom?"

"That'll depend on your grades in math."

My mother definitely had dreams for her children as well as for herself, but they weren't the kind that came with batteries.

ALL QUIET ON THE WESTERN FRONT

Forgive me, comrade, how could you be my enemy? If we threw away these rifles and this uniform you could be my brother.

Erich Maria Remarque,
All Quiet on the Western Front

My friends from West Germany were named Mario and Matthias; Mario lived in Munich, Matthias in a village near the French border. Our mothers had become friends during a backpacking trip to the GDR.*

After they met, the two young Germans sort of adopted my mother, like some kind of freelance version of World Vision. She sent them letters and photographs of her growing family and, in exchange, we received occasional care packages.

It was a big event whenever one of these packages came. There were hand-me-downs that had been outgrown, but were still too big for me; some new things for my sister; boxes of cereal; jars of Nutella; Nescafe for my grandmother and best of all, as far as I was concerned, toys.

That's how my collection of matchbook cars was dramatically enhanced, as was my popularity at school, where I profited from the general interest in things of that nature, which in Hungary were either expensive, rare, permanently back ordered, or whose existence was simply unknown.

* German Democratic Republic or East Germany—trans.

I bragged about my Western friends, showed off my new acquisitions, lent them to other kids or traded them, and in the midst of this materialistic frenzy, not a soul suspected that I had never even met the by now famous German friends.

The struggling East-West friendship was given a boost by an invitation from the West German families to visit. A formal invitation was necessary for a Hungarian family to get authorization to travel to a country whose government had not seen fit to sign the Warsaw Pact. It was common knowledge that innocent visits often turned into requests for asylum.

Even though it must have been tempting, we returned as planned at the end of the summer. Was it because of me? In any event, my participation in the diplomatic mission didn't exactly end up strengthening the cause of East-West friendship. Matthias was less committed to international solidarity than was his mother. It didn't take long to figure out that he had never been informed that his toys were disappearing from his shelves only to reappear on mine, and during my stay with him, he never let me get close to any of his enticing belongings except once when his parents ordered him to be nice to his friend from the East. After which I actually got to play with a single infantryman from his impressive army of tin soldiers, deployed over an entire room.

My German wasn't good enough to say, "You know, *mein lieber Freund*, it'll be mine anyway in a couple of months," so in the politely submissive role of a player who knows how to read the global political chessboard I accepted the unequal economic and political power relations that governed us.

Mario, my other German friend, was much more generous than his compatriot, especially seeing as how he was away during our visit to Munich. A diplomatic incident that I forgave when his parents suggested I try out his favourite plaything, a motorcycle. Not the kind that comes in a box of matches: a real kid's motorcycle, with a real gas engine! The photo of me riding that motorcycle with my pink sandals, my plaid shirt and my red helmet is worth all the money the trip cost my mother. The time spent on his bike became the most memorable of my life. Let's just say I didn't suffer from writer's block when asked on the first day of school to give forth on "the most vivid memory of your vacation."

During this trip, taken when I was eight, while I was trying to figure out how to wisely spend the thirty deutsche marks I had been given as pocket money, my mother was shopping for a country for us. She never said as much, but I'd be willing to bet on it. It would have been easy for us to emigrate to Germany. The country was accepting young families from the East not less generously than was Canada. We had contacts there, we were able to demonstrate some knowledge about things German, my mother spoke the language of the country and even had a German name. We would have been just a few hours from Hungary, life was easy, and the country, organized and rich. Integration seemed to be proceeding smoothly and immigrants received a level of support which would no longer be possible ten years later, with the massive flux of immigration that followed reunification and the signing of the Schengen Agreement.

It could have happened. Where immigrants settle is often the result of chance, a question of fate. The choice of a country – and even more a province and a city – is more random than you might think.

What would my life have been like if I had ended up in Germany, if my mother had taken advantage of the dying moments of the *Wirtschaftswunder* – Germany's post-war economic miracle – instead of choosing to emigrate to Canada?

Today, I'd be telling my story in German, explaining how I became German in my way. My collection of matchbox cars would have grown astronomically, my sister would have had posters of Nina on her wall, instead of Roch Voisine. My mother would be watching German soap operas, voting in German elections, living like the Germans… We might have even adopted the language as our common language at home, as is done by many immigrants in many unilingual countries, including in English Canada.

Then if Nina's songs, the soap operas, and German politics hadn't agreed with us, who knows, we might have simply jumped on the Autobahn in our brand new Mercedes and gone back to live in Budapest after the fall of the Berlin wall, a few years later.

"All Quiet on the Western Front," we would have said, and I would have ended up without any true German friends just the same.

FAREWELL MY COUNTRY

I left my sun
I left my blue sea
Their memories are reawakening
Long after my farewell

Enrico Macias, *Farewell my country*[*]

"Check it out, even Károly's here, and in a coat and tie no less!"

The unkempt hair stylist, skinny, in his late twenties, was my mother's only male co-worker. It was the fact that he was sober at six in the morning, more than his tweed suit, that impressed the handful of people gathered at Budapest Airport to witness the grand departure.

Alcohol waged havoc on his life like it did on thousands of other men of his generation, but he was indulged every morning by the women in the beauty salon, first among them my mom, who couldn't resist mothering him. Which explained his surprise presence among us that morning; sad, sober, and wearing his best suit.

At work, Károly's thoughtful co-workers cancelled his early appointments to give him time to clean up his after-party vomit, vomit in which he died of suffocation at a ripe young age, a few years later. I never saw him again, but he remains my only clear memory of our departure at the

---

[*] Translated from the French by Casey Roberts.

airport. Károly, with his scrawny body inside a tweed suit that was too heavy and too large and that he maybe never had a reason to wear again. With his heartfelt sadness at the departure of his co-worker, full well knowing that it takes more to replace someone dear to you than simply placing a job offer in the classifieds.

Departures cause big disruptions, and small ones as well. A life is made up of hundreds of tiny interconnections, most of which are insignificant compared to those of kinship and friendship. We tend to forget all but the most painful separations, but it's often the unmemorable ones that bring on the biggest bouts of homesickness. We have lost contact with the people with whom we interacted in the course of our daily lives; they gradually fade from memory over time without us noticing, but take up residence in our deepest selves without us connecting these losses to our aching feelings of loneliness. We are missing something: these daily presences. The florist at the entrance to the subway, the next door neighbour with whom we stop to exchange a few words, the people we meet on the corner, to whom we say "let's keep in touch," even though we don't really think we will, people whose names, faces, and even existence we have forgotten, but who were definitely there, extras in a scene of which we only remember the leading actors and actresses.

It's like two strips of Velcro. We perceive how tightly the two long strips bond together, but in reality, there are hundreds of tiny plastic hooks clinging to velour loops that function collectively to hold the two strips firmly together.

The atmosphere at the airport was suddenly somber. Teetering on the dividing line between the excitement of the preparations and the uncertainty of a new life, we all realized that nothing would ever be the same. For those who were leaving, of course, but also for those left behind.

To avoid any inordinate speechifying, people instead wise-cracked about Károly's coat and tie, and he good-naturedly sacrificed himself to serve as a distraction. With his usual shy smile, he went along with the jokes told at his expense that stood in for "we're going to miss you" and "we'll never forget you." The friendly teasing inevitably gave way to longer and longer periods of silence. As if each person had become a customs agent at the border of the land of melancholy, they silently opened suitcases stuffed with memories, and stone-faced, sorted them into two piles: those that would cross the border and those that would remain behind.

We would never again go hiking together in the mountains of Bükk, or spend our summer vacation at Lake Balaton, there would be fewer people at the children's birthdays and adult parties, Akos would no longer be there to fool around with the beauty salon's clients, and his sister would never become the Hungarian diving champion. The hikes would still take place, the vacations too, everybody knew that there would still be parties, but all were aware that they wouldn't be exactly the same as before. And Károly knew that my mother wouldn't be there any longer to suggest he give flowers to his fiancé on her birthday.

"It's time to get going, we don't want to miss our flight, it's not a Hungarian airline, this plane is taking off on schedule!"

I know that my father was there, but I have no memory of it. Not the last words he said to me, holding me in his arms, nor the suit he wore for the occasion. Did he have a beard or only a moustache, as I preferred? Was he wearing a tie? Most likely not. But he was sober, that I'm sure of, otherwise I'd remember.

Two strips of Velcro can adhere to other surfaces with more or less efficiency, but rarely with the same tenacity as when they compose their original pair. It's true that they need each other, but they can also grab on to something else if they can't find their true complement. One thing is certain, we will always need a few hooks and a bit of velour.

LIVING IN AMERICA

Somewhere on the way
You might find out who you are

James Brown, *Living in America*

Someone had told me that there was supposed to be a movie on the plane, amazing information that only upped my desire to fly for the first time. My excitement was tempered by my lack of enthusiasm for a massive change that I had not chosen and about which no one had even asked my opinion.

I knew there was no point in resisting, so in my role as a nice and well-behaved boy I kept my feelings to myself: my reluctance, my pain in having to leave my old life behind me and my fears about the new one in front of me. Complaining with a full belly, whining, comparing oneself to others were all considered spoiled child behaviour in my family. I knew what to expect. I listened obediently, without brandishing the Convention on the Rights of the Child when well-meaning adults around me said things like, "Children, you know, they adapt so quickly, it will be easy for them."

The whole idea of "flying on a plane for the first time in my life" helped me to put aside my grief. Don't they say that it's all about the journey, not the destination? Everything seemed to be in agreement with this maxim. "You're going to fly?!" was the first question usually put to me when someone learned of my impending departure. It was one of those childish questions with an exclamation point at the end, but for which children don't hold an exclusive monopoly.

Flying symbolized for kids and grown-ups alike social success, wealth, freedom, adventure: things that few people hoped to achieve – let alone managed to achieve – in my native country.

As the wheels lifted off the ground, these aspirations would be taking flight, aspirations denied to the builders of the socialist state, who had had to settle for the decent life that the regime was able to offer its citizens after decades of arduous reconstruction and stunted economic development in the orbit of the Soviet Union. For people who were content not to venture outside the limits set by the authorities, the result was a stable and predictable life with the guarantee of a job, an apartment, education, quality health care, a decent pension, leisure family time and limited, but adequate, choices in consumer products.

As for the destination – this Canadian America or American Canada – it was seen as paradise on earth, except that you needed heat in the winter. A remote and vast Switzerland, a place where political conflict, poverty (visible or invisible), or any other kind of problem that you might one day take seriously, was simply unimaginable.

That a ten-year-old child could fly – and to America at that – was something unheard of, an unattainable dream that many had shared before there was any premonition of the sudden dismantling of the Eastern bloc that would come just four years later.

Our entourage, consisting of classmates, friends, family, colleagues and neighbours, pestered us for every detail of our project, counted down the days with us before our departure, swinging between envy, jealousy, and vicarious pleasure; and some clung to the hope that the fact of having known us and helped us would benefit them someday. None of these curious folks showed the slightest interest in whether or not I wanted to go, regardless of the mode of transportation. The other children were zoned in to the positive aspects of my emigration, fascinated by the abundance waiting for me and the toys I'd be leaving for them; while the adults were convinced that breathing the – even cold – air of freedom would provide me with all the energy needed to live happily the rest of my days.

When they thought about America, despite the economic precipice on which capitalist imperialism teetered, as was reported by the state media, despite the belligerent tone of a Ronald Reagan brandishing the specter of a war his people had never experienced – Hungarians knew, even those most vulnerable to propaganda (their children) – that life was simply better there.

Our knowledge of life in America came from Hollywood productions that finally ended up making it to our country; films and television series that came out in Hungary years after their initial release, although we were aware, somehow, that there were certain productions we'd never get to see, except perhaps on pirated videocassettes.

Thanks to *The Dukes of Hazzard*, we knew that even small-town people in America had nice cars, jeans and a sense of humor, and thanks to *E.T.*, we knew that even aliens there possessed a bicycle – and even more incredibly – a home phone. We knew the Americans had plenty of TV stations, clean cities, big houses with gardens and pools, skyscrapers and beaches to go to after school.

"Are you flying on a plane?"

"What do you think we're taking? A tram? And the plane, can you believe it? There's even a movie theater in it!"

The excitement of boarding the plane and being able to look out the window and see all of Budapest, the outline of entire continents, the Atlantic Ocean from the sky, the clouds above, pushed aside the anxiety I felt in arriving, totally unprepared, at the starting line of this marathon that I had been forced to run.

You can imagine my disappointment when I realized as soon as I sat down in my seat, far from the window, that there wasn't really a theater on the plane, just a small screen suspended in front, on which they were planning to show a film during the flight. I drowned my sorrow in the unlimited supply of Coca-Cola, visited the cockpit (to which I was invited in my capacity as an adorable little boy), and thoroughly depleted KLM's stash of salted almonds.

The time in the air flew by too quickly for me to think about what I'd left behind. All the distractions had temporarily obliterated the fact that I wouldn't be going to the Museum of Transportation on Sundays any more with my grandmother, that I wouldn't be hanging out between the apartment buildings on Kárpát street after school with my Boys, that I wouldn't get to go with my father any more to the tavern and drink a glass of orange juice, I wouldn't ever get to go to the baths with my family again, never again go to the movies with friends to see an Italian film with Bud Spencer and Terence Hill.

The cabin lights were dimmed. I'd been waiting for a while with the headphones on my ears, the same set of airplane headphones I've kept ever since in the hope of finding receptacles that could accommodate its plastic plugs.

The sound of James Brown's *Living in America* poured into my ears.

How does it feel
When there's no destination that's too far

The movie was about an American boxer with a blazing heart. A character I had never heard of, whose mission was to face a Soviet giant in the ring. The American hero was poor and humble, running on courage alone, while his opponent benefited from unlimited resources committed to helping him win. A soulless (Russian) machine, programmed by a regime that despised personal freedom every bit as much as it did the enemy's freedom.

As the film and the plane both moved towards their final destinations, I realized that in this story – and in the story of my new life – the roles of the good guys and bad guys had been flipped. I had heard a rumour told by a classmate (who attributed it to a mysterious cousin living in the West) to the effect that, for Americans, it was the Eastern bloc that wanted war and not the other way around, but to have this confirmed at this moment of my life was a shock as brutal and necessary as the pounding that Rocky dishes to his rival at the movie's end, a few minutes before the landing of the communist colossus on the floor of the ring... and our Boeing 747 at the Mirabel Airport in Montreal.

I clapped enthusiastically along with the other passengers, changed sides, and suddenly realized that there would be no turning back.

BACK TO THE FUTURE

He was never in time for his classes...
He wasn't in time for his dinner...
Then one day... he wasn't in his time at all.

Back to the Future, poster

"Salon Vera Fodor," read the neon sign on Chemin Queen
Mary, north of Décarie, where my mother worked at her
first job, acquired thanks to the sponsoring of the former
Hungarian owner.

Thirty years after Soviet tanks had forced hundreds of
thousands of Hungarians to flee their country, it wasn't
uncommon to still see shops in Montreal adorned with
Hungarian names. Not just butchers and restaurants, but
also shoe repair shops, garages, dentists' offices, notaries,
and lawyers we knew were Hungarian, even when it wasn't
specified up front. The synagogue, a Catholic church and a
Protestant church organized community life, with its festivals and activities, according to a segregated system that
we didn't even respect at the beginning. My mother's new
husband was of Hungarian origin, and all of the people we
interacted with at first, including contacts that we quickly
made at school and in the neighbourhood, were too.

A Hungarian pediatrician treated the grandchildren of
the 56-ers as well as the few new additions to the community, like us. A mechanic in Outremont was known not to rip

off his fellow countrymen. At Délibáb, the Hungarian book-store on Prince Arthur street, we could rent old movies that my sister and I had never heard of before, but which we came to know by heart. On Wednesday at five o'clock on ethnic cable we could watch Hungarian dance performances recorded with a Betacam mounted on a tripod. On the week-end, a radio program poured out venom with Nazi overtones with impunity, made possible by the CRTC's shameful ignor-ance of Finno-Ugrian languages. Every other month, we went to see Hungarian artists perform while on tour in North American, in a high school auditorium, where my sister, my mother and I were the youngest people in the audience.

I can only imagine what it would have been like to arrive in a dynamic community with enough members to be able to occupy entire neighbourhoods and take their places in important institutions and sectors of the local economy. A community sufficiently organized to defend against the loss of its identity – through the handing down of its language and folklore – and to assimilate any newcomer, generation after generation, into a process of cultural osmosis between the host country and the country of origin, this hybrid entity that we would come to call a "cultural community."

Ours was aging, reeling, out of step with the Hungary that we had just left. We had not migrated to the futuristic America foreshadowed by *Back to the Future*, but to a scene out of post-war Hungary, filmed in black and white. During our early years in Montreal, our family and community life were like a Magyar version of *The Cosby Show* where the main cast as well as the supporting roles weren't played by African-Americans, but Hungarians. Although we were getting tired of it and occasionally dreamed of returning to the future, this new world did have its advantages.

When my mother opened her own beauty salon, the old country network would become indispensable to building up her clientele. A little boy (that would be me) distributing discount coupons at Snowdon metro for a bikini wax was relatively ineffective compared to the rumours circulating that my mother would offer a discount to anyone who could demonstrate their Hungarian origin.

She professed ethnic solidarity towards the merchants of the Hungarian diaspora, but in practice she much preferred to shop at the big chain stores: Cumberland, Canadian Tire, Miracle Mart and Steinberg, the first *native* places she made her own. We felt quickly at home in them, although little in these places reminded us of home: neither the product variety, nor the cleanliness, and especially not the quality and warmth of the service.

Corn Flakes replaced lard at the dinner table, and we hoped that if we were really really good and brought home excellent report cards, we would be allowed to have some Nutella once in a while at breakfast. At the Provi-Soir they sold three types of milk, none of which went bad before we had finished it. There were bananas everywhere, sold at affordable prices. There were AA batteries that didn't leak for our Sony Walkman (with a radio!). And we finally owned a remote controlled colour TV, which received more than one channel and even carried broadcasts on Mondays.

Pouring through the circulars and scouring the aisles, we liked to say, "In Canada, you can buy anything," before adding "you just need to have the money." But that already seemed more attainable than anything the dictatorship of the proletariat had led us to hope for. The Canadian Tire and Consumers Distributors catalogues replaced my favourite Hungarian novels as "must-read" material. I cut out ads for bicycles and computers and sent them to my friends in Hungary. With great success.

For my mother, finding the right product in the right store at the best price had become second nature. Also, the clever use of coupons, rewards cards, and rain checks. She no longer hesitated to take something back on exchange or return, to ask to be reimbursed, to try to get a discount even when past the expiration date. She staked out a position as always being in the right, as always in her role as a mother, but now also as "the client." She had become an expert consumer who after only a few months, held second candle to none of the native-born in this area of competence. Just like thousands of other immigrants before and after her.

We were happy just to stop for a few minutes in any of the larger grocery stores in immigrant neighbourhoods. To watch the fascinating spectacle that appeared before our eyes in these well-lit places. The chaotic crowd would come alive between the aisles and around the produce where the colours of the women's veils and saris mingled with the colours of the fruits and vegetables in a choreography where everyone writhed in Babylonian confusion. Like ants, who at a distance appear to be disoriented, but who when watched from close-up as they approach the nest, seem more or less organized within a system in which each individual fulfills its task with precision and without asking questions. Slowly but ever onward, in an environment that was in principle *foreign*, these immigrants filled their baskets – and roles – to perfection.

With each bar code scanned, with every beep of a cash drawer being opened, with every use of a rewards card or credit card, the meaning of 'economic integration' becomes clear, and reason given for people to think that most immigrants, even those who just arrived, integrate into their host society quickly and in an exemplary manner.

Presumably this is only the first stage of integration, but for many this is also its purpose. The truth is that in many respects, this degree of integration is sufficient to make the machine run, but it would be more honest to reveal its true design, as required by the Consumer Protection Act.

THE LANGUAGES WE ARE

"The more languages we speak, the more people we will be," said the wise man back home, but especially my grandmother who, according to this logic, was four people all by herself. The one I knew – Hungarian – was already fabulous; I could only imagine how much more when she spoke in German, French or English.

My grandmother learned German more or less at the same time as her mother tongue and never stopped using the Germanic expressions that betrayed someone's bourgeois origins in Hungary. Like many early twentieth-century Hungarian Jews, she had been raised in an assimilated family – though naturally pro-German – which can be explained not only by the poetry of Rilke and Yiddish influences, but also by the political and economic strength that this language represented under the Austro-Hungarian Empire.

This sincere fondness for German culture did not serve her family very well in Auschwitz, from where they never returned, but two generations later, I still had to painfully submit to private weekly German lessons my mother paid for out of her meager savings.

Of the four languages that my grandmother spoke, she was most proud of her French, a fact that she could scarcely keep concealed in spite of her humility, normally held as a virtue. She had learned it at a boarding school in Neuchâtel,

Switzerland, where she had been sent at the age of twelve, after the death of her mother. Her father wanted to ensure that the education of this only child of a good family would continue under the best conditions possible during the uncertain years of the interwar period.

The family history does not tell with what intensity my great-grandfather enjoyed the Roaring Twenties once released from parental restraints, but we do know that four years later, a new stepmother was there to welcome his daughter back from boarding school. She came back speaking French and advanced German, albeit now tinged with a Swiss flavour. A few years later she became a typist and stenographer, where she learned proper English.

Knowing that I was going to the French part of Canada seemed to mitigate her grief at being separated from me by an ocean. She now dreamed (out loud) that she would soon be able to correspond with me in French, while I was dreaming (in secret) of meeting Sophie Marceau at a house party.

Arriving in Montreal, where the debate over Bill 101 was raging, we were rapidly informed that the French spoken here wasn't real French, but a crude dialect, whose speakers were mostly ignorant racists on welfare. Heavy stuff. This disdain was all the stronger since the golden age of French had just arrived in Quebec, for the first time since the Conquest. It was fashionable to order a *chien-chaud vapeur tout garni.** The comedy troupe Rock et Belles Oreilles could mock French-speaking Quebecers who recorded in English in order to be respected in North America:

---

* Steamed hot dog all dressed—trans.

I want to pogne...*
Is it the reason that i speak in english?
I want to pogne
I do not want to speak my tongue
I just want to pogne
I know i have a big accent
But i want to pogne
And i have composed that song
I know the mathematic
America is a big market
If there is a more public**
There is more money in my pocket...

It was a time when each French word that replaced an English word, be it in the media, in commerce or on the job, was seen as a step towards equality, a concrete advance that would finally lift those who spoke French from the bottom of the social ladder where they had been historically relegated.

After the proclamation of French as the official language by the Liberal Party in 1974, and even more so with the adoption of the Charter of the French Language by the Parti Québécois in 1977, Quebec's vast French-speaking majority grew in confidence. Their new strength and consciousness inevitably provoked a heated response from powerful English interests, who tapped immigrants to be their not very advanced vanguard and force a retreat. For the English, the battle would be henceforth focused on the conquest of new immigrant communities whose previously acquired language identity (English) was now in jeopardy due to Bill 101, which required their children to attend French schools.

---

* I want to be popular, to make it—trans.
** Larger audience—trans.

Their Canadian-Hungarian foot soldiers, drawn from a mostly English-speaking wave of immigration (like most Italians, Jews, Greeks, Portuguese, and Chinese in Quebec) would happily be the first to volunteer to go to the front. To listen to them, we had realized from the start that Canada was the only place on the planet where speaking French was not prestigious.

I came to the conclusion that being forced to learn French would certainly make me a different person, but that this new person would not necessarily be more respectable. I only hoped that my grandmother would love him just as much as before.

AN AMERICAN EPIC

Digging, extracting pieces of the past from the earth – in order to reassemble them like a 3D puzzle – to give concrete form to history had been a dream of mine as far back as I can remember. Not like *Indiana Jones*, which hadn't yet been released back home. It was probably a side effect of visits to the Museum of Fine Arts in Budapest, where the basement was full of ancient treasures. Maybe it was because of my fascination with the pyramids, or my love of stories drawn from Greek mythology, or the illustrated book on the early Magyar tribes that I still like to flip through thirty years later.

Anyway, when someone would ask me about my future plans, I had my answer ready-made, original and striking: "I'd like to become an archaeologist." Once in Canada, the answer didn't really impress our entourage of more established Hungarian immigrants. Here, the profession of archaeologist does not exist, I was informed in a tone that brooked no response: "What do you think you'll find in the soil of a country that has no history, teepee poles?" they'd say, obviously little intrigued by past Native American civilizations. Usually, First Nations were only of interest to immigrants as a trump card in an argument over the legitimacy of the desire of Quebecers to build their own country and impose their language on this colonized land.

"Here you must become a dentist if you want to make money."

My hope for my chosen career was given a boost by the discovery of the existence of a wax museum not far from our first apartment on Victoria Street. On Queen Mary, right across from St. Joseph's Oratory, dioramas evoking scenes from the Bible and the history of French Canada were displayed.

For those who like to acknowledge "the contribution of cultural communities," the museum was founded in 1935 by sculptor Albert Chartier and painter Robert Tancredi, both from France. They had to struggle with the religious authorities who feared that this new business would negatively impact on theirs, since they had just invested in the massive building that towered over Mount Royal where they sold St. Joseph's oil. They must have been more or less reassured, business remained good, even enhanced by the hundreds of thousands of pilgrims and schoolchildren who were attracted by the works of the two artists.

I had always loved museums, but this one was confusing. No artifacts in display cases, no paintings on the walls. In tiny rooms, life-like scenes, murky, nebulous for the immigrant child that I was. Scenes of baby Jesus and grown-up Jesus, Moses's flight out of Egypt – or was that actually Jacques Cartier? Jeanne Mance who nursed the Iroquois under the approving gaze of John Paul II and three astronauts.

These bewildering images made a very strong impression on me. I vowed to return to put order into my new Quebec mythology, but the authorities decided I had seen enough and closed the doors of the museum shortly after my visit. The premises were transformed into retail space, a conversion nearly as radical as the conversions being carried out by the Jesuits in a diorama that was about to disappear.

Statues of Mary Magdalene, the Canadian Martyrs, founders and first settlers of Nouvelle-France, the British officer hidden under a sheet by Marguerite d'Youville, statues of Brother André and Maurice Duplessis gave way to the diners of a vegetarian restaurant and a pharmacy. I'd have to face the obvious, they were right, there was nothing about Quebec you could sculpt in wax, taking into account their limited history.

For adult immigrants, there was a compulsory citizenship test where the most difficult questions were: 1) Who is the head of state of Canada? (the Queen of England, not Brian Mulroney), and 2) What is the capital of Manitoba? (Winnipeg and not Regina). There wasn't much offered to engage the curiosity of young people – immigrants or not – unless you count *Heritage Minutes*, one-minute historical videos produced by the federal government.

At the time, the only way you were exposed to history in primary school was through the comic-book adventures of Asterix and Lucky Luke. In the eighth grade, there was a course that reviewed the history of mankind starting with Cro-Magnon man, without managing to get to his descendants in the twentieth century. In tenth grade, we finally had a course on Quebec *and* Canadian history in which Mr. Hamoun explained who was who among the metro stations of the Green Line, and even took us around Parliament Hill in Ottawa. He did an admirable job in just a couple of hours a week, in front of an audience much more difficult to conquer than Montcalm's troops on the Plains of Abraham.

My real understanding of the struggles of the men and women who built this country came from the historian Jacques Lacoursière, whose fascinating television series on Radio-Québec, *Épopée en Amérique*, (An American Epic), I even recorded over my old Seinfeld shows. But it came too late to influence my choice of careers.

The finely sculpted entrance arch giving onto Chemin Queen Mary is now condemned and serves as an improvised bus shelter. The inscriptions "Musée," "historique" and "canadien," carved in low relief, have continued to erode with the changes of the seasons and the collective memory. My dream of becoming an archaeologist was gone forever, abandoned to the consensus that in my new country, the past has no future. Now, when I wanted to please adults who cared about my career choice, I answered "dentist."

My future in America was sure to be an epic all its own.

FOR BETTER AND FOR WORSE

We arrived in Quebec in the last century, some of us as far back as the one before that. Like all immigrants of that time, we expected that its land had been cleared, its roads built, its cities erected; but when we arrived, the information highway was still yet to be built. This highway – Skype, Facebook, texting, satellite television and radio – is capable of linking today's immigrants to their past in real time and of giving them the illusion that they haven't really left the old country.

On a daily basis we were confronted with the distance between ourselves and what we had left behind. We were never allowed the reassuring and comfortable feeling of being able to take advantage of the best of both worlds. The cultural gap and sense of distance grew inexorably greater as each week passed in our new homeland. We had left one world to come to another, there was no avoiding it.

If you wanted to know what was going on back home, you couldn't rely on the local media, rather stingy when it came to international news. And when they did get around to talking about our country, we could only thank our lucky stars that we weren't there anymore. Like during the reports on the Chernobyl explosion, radiation we had barely avoided.

We rarely heard about anything of less import, and when we did, it was well after the event. Immigrants are interested in what's happening in the soap operas from back home, the results of their soccer team's matches, the vicissitudes of the old country's politicians, gossip about its stars and their former colleagues, friends and neighbours. By the time such news finally arrives weeks later, distorted by rumour and passed along by word of mouth, it has lost a great deal of its significance and seems increasingly remote.

We had no choice but to give up some of our habits, acquire new hobbies, adapt to life here and gradually open up to the local culture. A little bit at a time. We had to begin by *arriving*. We might be eating less breakfast meat, but that didn't mean we were rushing out to purchase season tickets at the Théâtre du Nouveau Monde. For starters, there were random hits from the zapper; we chanced upon an Expos game; episodes from *He Shoots, He Scores!, Inspector Gadget, The Cosby Show, Top Jeunesse* with Roch Voisine and *The Price is Right*; and the funeral of René Lévesque.

Although this cultural menu wasn't all that enticing at first glance, we had to sink our teeth into something. Life forced you into discovery mode. Basically we had no choice but to integrate ourselves into something *here*. It was still possible to live more or less reclusively under the shelter of our "cultural community." But this community, with its cultural centers from *here*, its newspapers published *here*, its radio shows produced *here*, had however its roots sunk deep into its Montreal sanctuary.

In terms of communications, we were closer to the nineteenth century than the twenty-first. It might be true that Pony Express or telegrams were no longer the key factor in maintaining contact with Hungary, but the unpredictable Magyar Posta and the skyrocketing rates of Bell Canada held monopolies on our homesickness. Our contacts with home were mainly therefore by mail. Phone calls were reserved for emergencies and, once a fortnight, for a call to our grandmother, who had become with age and the shock of our departure, increasingly anxious.

For the investment to be profitable, the operation had to be methodical. We scheduled a time, reminding her that 1 p.m. for us was 7 p.m. for her, not the other way around; three people in three different rooms picked up three different phones at the same time so we could all listen in and take our turns speaking. My sister and I had to prepare our talking points.

Guess what? I have a Yugoslavian teacher (yes, he knows I'm Hungarian and he likes me all the same); my sister has an Indian friend (no, not Native American, but Indian from India with an earring in her nose and a black dot between her eyebrows); I take my lunch to school, there's no cafeteria (yes, I eat the whole sandwich that my mother makes for me); the city's downtown is jammed with skyscrapers, like New York in *Crocodile Dundee* (it's a super cool movie); we met a Hungarian family, you know their grandmother (she is kind of ditzy).

"OK, children, promise your grandmother that you'll write, and then hang up. It's our turn."

The adults then finished their conversation, staying within their time limit. Once I only pretended to hang up. Secretly still on the line, I think I heard my mother cry for the first time in my life. It seemed clear that her hasty marriage had soured, as might have been predicted.

Was it worth it to get married in order to immigrate to another country. I don't know. This aspect of our adventure, rarely mentioned out of shame, or maybe modesty, would never be discussed. What is certain is that this path to being accepted is infallible and takes less time than requesting asylum or becoming an "economic" immigrant, but it is no less bumpy. In any case, our old country had already become little more than a virtual reality; we had come here, turning back was unthinkable. We were here to stay. *For better and for worse.*

MR. NICOLAS'S CLASS

"Hello, my name is Mr. Nicolas and I'm from Yugoslavia," began Mr. Nicolas, who came from Yugoslavia. Specifically from a village at the crossroads of Hungary, Romania and Serbia, whose multiethnic population belonged, at some point or another over the previous century, to four different countries. Let's say he was predisposed to teach a welcome class, even though he didn't have a diploma in intercultural education from UQAM.

Next, the students introduced themselves. Hello, I'm Hsiao-Vahid-Thi-Ernesto-Sandra-Charon-Tara, and I come from Hong Kong-Iran-Vietnam-Honduras-Sri Lanka-Israel-Jamaica, recited the students, each rising in turn to divulge this essential information.

The class was like a mini-UN, only without any members from the Security Council, the OECD or the G7. No French Quebecers either, or little Eskimos, as I had imagined rubbing shoulders with at school. The only representatives were countries that sing the beautiful melody of the symphony of nations out of key. We may have been among the haves in our countries of origin, but once here, that was no longer the case. We were the castoffs from conflict zones and the third world.

We were the offspring of families who fled from civil wars, dictatorships and poverty in the 1980s. Not really poster material for promoting the "economic immigration"

that was supposed to rescue the Quebec economy during
the severe recession.

In any event, before we could do anything to save the
Quebec economy, we had to increase our own productivity
and learn the basics of French in a multi-level class where
the nearly illiterate were mixed in with witty Eastern
Europeans. The purpose of the welcome class was to learn
enough French so that you could function in a regular classroom within two years. Whether that was enough time or
not depended on the proximity of your mother tongue to
French, your level of prior education and your pace of learning; but it was nevertheless axiomatic that grammar would
be better absorbed if its teaching was accompanied by the
constant recognition of our origins.

With a flag planted by each student in the inkwell of the
our desks, a cassette of music and a baked dish from their
country brought to intercultural day, the new Quebecers
were armed with all that they needed to open their
Bescherelle, the trusty pocket French verb conjugator. The
celebration of my different-ness began right on the first day,
with a modest ceremony where I was asked to pin a miniature flag on the world map, on which the other students
had already marked their birthplaces.

Standing in front of my new classmates, clutching a sharp
tack that Mr. Nicolas had given me, nothing could have been
easier. But something was off in the way the world map was
displayed. The Americas were centered in the frame, bizarrely
cutting Asia into two, which wouldn't have been that bad,
but that meant that Europe was, as a consequence, squished
into a corner. Feeling the pressure mounting on my tiny
shoulders, too much attention falling on my too-little person,
my throat constricting in my buttoned-up shirt, stumbling
on tiptoes in front of this damn wrong map that was in any
case too high to reach, I completely lost my bearings.

Laughter rang out, quickly smothered by a look from Mr. Nicolas who had never dreamed, when he asked me to perform this simple gesture on my first day of class, that it would result in such sharp humiliation for me and simultaneously for the reputation of the quality of our Eastern European educations. Just as I finally found my target he put an end to my ordeal, assigning me a vacant spot on the map, before I could demonstrate my actually respectable geographical knowledge.

My first day of school was a disaster. Back behind my desk, flushed with shame for leaving the impression that I didn't have a clue where I was from, after those few seconds that were already too many out of my life in Quebec, I could at least find comfort by pondering this new way of understanding the world: the idea that its very center had relocated to the same exact place as had I.

THE TRIAL

A calculator watch that had been given to me as a gift was the most valuable thing I owned. This luxury object had the power to set its possessor apart from the mass of proletarian children in Hungary. It was black, made out of plastic, and had gray rubberized keys. I never took it off except to take a bath, in math class, and occasionally to sleep. But after some exceptionally heavy use, a small crack appeared on its screen and then I also took it off for phys-ed.

I couldn't have imagined that in this country of freedom and abundance, where as we said fences were made out of salami, something so sickening would happen to me, but only a few weeks after my arrival in Quebec, in the chaotic midst of a class change, the watch disappeared from the bench on which I had carefully placed it during my gym class. I had barely dried my tears when, a few days later, I saw a student during recess showing off his new watch, which was mine without a doubt.

Faced with the indifference of my new schoolmates, unimaginable a month earlier, I moved to confront him, but I didn't know the necessary verb to articulate the liberal principle of private property. He pretended not to understand the meaning of my antics, but I saw in his panicked eyes that he was well aware of the seriousness of the situation. When he refused to give me what justly belonged to me, I had no way to convince him of the legitimacy of my claim except to violently throw him down to the asphalt in the schoolyard. This conflict resolution process did not bear fruit and instead, earned me an invitation to the principal's office.

The cultural and linguistic disconnect was total. It took me a moment to realize that once inside her office, I'd be the one on trial, since I'd been the initiator against a younger student who had been unable to defend himself. The interrogation, conducted by the principal and a teacher, was complicated by my bafflement at this obvious injustice and their inability to understand my stammering French. Humiliated by this Kafkaesque ordeal, I tried to plead my case with my limited vocabulary, explaining how important the calculator watch was to me, its history and the most important detail: the small crack in the screen that should justify the bringing of charges against the real culprit.

My frustration grew; it seemed as though my jury did not and could not understand a single thing. In a moment of lucidity, I took out a sheet of paper and drew the watch from memory. In exacting detail. I knew the location of each key and button, each legend inscribed on its face. I added the crack and I insisted that the little thief be asked to do the same before the jury reached a conclusion as to whom – him or me – the object should be returned in all fairness!

We never made it to the hoped-for moment of humiliation and sweet revenge. I still regret it. The principal opened her desk drawer and removed the exhibit; the two women studied the watch for a couple of seconds and then looked at my drawing, and trying to stifle their smiles, handed me the calculator watch, never apologizing for the judicial error they had committed. They gave me a little sermon on how nonviolence was the policy in schools in this country, but I wasn't paying any attention.

Whereas in my French class, I was now all ears.

"NIGGER BLACK"

Basically what good does it do anybody to be a nigger?
Nothing. Because basically, they're no better than us.
They're not better, because if they were better, they
wouldn't have been made the way they are but they'd
have been made the same as us.

Yvon Deschamps,
Nigger Black (satirical monologue)*

The school's name has been engraved on its front wall in red-brick English since 1932, the year it opened its doors to serve the Snowdon neighbourhood, the rich English-speaking section of Côte-des-Neiges that real estate agents call "Westmount Adjacent."

In this wooded area, in a small circular village, the Iona School was surrounded by luxurious houses. Each one was unique, built according to the tastes of its first owner, and they ranged around the school on a street aptly named Circle Road. Their lawns were immaculate and none of the occupants thought that their neighbour's grass was greener. The school integrated perfectly into its environment with its ivy covered brick walls that, in North America, miraculously added value to the attached building.

This perfect architectural integration did not extend into the domain of human experience. Families living in these homes stopped sending their children to the school when it

---

* Translated by Casey Roberts.

was transformed a few years earlier into a French school, with the entry into force of Bill 101. As the new students were arriving by school bus from the poorest areas of Côte-des-Neiges, the neighbourhood kids were being driven to English schools in Westmount, Côte-Saint-Luc or Hampstead in their parents' luxury cars. That is, the ones who hadn't already applied for asylum in Ontario as did thousands of English Montrealers after the election of the Parti Québécois and René Lévesque in 1976.

Like every other immigrant child, I was required to attend French schools, and I had been assigned to the Iona school because there were still places in its "welcome classes." That was fine by me. I considered it a typical American luxury to have a school bus stop in front of my house every morning whereas back home, I had gone to school alone on the subway and the bus. I could write home to my friends that having failed to obtain a remote controlled electric car, I had instead acquired my own chauffeur. And just like in the movies, he was black!

Growing up in Hungary, the only black people I knew were in the movies, where they either played the bad guys or the police, or chauffeurs or the sax. That was before I came to Montreal and noticed that they weren't always bad guys, and seldom were they police (as for the sax, I didn't know). But by all evidence, chauffeurs, yes.

We were no longer allowed to say "*néger*," as we called blacks in Hungarian, it was considered a big insult. Given the proximity of the word to the French word "*nègre*" and the English word "*nigger*," we had to quickly revise our vocabulary when talking in public, even in our otherwise incomprehensible language. A first effort to adapt to the diversity of our new country.

There is a misconception that the host country learns to live with diversity thanks to its immigrants, but it is often the opposite. Immigrants tend to come from towns and villages with homogeneous populations or from regions where hatred of a neighbouring community is acceptable. When they arrive here, they have to learn to deal with "differences" for the first time in their lives. The culture shock is a lot milder for someone from Abitibi who comes to Montreal than it is for a Jamaican.

In my welcome class there were three or four black kids who seemed normal enough to me, one was even really nice. Although I must admit, I was amazed to see that he couldn't handle the heat any better than we could. Most surprising to me was how quickly different skin colours had become just part of the landscape in this multiethnic school. I'm not trying say it was nothing. We often designated each other in terms of our origins (especially when using the third person), but it was rarely malicious. It wasn't exactly Martin Luther King's dream come to life, but I don't think he would have been overly disappointed.

My sister told me that a black kid at school had made some moves but that she had brushed him off, although I did notice that she had bought herself a LL Cool J cassette. Even my mother made friends with an African, a rare event among adult immigrants. A foreign student who, in order to pay for his umpteenth postdoc, distributed *The Gazette* in Westmount and got up every morning at four a.m., seven days a week, winter and summer, without a break. It seemed as if he wasn't really living in the tiny basement flat downstairs from us, but rather in a novel by Dany Laferrière.

There were some somewhat less friendly people too; like the boy at school, who true to the Hollywood stereotype, terrorized any student who crossed his gaze. The existence of this bully contributed to my education, and not just on the subject of interculturalism. By denying me oxygen for a few long seconds, he made sure that I learned that *"Je regarde où je veux"** is not the right answer to the question "What are you looking at?" This episode offered me the opportunity to reflect on the benefits of dropping out of school (and on the limits of cultural relativism).

It's the antiracist rationale *par excellence*: all cultures have their tightwads, their thugs, their aces, they told us, and they were right. From the perspective of the Intercultural Affairs Office of the Ministry of Education, that should have settled the debate. But what could you say about the black person who mugged you, the Chinese kids in school who got the best grades, the Jewish person who had scammed you, the Latinos who were the best dancers, the Quebecer on welfare, the alcoholic Aboriginal, the annoying Frenchman? When the prejudice reveals itself to be *basically true*. This is when the second part of the idea comes into play, the sociological perspective, an argument that we might someday be able to work into our essays and oral presentations: It's society's fault. Not to be a pest, but once again, what should we do when the poor single-parent backwoods family living in public housing proves to be respectful and respectable? How can you avoid creating social stereotypes while trying to fight against racial stereotypes?

Mr. Nicolas had an approach to help us get rid of the prejudices we brought into the classroom from our countries of origin or hot off the playground. "Are you carrying any prejudices in your luggage?" wasn't a question usually asked at customs, but he was determined to confiscate them as quickly as they appeared. It was necessary to intervene early, with patience and skill, without rushing the children and their parents too much, while, simultaneously, the system encouraged everyone to affirm their every bit of difference. His

---

* I look wherever I want—trans.

approach, whose rhetoric could not be argued with, was simple and effective.

He didn't hesitate to designate us by our origins. He constantly spoke of his little Chinese, his beautiful Chilean, his brilliant little Hungarian, but never compared us to each other or validated us on this basis, never left the impression that we could rank the "races." He trivialized our differences rather than emphasizing them, especially when there was obviously prejudice involved.

"Who did this? Mr. Nicolas asked me, looking at my red neck.

"That big black guy over there! They're just a bunch of..."

"The tall boy from the class next door?"

He had interrupted me in mid-phrase, both to enrich my vocabulary and to imperceptibly model something important for me. That's what great teachers are like, you're not aware of it when they send you a little bit of what makes them who they are.

Only a little bit, because I've erred a few times since. Anyway, according to the usage in common in the Montreal immigrant environments where I spent my youth, I continued – and still continue – to designate people according to their origin and sometimes the colour of their skin. My neighbour is Chinese, the other one's a little bit of everything, my grocer is Portuguese, my dealer is black. None took or take offense, even if your anthropologist daughter, raised in Saint-Bruno, believes otherwise.

Rest assured: By the time, decades later, that I returned to my old primary school in suit and tie, as a school commissioner and chair of the intercultural relations committee of the school board, I had learned all the acceptable vocabulary to describe "immigrants;" these new Quebecers, immigrant Quebecers, first or second generation "allophones," people whose mother tongue was neither English nor French; the

Italian, Chinese, Arab, any kind of multiword identity that ends with a hyphen and Canadian or Quebec people; members of ethnocultural communities; ethnic and visible minorities; our fellow citizens from diverse backgrounds; I knew all the politically correct terms that no immigrant uses except when speaking into a microphone.

Mr. Nicolas, who had not yet retired, was still as proud of me, his little Hungarian, as if I'd been his own son. That was good enough for me.

THE HALF-JEW

What does the word "Jew" mean, mama? Would it be better if we weren't Jews? But then, I wouldn't be able to wear my yellow star any more, and didn't you tell me, mama, that it's only big boys like me that get to wear them?

Little George in *Elysium*,
a film by Erika Szántó (1986)*

I learned the hard way that you shouldn't kid around with that particular subject, so please believe me: it wasn't until I was nine, in the décor of concentration camp where a devious Nazi doctor conducted experiments on children, that I learned I was Jewish. Half-Jewish, to be precise.

The gym where we were being tortured under the terrorizing eyes of soldiers in SS uniforms, the operating room where they administered sometimes lethal injections, wasn't in Auschwitz but in an outlying district of Budapest, in a film studio where they were shooting an art film. I lost out on the leading role to my friend Zoltán, who then worked things out so that our classmates would be hired as extras in exchange for a modest pay check, a bit of fame and above all, a few days off of school.

My mother, who early in her career was a professional makeup artist, had made sure to be on the set. She was well

---

* Translated from the French by Casey Roberts.

positioned to overhear the stupid jokes me and my friends
were telling during the interminable breaks between takes.
In the little vignettes we acted out we were pretending to
be stingy Jews about to be gassed. You didn't hear me say
it, but we *were* pretty hilarious!

I'm not telling you them because I don't have the right
to repeat them. On the spot, my mother took me aside and
roundly chastised me, ordering me with all severity never
to repeat such garbage. And she added: "I'm telling you, so
listen up, you're a little Jewish yourself. Half."

In a country where in certain circles anti-Semitism is
deeply rooted, and where a national introspection had not
occurred after 1945, it was an urgent matter to clarify the
family rule concerning religious identity. When your grandparents were part of the one-fourth of what was originally
400,000 Hungarian Jews who survived the war, discretion
remained the best strategy. (Officially, they had converted
to Christianity, like other Jews who had gone into hiding,
and never went to the synagogue except under the greatest
secrecy.)

My mother didn't say all of that right at that moment,
she simply stated, "We don't talk about our religion nor
about anybody else's. If somebody asks you, we're atheists;
if someone says you're Jewish, you're 'half-Jewish' and never,
ever, tell or laugh at jokes about Jews. Am I clear?"

"Are you half-Jewish too?"

"I wasn't lucky enough to have a father like yours."

The nuance between Jewish jokes and Jewish humour
was thereby forever illuminated. And when a little boy,
dressed in white underpants and a t-shirt, appeared briefly
later in the film, visibly traumatized, his convincing performance couldn't be so much ascribed to the work of the
director with the young actor, as it was to the shocking news
and stern dressing down my mother had given me.

You see, she ruled her single-parent family with a firm hand, and so there was no way I could reconcile my knowledge of how hard she worked between one shift and the next with the heavy demands of dominating national policy and world finance, as the pervasive anti-Semitic discourse would have it. Even so, my fifty percent of Jewishness had to be scrupulously kept to myself.

Until our arrival in Quebec. Once here, I multiplied the fraction by two to get accepted and correctly classified by Statistics Canada, our new friends and my neighbourhood playmates in Côte-des-Neiges. Two Jewish Moroccan brothers warmly welcomed me into their gang, once my Jewish identity – Ashkenazi, but still – was revealed.

In Mackenzie park, my membership in the chosen people made sure I was one of the first, um, chosen, when we formed up baseball, hockey or soccer teams, thanks to the patronage of my co-religionists. The other advantage of being poor one-hundred-percent Jewish immigrants was one-hundred-percent free access for the whole family at the Westbury Jewish community sports center, with its pool, its ping pong table and badminton and indoor basketball courts. At the sight of all this equipment, we understood for the first time since the destruction of the Temple of Jerusalem by Emperor Titus, that being openly Jewish could have its advantages.

An advantage that I thought seriously compromised for a few long seconds the day I came face to face with the Israeli boy from my welcome class who I already was trying to avoid at school whenever possible. He was at least two heads taller and two years older than me. I suspected that he had already completed his military service. He intimidated the kids on the dodge ball court, even when he didn't have the ball in his hands and even when we were on his side.

The Israeli looked at me as if he had just discovered that I was a Greek polytheist.

"You, *Jewish*?" He said, astonished, without waiting for an answer and without adding anything before turning away.

I didn't know what to expect, but on the following Monday, playing dodge ball in the school yard became a safer sport. For me, at least.

Reassured, I began to quietly describe myself as Jewish – under my breath – when I thought that this information would complement my Hungarian identity advantageously. I realized that you couldn't work the math with half identities in multicultural Canada, but they could be summed to infinity.

At the end of the film in which I appeared, the young character played by my friend has obviously been murdered – unsurprisingly for the few Hungarians in the audience, most likely other Jews who still felt like they still had to hide their cultural identity forty years after the events. They couldn't imagine that at just that moment, somewhere in America, a Hungarian Jew could proudly proclaim his identity, that it could serve to liberate him from a prison that he couldn't have imagined ever being in.

WORKERS OF ALL COUNTRIES...

My Hungarian comrades kept sending me letters for a while, though they came at increasingly longer intervals. I got messages from professors, the latest gossip, and some photos, including this one, taken while I was still one of them.

The basketball and handball court lines painted on the floor, and the gymnastic equipment hanging on the wall bring it all back.

Arranged in a half-circle, the students watch a show, with all seriousness. Ranked by class, standing at attention, hands clasped in front of them, they wear the uniform reserved for special events scattered throughout the school year: back to school day, awards ceremonies, official celebrations, class photos. White shirt and black trousers for boys, skirts for girls. And the iconic accessory, a knotted blue triangular kerchief for the Scouts (the younger students) and a red one for the Pioneers, starting in fifth grade. You can't tell from the photo, it's in black and white.

In front of the wall bars, a student plays a drum, slung over his shoulder. He has been beating the military cadence as the students enter, class by class, starting with the first graders and ending with the eighth grade classes. The Hungarian flag stands in the corner, and they begin by saluting it, followed by the singing of the school song, and then the *International*. Next to the flag, also standing, are the members of the School's Communist Youth, which serves as the student association, accompanied by a woman, the Party representative of our district. They had just given the opening remarks, and they would come back at the end for some closing remarks. The red flag with its hammer and sickle rests on the floor, waiting for its moment.

In the background, standing on a bench, the eighth graders recite revolutionary poems, with adult seriousness. In front of them, there are two groups of costumed children. On one side, wearing feathered hats and white dresses, aristocrats waltz under the approving eyes of the Czar, in the opulence of a masked ball in the Winter Palace in Petrograd. They dance, carefree; while from the foot of the Palace walls, we hear the rising chant of slogans. The people are massed, impatient and increasingly loud. The crowd chants to the rhythm of the great national poet, Attila József.

> Long live the workers, the peasants,
> safe from the scheming of the bourgeoisie,
> millions of feet will trample them,
> Onward! the masses, forward, forward!*

The narrator recounts the story. We are in the future Leningrad, on the night of November 6-7, 1917, in October according to the Gregorian calendar. The proletariat suffers, crying out. It will soon launch an insurrection against the Palace, symbol of all the injustice that afflicts it. We are there at the heart of the most important moment of history, according to the Hungarian regime, proud inheritor of the legacy of the Bolshevik Revolution.

The people don't let up: "Work and bread! Work and bread!" The small group of students in front of the dancers is in agitated motion. The student who seems to be their

---

* Translated from the French by Casey Roberts.

leader, wearing overalls and a black beret, standing in the center of the workers choir, left fist raised, is me.

Seeing the photo, my heart tightens in my chest. It has been exactly one year. I had just participated in my first Halloween, at my new school in my new country. I was one of the few kids who had come to the school party without a costume, a party for a holiday that I didn't know much about and that, frankly, seemed childish and ridiculous.

I was homesick. I had discovered *a posteriori* an inordinate interest in everything I had left behind, including boring official celebrations. I don't like abrupt change and I didn't like all the chaos in which I found myself. Basically, I never liked revolutions. Standing next to superheroes and princesses, my Bolshevik costume would nevertheless have made an impression.

THE MAN WHO FAILED

*He promised to be at home by eleven o'clock, bringing
his school-report. Why, he doesn't want to go home at
all. Has he got a home, the Man Who Failed?*

Frigyes Karinthy, *The Man Who Failed**

Five ("outstanding") was the highest grade they handed out
at my school in Hungary. The grade below, 4 ("good"), would
have made me happy in every subject except physical education and technology, where I'd be aiming for 5s, and math,
where I'd be happy with a 3 ("average"). I had applied myself
with more passion in history and literature than in Russian
or chorus, but it wasn't reflected on my report card. When
attendance and behaviour were factored in, my very average
average sank even further. I was never a very good student.

If you got a "1" (unsatisfactory) on your final report card,
even if only in one class, you had to repeat the year. And
you'd be rebranded as a pariah, a disgrace to the school, a
kid who had "flunked." In fact, it almost never happened,
and then only in serious cases, even if the threat of it happening kept the more susceptible among us in a constant
state of terror.

I'll spare you the rich list of possible Hungarian fighting
words you could call on in a confrontation, but "you

---

* Title of the Hungarian original: *Tanár úr kérem*. Translated by
István Farkas.

flunked" was near the top. It was so fraught with consequences we didn't dare use it when the designee had actually
flunked. Especially since the kids who flunked tended to be
bigger and more brutal than the rest of us and had nothing
to lose in a school system where everything laggard was
treated as irredeemable. Moreover, we preventively frater-
nized with the thugs of the upper classes, knowing there
was always a chance they'd be sharing our desk the next
year.

By the end of sixth grade, I had been in Quebec for a year,
and in a regular classroom for only a few months. School
was easy for the first time in my life, despite my language
handicap. I had enough French to be understood, despite
my limited vocabulary, but its many subtleties (masculine,
feminine, grammar and spelling, its restricted syntax)
represented huge challenges, which still show up today.

But the rest was for me a real joke. The Quebec primary
school couldn't compete with the requirements, authori-
tarianism and seriousness of schools in a country like
Hungary. Three elements with which I have always struggled, so I wasn't about to complain. In a multiethnic
environment where students' strong language is rarely
French, regular classes or not, the requirements were even
lower – in principle to my benefit – but in reality only serving to reinforce a handicap for which the convenient solution was the almost systematic practice of requiring
immigrant students to repeat a year.

The classroom seemed more like a daycare, with our little
drawings tacked to the walls and a constant hubbub. Our
days were punctuated by quiet times, breathing exercises,
breaks for gargling with fluoride, other breaks to drink
some milk, an hour break for lunch, trips to the library
where I could read *Smurfs* comics without anyone hassling

me about the value of my literary choices. Then, when we were finally seated and mostly quiet, we would learn our division tables and the names of the planets. Which is by way of showing how the whole thing was a joke – to which I added a few of my own – to the pleasure of some, but to the consternation of the teacher.

There wasn't a schedule, except for gym and English. There weren't any tests, and report cards offered a level of precision limited to two possibilities. Either column "S" for "satisfactory" or column "U" for, you guessed it, "unsatisfactory." And three lines where the teacher informed our parents if we had lately been well behaved.

When I got my final report card, I learned, for example, that I had had a course in geography (or something like that). The grade I got was surely on account of the afternoon when we had been asked to use stencils to draw the continents with crayons.

I had carefully coloured, without crossing the lines, as seemed logical, Africa black, Asia yellow, America in red and Oceania in blue, and had left Europe white. This was possibly a mistake, because I got a U in the subject. The same grade was given to me for my behaviour, for English and French, and some other subjects to which the S's in math, dodge ball and arts and crafts were insufficient counterweight. So, tragically, the U's outweighed the S's, and there was just one comment at the bottom of my report card: "Required to repeat 6th grade."

I had flunked and I had failed. *[I am] surrounded by a lethal vacuum, a meaningless existence, a world of cold injustice.* I felt like I was the most disgraced kid in the school at the end-of-year party and would surely be a pariah throughout the make-up year, and probably for the rest of my existence in this fucked-up country.

STEP TWO: FIND YOUR WAY

EVERYONE NEEDS A SOUL MATE

"It's for his own good, it's for his own good, but listen. It's idiotic that they routinely make immigrant kids repeat a year!"

I had been promised that the recent humiliation I had suffered of being made to repeat sixth grade would be kept a secret, but a friend of my mother's got wind of it. The Hungarian-born woman was scandalized by my failure, but unlike some others, she directed her fire at the Quebec education system, not at me. I liked her a lot.

"His French isn't perfect, but there's no way they can hold back such a brilliant child (her words), you have to challenge the decision." Challenge an official decision? At first hesitant, my mother decided to take her advice: we immediately went to visit the secondary school that my sister was already going to.

Mr. Dahan, the assistant principal, greeted us with a stoic air that boded poorly. He was a Moroccan Jew (we had begun to excel in ethnic identification) and my mother deftly slipped in that I would be spending my summer at a Jewish community summer camp. This information seemed insufficient to justify my enrolment because he asked me to take a test right in front of him. After twenty minutes, I handed him the questionnaire. Mr. Dahan scanned my answers, occasionally raising his eyebrows, and with them ending in the up position, he informed me impassively: "It's good, young man, you can start in September, no need to inform your primary school." It didn't seem quite kosher, his way of doing things, but we weren't asking too many questions, especially since we didn't, you know, keep kosher ourselves.

Going into secondary school without a diploma from primary school didn't bother me that much, but the thought that anybody would find out terrorized me. What if my name wasn't on the list when they took attendance in the morning? And what if they then immediately sent me back, in front of the whole school, to redo colouring-in-the-maps in sixth grade.

Even though I had managed to avoid my own worst nightmare, I wasn't yet out of the woods. Every newcomer – whether to a school or a country – knows that getting in is only the first step in *finding your way*. A guaranteed place in a new school was no guarantee that I would be accepted. Especially since the local integration strategies seemed nebulous to me, and as far as I could understand them, would only work against me.

Even in homogeneous environments, on the first day of school all the kids are looking to find a group they can hang out with. The new students desperately seek out familiar faces or other kids whose sense of style or social class vaguely resembles their own, as far as might be determined by whatever had been snuck past the school dress code. Everyone's looking for the slightest opening they can grab to make initial contact and to avoid having to eat lunch by themselves. In a multiethnic environment, this pressure to find a friend, this challenging race to outrun shame, is accompanied by cues provided by the ethnocultural attributes of one's new schoolmates (skin colour, everyday language, accent, religious accessories).

I was the appointed loser in this integration-association game. My shoes, bought at Pitt's, didn't make a big impression because the few faces I could recognize were indifferent to me, and the school's Hungarian community was for some reason practically invisible, not counting my big sister who I could only rely on as a support of last resort. The school wasn't too concerned about my social life either. The first day, I was assigned a schedule, a homeroom and a locker, but no integration activity was planned, except for a dry explanation of the school rules. I understood that I would be on my own here and that I'd best not disturb the authorities during the next five years.

This dark universe suddenly lit up a few weeks later, during my art class. Through a kind of epiphany: the magical appearance of a girl with platinum blonde hair in an aquarelle wash, Prismacolor ultramarine (W2902) eyes, and a mouth, outlined in fine point charcoal that was constantly trying to compose itself into a smile. It seemed as though the exquisite sketch had sprung to life from the sketches in my Canada Notebook, whereas in reality, she had just come from Switzerland.

Her name was Justine.

That she didn't come from the devastated corners of the planet like us, but from the peaks of the Alps, was already exotic; even more surprising, she lived in the neighbourhood near the school, in the affluent Town of Mount Royal, whose residents generally avoided sending their children to our public school, even though it bore the name of their municipality.

Clearly, her parents were unaware of a fundamental piece of knowledge necessary for the social success of their daughter in this land of welcome. In Quebec, if you are able to set aside two or three thousand dollars a year, you qualify to enrol your child – if he or she isn't too dumb – in a private secondary school. It's a perfect system for making sure that the upper and middle class reproduces itself, by offering

enriched education to their children, without the disturb-
ances of the lower classes. The better-off immigrants generally take advantage, happily imitating the behaviour of the
local elites.

The normalization of this anomaly persists precisely
because it benefits those who have the power to change it:
first of all, businesspeople and professionals, but also government officials, journalists, politicians, academics, and
artists whose objectivity on this subject melts away like the
snow in spring out back of their Eastern Township cottages.
And for those among them who might suffer a twinge of
conscience, there is a very convenient in-between solution:
public schools oriented towards a special vocation for their
offspring who are, well, equally special. A perfect system,
as I said.

I spared Justine this line of thought, but I nevertheless
did my best to help this girl from Switzerland – my first
good reason for going to secondary school – feel at home.
I leveraged my three weeks of strategic advances in school
and my eighteen months' experience as an immigrant to
Quebec, to her delight, I think. Anyway, we got along really
well. We compared our experiences and our observations
about our small corner of the universe. We weren't talking
about things like op-eds in *Le Monde diplomatique*, nor
about shows that had been on TV the night before. She had
a mind of her own and didn't see why speaking in public
with a boy should subject her to mockery or teasing. The
short version is that I quickly figured out that she didn't
date, as opposed to the girls just emerging from six years
of extended kindergarten. I had found something of a soul
mate, after all.

I don't know if it was our comparative discussions of the
three school systems that we knew that put a flea in her ear
(behind which she was constantly trying to discipline a

recalcitrant curl), but she didn't return to school after the Christmas break. Her parents probably realized that the level of instruction had to be necessarily dumbed down in a school where the native and everyday language of the students wasn't the language of instruction. In any case, they corrected the mistake they had made of having sent their daughter to the neighbourhood school, situated in this parking lot for immigrants from Côte-des-Neiges and Parc-Extension, and enrolled her as designed, in a high-performing expensive private French school.

We never spoke again. Once I saw her at the entrance of the Snowdon metro. She was taller and more beautiful than I remembered. She was surrounded by a few friends, girls and boys who probably shopped for their upscale clothes on rue Laurier. They were laughing at stuff I wouldn't understand and getting ready to go somewhere where I would probably never be invited. I was returning from Mount Royal where I had gone sliding with a friend. I don't know if it was the embarrassment of her seeing me with my crazy carpet rolled under my arm or the fear that she'd pretend not to remember me, but I avoided the whole situation by pulling my scarf up over my nose.

The worst thing wasn't school as such; I ended up finding my place, some friends and some other reasons to go. The worst thing was the knowledge that there were *better places* and more humiliating still, that kids in those schools were aware that there were *worse schools*. And among them, this girl named Justine.

GOD, WOODY ALLEN AND ME

Why pork was proscribed by Jewish law is still unclear, and some scholars believe that the Torah merely suggested not eating pork at certain restaurants.

Woody Allen, *God, Shakespeare and me*

Coming from a family in which our practice of Judaism was limited to putting matzo balls in chicken broth and religiously watching Woody Allen movies, I found myself feeling like an imposter in Montreal's Jewish society. While learning the habits and customs of what was said to be "my community," I lived in constant fear of being unmasked.

Like the time in the synagogue at the bar mitzvah of my Jewish Moroccan neighbour. Holding the Torah, I piously pretended to follow the ceremony, nodding, trying to imitate the murmuring of the congregation, trying to follow the Hebrew text. I thought I had the situation completely under control until the man sitting next to me eventually gave me a nudge to let me know – with a small grin, seeming to say "nice try, buddy," – that I was holding the sacred book... upside down. That's when I knew I was living dangerously.

That lesson and the whiff of danger served me well later on, especially at the summer camp I attended in the early summers of my not-always-so-tender youth.

The summer camp was run by a Jewish organization and, unlike me, most campers were from the affluent neighbourhoods of Montreal and attended Jewish private schools. Like most Jews of Quebec, they were not particularly religious. But at a minimum, they emphasized the major holidays, knew what to do in a synagogue and called themselves kosher. Their practices varied according to family traditions, but let's just say that they didn't eat ham and cheese sandwiches in front of their rabbi during the Yom Kippur fast.

At the very least, you had to say you kept kosher, and keep it to yourself that you ate pork at home. Every community has its more or less stringent identity requirements, and this, among Montreal Jews, was the basic marker to differentiate the "them" from the "us." It wasn't as bad a sacrifice as that asked of Abraham, and it was also easier to fake than whether or not your penis was circumcised – but that's another story.

The place was beautiful, situated on a lake on a large wooded property in the heart of the Laurentians. Apart from a few differences, it was a summer camp like many others in Quebec. But here, the day began with "O Canada" and ended with the Israeli national anthem, along with the solemn raising of the flag, without setting off the irony detector in this community that was otherwise so paranoid about any form of indoctrination or manifestation of nationalism.

The camp didn't have an overly religious character, the singing of a prayer preceded the meal, and on the Sabbath, other than a religious service for which it was necessary to wear a shirt and kippa (baseball caps were tolerated), there were no organized activities.

Intercultural activities consisted of reciprocal visits with a neighbouring ultra-Orthodox camp, opportunities to play baseball with the boys with side locks and participate in (gender-segregated) Jewish dances as a manifestation of our solidarity with our brother (and sister) coreligionists.

Surrounded by a forest, with only cafeteria food to eat, away from civilization, being able to enjoy a bag of chips, some gumdrops, or a chocolate bar fell within the definition of luxury. As the days and weeks passed, the reserves set aside were becoming seriously depleted. The thriftiest campers strangely rose in popularity and the number of cases of theft and racketeering also rose in measure as the stocks – and our pocket money – declined.

The real kingpins were those whose parents had a cottage in the area. They could easily replenish their stash when supply became short. The other route of entry for the coveted items was provided by the counsellors, who you had to regularly bribe and then pay in advance of delivery – but without necessarily being able to get your money back if the delivery fell through.

There seemed to be only one law in this bad Jewish western: it was strictly forbidden to bring non-kosher food into the camp. Under penalty of forfeiture, the packages of new arrivals were routinely checked by the competent authorities to see if the little kosher logo was on the outside.

For me, more of a rebel and less concerned about morality, the work around was simple enough. I found how to get around the system without having to reach into my pocket. I discovered where the counsellors kept the confiscated goods, which they helped themselves to with few scruples. Sometimes you catch a break in life. While everyone was observing the Sabbath (and no one was minding the stash), I slipped away to take advantage of this manna from heaven, munching on junk food while reading *Lucky Luke*, all the while keeping my knowledge of this secret world, a secret.

I might end up in hell, but that's a risk I had decided to take while still very young. "Desperate times, desperate measures," I'll plead in due course before you-know-Who. If this proves insufficient, I might dare add that He should know better than the team He has managing His business in the Laurentians:

> We are human beings intermingled together, here in Quebec, and anyway, could we, for the love of God, enter Paradise without having so many restrictions – superficial, costly and ridiculous – imposed on us; so many ways to identify those who share our beliefs and those who do not, so many codes and uniforms to separate the worthy from the unworthy? So let me in, despite the fact that when I was twelve, I helped myself to quite a few Jolly Ranchers at camp! I was only just beginning to understand the complexity of being Jewish.
>
> And one last thing… tell me, we're not the only ones in there, are we? Otherwise, forget it, Man, I'll take the other door.

THE GAZETTE

In the Budapest of my childhood, you could get a couple of *fillérs* (pennies) per kilo for newsprint brought to the sorting center. Glossy paper paid even less, but if you include what we got by bringing in returnable bottles, it was the most reliable source of income for Hungarian children.

There were a lot of daily newspapers, although they weren't too meaty, and to increase our revenues, we would moisten the middle of the stack to pad the scale; you had to keep your eyes open, check around garbage cans, ask relatives and neighbours if they had any old newspapers lying around.

The loose change found by zealously checking the coin returns in vending machines and broken-down public telephones topped up my income. Sticking to this routine slowed me down when I had somewhere to get to, but significantly increased my savings, which in any case, I never spent because I didn't have any precious goals in life.

When I came to Montreal and saw the heft of its newspapers, especially on Saturday, I started dreaming of my golden retirement. What I understood was that in Quebec, people were so well off that they didn't need to recycle paper, they simply threw it in the trash. On the other hand, they had to work.

Thanks to my mother's clients, who were an inexhaustible source of information, I managed to get my first honest job when I was twelve, while in no way giving up on my planned future in IT: I became a paperboy.

Every morning before school and on Saturdays, in rain and snow throughout the school year, it was thanks to the hard work of me and my sister that the inhabitants of one stretch of Victoria Street west of Queen Mary (even and odd sides) benefited from the diversity of viewpoints offered by *The Gazette*. We got to keep ten cents per copy delivered, and we had to collect the money at the end of the month by going door-to-door in the evening.

Slowly but surely, the pennies added up and we were able to harvest the fruit of all our labour: two round-trip plane tickets to finally get to spend our holidays in Hungary, two years after our departure.

This story intrigued a family friend in Hungary, who during the holidays that followed, conducted an interview with us for Hungarian Radio where he was a freelancer.

We told him about our first couple of years in Quebec, from our limited perspective. How is school (easy, they don't teach anything very complicated), learning languages (French better and better, less so English), how's the weather (it's cold), does your mother work (she just opened her own business), what do you miss the least (too much school-work), what do you miss the most (our grandmother and our friends).

"Just one last question, how much did they cost, the airline tickets?"

"Eight hundred dollars each."

"And how did you pay for them, by bringing newspapers to the sorting center?" he went on, even though he already knew the answer.

"No, by delivering them."

I'm still not certain what conclusions the audience and the journalist were able to take away from our unguarded answer. The unimaginable opportunity that existed whereby a child could earn such a sum of money, the cruelty of a system that makes its children work or the irony of these barely departed emigrants whose greatest dream is to come back?

FRENCHEMENT BETTER!

It didn't take me long to realize that at my multiethnic French secondary school, you had to speak English if you wanted to be "*in*." This was long before becoming, you know, "perfectly bilingual," became a high priority societal and educational objective in Quebec, and not only among immigrants.

In my school, run by the Protestant (English) school board, the "Québécois" were primarily madams who worked in the cafeteria, secretaries, janitors and prisoners on probation who came to our school to discourage us from taking drugs. There were also teachers "from the majority," only, they were in the minority. As for students, only a handful of "*pure laine*"* landed here as castoffs in this inhospitable land: typically Mormons and Jehovah's Witnesses whose parents did not wish to have them educated in so-called Catholic schools.

Although the school board at the time was run by English-speaking Quebecers who still hadn't gotten over the founding of New France, let alone draw inspiration from the election of the PQ ten years earlier; and our principal, Mr. Asimacopoulos, did not speak a word of French, the teachers were militant enough to want to somehow try to make French the common everyday language in the school. Ambitious program!

---

* Dyed in the wool, possible synonym for *Québécois de souche*— trans.

The ideal promoted by the Charter of the French Language had to all appearances been reached (any number of moving stories about the success of Bill 101 and the integration of immigrant children could have been filmed here), but in reality, French was only used in class and among small circles of friends among the most popular in school – the more or less *cool* kids – made up mostly of Lebanese, Vietnamese, Latinos, Haitians and a hilarious little Hungarian boy I hope you will meet some day. Otherwise, the dominant language of daily life was English. Through the magic of power relations, it was English that conveyed authority and was the language of *winners*, although in fact more students could speak French than English.

In any case, for the vast majority of the students I knew, those years under Bill 101 were simply a necessary step on their way towards CEGEP, a degree and a job that would of course function in the international language of business (and by definition that of success). At best, they were a great opportunity, perhaps the only one, to learn the *"parler de circonstance"** of Quebec and discover *"les chants rauques de nos ancêtres et le chagrin de Nelligan."***

The passive resistance of the students to Bill 101 was the use of Franglais.*** Under the pretext of the difficulty of learning a language other than our mother tongue, we peppered our French sentences and phrases with English words and expressions, drawing from a language which also wasn't our mother tongue, but whose use sustained the illusion that we were both *cool* and cosmopolitan.

---

* Everyday language—trans.

** *The raucous songs of our ancestors and the grief of Nelligan*, lines learned from studying one of Quebec's greatest poems, "Speak White," by Michèle Lalonde, the reference being to Émile Nelligan, Quebec's most admired poet—trans.

*** Also known as Frenglish: a mix of the two languages—trans.

Active resistance went so far as the students walking out of school, waving signs challenging the directive seeking to impose the use of French during extracurricular activities. The English media covered the event, but failed to mention the students' second demand: the abolition of the school uniform.

You will therefore understand how ambitious it was to think that French could be imposed in such an environment. In these places, not even Dr. Camille Laurin* would dare administer his cure for making the school one hundred percent French.

To be fair, the people working in the school knew that the project of making French the everyday language would be difficult and sensitive, although absolutely essential to the success and integration of these immigrant students. To maximize the use of French, the school authorities applied both the carrot and the stick, sometimes vigorously, sometimes with resignation, sometimes with naivety. And sometimes too, with skill and intelligence.

The stick was represented by the constant calls to order that eventually blended in with the ambient noise: don't forget your homework, don't run in the hallways, put your hats on before going out, please, French is spoken at school. In the absence of any real consequences, let's just say that the last rule had about the same effect as the others: the important thing was not to look too nerdy in the school yard, even at twenty below.

More cleverly, "the imposition of a common language" led to the establishment of extracurricular activities where the use of French was intended to be as rewarding as it was indispensable, conducted by teachers without sufficient

---

* Dr. Camille Laurin, PQ minister and guiding force behind the French Language Charter—trans.

resources or support, who each deserved a medal from the French-only partisans of the Saint-Jean-Baptiste Society of Montreal.

The carrot was also applied through subtle approaches designed by intercultural relations specialists to promote the use of French in school, as was the case during a poster competition we were invited to take part in.

"Who wants to participate in a poster contest to promote the use of French at school?"

Suddenly, a fly flew across the room.

"Well, you don't really have a choice, but hey, there's a prize."

My team's collective intelligence delivered up a tasty *"Le français est frenchement meilleure"* (French is frankly better), a take-off on a popular milk commercial (*Le lait est franchement meilleur*) and a play on the French word *franchement* and *fraiche* (frankly and fresh). Frankly, we were pretty pleased with ourselves.

Not bad, eh? Perfect, we thought, for the "special jury mention for the transgressive originality of the use of the language in a multilingual environment." If only... Even though we had demonstrated a subtle sense of humour and made a case for the effectiveness of irony, the decision was clear: a poster to promote French must be in French, period. Our work was therefore morphed into the unconvincing slogan *"Le français est francément meilleur."* (the argument being that at least the word *francément* existed in French, well, if you lived in the thirteenth century).

As you might have guessed, we didn't take away a prize, unless you count a deep conviction that in the effort to win the cause of French in Quebec, bureaucratic intransigence is not guaranteed to get better results than being a corny Pollyanna.

The truth, which I couldn't admit under threat of marginalization, is that the complete imposition of French would have been just fine for me. A bilingual space inevitably creates inequalities and injustices at the expense of those just entering who do not master the dominant language. In a single language system, I would have concentrated on mastering a single language with which I might have become *in*.

THE ENIGMA OF THE RETURN

*We are disappointed to have become what we have
become. And we understand nothing about this strange
transformation that took place without our knowledge.*

Dany Laferrière, *The Enigma of the Return**

I arrived in Hungary alone for the holidays. The savings
on my reduced fare justified my getting out of the last week
of school; anyway, it was done often enough and the school
didn't ask too many questions.

"Do you still have to wear your Pioneers uniform when
they hand out the report cards at the end of the year?"

"Those days are all over. Come on, everyone'll be there!"

Like the others, I put on a nice shirt and bought a bou-
quet of flowers for my old teacher, before attending the
graduation ceremony.

The posters urging the youth to work to build socialism
still clung to the walls in indifference, but the most striking
change upon entering my old school wasn't political. Now,
not only the boys, but also the girls, more beautiful than
ever, came to kiss me on both cheeks. It wasn't so much a
sign that the regime was maturing, rather, that we were.

The kisses rained down when I arrived at the small humble ceremony, where the students gathered for one last time
after eight years together. Some kids had dropped out,

---

* Translated by Casey Roberts.

replaced by others, a girl had left for Kuwait with her parents and I had emigrated to Canada; these were the only changes in the group not attributable to puberty.

I sat down at my old desk knowing that I wasn't going to receive a diploma. I listened to the cheerful conversations without understanding the references, without knowing the anecdotes. I seemed to have missed out on everything; basically, nothing interesting had happened to me in the past three years despite my emigration to America. The distance seemed to have permanently widened; going back, even in my imagination, had become unthinkable.

A year before, every little scrap of information I had sent them from the West caused a sensation. Now, it wouldn't have impressed anybody to find out that you could buy 6-paks of Coca-Cola or that the sequel to *Back to the Future* was out. A McDonald's had opened in Budapest, a first in the Eastern bloc. Western brands, cars and videos had gradually made their appearance, giving the impression that everything would soon be as good as it could be in the best of all worlds. For my friends, it was the beginning of a new era. They were about to enter junior college. For them, everything seemed possible. For me, returning to secondary school in September promised at best a new intramural stick hockey season.

Here, a new world, full of promise, was looming on the horizon. A liberalization that was economic, but also political. The announced opening of the border between Hungary and Austria literally created the first breach in the Iron Curtain, which would render the Berlin Wall archaic a few months later.

The influence of the authorities had weakened slowly but steadily since the end of Stalinism, which had led to the 1956 revolution but, in this year of 1989, the weakening of the regime had become meteoric. Big Brother didn't know where to turn his eye, he had become the little brother we no longer hesitate to openly defy, even the most disempowered among us. Even fourteen-year-old kids.

The discussion was fuelled by the approach of the ceremonial reburial, this time with dignity, of Imre Nagy, the martyr of the 1956 revolution, the former prime minister hanged by János Kádár after the events. Kádár, head of state for thirty-three years, would die the following month among relative indifference.

What is to be done? they wondered in the higher echelons of power. But no answer would be forthcoming from Lenin, whose huge statue had been removed from where the enormous demonstration was going to be held. "For urgent restoration," said the statement of the Party, in the newspeak it continued to rely on. The vacillations of the highest leaders left room for predicting both the best and the worst. It was a few weeks after the bloodshed in Tiananmen Square. There was concern in the western media that riots and Soviet tanks were going to ruin my vacation. Not me. I knew that nothing like that was going to happen. The mood of the people, the carefree optimism that I could see in my young friends – but also in their parents – foretold the end of an era.

"Your mother told me to tell you not to go near there," my grandmother warned me.

"No, no, I have a rendezvous with my cousin."

In fact, it was with history.

I saw a silent crowd scroll by. Their faces, proud and serious. Old women with their headscarves, white carnations in their hands, men with moustaches wearing suits and ties, university students with styled hair and jean jackets trying to seem vaguely western. I saw a poster demanding the departure of the Soviet army. I saw Hungarian flags with holes where the hammer and sickle had been. I saw visibly moved faces shining with light move forward in small steps towards Heroes' Square which turned out to be, in this dense crowd, unattainable.

I went home to listen to the live broadcast of the event – uncensored – on my grandmother's old black and white TV. The image was jumpy at times, you had to keep getting up to adjust the scrolling horizontal lines. I had forgotten how exhausting communism could be.

"I can't wait 'til you have a remote-control colour TV, Mamie, that's the only kind there is in Canada, you know."

"Wasn't it just announced that they'll soon be growing on trees?"

THE MUSKETEERS

*"Gentlemen," said d'Artagnan, "allow me to correct
your words, if you please. You said you were but three,
but it appears to me we are four."*
"But you are not one of us," said Porthos.
*"That's true," replied d'Artagnan; "I have not the
uniform, but I have the sprit. My heart is that of a
Musketeer, I feel it monsieur, and that impels me on.*

Alexandre Dumas, *The Three Musketeers*

The banquet was sumptuous. The music was loud, a belly
dancer gave a passionate performance, the alcohol flowed
freely. Lively discussions animated the tables, and more or
less raucous laughter filled the restaurant. Between courses,
the fencing master stood up and called on one of his students, poured him a glass of wine and highlighted his most
significant achievements of the year.

The "Les Mousquetaires" fencing club was marking its
sixtieth anniversary, but absent its founder who had died
the previous year. They paid tribute to him. Master
Desjarlais had made the club the standard bearer in the
discipline in Quebec and Canada. Thanks to him, fencing
had escaped from the military barracks and cape and sword
novels to quietly become more accessible, and the Province
of Quebec Fencing Association had become the Fédération
d'escrime du Québec. I never had a chance to meet him,
but we surely had one thing in common: the pleasure of
having read, as children, Alexandre Dumas. For him, it had

been in the original language, on another continent, nearly a century before me, but there are certain works that transcend eras and borders.

I had landed in the iconic armoury a bit like how d'Artagnan, the young cadet, had arrived in Paris to join the king's musketeers with his precious letter of recommendation. The only similar resource I had on hand were the good words of a former member, a Hungarian woman who was one of my mother's clients, supplied when told about my dream of becoming a fencer. The mere mention of her name earned me a wary grin, a bad omen as regards my acceptance into the select group and my Olympic future. I was just hoping that our common origin was not the cause of this timid welcome. (I later learned that she was cheerfully hated there on account of the fact that she held a monopoly on the resale of fencing equipment, which went for exorbitant prices.)

Anyway, they gave me a mask and a foil, and I had my first lesson as the rumour spread about the newcomer, a small Hungarian with a strong accent who rolled his French "rrrrr's" for a couple of ticks too long.

I passed the test, but the true baptism of fire was waiting in the club lounge. When I opened the heavy door, the smell of sweat mixed with acetone – used to strip glue from the metal blades – washed over me. Decrepit steel lockers lined the wall. Overhead were dozens of trophies, held in place by the weight of the dust. On the other side, a large window with dirty panes gave on to the gym below. A loud *"tabarnak de putain de marde"** came from the armoury at the back of the room, where someone was repairing a sword with a saw, a shaper and a couple of kicks to the workbench.

---

* A colourful stream of Quebec swear words.

The fencing master assigned me a locker. "There's a foil in there, it's yours, but I don't want to see your stuff lying around, eh?" The tone was cheerful and the gesture magnanimous, but the rule was absurd. *Everything* was lying around the place. Big sports duffel bags and pieces of equipment, shields, blades, dirty t-shirts, socks and shoes littered the floor. A massive desk in the middle of the room was covered in paperwork, uncashed checks, precious official rankings. And half a dozen fencers were also hanging around in the room, instead of working out, recounting in manifest good humour a variety of martial (and non martial) exploits.

Crossing the couple of steps that separated me from the group was the ultimate test, and the most terrifying.

It proved to be the easiest. They were warm in wishing me "welcome to the club." Both the guys and the girls shook my hand and introduced themselves in turn. I was able to let my guard down. Even d'Artagnan, with his fiery temperament, would have failed to provoke these new companions into a duel. I took my place in the circle, slightly behind the others, and they continued with their stories, while I pretended to understand.

To think back, they might have accepted me out of necessity and didn't have a choice whether or not to be welcoming. It wasn't that easy to recruit new students. Most candidates who would have had the misfortune of being brought here by their Outremont parents might have made a hasty retreat. The addition to the troops of such a formidable potential as mine – in the veins of every Hungarian flows the blood of a swordsman – was ultimately welcome. I must say that it could have been much worse: I could have come directly from the neat and tidy Centre Claude Robillard.*

---

* Training center for elite athletes—trans.

The natural camaraderie of the club contrasted to the silly and superficial rivalries that unfolded daily at my secondary school, whose motto, "Every man for himself," couldn't begin to compete with the "All for one, one for all" of the Musketeers.

Another difference from the rest of my life: here, everything was in French. The conversations, of course, but not only. Each piece of equipment, every movement had a French name, the spectators shouted "*Allez, mon grand!*" instead of "c'mon, let's go!" And the results from the competitions were printed in *La Presse*, not *The Gazette*. Even at competitions held outside Quebec there was a proper respect for the French fact. The dominance of Quebec athletes was a partial explanation, as was the unabashed self-confidence of this first generation of young people born after the Quiet Revolution. It's also true that French was the official language of the sport and even English Canadians in Ottawa, Calgary and Toronto submitted to it without challenging this *lingua franca* before the judges of the Supreme Court.

This tight-knit community was certainly not *pure laine*. There were a number of athletes with different origins, but the French Canadians "of good stock" were the majority. With this jovial band I spent the most beautiful moments of my youth in Quebec. In exchange for my extraordinary personality, I was able to take advantage of my friends' basements, offers of extra tickets to the Théâtre du nouveau monde, their cottages in the countryside, the lifts from their parents and regular cups of hot chocolate from their moms. With them, I travelled abroad and across the country, from Vancouver to Newfoundland, via Chibougamau and Magog. I proudly wore the colours of Canada and Quebec, but basically, my allegiance has never been to anything but the Musketeers.

Some fifty people were gathered for the anniversary banquet in a couscous restaurant on Parc Avenue: athletes, volunteers and some old-timers. The event capped the end of another successful season. I had been sharpening my own gear for a couple of months without winning a medal or anything that would seem like a sporting achievement, but I enthusiastically joined in singing traditional refrains to the deserving recipients.

We were eating dessert when, suddenly, a glass of red wine was placed in my hand and I was urged to get up on my chair. Ever the eager recruit, I complied. I raised my glass well over my head without spilling it, and true to the mixture of Latin and slang from the popular happy drinking song, inclined the glass towards my "frontibus and nasibus and mentibus and flexibus and ventribus and sexibus and glug, glug, glug, down the hatch just like the rest of us, just like a real drunk (you can't tell except for his red face)." Then I heard my new brothers- and sisters-in-arms join in song, *for me*, singing the words I had longed to hear from the moment I had first come to Quebec and that still move me: "He's one of us!"

ON QUEEN MARY

At the video store, I spoke to the clerk in the language of the movie I was renting, usually in the original version. In other stores on Queen Mary, it depended on the language of the merchant.

With the Jews at Cantor's bakery and R.E.A.L. Bagel, I spoke English, same with the Chinese florist and the Indian drycleaner. In Cumberland pharmacy and at Steinberg's, it depended on the cashier, but I preferred French. Not out of love "for the beauty of the language of our land," let alone linguistic militancy. It was simply the language that I spoke best and it spared me embarrassing misunderstandings with the fast-moving cashiers and the customers in line behind me, who I was afraid would become impatient. It was only in French *pâtisseries*, with the Occitans in the *pâtisserie* at Calvados groceries and at the Provi-Soir that we would speak the language of the fare attendant at the Snowdon metro without hesitation.*

Ten years after the imposition of a single language on all outdoor signs, the "French face of Quebec" had come to dominate the city's facades, even on this street where English once reigned as Queen Mary of yore. Only now you

---

* Ironically, though living in a place where the predominant language is French, many people for whom French was not their strong language would only speak French in business establishments that were "obviously" French, like *pâtisseries,* but English to people who were performing their jobs in French, like the fare attendant—trans.

had to go inside the shops to find out what language was spoken inside.

The sign law had the merit of being clear, which avoided the messiness that would follow with the addition of the predominance of French rule. It was more respected at least in part because the militants were vigilant, sending complaints to the Office de la langue française whenever they found an English word on a sign, and slapping "Obey Bill 101" stickers on the windows of offending merchants. Of stickers that are difficult to take off, I know something, because my mother's beauty salon received a sticker treatment due to a post-it note stuck on the door saying "back in 5 minutes."

At my mother's shop, clients mainly spoke English and Hungarian, as they did with the other merchants from Hungary: Adler, the tailor, and Eva's corner store. The latter being the seedy convenience store north of Décarie – with a blinking orange neon "Bière-Vin-Cidre" sign – that I avoided because of its owners, a cantankerous couple, for whom I ultimately ended up working for two years after school at five dollars an hour "under the table," so ten dollars a night plus a fifty-cent tip that I got on a delivery. A small fortune that I deposited immediately at the Bank of Montreal ATM across the street, which was used to pay for my fencing equipment and trips.

To earn the money, I mopped up, brought up the beer bottles from the basement, took down the empties and did the deliveries. That was at first, before they discovered my indisputable talent for customer service, which when encouraged, finally added some warmth to this place to which the customers were only faithful due to their addictions to tobacco, lottery tickets and booze.

My mastery of the French language was not inconsequential to my success, but it was mostly due to my talent for guessing the customer's language. A challenge not so complicated considering I had lived in the area for years, and also it must be said, because English was the right guess two times out of every three. I was rarely wrong, but the mistakes were embarrassing. I then adopted the clever solution of an enthusiastic *"Bonjour!* Hi!" The most influential innovation in the commercial history of Chemin Queen Mary since the dismantling of the tram.

The return of bilingual signage brought in its wake the standardization of bilingual greetings, bilingual circulars, bilingual government services and bilingual sixth grade. Immigrants would no longer have that short moment of hesitation when entering a store when you remember that in Quebec, oh yeah, it's true, the official and standard language is meant to be French. As for French-speaking people, *"Bonjour/*Hi" serves as a reminder that their country, at least in Quebec, is in fact bilingual.

So it's perhaps thanks to me that this became the universal greeting in Montreal shops, except that in my case, if it helps to get me pardoned, it was the French greeting that was added.

THE NOT-SO-NICE DANCE

I can't help it, it's not that it's right
But if you're in my path
First I extend my hand
And then I finish with my fist

Félix Leclerc, *"La Danse la moins jolie"**

The field trip to the *cabane à sucre* or sugar shack was the only Quebec tradition usually included in the school calendar. The landscape rolling by that we saw through the windows of the yellow bus taking us to the sugar bush provided for most of us our only glimpses of what was called "the regions."

A number of teachers included Quebec works in their course outlines, although there was no ministerial requirement to do so. Otherwise, activities to discover Quebec culture were based strictly on the voluntary initiative of those teachers who, worthy successors of the Jesuits, were trying to transmit a little bit of their culture "positively" so as to avoid the unfortunate fate of the Canadian Martyrs.

Madame Desruisseaux, a young French teacher full of idealism, organized trips to Quebec City and Lac-Saint-Jean. Another took us to the theater. Another tried to get a student radio going and encouraged the volunteers to play some Quebec music occasionally. Another created a student

---

* Translated by Casey Roberts.

newspaper, *Le Salmigondis*, at the same time teaching us this great French word meaning hodgepodge that described the paper's contents so well. Some organized homemade versions of high school academic television quiz shows such as *Génies en herbe*, that a school such as ours did not have the resources to participate in.

During that time, others pursued an "intercultural approach," whose strategy was to organize activities highlighting different cultures and subtly slip in some Quebec culture.

In more homogeneous settings, the objective of these intercultural activities was to gain the acceptance of non-immigrants to immigration by demonstrating "the richness of diversity." In mixed environments there was the additional objective of encouraging meetings between the old tree stumps and the new seedlings. But in our school, where there weren't any French students, the idea was to show the children of immigrants that they belong in their adopted country, where there is an openness to their culture, and so to them; and by so doing, encourage the children's sense of belonging to Quebec society. In every scenario, learning to "live together" emerged as a process of discovery not so much about our similarities as of our differences.

Oddly, the contents of these intercultural activities vary little in relation to the degree of heterogeneity of the setting in which where they are conducted. They all reinforce stereotypes and contribute little to cultural enrichment, because what they are showing about different "cultures" remains on the superficial level. The activities are not designed to help you discover contemporary life in the various countries, their literature, their classical or contemporary music, the daily life of their inhabitants, the diversity of their populations, their history, policy issues or even their tourist attractions; but simply to reduce them to a couple of folkloric clichés or songs, so as to be able to say: Isn't it great how open we are to each other?; it's so awesome how we all have something different to offer.

In our secondary school, this approach was reflected by the flags of all the countries hoisted in the lobby, next to the *Fleur-de-Lys* and the Maple Leaf. And the photos from the five continents decorating the walls of the hallways with portraits of students in the style of "United Colors of Benetton." On the door of the secretary's office, around the sign that said *"Bienvenue,"* they added multilingual translations that made us feel really *welcome* and *bienvenido* and *nalvaravu* when we were called in to the principal's office.

There were of course, as everywhere, performances of songs and skits during which the organizers were impressed by the diversity of the presentations while managing to ensure that some of them were in French. We never complained about these not very demanding and often fun initiatives. Especially when as a result, we would be excused from class. This was the case when, during my third year at secondary school, things took a turn for the worse during just such an activity.

One afternoon, the whole school was invited to watch a professional folk dancing troupe in the auditorium. On stage, they performed dance numbers from different countries. When the dragons appeared, the Chinese students applauded; next, a Haitian dance, with the young Haitians standing on their seats; and so on, each time in a healthy competitive spirit that was fun for the dancers and surely brought satisfaction to the organizers as to the success of the event. During the Greek dance, the troupe brought the house down. I was planning my reaction as soon as they announced a *csárdás*, already imagining the comic effect that would be caused by my solitary celebration of diversity, standing on my seat in the middle of the floor.

"And now, our last number."

I expected that they would announce a dance special for its originality, rhythm and beauty, a traditional Hungarian dance, but instead was promised "a dance from right here."

"And now, just for you, dear students, a Quebec gigue."

The disappointment of not being able to experience Hungarian folklore seemed widespread because the room was spontaneously invaded by boos. The dancers, probably all from Quebec, and certainly energized by the curiosity of other cultures to put on such a show, froze before the cold reaction, and eventually, after a few long seconds, when calm returned, began the first hesitant steps, under the catcalls of the teenagers who left the room despite the intervention of their teachers. I might have been one of them.

After this sad spectacle, Mr. Milleret, a charismatic French-born teacher of history, took the initiative to visit the classes. He served up a strict lesson in morality, the most assertive discourse on immigrant integration I have ever heard and one that would make the hair stand on the heads of the members of the Tolerance Foundation.

"You are here in Quebec, welcomed by Quebecers, you have a duty as immigrants to show a minimum of respect for Quebec culture," he said in brief, with a tremor in his voice and a gravity that increased his eminence in front of the class – which for a moment – was trying to make itself as small as it could.

He didn't add, "And if you are unable to do that little bit, go elsewhere or go back to your country," but he certainly thought it.

1990

It's time for the broadcast
In 1990
It's the time of 24/7 media
In 1990
It's the era of consciousness

Jean Leloup, *"1990"**

God only knows that the summer of my fifteenth year was endless. My few friends were mostly off travelling or had moved. I hadn't found any work other than my *Gazette* route every morning. In anticipation of those long days, I always grabbed a copy of the newspaper, mainly for the sports, *Calvin and Hobbes* and Josh Freed's columns.

Nevertheless, when you're already over your workday by seven o'clock in the morning and you've got nothing to do, time seems to slow down. For me, but also for the politicians of the time, both in the world and in Quebec. It was 1990, the dawn of the information age which would, according to Jean Leloup, "leave us all speechless."

Something was happening on my old continent and in the world. There was the collapse of the Soviet Union and the collapse of Yugoslavia; the desire for independence of their former subject peoples had burst these two federations apart to give birth to new independent countries. Former

---

* Translated by Casey Roberts.

democracy activist Lech Walesa became president of Poland; the Czechs and Slovaks were beginning an amicable divorce while free elections were announced in the former countries of the Eastern bloc. It was also the year of the release of Nelson Mandela and the end of apartheid in South Africa. There was the reunification of Germany after the fall of the Berlin Wall.

Freedom, this word was being flashed on the cathode-ray tube pages of History, live. I spent time watching with rising enthusiasm the astonishing news that unfolded day after day on TV. Live reports, specials and non-stop commentary that heralded what would become information processing a few years later with the arrival of the 24/7 cable news cycle.

There was something going on in the world, but so too in Quebec, I understood. What was happening here would keep you on the edge of your seat with as much excitement as the Gulf War. Every day on the news, we could see the First Nations, defending their territory, armed with Kalashnikovs, right outside Montreal. Meanwhile, in Canada's capital, the plot twisted and turned around the Meech Lake Accord, which intended to give special status to Quebec in the constitution as a "distinct society." Conservative Minister Lucien Bouchard resigned to create the Bloc Québécois when the accord was rejected. There were the rants and bluffs of Bourassa, Mulroney, Trudeau and the premiers. The negotiations to save or nullify the agreement were becoming increasingly untenable, not only for the politicians but also for those who watched as time ran out.

Since I was by myself, it wasn't easy to sort things out, but at least thinking about it helped to pass the time.

Every so often, I'd go see my closest friend, who lived deep in the suburb of Pierrefonds. I had to take the metro, train, and a bus when his big brother didn't want to pick me up at the station. The father, who had settled in Quebec in 1979 on the eve of the first referendum, had the bad habit of monopolizing the TV in the basement where we usually played Nintendo. Which had the benefit of making us go outside, and then after we'd gone around the block, to enable us to follow the ongoing political saga accompanied by real-time explanations and comments from the point of view of the rather informed he was.

Like many others, he had neither emigrated to Quebec to make a revolution nor to discover the experimental theater of Pol Pelletier, but you could nevertheless sense in him a desire to understand his host society. I should also say that his open-minded comments incited me to relativize the prevailing consensus of the people around me, who generally considered *Passe-Partout** as something like a breeding ground for the Fourth Reich.

During this hot summer, I tried to put the timeline of the recent history of Quebec into some kind of order: the PQ voted into power in 1976, the adoption of Bill 101 in 1977, the 1980 referendum, the patriation of the Constitution in 1982 without Quebec's consent, the election of the Mulroney Conservatives in 1984 promising a path to its acceptance "in honour and enthusiasm," René Lévesque's "good risk" worth taking the following year in spite of opposition in his own ranks, with the whole thing culminating in the resounding failure of the Meech Lake Accord. This was a humiliating setback to nationalist federalists in Quebec. That's where we were in the summer of 1990. It was the epoch that gave rise to all the hopes and all the discussions that have continued to inspire and excite me ever since.

---

* A made-in-Quebec French-language answer to *Sesame Street*—trans.

When, the day following the rejection of the agreement, we heard Bourassa proclaim that "English Canada must understand very clearly that whatever is said and whatever is done, Quebec is now and forever a distinct society, free and able to assume its destiny," and saw Jacques Parizeau cross the Blue Room of the National Assembly to shake his hand, I felt – even at fifteen years of age – that big things were coming.

Things I wanted to see happen, and not just on television. An excitement to see the changes taking place, nearby or far away, overcame me. At the turn of the decade and still in my teens, I was forming my own opinions about this world in which everything was drawing closer together. I too wanted, in this *era of consciousness,* to free myself and – whatever they said, whatever they did – become more and more independent and ready to assume my own destiny.

THE "QUÉBÉCOIS"

I once saw a National Geographic documentary about one of those American prisons where daily life, with its social and illicit activities, is strictly organized along ethnic lines. Generally accepted by both the prisoners and the administration, it is a fundamentalist version of the multiculturalist ideal that in a multiethnic environment, general harmony will be achieved if the individuals who populate it are reduced to their ethnic, religious or racial affiliations and that this clan-like categorization take priority over any sense of belonging to a bigger collective. In the hell of these prisons, the inmates are not only locked behind bars, but also within the prison walls of their genetic code that they believe is their ticket to freedom.

Once the question of belonging is defined in this way, everyone has a place and a role that is recognized as much by the forces of order as the forces of disorder. At first driven by the need to survive, these outcasts of society find in their ethnicity a source of pride, income, protection and comfort. They give up trying to free themselves from its constraints, imposing it on their followers under the approving gaze of the guards, who are happy to reign over a microcosm in which the general interests are automatically fragmented, ensuring that this racist way of functioning continues and is systematized.

In the Californian prison that was the subject of the broadcast, 150 prisoners are crammed into a dorm with three bunk beds stacked one on top of the other, housed in a gymnasium. In this open space (open to all dangers), ethnic rivalries are even more pronounced – always tense, sometimes fatal. Without the protection of the bars, each person has even more need of those who are the same colour as him, in order to survive.

At the beginning of the documentary, we follow the arrival of a new African-American prisoner. Upon entering the gym, he stops, surprised by the inhuman layout of the facilities and, especially, by the absence of blacks in his field of vision. He instinctively knows what to do. Under the terrorizing gaze of Latino inmates, the newcomer desperately seeks his clan. Feigning self-assurance that fools no one, he moves forward, hesitantly, in the face of some nasty smiles, before finally asking, desperate, "Where are my people?"

His relief is palpable when he finds, several minutes later, a dozen blacks in the hall. There, regardless of the city and the neighbourhood they had come from – and even, regardless of their criminal colour – they are welded together as they would never be outside the walls.

The "Québécois" who started secondary 4 at our school probably felt a bit like that on his first day of classes.

Except he never did find his people; he was the only one of his clan. Worse, his species seemed on the verge of extinction, or at the very least, threatened in this not very natural, sometimes hostile social environment that was often suspicious of the French-speaking majority in Quebec.

Being a typical specimen didn't help him gain acceptance. With his too large shirts, which he wore hanging out over too-faded black jeans, his hair too long, his voice too loud, his accent too strong, his name too composed, he was too much. Not too welcome, for some.

In French we called him "the Québécois." In English, "the French guy" or "the Quebecer." But I heard some people call him – even to his face – "Pepsi," "Parizeau," and "frog," contemporary unofficial but commonly used names to describe the *Québécois de souche*.

His marginality was suspect and ridiculed despite all the preachy words about the beauty of differences and the importance of anti-racism that we discussed to pass the time in our ethics and religious education class.

In this sea where any opportunity to celebrate diversity was exploited, he was the most different fish. In this little universe fashioned by the conformism of American popular culture, marked by an overriding materialism and the styles it imposed, his brash presence reminded us that there was another cultural model that all of a sudden was standing in the way of our pursuit of the American dream.

The "Québécois" didn't find it weird to bring his sandwich on home-made bread, take a toilet paper roll out of his backpack instead of a Kleenex, wear a tuque at minus twenty or to have missed the Montreal Canadiens game the night before. He proudly explained that he didn't have a TV at home, that he bought his clothes at Village des valeurs, and wasn't ashamed of being bad at English. For most of us, his rejection of these symbols of wealth was unthinkable. In poor and immigrant communities, the nicks, scratches, styles, and bling of American celebrities were what was respected. By rejecting them, or worse, by displaying the symbols of poverty, he transgressed a taboo, a convention that was the main cultural binder in these ponds: consumer society.

Obsessed over external differences, we don't realize how a multiethnic environment can be a homogeneous reality. In these schools, "where people speak 150 languages and where we come from so many countries," diversity is often much less on display than you might expect. You would have asked us what movies, music, books, TV shows, food or hobbies we liked, and you would have got roughly the same answers. Ditto for our political views. And this is where his difference rubbed the most.

It was the era of highly effective challenges to Camille Laurin's Bill 101, conducted by an English community more determined than ever, which brought increasingly untenable pressure to bear on the provincial Liberals under Robert Bourassa. In response to the announced compromises, a vast mobilization led by nationalist groups, unions and the PQ, with the slogan "*Ne touchez pas à la loi 101* (Hands Off Bill 101)," peaked that year with a massive demonstration in Montreal.

The general buzz made its way into some of the secondary schools in Montreal, which gave rise here and there to small demonstrations in support of the Charter of the French Language. In multiethnic schools where there was still a substantial minority of *Québécois de souche*, they were organized (with the backing of the Société Saint-Jean-Baptiste de Montréal) to ensure their language was respected – or to make sure that *they* were respected at the very least. Because even the young people understood by then that Bill 101 didn't aim so much protect the French language as it did those who speak it.

Which could not have been better illustrated than in our school after the arrival of the "Québécois." Especially since he refused to "fit in," to accept his status as a minority. His refusal to blend in, to erase the most visible part of his identity, his refusal to disappear that was more disturbing than his Sorel boots, though oddly, this very attitude tempered the ridicule of which he was the object.

He was determined to make himself respected and didn't hesitate to tell his declared enemies to get lost, with some success. He even defiantly expressed his political ideas. Others might have let themselves be intimidated, but not him. He plastered his agenda and his locker with *fleurs-de-lis* and, even more provocatively, with stickers with the unmistakable numbers 1-0-1. He wasn't about to negotiate the denial of his origins in order to gain acceptance by his peers.

A rare enough phenomenon in this puritan environment, he even got a girlfriend, a beautiful Jewish girl from Latin America, Brazilian, I believe, who was attending a welcome class, surely too recently immigrated to understand what kind of pariah she was fooling around with in the dark corners of the basement.

The "Québécois" disappeared a year later, as mysteriously as he had arrived, and we never saw him again. Although, I did. Shirtless and in my boxers, on a Sunday morning, years after I had finished secondary school, when I came out of the bedroom of my girlfriend, who was going to UQAM. I learned that he was the cousin of her roommate, dropping in for breakfast in the apartment in Centre-Sud, an area that I had never heard of back in the day when we went to the same school.

"Hey, Akosse the Greek!"

"*Ben non*, you *maudit* Québécois, you insult me, I'm Hungarian."

And my friend breaks in, taken aback by this unlikely scene: "Look, in Quebec we're all Québécois!" She was partly right. And anyway, maybe the young man had contributed, through his refusal to submit, to the fact that I no longer find any shame myself in being designated years later as "the Québécois."

They say that prison society has its own organization, laws and power struggles, but they're wrong. In fact, it is only a reflection of the values of the society that created it. This also applies to its schools.

MADAGASCAR POWER

The focal point of the first-page photo in my Grade 11 Yearbook is a Greek flag proudly borne by the students of Greek origin who formed half of the school. A reality that these children and grandchildren of immigrants obviously did not want forgotten. Yet flag or no flag, it would have been impossible to forget.

"The Greeks" dominated the school by their numbers and by their *esprit de corps*. The principal was Greek, like many of the teachers, as well as the most prominent students displayed on the Board of Honour, in the detention halls, winners and runners-up in beauty and popularity contests.

Graffiti scrawled on the walls and lockers proclaimed *"GREEK POWER."* It was not a reference to a gang, but an affirmation of a community, a simple reminder of the balance of power in the place. Others affirmed themselves too, of course. Latinos, Vietnamese, Lebanese, Haitians, West Indians and Jews stuck to their own groups during activities and in the cafeteria, but the Greeks dominated over the smaller communities and free floaters, left on the side of the road by communitarianism.

Along the ethnic fault lines, there were occasional conflicts, rarely violent, but the prevailing good-natured communalism, accepted by all, kept daily life flowing harmoniously. Ethnocultural borders were not completely impermeable, but when it came to enjoying the privileges of the dominant group, its lines were jealously guarded.

The biggest advantage in being Greek was membership in the Orthodox religion which de facto provided extra days off of school, denied to the rest of the fools who did not believe that the Holy Spirit proceeds not only from the Father but also from the Son.

Because of the discrepancy between the Julian calendar and the Gregorian calendar, the Greek holidays fell on school days during which our principal, many teachers and half the students were absent. The numerous substitutes and remaining teachers didn't plan any class activities or exams for the occasion and, most importantly, no attendance was taken. One possibly passive way to protest against this accommodation they didn't yet have the impudence to call "reasonable."

These days were like all-day recesses, as if an apocalyptic blizzard had prevented half the students from going to school, and the other half from leaving. I tried anyway. Accompanied by my gang. This very exclusive ethnic gang consisted of my good friend who came from Madagascar and myself. We baptized ourselves "Madagascar Power" by a majority of votes (with one abstention). Our only achievements, for a long time, were the etchings – scratched into the top of our desks by the points of our compasses – of the name of our gang, alongside the more common "I Was Here," "School Sucks" and obviously "Greeks Rule."

Our ultimate act of daring may have been our unauthorized participation in one of these Christian Orthodox holidays. We decided to take advantage of the relaxation of supervision to skip school, as did several of our Greek comrades, who weren't fooling anybody. Since we hadn't received any specific religious education, the celebration of Good Friday took the form of sitting in the stands at the nearby arena eating poutine and passionately contemplating the private school girls, enrolled in sports studies, practicing double toe loops in tutus at center ice. The pious observation was soon disturbed by the habitual high-energy of a gang of Haitians from school who had had the same idea as us, but without the goal of passing this day of commemoration of the crucifixion of Jesus Christ in contemplation.

It was a way of seeking and finding trouble in the person of the Assistant Principal, Mr. Dahan, high priest of discipline, who didn't want a scandal to erupt on one of these feast days that could risk calling into question his day off on Yom Kippur. Warned that half of what he had left of his students were hanging out at the Town of Mount Royal arena, he, with disproportionate zeal, launched a surprise raid, setting off a general retreat. Getting caught in a stampede can be a terrifying experience, and we regained our wits only to discover that we had been arrested, crammed into the back seat of a car along with three Haitian captives. It was Mr. Dahan's old rattle-trap.

Along the way we couldn't help anticipating a painful meeting in the principal's office and, later, at home, a sentence without appeal. The car stopped in front of the school and our Haitian accomplices, more amused by the situation than we were, dressed as always in respect of the dress code of the American ghettos, pulled their hoodies over their heads and began play-acting a group of brothers getting out of a police car in front of the tabloid photographers. We got right into it, following their lead. Heads down, faces nestled in our elbows, for a few moments, we were members of a real gang.

The scene wasn't photographed for the yearbook. An image like many others that could have been poster moments for intercultural solidarity.

Our gang was officially dissolved by necessity; in any event, our time in secondary school came to an end. But not so our friendship. It still endures decades later, despite

the fact that one of us came from Africa and one from
Europe, that one of us is Jewish, the other Muslim. Facing
life together binds people more tightly to each other than
the blood flowing in their veins, it seems to me. We didn't
have a dress code or code of conduct except for the universal one held by all friends in all countries from all backgrounds who share values, memories and common interests.
We also had a conviction that these interests and values
could, if promoted and if space were created for them to
materialize, transcend differences of cultural origin. This
public school even offered the opportunity – especially to
those with the capacity and the desire – to shake off their
ethnocultural straitjacket.

But in the graduation photo, an attractive portrait of a
hundred multicoloured faces, the modest resistances to the
ambient communalism are imperceptible, hidden by the
omnipresent blue cross of the Greek flag.

THE APPRENTICESHIP
OF DUDDY KRAVITZ

*"Not the most delicate boy in the world, is he, Yvette?
He'll never marry you. A Hebrew never marries outside his own race. He's callow. His manners are
unbelievably gauche. Why, he hasn't the first notion of
how to treat a woman. What on earth do you see in
him?"*
"Plenty. Here he comes."

Mordecai Richler,
The Apprenticeship of Duddy Kravitz

I learned how to flirt with girls when I was seventeen, first
as an interpreter.

It was at the summer camp in Sainte-Agathe which, since
1921, had been delivering happiness to Jewish children and
teenagers, and where, in spite of having found this happiness during my first summer in Quebec, I returned as a
counsellor at the end of secondary school.

Above all else, I rediscovered there the Laurentian flora
and the English-speaking Jewish fauna that I met five years
earlier. They returned summer after summer, like the geese
that as a child I watched after supper land on the lake, alone,
in silence. A peaceful spectacle, far from the taunts of the
campers to whom I was too foreign, forgetting after a few
generations what it's like to be an immigrant.

The counsellors didn't come because they had to, and certainly not for the three hundred dollar salary. Except maybe me, who had nothing that paid any better, and my fellow counsellor I met there, Bobby. He, like most of the staff came from a well-off family, but his parents had turned down his proposal to spend the summer hanging out in the basement of their huge house in Côte Saint-Luc and the bars on Crescent Street.

The atypical duet that I would form with this impudent boy – a good guy – allowed us to extend our adolescence an extra two months. We had nothing in common except the perverse pleasure that we took in flouting the rules. And our interest in girls. Two art forms of which he was the undisputed master and I the meek apprentice, meaning that my job was to save his shorts while he tried to figure out how to unbutton those of our female colleagues.

I watched his method with a certain admiration. His feline approach, his steps light and sure. His way of directly approaching girls. His ability to adapt to the ambient room temperature. His talent for finding common interests when there weren't many. His belief that the hunt was more a matter of instinct, a mixture of charm and improvised genteel provocations, than the application of carefully prepared recipes.

He wasn't a total success. His reputation preceding him, the camp girls watched Bobby from an increasing distance. He wasn't exactly a nice Jewish boy, a future lawyer, doctor, or at worst, a real estate agent to whom their parents would gladly wish *Mazel Tov* after he broke the ceremonial glass with a stomp of his foot at their wedding. Suitors were not lacking, a little something between boys and girls upped the summer heat. Experiencing a first great love story, maybe your only one, getting a boyfriend or a girlfriend, was the dream of campers and counsellors as is the case at all summer camps.

It was fortunate because one of the main objectives of the camp, as of any community enterprise, was to encourage intra-community marriages. It took over this task from the schools, synagogues and associations where the community forged its identity. In addition to the transmission of language and common traditions, the most essential instrument for ensuring the cohesion and survival of a group is the formation of couples. Camp management didn't have to program weekly orgies after Shabbat, although they did impose some restraint in the public demonstrations of young love, but it also knew that the more this environment was restricted to outsiders, the more the objective would be fulfilled naturally.

And as for that, camp management was confident. The only outsiders were there by strict necessity. The campers, counsellors and managers were Jews, but the workers were as in any good (vacation) colony, natives. They were invisible to us. Except maybe for this one beautiful blond girl, responsible for maintaining the lavatories, not without contempt called the "Toilet Lady." Anyway, for my friend Bobby (and I confess, for me too), she was far from invisible.

This Québécoise could also see through his game, but she wasn't put off by the possibility of a romance with a handsome foreigner, adopting a liberated woman kind of attitude that often, in the eyes of conservative ethnic minorities, is interpreted as a degree of levity inappropriate for a long-term relationship (and vaguely despicable), but very practical for the short term.

The manifest efforts of my friend to venture outside the box did crack up the other campers, but Bobby's problem was his unilingualism. A completely relative handicap that he didn't feel forced to justify – like so many others – by citing the alleged refusal of the Catholic clergy, under Duplessis in the 1930s, to admit his grandparents to French schools. The same guy who had unsubscribed the French channels from his cable package stated clearly that he could care less about learning this language, useless in his world.

The ability to form a complete sentence in French might have been useful to him for the first time in his life, but he found a solution because he always found a solution, and appointed me as his personal interpreter.

"Hi, my friend's called Bobby."

"I've known that for awhile…"

"He knows yours is not 'Toilet Lady,' he's just joking around, he wants you to know."

"Okay."

"Do you want to smoke a cigarette with him in the woods? There's a fun spot he wants to show you."

There, an old picnic table was our meeting place when our breaks fell at the same time. I translated their conversation, whose limited vocabulary didn't require that I bring my pocket Webster's. Although I made a few mental notes, admiring Bobby's boldness and increasingly jealous of its effects.

"Do you realize that we are reliving a scene out of *The Apprenticeship of Duddy Kravitz* by Mordecai Richler? We're only a few kilometers from where his famous novel was situated, Lake St. Louis, where Duddy meets Yvette, a Québécoise from Sainte-Agathe who falls for a Jewish boy as handsome as he is calculating. It also happens to be where the poet Gaston Miron was born…"

Well, that, I didn't say to him, or didn't know, and even if I had, I would never have strayed from my mandate as an interpreter to share my literary observations. In Quebec, the ignorance of culture *was* the common culture. They didn't teach young people about Richler or Miron, not in private Jewish schools nor in Montreal immigrant secondary schools nor in the public schools in the Laurentians.

His charm was working nevertheless. He was exotic; blond, English and Jewish, from Montreal above all. The big city on the other side of the Porte-du-Nord where she had only gone once or twice, but that was a destination as intimidating as the blue eyes of her Outlander.*

"What kind of music do you listen to? I'm mixing, you know."

"No, he's not a musician, he means that he's a DJ."

"Do you go to the Princess Club in Sainte-Agathe? If you come to Montreal, I'll show you some cool places."

And of course, the ultimate question, the one that stood waiting in ambush, waiting for the sniper to finally squeeze the trigger:

"Do you have a boyfriend?"

"Nothing serious, and you, a girlfriend in Montreal?"

"He finds you beautiful, he says you have beautiful hair."

"You too."

"..."

"Me?!"

At this point, they excused me from what may have constituted advanced lessons – and Bobby, like Richler's character, did not include the use of the mother tongue of his ephemeral conquest.

Bobby was sent home on twenty-four-hours' notice for having provided beer and cigarettes to the campers. She never saw him again, and he left me the task of saying goodbye. She had tears in her eyes that I wasn't able to assuage. I didn't make it to the goodbye module in my apprenticeship with Bobby, a piece of the puzzle I'm still missing.

On the other hand, my basic training came in useful for getting to know some Québécois girls. If I have surpassed

---

* Reference to the classic Quebec novel *Le Survenant* by Germaine Guèvremont entitled The *Outlander* in English.

the master in some respects, it's probably due to having more respect for women in general (I like to think), those from here in this case, a sincere interest in their culture to which I felt less and less foreign, thanks to an important asset, one that Bobby lacked as much as Richler: a knowledge of the other person's language that helps move intercultural relations in a positive direction by providing a minimum basis for mutual understanding.

SNEEDRONNINGEN

But it is so hard for me to speak your language.
If you understand crow talk,
I can tell you much more easily.

Hans Christian Andersen, *The Snow Queen*

I'm not boasting or trying to make you feel jealous, but I once became friends with a Danish woman with whom I shared an interest in education, Quebec and French. She had beautiful red hair.

She belonged to an association of French teachers in Denmark, founded by her father decades earlier, and was particularly interested in Quebec culture. The association wasn't intended for professors from major universities or upscale colleges. Its members taught in regular public high schools around the country.

She'd be kind of like a German teacher in a secondary school in Baie-Comeau who was especially fascinated by Austrian culture… and who had travelled to Vienna on her vacation to deepen her knowledge of the place. Even if I didn't know the colour of her hair, I'd be curious to meet her.

My friend didn't seem to be the only one of her kind. When I met her, she was accompanied by a delegation of twenty-five teachers who had come to Quebec for meetings and workshops on Quebec culture and literature. I don't

---

* Translated by Jean Hersholt.

know if their teenaged kids are taking Ritalin or smoking joints before entering their French classes, but what I do know is that they are reading Anne Hébert and listening to pop singer Daniel Bélanger "dry his sister's tears."

As for me, I was and am rather ignorant about Danish culture. I've seen some Lars von Trier films, I've read Andersen's tales, those Great Danes make me laugh and I love the brioches, but it never occurred to me to take Danish. As with many languages, I get along just fine with translations, subtitles, dubbing. And when I travel, a few words and everyday phrases. Do you see how narrow my mind can be?

I am always appreciative of the kind of people, rarely enough encountered, who have learned a foreign language just to satisfy their curiosity. We often extol the young immigrants "who master three languages," like me supposedly. Fortunately, Statistics Canada doesn't administer language tests because it's not always completely true. Like other immigrants, I can't write a letter in my native language without mistakes, and even if I could, being able to do so wouldn't deserve a great deal of merit. Not like what should be given to the young Quebecers who learn Catalan, German, Russian, Spanish, Mandarin, Portuguese or Arabic merely out of passion for a culture that is foreign to them, in spite of the lack of encouragement from their parents or our education system to do so.

Like the students of this Danish teacher. When I spoke to her about Andersen, to make myself look good and show that I also could be interested in her culture, she let out a deep sigh. "You know, we keep recycling Andersen until we've kind of had enough. It must be the same for you with Tremblay, Nelligan or even a French writer like Victor Hugo."

"Uh… yes, for sure, though in fact, it never gets to that point. Here in Quebec, we want the young people to just read stuff that interests them, you know, books that are close to their concerns and accessible to them. And conveniently also available at the video store. We certainly wouldn't want to chase them away with classics that could harm their self-esteem or turn them off to school. We have a big dropout problem in Quebec, you know..."

To change the subject – and preserve the honour of the motherland – I told her about a poem by Michel Garneau I had read in college and, suddenly, she was once again fascinated by Quebec. And me by her hair.

Thinking back on it, I suddenly regret not having asked her to marry me. Not necessarily so that we could have had frizzy red-headed children, but to have been able to pass on to a new generation her culture of openness. A culture that opens us to a world so vast that it exposes the narrowness of our own. She would have been the perfect model. Like her father and his colleagues, who worked every day to manifest the idea that the beauty of the world cannot be expressed in one language alone, always the same, and that a poem by Anne Hébert can even speak to the goof-off seated in the last row of the class of a regular high school in a Danish village.

I've often thought about her. When I travel, especially when I meet young backpack-carrying Quebecers so open to other cultures, but unable to talk about their own; who identify themselves as citizens of the world ever since they got drunk with two Australians and an Italian in Barcelona; who are convinced that their salvation, and that of their compatriots, will be gained through more English, and nothing but English; and to whom the incongruous idea never occurred to try to talk to the people of the world, without intermediaries, in their own language.

Obviously, this still requires having something to say. As for me, I started by reading, like this Danish Snow Queen, some novels written here in Quebec.

HUNGARIAN RHAPSODIES

RHAPSODY

I.

A. *GR. ANTIQ.* Epic poems sung by *rhapsodes*, singers who went from town to town.

B. *Pej., Old.* Work in verse or prose composed of various poorly connected elements.

II. *MUS.* Free form instrumental or orchestral work, consisting of juxtaposed themes, folk or regional inspiration. *Hungarian Rhapsodies of Liszt.*

Centre national de ressources textuelles et lexicales

After the change of regime in Hungary, the newly announced compensation program for property confiscated by the communist regime represented for many, during the 1990s, the first tangible benefit of this democracy, this freedom, so promised and hoped for.

My mother questioned my grandmother about the fate of pre-war family properties. "Did you sell the apartment where you lived in Budapest before collectivization or was it confiscated? And the country house and the land where you told us you spent your summers? And the one from your childhood, that huge villa of your parents, so spacious that the Germans requisitioned it as their general quarters, is there any paperwork?" It was a lot of details requested of Mamie who, at the time, was confusing me with my grandfather who had died eighteen years before my birth. But my mother, whose dream of spontaneous enrichment had not yet been realized in Côte-des-Neiges, hoped that maybe it was still possible in the country she had left.

"It's been a long time since I worried about any of that," pleaded our only witness from back then who was still alive. She had already put the old family villa out of her mind fifty years ago; it certainly wasn't something she thought about now that she shared a tiny room with a stranger in a retirement home in Budapest.

The lucky ones, like my mother's friend, found traces of their property. This friend, after years of administrative procedures, documents to produce and forms to fill out, finally won her case after she had given up all hope. In return for the confiscation of a large farm with a house where her family had lived until the state had taken possession of it, she received compensation for her losses. The check enabled her to buy a panini maker. I'd seen a similar model at Canadian Tire for $19.99, plus tax. Even my mother, who nevertheless encumbered any flat surface of her kitchen with useless gadgets, hadn't wanted one.

This quest seemed futile: I had always known that my legacy would never be financial, which didn't bother me. Especially since I didn't really know how to relate to any aspect of my past. "I'm Hungarian, I'm Hungarian, stop harassing me," was the cry from my everyday heart. My foreignness began to weigh on me. In the years following secondary school, I met plenty of Quebecers for whom the immigrant was still a curious beast. Being asked the same questions about my background over and over again was starting to annoy me.

I would have liked to go by the name "Martin," unnoticed, to avoid provoking a barrage of questions at the beginning of any social interaction. This was rarely done out of morbid curiosity, but neither was there much genuine interest either. Still, I preferred the questions to the difficult discussions where my difference was a pretext for a debate on the ethnic vote, the Israeli-Palestinian conflict or the collapse of the USSR.

"Sorry, my stop is coming up, we'll continue this as soon as we can, I promise!"

"Me too, I have to get off here."

I learned that I couldn't get out of it all the time and I saw myself more and more as a kind of ambassador whose role – although often annoying – was to market his country. I brushed up on some facts and became good enough, I think, to explain the grand lines of the history, current events, literature, cuisine and language that define the originality of my native culture. Not necessarily in a super comprehensive and erudite manner, but I tried to avoid the usual hodgepodge of clichés, exaggerations and approximations often delivered by overly proud immigrants when they speak of their country. I even started to find myself interesting...

I had also begun to gather some tangible vestiges of my roots (as the last of my ancestors departed). Books, pictures, family artifacts. The photo of my grandmother in a bikini in the 1930s, my grandfather as a uniformed officer, subway tickets from my great-grandfather (expired in November 1920). My grandmother's first shoe, cast in bronze. An antique history of Hungary, my father's collection of cigar cutters, his flask with our family name engraved on it...

I would use any of these objects as an occasion to tell about *my* Hungary, which doesn't exist on any map or in any book. The courteous curiosity of my interlocutors often became sincere, profound, friendly, loving. I'd work the objects into stories of my youth, relate them to the books I read early on, the works of Hungarian culture that I discovered and then gradually rediscovered. I would show people Vasarely's graphics, play recordings of Bartók, Liszt, popular singers. I'd recite the poems of Attila József, I got people interested in reading the novels of Magda Szabó, Frigyes Karinthy and Ferenc Molnár, and to this very day, on my birthday, we throw some Debrecen sausages bought at Fairmount's on the grill.

My stories became the reflection of my new home, of my life, of my memorabilia and anecdotes. I had walked into the looking glass I held in my own hand. The scattered stories, these various poorly connected elements, came together into a more or less harmonious whole. They forged my identity. They were my rhapsodies, my rhapsody, not Hungarian but Quebecois.

At some point I was the one who started to be annoying about my heritage, probably a legacy from my mother.

STEP THREE:
ARRIVE AT THE BEGINNING

THE LIFE BEFORE US

The choice of the CEGEP* I'd end up going to was more attributable to the magic of the Z-rating than to any late-blooming teenage rebelliousness, much less feelings of patriotism, as my mother feared. Like most immigrant parents, she would have preferred me to choose to pursue my education at an English CEGEP, like eighty percent of my former classmates.

I pleaded that my English wasn't good enough despite all the American TV I had watched, whereas I had attained a certain mastery of French. It was true, even if it wasn't reflected in my grades, and it gave me confidence to face the future. A blind confidence that was, however, more typical of a teenager.

Through the application of the mysterious formula of the Z-rating (now R), to which the Ministry of Education held the only key, it was determined that I would spend two hours on the bus every day on the round trip between home and the CEGEP. To a neighbourhood I hadn't known existed: karma for my years of being a dilettante in secondary school.

Whatever! i was far from being a dropout. This wasn't much of an issue In my community. We were never even told that leaving school without a diploma was an option.

---

* CEGEPs, which are only found in Quebec, are colleges that provide post-secondary education, either professional or pre-university.

Awareness campaigns at the time were primarily concerned with respect for differences and *Canada's Food Guide*. We were also asked to avoid drugs and acid rain as much as possible. To be sure, students disappeared from our classrooms from time to time without anyone seeming to worry too much about it. Maybe they had figured out that as long as they weren't learning anything in school anyway, it might make more sense to go work in a corner store or sell dope. Which would be the logical consequence and a correct understanding of the school's utilitarian orientation.

In secondary school, there had been a tacit understanding between students and teachers: the latter pretended to teach and, in exchange, the former pretended to learn. I wasn't too bad at that. The minimum requirement in exchange for our diploma was to not fool around too much at our desk, which for me was the complicated part of the deal.

Take for example our home economics class. Objective: to turn us into happy homemakers. Potential usefulness: very large. Learning: limited to the baking of muffins. Implicit educational philosophy: do not frighten teens with vegetables and risk alienating them from the kitchen forever. The same fashionable strategy was applied in our French classes where they avoided traumatizing us with books, so as not to turn us off to reading for the rest of our days. Success: mixed.

Immigrant children from immigrant schools were not the only ones afflicted with cultural poverty when they arrived at CEGEP. Obviously, there were students who were cultivated, studious, and interested; they had also existed in my secondary school, with the difference being that at CEGEP the teaching was oriented towards them. The teachers had time and space to devote themselves to their passion, unlike their secondary school colleagues for whom it was impossible, overwhelmed as they were by managing their classes and dealing with the disinterest of their students. Here, they were indifferent to our indifference, but not the other way around.

Like this professor of literature, a poet-rocker, whom I liked in his friendly cantankerous role. I saw him lose it a couple of times on account of our literary ignorance, memorably the day when a student asked about Arthur Rambo* in relation to one of his assignments. "Which Rambo man? I've seen most of them."

I could only agree when he pointed out the weak literary awareness of some of his students. I probably had read three, four novels at most throughout secondary school. Between Claude Gauvreau's tormented poems recited on *La nuit de la poésie* (1970) that I had recently discovered on VHS, and the poems of the Hungarian *terroir* that I had been required to recite by heart in front of the class in primary school, I had literally never been exposed to poetry in school.

He wasn't any more eccentric than the average prof at this CEGEP, where you had to belong to the Fourth International to teach (at least in the humanities department where they didn't teach math), and where some of them smoked in class and looked like they had just set off a bomb on behalf of the Front de libération du Québec. There was one rather erudite prof, a walking encyclopaedia of art history, who took me and a few other students to the Pointe-à-Callière Museum on her time off. There was also a Raëlian bishop guide who, notwithstanding his writings on the benefits of collective masturbation which had caused quite a stir, was frankly a good teacher.

Strangely, I have few memories left of the people I knew or of my everyday life during those years. I went to my classes with a new sense of pleasure, but the rest of my CEGEP

---

* Arthur Rimbaud, nineteenth century French poet—trans.

experience, such as rolling joints and learning the Morin Code* is kind of foggy. But it did open me up to another world, one that the Ministry of Education had cleverly kept hidden from me: Quebec.

Once her Westmount clients were reclined in their comfy chairs with no choice but to follow the tribulations of my life while they were getting waxed, my mother would have liked to have been able to say that I was going to an English CEGEP. Vanier, Dawson, Marianopolis: the three possibilities that would have led me to McGill or, next best, Concordia. In other words: to social success, to the success of our immigration.

"Cégep de Rosemont" – even smoothed out to Rosemount College – inevitably raised the very eyebrows that my mother was trying to pluck. Everyone was worried about my future. A French CEGEP in a French neighbourhood with French students and professors wasn't very prestigious or promising, and besides, it was dangerous for my young mind, susceptible as it was to influences.

"I worry about who his friends are, he's changing. He's in his first semester and he's already talking about the failure, no, not of his courses, but of the Charlottetown Accord, because, listen to this, 'the proposal is insufficient for Quebec.' And he's going to vote for the Bloc and Lucien Bouchard next year. Lucien Bouchard, can you imagine? I don't understand what he's doing, what he's reading, what he's saying. He's too enthusiastic about his courses, I can't even recognize him any more…"

"At least he doesn't take drugs," replied the pitying voices, trying to be comforting.

"Maybe not, but he reads *Le Devoir.*"

---

* The French version of Robert's Rules of Order—trans.

A DAY IN THE LIFE OF A DEPUTY RETURNING OFFICER

For his part, Amerigo had learned that change, in politics, comes through long and complex processes, and you couldn't hope for change overnight, as if it were a stroke of luck; for him, as for so many others, acquiring experience had meant becoming slightly pessimistic...

"To transform a room into a polling place," Italo Calvino wrote, "only a few objects are required." Curtains for polling booths, ballot boxes, ballots, pencils and some posters. We put everything in nondescript bare rooms, added a few chairs for the staff (returning officers, clerks, party representatives), who surrounded by these even more bare and nondescript objects, assume "the impersonal appearance of their function."

I assumed that appearance for the first time in 1994, on the ground floor of one of the Rockhill Towers that disfigure chemin Côte-des-Neiges. It was during the provincial elections that would bring the Parti Québécois back to power with Jacques Parizeau as its leader. It was this very passive role that led me – somewhat by chance – towards an active life in politics.

At first, I did it mostly for the money. I had heard that they were paying more than one hundred dollars a day for sitting in a polling station "doing nothing." In my defense, I wasn't exactly rolling in money: I needed the twenty or

fifty dollars I earned here and there – as a fencing coach
or referee, clerk or babysitter – to supplement the loans
and bursaries that I lived on at the beginning of my adult
life.

Having a chance to be in the front row of – or to be an
actor in – an important political event meant as much to
me as my paycheque. Earning a living without having to
work and changing the world effortlessly were my two more
or less avowed goals in life, and this job proved that my
dream was achievable, no matter what my mother or guid-
ance counsellor thought.

To get the job, you had to be referred by a political party.

At the PQ election offices, nothing was asked of me other
than my address and phone number. The woman didn't
react when I mechanically spelled my name and eagerly
emphasized my sovereigntist sympathies. For that matter,
the name of the candidate in my riding didn't seem that
Péquiste either. "Salomon Cohen, Parti Québécois" seemed
like a bad joke. Or a good one?

"The training of the election staff is tomorrow night, if
you don't show up, you don't get the job."

My career as an involved citizen could begin. Ten years
later, It would be me providing the training.

It might seem pretty boring to sit on a folding chair
watching a whole neighbourhood file by for twelve hours,
but the optimistic observer of democracy would have plenty
to sink his teeth into. He would be astonished at the seren-
ity of the place, even when the stakes are the creation of two
countries out of one. He would notice that "the variousness
of life enters with them" when the voters enter, the diversity
of his fellow citizens, even in the most homogeneous rid-
ings. He would tell himself that it's a pretty good thing that
everyone has an equal voice in a democracy, even people
like the disoriented old man who wants to know where Jean

Drapeau* is on the ballot and someone else who doesn't understand a word of French or English.

The cynical observer of the democratic exercise would, on the other hand, notice the shuttles bringing people to the polling station who, without this logistical support, would have had neither the notion nor the heart nor the strength to vote, much less the lucidity. He would see the fake smiles and the over-the-top confidence of the candidates who are there one last time to shake our hands (and call you "son" but forget your name the day after, as singer-poet Félix Leclerc would sing). He would note the futility of the vote for the numerous voters whose votes will not be represented at all by the first-past-the-post system. And he would notice all the names, especially of young people, who when the polls close will have yet to be crossed off the voters list.

But when the polling station closes, our deputy returning officer feels the satisfaction of having accomplished a duty; that the task of voting, like that of mechanically handing out ballots, makes sense – and his life does too. When he gets home, where he will follow the electoral results throughout the night on television, well past the solemn announcement of Bernard Derome,** the deputy returning officer tells himself that even if the results hold up, the regularity of this exercise, the very existence of the right to vote, the mere fact of granting this voice to each of us invests the citizens with a certain duty and a certain power. And that by giving to each and every person this trust, the opportunity to express their opinions through the ballot box, we can, we might, we should be able someday to truly make a better world for everyone. Then, opening the newspaper the next morning, reading the headlines, the analyses, the editorials,

---

* Mayor of Montreal from 1954-1957 and 1960-1986—trans.
** Long-time Radio-Canada election night anchor—trans.

the open letters, he assures himself that the birth of this better world didn't hinge on the results of any one election, no matter how important. He realizes that the next election is somewhere down the road and wonders if he couldn't do more, participate more, in the great march of humanity.

A little while after my first experience as a deputy returning officer, maybe during my second, I attended a meeting organized by the Parti Québécois in the basement of a church in Côte-des-Neiges. After which, I returned often, I confess.

"I can help out between the elections too, if you want."

"Sounds great, we need young people *like you.*"

I didn't ask what that meant exactly. In any case, I found my place in the party's structure over the following years, somewhere between those brave "front-line activists," indefatigable servants of the cause, and the up-and-coming young politicians no less lacking in ideas. The "Community Involvement" section of my CV started to grow. After the PQ, it was the student newspaper at the university, then the student groups, the boards of directors… From which I gained experience, friendships, a social life – not really money – and more than anything a reassuring feeling that I was accomplishing something and that I had my place here like everybody else.

I ended up with a decent return on investment from all those years of activism, rest assured. My first serious job demanded "a broad knowledge of political organizations and an interest in civic engagement." My responsibility was to develop projects to promote the civic engagement of young people. "Take a position!" I would say to them through posters, guides, symposia, conferences, training and activities of all kinds.

Ten years after my first experience as a deputy returning officer, it was my turn to train the electoral workers, but in reality I was working with teenagers. A small group of students was asked to transform the cafeteria of their second-ary school into a polling station and organize a mock election. It was part of a project I had created and coordin-ated for years. Poetically named "Électeurs en herbe" (trans-lated not so poetically into English as "Voters in training"), it grew to the point that hundreds of thousands of future voters across Quebec have been able to have their first experience in citizenship thanks to this initiative (and a little bit thanks to me).

During these workshops with the young people, I didn't dwell on electoral mechanics. Rather, we discussed the functioning and dysfunction of our democracy, the mind games and the real issues of the campaign, politicians and politics, and the disengagement of a growing part of the population. I listened to them speak of their cynicism and their idealism. I empathetically observed their indifference and their zeal. I was sometimes astonished at their ignor-ance, other times by their perspicacity. I tried to moderate some and awaken others. I knew that the indifferent had time to become interested; the ignorant, time to learn; and the cynical, time to discover their ideals.

I was also well aware that setbacks were possible, and I tried to be reassuring. In short, I told them that to trans-form a room into a polling station a few accessories are enough, but that transforming our democratic life is more complicated and we must do everything we can to avoid becoming one.

> On the other hand, there was the moral question: you had to go on doing as much as you could, day by day. In politics, as in every other sphere of life, there are two important commonsense principles: don't cherish too many illusions, and never stop believing that every little bit helps.
>
> Italo Calvino, The Watcher

THE WORDS OF A MAN OF HIS WORD

You have a job to do, and only one: organize yourself so that society allows people to flourish and satisfy their needs. Everyone, no matter who we are, must have an equal opportunity to eat, work and be cared for. This is what I've worked for all my life. It's your turn now.

Michel Chartrand, *Les Dires d'un homme de parole**

MICHEL CHARTRAND
OUI-UQAM CONFERENCE
SEPTEMBER 28, 1995
LOCAL RM-120

And on the back, these words from La Boétie:**

THEY ARE GREAT BECAUSE
WE ARE ON OUR KNEES.

The information was printed on the stack of blue leaflets handed to me at seven o'clock in the morning at the OUI-UQAM office where I had come to launch my career as an activist. There was one brave soul staffing the office at that early hour, but the décor, complete with posters, scattered newspapers, overflowing ashtrays, walls lined with *fleurs-de-lis*, slogans, images of René Lévesque and *Les Patriotes*,

---

* Translated by Casey Roberts. "The Words of a Man of His Word".
** Étienne de La Boétie, sixteenth century French political philosopher—trans.

could easily conjure up the image of the dozens of activists who had been, well, quite active late into the night, dreaming, under a cloud of smoke, of freedom.

I wouldn't have dared to actually walk through the door and join the group during that referendum campaign, even though I now shared their dream, convinced that we cannot live in harmony on the same territory without sharing the historical aspirations of the host society. And that the immigrant who no longer had to choose his loyalty would feel better and would in time be better accepted in an independent Quebec, freed from its schizophrenic identity.

The most experienced were distributing the leaflets at university entrances, handing out the invitations to students rushing by, others daily volunteering to staff a kiosk next to the cafeteria, and others going from class to class making sure that everyone was registered to vote. This exercise seemed extremely embarrassing to me, and I was glad to be given a solitary task, which was to go from class to class in the lecture pavilions on the outskirts of the campus before the students' arrival and leave little handouts on the desks, a perfect assignment for the young academic and revolutionary apprentice that I was.

They say that every action counts, and I've done hundreds. One month from the referendum, prospects were dim for the sovereigntist camp. At the beginning of the campaign, the polls showed support for the Oui running at forty to forty-five percent and it was feared that the results could prove fatal for the independence movement in the event of a defeat similar to what had happened in 1980.

I had lots of good ideas for reversing the trend, but when I tried to speak up, the Oui-UQAM sergeant-recruiter politely told me that they were primarily interested in my talents as a leaflet distributor. There weren't as many volunteers as the general state of agitation over the referendum might have suggested. In any case, as always, there were certainly more candidates for the position of general than those who wanted to serve as privates. Handing out leaflets was to be my contribution in the fall of 1995 to making Quebec its own country. I didn't yet know that it would almost change the course of history.

My work as a volunteer had obviously borne fruit. The room where Michel Chartrand's conference was being held was jammed to the rafters. The crowd spilled out into the hall, speakers had to be set up in the classroom next door, from which boomed the inflammatory words of the old trade unionist, who was serving it hot and spicy to the attentive and enthusiastic youth. Nothing and no one intimidated him. Neither the powerful in this world nor the English, and certainly not independence. "I do not agree with all those who say it would be appalling. What would we miss? Scented and floral toilet paper? We'll use *The Gazette*."

A first wrong note had shaken the smooth-running campaign of the *Non* camp. One of their spokespersons, Standard Life Assurance executive Claude Garcia, a powerful figure in business circles, let himself be carried away by the prospect of a decisive knockout by Canada against Quebec's aspirations. "You must not just win on October 30 [against the separatists]," he said, "you have to crush them." Had the true face of the federalists, who claimed to be so tolerant and to be acting in defense of Quebec's interests, just been revealed? In any case, the sovereigntists didn't let this get by, and Quebecers in general didn't like the idea of being humiliated after thirty years of progress, even those who, facing the possibility of losing their precious Canadian passports thanks to Parizeau's maneuvering, were panic stricken at the thought of not being able to go lie on the beach in Santa Banana.

It just so happened that Garcia was also chairman of the Board of Directors of the Université du Québec à Montréal. We were informed of this in the middle of Chartrand's conference by a feisty and charismatic OUI-UQAM organizer. We had to demand Garcia's expulsion from the university, which belongs to the people, he asserted. Immediately! The audience, already wound up by Chartrand, was ready to expel Garcia summarily, which in any case seemed to be the plan. But "the man of his word" wasn't happy to be interrupted, and his agreement that we should "kick this asshole's ass" only came once he had finished saying what he had come to say.

At the exit, I was handed a sign, the first (in a long series) that I was to carry. The signs had been quickly thrown together with the concise slogan: "*Garcia, dehors!*" ("Garcia, out!") Chanting this exclamatory sentence, carried by the crowd, I passed from the backstage to the battle lines of politics and, just saying, my photo even appeared in *Le Devoir* the next day. Because yes, the media and their cameras were waiting for us at the rector's office. As were the members of the student association and the rector, Claude Corbo. The only person missing at this surprise party was the honoree, which we strongly regretted. We would have preferred that Garcia be in the boardroom so that we could toss him out.

He never showed, and he submitted his letter of resignation to UQAM a few days later. It was a first battle won by the *Oui* camp, and a turning point that lifted the polls and people's hopes for victory. A little bit thanks to my leaflets, as you have no doubt realized. I ended up learning that the whole affair – the conference in a fairly small room, the protest, the placards, the media, the student group that had spontaneously decided to march on the rector's office – had been choreographed, and had even been approved by Jean

Royer, chief of staff for Jacques Parizeau, who feared the radical actions of the new-gen sovereigntists. Although Chartrand's stubborn insistence on finishing his speech had nearly derailed the whole plan.

During my university years, I grew closer to the vanguard of the student and political movements that impressed me so much. I also knew their advisor was a communication professor who invited them over to his apartment to discuss and smoke. His name was Pierre Bourgault.*

With this first experience, I finally walked through the door and joined the students movement: I could see it was open, if only just a crack.

It is true that their offices were often staffed by *Québécois de souche*. But the sense of homogeneity didn't flow from a language or cultural affinity. We shared a common vocabulary and not just a single language, a historical moment and not necessarily a history, an organizational culture and not just a culture. To participate in a group like this, you have to learn how to decode what people are saying, to tame them – to merge into the group – to integrate, in short. Sharing an objective and common interests, no matter where one comes from, allows newcomers to find their way in. Integration into a culture often involves belonging to one of its subcultures.

I believed for a long time that it was I who had taken the first step. Immigrants are often like that. But think about it. Would I have had access to this universe without the presence of the kiosk in the center of the university, without the warm invitation to lend a helping hand? The dedicated young man who sat at the kiosk and handed me the leaflets would tell you, now that he is a little less young, that it takes both.

---

* Also actor, journalist, essayist, and direct-action sovereigntist since the 1960s—trans.

MONEY AND ETHNIC VOTES

We missed, but not by much, a few thousand votes.
Well, in a case like that, what do we do? We spit on our
hands and start again!
  It's true, it's true that we were beaten, but funda-
mentally by what? By money and ethnic votes, essen-
tially. So it means that the next time, instead of sixty
or sixty-one percent voting Oui, *we will have sixty-*
three or sixty-four percent and that will suffice. That's
all. But, my friends, in the coming months, we're
going... Listen: there are people who have become so
afraid that the temptation to take revenge is going to
be very strong!

Jacques Parizeau, speech on October 30, 1995

The first thing the immigrant does when he reaches his
destination is to seek out his own kind. He's been told, "Call
the friend of my aunt's cousin, he's in Montreal, he'll help
you get by."

My family and I regularly played the role of the Ministry
of Integration; setting out tea, sausages and pastries, a directory of the Hungarian community in Montreal, maps of
the metro. Don't buy a car right away; rent a five-and-a-half
in Côte-des-Neiges, it's not too expensive. Go see the Jewish
organizations, they'll give you some help and a few hundred
dollars. Take our old telephone, we don't use it anymore;

---

* Translated by Casey Roberts.

buy a used TV, but for anything else, go to Miracle Mart and Canadian Tire. While waiting to find work, sign up at a COFI* where they teach French, and you get paid to take the classes.

Thanks to my knowledge of French and the fact that I was generally more involved, the role of talking about Montreal and Quebec increasingly fell to me. Beyond practical advice, this was an opportunity to talk about Quebec culture to immigrants who had usually never been here before and who had only a vague idea about it. Genuine curiosity was often accompanied by a healthy distrust. "Will we be accepted?" was their basic worry. The expectation of the immigrant is not so much to be invited to the neighbour's sugar shack as to be certain that he and his family won't be looked down on or blamed for the frustrations of everyday life.

I often found myself having to demystify prejudices before they became enshrined. About people's lifestyles, how they educate their children, Hungarians in Quebec, other immigrants and, above all, about the *Québécois de souche*. It only takes one bus driver responding too brusquely in *joual* to validate prejudices about this backward Quebec, hostile to foreigners.

The hardest thing to get across was that "the French," as they were called, were not a minority in Montreal and that this was even more true if you took the province as a whole. Knowing this counterintuitive fact is essential for an immigrant in Montreal to understand the cultural and political dynamics here, but it often only adds to the initial mistrust. The idea of a Canada "where everyone comes from somewhere else" is reassuring. In theory, it allows the immigrant to become part of the majority, automatic-

---

* *Centre d'orientation et de formation pour les immigrants*—trans.

ally and effortlessly. The opposite idea, of a people inside Canada that wants to become the majority (on the basis of its own characteristics), is, on the contrary, destabilizing and challenging.

"I'm telling you, we can live in a French Quebec, and even enjoy it. If I like living here, it's a little thanks to *them*. I have 'French' friends, they travel, study, read. They're not like you think, they're fine, I swear. There are good TV shows in French and good singers. I'll show you."

"He even listens to baseball in French. On the radio!"

Explaining the rules of baseball was among my favourite tasks, but too complex – during the early stages of integration – to get into why the hit and run was a good strategy when it's three-balls-one-strike-nobody-out, not to mention the poetry of Rodger Brulotte.*

Out of such visits lasting friendships sometimes emerge, especially with people from a socio-economic background similar to our own. This was the case of one family in particular, whose main attraction was their only child, who, like me, was sixteen when I met her.

They settled in an English-speaking neighbourhood, the husband worked in a small factory, the mother was a salesperson in a store in Lachine, and the daughter, a technical school graduate. Since Bill 101 didn't apply to small businesses, vocational training or, in practice, to the West Island, none of the three had therefore learned French. But from the point of view of statistics produced by the Ministry of Employment and Social Solidarity, their integration was perfectly successful. Their modest salaries didn't bring in tons of taxes (sales taxes, a little), the grandparents hadn't come with them to add to the burden on the health care

---

* Former Montreal Expos colourful play-by-play announcer— trans.

system. In short, apart from universal basic services, they were not clients of government programs. For government managers and politicians, this is key.

They came over often and became our best friends. They were as fascinated as I was by politics, especially in the turbulent post-Meech period. They ended up scared to death about "separation" when confronted with the determination of Lucien Bouchard and Jacques Parizeau, who the English media depicted more or less subtly as enemies of immigrants and of reason. We were in the middle of the historic match between Quebec and Canada that took place between 1992 and 1995. The pregame warm-up was the defeat by referendum of Quebec federalists who supported the Charlottetown Accord. The first period would be the election of the Bloc Quebecois in Ottawa; the second, the return to power of the Parti Québécois; and the third, the referendum on sovereignty.

They appreciated my explanations, my patient pedagogy, my point of view that I think helped to sort things out somewhat, but it was becoming increasingly clear that I was on the other side. It should also be pointed out that I was used to it. In English-speaking and immigrant milieux, there is such unanimity of opinion on the "Quebec question" that people are glad to have the chance to meet someone who thinks differently than they do. These unique moments are there to be enjoyed. Not so much for the rich exchange of ideas, but because they shine light on the faulty reasoning of your adversary and help solidify your own sense of the truth. They kept thinking that something must be wrong with the picture, since I didn't exactly match the enemy profile. Basically, if you weren't *Québécois de souche* or crazy, you'd be against Bill 101 and for *Non*.

It seems to me that it was by assuming the responsibility of presenting Quebec to people from elsewhere that I really came to love and adopt this land as my own. And it was out of a sense of duty to defend it that I became a sovereigntist. I became increasingly anxious about the future of Quebecers from hearing Anglophones and immigrants talk about them. I just felt like saying: "Separate, group, before it's too late."

At the time, our friends had not yet become Canadian citizens, but it wouldn't take long. A little later, with the signing of the Canada-Quebec Accord, "economic immigrants" would be selected by Quebec based on a self-administered point system. When the "applicant" earned enough points, he or she received a "selection certificate," and when the federal government added its seal – an often lengthy formality – their family could become Canadian. To get a passing grade, the key assets were relevant training, a young family, and knowledge of English to a lesser extent of course, knowledge of French. It was this last criterion that posed a problem for the father, designated to take the exam on behalf of his family. His initial desire to learn French had sort of melted away as the task became daunting and English, useful. When we are able to get by in a certain language, it's not in our interest for society to function in another. And when our interests are involved, it's easy to find excuses.

To make a long story short, he had been here three years and hadn't learned French, and he was summoned to take a French test in a couple of weeks. I was the only person who could help him avoid a refusal that would have been tragic for him, his family and our friendship. The requirements were ridiculous, and despite my special lessons, failure became predictable. In desperation, we started looking for a better strategy. The Quebec Ministry of Immigration gave us a break: "*Monsieur,* your test will be administered by telephone."

The Immigration-Québec officer had a friendly tone, like that of a public servant who wants the applicant to pass the test, unlike, say, her colleagues responsible for conducting driver's license exams. At Immigration it's all about quotas – by year end, it's imperative that they have accepted the forecast number of immigrants, while the Ministry of Transportation has a comparable degree of focus on, say, tariff revenues and, incidentally, improving safety on our roads.

The operation proved a real breeze. We connected two telephones with an extension cord. My handset on mute, I listened to the questions in French: "What is your occupation? How many children do you have? Where were you born?" I whispered the answers, which he nervously repeated, more or less, after me. After ten minutes, he was congratulated by the officer and as the interview came to an end, when, to indicate the verdict I lifted two thumbs up, he collapsed in tears into my arms like a child, repeating, without my help, "*Merci madame, merci madame, merci...*"

It was merely incidental, but lady luck smiled again. When his file was transferred to the federal government, it was processed in record time. It was just a few weeks before the referendum and the small family, like thousands of others in the same situation, obtained citizenship and their inclusion on the electoral list just in time for the historic vote.

To make their decision, they no longer needed me, nor to listen to the appeal for the ethnic votes of Montreal made on Tuesday, October 24 at a press conference during which Athanasios Hadjis of the Hellenic Congress, Tony Manglaviti of the National Congress of Italian-Canadians, and Reisa Teitelbaum of the Canadian Jewish Congress appealed to "their communities," four hundred thousand people and six percent of the electorate they claimed, to vote

Non. Our friends had long ago made up their minds and they voted in step with the vast majority of immigrants.

The evening of October 30, this brand new Canadian family was able to celebrate the fruit of its first democratic contribution to their new country. Meanwhile, even though I had recounted the ballots one last time at the polling station on Van Horne Street where I was a deputy returning officer, nothing had changed, only twelve people had checked *Oui* out of over two hundred.

Later, when I met my friends once again, it was clear that while Canada's borders hadn't changed, the distance between us had. The relationship that we had previously enjoyed – me the host who explains; they, the visitors open to discovery – had disappeared.

Our political discussions resumed on a cordial basis. They never ceased to show their indignation over the – Oh My God – sickening words of Jacques Parizeau about money and, worse than that, "the ethnic vote." Obviously, they couldn't contest the reality that he described, they knew full well that the near unanimity of non-Francophones had been instrumental in ensuring the razor-thin federalist margin of victory. Immigrants don't see a problem in analyzing the results by ethnic origin. Nor do the commentators, politicians and policymakers who play the offended virgin on TV but who we can easily imagine behind closed doors – with their thin-lipped smiles – examining electoral lists in old French-speaking neighbourhoods, finding, in election after election, more and more foreign names to appeal to.

They complained that they had been singled out, not considered full citizens in a free country. They found it outrageous and racist, and thought it was pretty much a case of "sore losers." They were not entirely wrong, but for me, their indignation rang hollow, little more than thinly-disguised triumphalism. They were happy and reassured by the results, convinced of having been once and for all on the right side (of history), and I, inevitably, on the wrong side – as a result of my naivety, they said gently.

Parizeau's speech transformed the victors into victims. He provided unexpected ammunition to his opponents whereas he should have *spit in his hands and gotten back* to work convincing the unconvinced, and at the top of the list, the new generation of French-educated children of immigrants, of the relevance and legitimacy of the sovereigntist option. The children of Bill 101 who had become adults, having just reached voting age. To convince them that it is they who, next time, would have the power to make change. To tell them not to be the political tool of the federalists, to choose their future freely, vote *Oui*, vote *Non*; that they have the right to doubt, to procrastinate, to change their mind... like any good Quebecer. Instead, talking about mobilizing immigrants to combat sovereignty became Quebec's greatest political taboo.

I had less and less desire to talk politics with our friends. I just seemed to be hearing the trolling echoes of CJAD radio, the opinions of the people in their neighbourhood, their community. I had to accept the reality: basically, I was hearing what the vast majority of our fellow Canadians thought; their new fellow citizens of their new country which they had saved, their new country still intact, a country that filled them with pride and the fierce determination to defend it.

Basically, the integration of these immigrants was a great success. Because of me. Essentially.

THE TIME OF THE BUFFOONS

It is in Quebec, in 1985. Every year, the colonial bour-
geoisie gathers at the Queen Elizabeth Hotel for the
Beaver Club banquet. Here, no have nots, just haves.
At the head table, with their fake beards and cardboard
hats, the lieutenant governors of ten provinces, busi-
nessmen, judges, shopping center Indians, white-
skinned African kings who speak bilingual. Like in
Ghana, they celebrate the old British system of exploit-
ation. But we're here. Here, the masters play the role
of masters, the slaves remain slaves. Each person has
their role! This is the history of Quebec in slow motion.
The whole reality of Quebec at a glance: clear, crisp for
once, as if magnified under the microscope.

Pierre Falardeau, *Le Temps des bouffons*[*]

"We discover the reality of immigration through fascinating characters: immigrants who chose Quebec and the
struggle for the independence of their new country. They
are beautiful, they are young, they are articulate and intelligent. I love these people. These are my brothers, my children, my comrades."

Filmmaker Pierre Falardeau was speaking about the
documentary *La Génération 101* by Claude Godbout, in
which I was one of the "stars." It dealt with some young

---

[*] Translated by Casey Roberts from Pierre Falardeau, "Notre schizo-
phrénie," *Ici Montréal,* October 16, 2008.

people like myself, militant sovereigntists for the integration of immigrants and for the French language.

I discovered Falardeau at UQAM, where he came to lecture after the referendum, calling on the students not to
give up the "fight for freedom." He angrily denounced the
hypocrisy of the *Non* camp, who after flying and bussing
in flag-waving demonstrators for free from Ontario to
express their "love" for Quebec, deployed in the wake of the
referendum their so-called "Plan B" which was clearly lacking love. The hoped-for constitutional changes were replaced
by the mass distribution of Canadian flags, federal sponsor-
ships, encroachment on Quebec's jurisdiction, a reduction
of federal transfer payments and, above all, a "Clarity Act,"
which following a politicized opinion of the Supreme Court
subjected the will of Quebec to Canadian power.

A group of admirers took advantage of the Falardeau lectures to solicit funding for his film project about *Les Patriotes*,
entitled *15 février 1839*, that according to him, "Ottawa's
henchmen" at Telefilm Canada were blocking. They also sold
his short film *Le Temps des bouffons,* which in the words of
writer and trade unionist Pierre Vadeboncoeur, "overturned
monuments to get at the crawling worms." Filmed in 1985, it
wasn't shown until 1993.

I immediately took a liking to him, with his colourful
spirit, his confrontational poetry that at times hid his sensi-
tivity and depth. I loved his love of the common people. His
respect for the popular language. He admired *Les Patriotes*,
who had taken up arms and died for their ideas, but also
the anonymous *coureurs des bois*, the farmers who had
cleared their land in abject poverty; or in *Le Steak,* workers
who chose to fight when they had no other way to maintain
their dignity. For him, the history of Quebec was the history
of a people exploited by the British and betrayed by its elite.
A Manichean world, true, but sometimes a sketch is more

recognizable than a detailed painting with all its nuances. Falardeau was clear. He railed against the *"bon-ententistes"* who advocated resolving differences through goodwill but who despised the working people from high in their lofty perches, *"La grosse Presse"* and university chairs, at the risk of falling into shortcuts and unnecessary insults.

When he talked about me in his column, saying we were on the same side, even members of the same family, I was flattered and touched, much more so than when I became the poster child for sovereigntist immigrants for a couple of months. Writing about the film *La Génération 101*, which portrayed young immigrants who had learned French with difficulty, he said that he understood "that most of them don't want to identify with a nation of losers who prefer to sit in their minority shit, with their ass between two chairs, unable to stand up and take charge. There is a price to pay for living on your belly: everyone gets to wipe their feet on your back."

The column in question, "Our schizophrenia," caused a big uproar but, surprisingly, not because the author concluded: "When I see that the majority of immigrants choose to continue their studies in English, I become ill. When I invite people to my home, I hate not knowing if they're going to screw me in the end. Parizeau was right." No, it was more because of the postscript in which he denounced environmentalist David Suzuki, who had said he was "disappointed" that Quebecers had voted for the Bloc and contributed to the election to the House of Commons of a Conservative government. "We've had enough of your colonialist contempt." And then, continuing on to describe him as "the bearded little Jap, just another shit disturber from the West Coast,"* a veritable Professor Sunflower of ecological enlightenment.

---

* *Toronto Star.* September 27, 2009.

David Suzuki embodies the image of Canada as it likes
to see itself. A self-made man of immigrant origins, fully
assimilated but proud of his difference, it is this Canada of
diversity that loves the planet and that the planet loves. He
is a national hero, our Yuri Gagarin, our Davy Crockett,
our Marilyn Monroe. These kinds of heroes are often simple people, who start out only doing their job, but end up
on a pedestal from which they can sell the official ideology
of a regime. In his case, travelling salesman for investments
in "liberal values": multiculturalism, charter of rights, individual success. A real bargain, not to be missed. No one
would dare poke fun at these trappings of Canadian
nation-building, which include its royal family, its
Governor General, its military leaders, its Hollywood stars,
its smiling astronauts, its hockey legends, its one-legged
runners with cancer. No one except, of course, Pierre
Falardeau.

As could be expected, perhaps even by himself, Falardeau
was pelted with stones in the public square. He was accused
of every kind of evil, of racism for sure. When one is talking about the emperor's missing clothes, it is irrelevant to
point out the colour of his penis. That's literally all they
could talk about. This time, the accusations came from an
unexpected direction: it wasn't the federalist, English-
language or ROC* press... Most of the detractors, as illustrated by an open letter published in *La Presse* in response
to Falardeau, were from the new generation of Quebec leaders, mine in fact. A different group of poster children, who
instead of defending Quebec's distinctiveness, celebrated
Suzuki's universal appeal, but above all his individual success and his difference.

---

* Rest-of-Canada—trans.

They made sure to highlight Suzuki's origins: "From childhood incarceration to Canadian icon, David Suzuki has transcended the barriers of this country and its identity to carry a vision: the dream of a just humanity and harmony with the environment that supports the sacred balance of life on Earth. For that he deserves our respect and gratitude."[*]

To suggest that Suzuki is an enemy because he is Japanese is messed-up, right on the edge of xenophobia, true. But to think that his merit is due to his origins isn't that different. The glorification of differences and their denigration are often two sides of the same coin.

The denunciation cleared the smoke out of the room. It was not going to be "yes, but Quebecers have the right to vote freely without suffering the recriminations of the ROC, and the Bloc Québécois can defend the interests of Quebec and the environment." Nada.

That must have been the thing that made Falardeau fume, more than being treated as a national pariah again. This refusal to recognize the relations of domination that exist in Canada at the expense of Canadians of French origin must have delighted the members of the Beaver Club, who these days invite to their mundane *soirées* these new knights of virtue, who assume the colonial era is ancient history, though if they could see through the studied eye of the reviled filmmaker, they would realize that despite their respectability they are seated far from the head table, next to the "waiters in formal shirts and sashes, water carriers dressed up as champagne servers."

---

[*] Translated by Casey Roberts, from "Une source d'inspiration," open letter published in *La Presse*, October 24, by Laure Waridel, Steven Guilbeault, Stephen Bronfman, Désirée McGraw, Hugo Latulippe, Karel Mayrand, Hubert Reeves, Bernard Voyer, André Boisclair and Les Cowboys Fringants.

For advocates of the constitutional status quo, everything was back as it was supposed to be. Each seated at his place, the table set, the cohort smiling. A new time of buffoons could begin.

I still fantasize about being on the blacklist in the company of Falardeau the pariah – my brother, my father, my friend – and alongside those who refuse to say "*Applaudissons-nous* (Let's all applaud for ourselves.) We are magnificent people. You are as beautiful as I think I am."

THE HUMAN ZOO

Did you know there are lots of Filipinos in Montreal and that there's Filipino food, Filipino parties and Filipino churches? Fascinating, isn't it? There's even Filipino kara-oke. If you want to observe them in their natural habitat, get off at Plamondon metro and check them out discreetly, quietly. If you are lucky you might even get to see them with their offspring (also Filipino).

It is these most unextraordinary kinds of things that the media are more and more interested in telling us about, preoccupied by diversity and convinced that it is through the celebration of their folkloric traits that immigrants will come to be accepted by the "majority." Through blogs, travel journalism, books, TV shows and radio, the public is besieged by invitations to "travel around the world without leaving the city."

In another epoch, these urban reporters would have loved the colonial exhibitions, human zoos where they put entire families brought from India, Africa and Polynesia on exhibit in Amsterdam, Paris and London. The public was invited back then as well, to "go around the world in just one day" in pavilions where their villages had been artificially reconstructed. Eighty years ago, the same think-ing that conceived these exhibits would result in the dis-placement – in unsettling unanimity – of tens of millions of people just as open to diversity and fond of exoticism as the audience for these travel accounts.

The difference is that the civilizing mission is now reversed. Formerly, it was the "westerners" who "brought light" to indigenous people; nowadays, it is the latter that open us to the world. Yesterday, the colonies with their indigenous people were presented as symbols of the superiority of our civilization, just as our cosmopolitan cities with their immigrants are portrayed today.

"We're all humans!" It was necessary to proclaim at the time, as today, I feel like we should say: "We're all citizens!" Oddly, the promoters of modern human zoos, after breaking society down into a thousand pieces, then proclaim, "We're all immigrants!" in order to find common ground. A catchy slogan that exempts immigrants from the process of integration and implies that Quebecers, the descendants of French settlers, are not really at home, that their culture in fact doesn't exist, so that it has no precedence over the others. Well, wasn't that what the colonizers said about the indigenous people?

Playing on the sense of the word "migrant," let's put everyone into one diversity container: Louis Hébert who landed in Nouvelle-France four hundred years ago, the Scottish multi-millionaires who came and started factories in Montreal in the nineteenth century, the newspaper columnist who after finishing CEGEP moved from Lévis to Montreal, the Pashtun refugee living in Parc-Extension since last year, the squeegee kid from Halifax who's spent the whole summer minding my closest intersection. And me. Which authorizes them, to show their openness to other cultures, to reduce me to an insignificant eater of Hungarian sausage.

It reminds me of the child who wants to start over again with a puzzle just when it's finally assembled. "Look little buddy, the picture won't get any more beautiful and we might lose a few more pieces."

Neither will explaining that they too are not at home effectively discourage certain xenophobic minds from telling "the importees" to go back to their country. Social peace and the acceptance of others will not flow from childish back and forth.

"My father was here before yours, nya-nya-n-nya-nya."

"My father says yours stole his bungalow from the Indians; put that in your pipe!"

Apparently I'm too old and lacking in wonder (which disappeared somewhere around Snowdon metro a long time ago), to choose to spend my weekends discovering "Montreal's diversity" by taking in a voodoo session or getting my eyebrows plucked by a Laotian beautician, proposals that I heard on Radio-Canada. Here it is not so much the subject that is insignificant, it's the infantile approach, populated by caricatures and necessarily condescending. "Try some of what that nice woman made, isn't it a delight? I tell you, our immigrants are really different, but good people all the same."

It is pretty delusional to think that we learn something about Mexicans by drinking tequila or Swedes while being massaged at the Scandinavian Spa in the Old Port. Nor would we get to know Quebecers by attending a Mass at Saint-Joseph's Oratory, but that would at least be progress.

Look, I'm always up for a great restaurant and a show from a far-off land. But stop pointing to it with such excitement, I'm aware they exist. I don't think I'm the only one. Are there so many people in Quebec who only listen to Michel Louvain on their snowmobile on the way to the sugar shack, to the point where we should be worried about it and design programs to explain to them the virtues of shish taouk?

You see, over there, the Filipino woman sitting on a bench in Mackenzie Park, near Côte-Sainte-Catherine metro? It's despair sitting on a bench, as Jacques Prévert once wrote:

> You must not listen to him
> You must pass him by
> Pretend you can't hear him
> Act like you don't see him
> You must quickly pass him by*

She's never heard of a Quebec crooner named Michel Louvain, never rode on a snowmobile and has never been to a sugar shack. And she has never watched your feel-good travelogues. But this is not a good time to bother her, she's got other things on her mind.

I am certain that there are literary masterpieces waiting to be written about the inspiration she will need to find, for instance, listen carefully, every morning before going to take care of the Johnson household on rue Victoria, Westmount, feeding their dog, taking their children out for a play. I am convinced that it's the same inspiration that keeps thousands of other women of all origins going every morning, each in their park, on their bench. I wish they could one day meet, come together, so that we could all hear what they have to say. I am sure that in order to do this, we must first let go. Let go of the quest for difference that seems to obsess us so much and that hides so much of our humanity.

Indeed, there is something positive about this morbid observation of "cultural communities." It can lead to amaz-

---

* Jacques Prévert, *Le désespoir est assis sur un banc.* Translated by Casey Roberts.

ing discoveries, such as when observing macaques at the zoo. The more one looks at them, the more one realizes that they resemble us... and the more one wonders what's the point of the damned cage?

LAND OF OTHERS

If we don't want to preserve our French-Canadian roots then I don't see why we want independence. For me, this idea, like others, is contradictory: the desire to live together, but at the same time, to preserve the cultural heritage of the majority, which is rapidly disappearing.

Bernard Émond, about his film *La Terre des autres*[*]

Once, I saw lots of Haitians at the Salon du livre de Montréal (Montreal Book Fair), and I'm not talking about Dany Laferrière or security guards. They were especially visible instead of being scattered among the hundreds of booths, because they had all gathered in one place, down the hall. The moment was exceptional because, as I understood by following them, the "Salon had decided to honour Haiti by offering the public an opportunity to discover and appreciate the inestimable richness of Haitian literature."

I was happy because there was red wine gratis and the poems of Rodney Saint-Éloi. A little buzzed by the spleen creole, I began to calculate the number of years it would take before we would so honour all the countries of the world – starting with Hungary of course – whose inestimably rich literature deserves its own little cocktail party and the presence of a minister. I lost count because said minister

---

[*] Translated by Casey Roberts.

spoke in a too loud voice about the importance of ties between Quebec and Haiti, which is a very very good thing, and then another speaker stepped up to stress the "importance of opening up to cultural communities."

It was the right place to ask the question. There are no better places to see the disconnect between the majority of immigrants and Quebec culture than these traditional institutions. Without exception, the audiences in public theaters and at movies from Quebec, in the museums and concert halls of Quebec – and I speak from what I've observed in Montreal – is pretty homogeneous.

We get it that recently arrived refugees from Bhutan don't spend their weekends at a book fair as a family activity; and I accept as well that the person who fled the Salazar regime in 1972 would rather take care of the groceries and his old mother. But where are the hundreds of thousands of immigrants who tell Statistics Canada they speak French, the second and third generation immigrants, the children of Bill 101, the people supposedly open to others (and the world) who are said to be well integrated and "as Québécois as you and I"?

Some people say that it's the cultural institutions which aren't open because they're not representative of the population's diversity. Yet I was actually really there at the book fair, and I don't remember anybody checking my birthplace before letting me in. It is always insulting to be accused of crashing a party just when you start having fun, and felt welcome there.

So before getting caught, I continued to tour the book fair.

That was where I met the filmmaker Bernard Émond, awakener of consciences and sworn opponent of the petty bourgeoisie if ever there was one, sitting on his stool, quietly waiting for someone to stop and ask him for his autograph, a compulsory exercise which seemed to obviously be against his nature. I wasn't shy to volunteer.

I'm not a groupie by nature, but the intelligence and sincerity of this man touched me deeply. Just the day before, I had read his interesting take on Quebec "where everything is a matter of taste, where all opinions are equally valid and where clicking on 'Like' or 'Unlike' seems to be the pinnacle of citizen activity."[*]

With the help of the red wine, it's possible I was a little over enthusiastic. I spoke for a good ten minutes without really succeeding at going further than the usual courtesies, beyond any reasonable purpose: I loved your movies, I'm looking forward to reading your book about which I've heard a lot of good things and I enjoyed your column yesterday. I felt like I had embarrassed more than bothered him.

I would have liked to have said more. To talk to him, for example, about an interview where the discussion about one of his old documentaries, *La Terre des autres*, had led him to say: "There is something in the idea of a cosmopolitan Quebec that I like a lot and there is something in the old French-Canadian heritage that I like as much. So how do we reconcile them?"[**]

I would have liked to reassure him. To say that reconciling the two was possible and that his sensitive camera was making a contribution. His film *La Neuvaine* (*The Novena*) moved me to tears even if all of the places, people and history are in principle outside my experience. I was born far from Petite-Rivière-Saint-François, I've never lived more than five minutes from a metro station – much less in a vil-

---

[*] Bernard Émond, "Le chemin de l'honneur," *Le Devoir*, November 16, 2011.

[**] "*La Terre des autres*, film-piège," *Chaire René-Malo en cinéma et stratégies de production culturelle (UQAM)*.

lage – the little religious education I received was Jewish, and I'm a devout atheist. Except.

Except, when Francis, the pious character in the film, gently replaces the pillow of his sick grandmother – despaired that we cannot heal the people we love – I couldn't help but think that my grandmother, alone, thousands of kilometers away, would have liked just before dying, to have had her little grandson do the same.

The works in museums, theaters, cinemas, and bookstores attract attention when they reveal a part of oneself, something that is universal in human experience. I'm particularly attracted to Hungarian works, I must admit. I understand the attraction for immigrants of anything that reminds them of their roots. Today, when I go in a bookstore, I automatically stop in front of the Hungarian novels and I look to see if there are any films from my native country playing at the Montreal International Film Festival, even if it's rare that I actually go and see one. To tell you a secret, during the Olympics, I find myself sitting on the edge of my sofa before the Hungarian shot putter's final attempt.

Like all Hungarians, maybe like many immigrants, I still have this little chauvinistic side, convinced that people would appreciate the products of my culture if only they understood its language. And maybe the sadly homogeneous public participating in Quebec's cultural institutions can be explained by the fact that Quebecers lack this kind of self-confidence. It nevertheless took *some* to ensure that new generations of immigrants learned French; it was a good start. It will take just as much courage for Quebecers to say that their culture has something to give to the world, starting with those "others" who find themselves on its land.

MULTICULTURALIZATION

Jacob Tierney, a young English-speaking Montreal film-maker, criticized Quebec cinema as being too francophone and "white, white, white." Despite the crude nature of the accusation, there were those who applauded, and some took it further. This happened in 2010.

Among the examples he offered to support his thesis, there was *C.R.A.Z.Y.* by Jean-Marc Vallée and *Polytechnique*, a Denis Villeneuve film cited as being one of those Quebec films that reflected a Quebec turned in on itself and stuck in the past, that glorified nostalgia. In other words, making film in French about an event that occurred in Quebec twenty years earlier starring Karine Vanasse was to fall into an unconscious kind of racism.

The message did not fall on deaf ears. Villeneuve seemed to come down with a bout of bad conscience, rushing off to the Middle East to shoot, quickly, well, a little masterpiece that nearly won an Oscar – *Incendies* – with lots of Arabs like Maxim Gaudette and Mélissa Désormeaux-Poulin.

Do you know what we call this prevailing trend whereby anything produced should reflect "the new reality of Montreal's diversity in the contemporary Quebec of the twenty-first century"? Multiculturalization. It's everywhere: on TV, on radio, in newspapers, in advertising, in magazines, but not sufficiently in the cinema, you see, and it bothers a lot of people who want what's best for you (but above all, what's best for me).

They're worried that ordinary immigrants like me supposedly would really like to love Quebec cinema, but can't because they don't see themselves on the screen. Like the young Haitians from Montreal who, according to Tierney, can't identify with an actor like Luc Picard because he's white and he speaks French, proving beyond a doubt, you know, that someone somewhere is a racist.

I have a feeling that you're not following me. I should have started with what a cinema that represents diversity might look like.

The idea is to make a film as if we were designing a brochure for Canadian Heritage. Ensure that there is always a black, an indigenous person, an Asian, an Arab (who might also seem Pakistani or Latino) and an attractive person with blond hair, surely gay, sitting in his wheelchair with a basketball on his lap. If the portrait of your gang of friends – or the poster of your film – does not look like that, then that's messed up and you should have a guilty conscience.

Don't try to understand it too much, that might ruin your pleasure. Believe me, it's an oddly refreshing way to appreciate the local cinema. Before, I was superficially engrossed in the acting, the screenplay, directing and even in the subject. Today, I judge a film by the number of blacks in it. And to be in step with the times, it's supposedly important that they be shown as much as possible in NDG, Westmount and in Mile End, the ghettos where the main victims of our ethnocentric cinema are miserably languishing.

Well, I didn't realize any of that before, either. For me to appreciate Quebec cinema, I don't think it would take the release of a movie about the tribulations of a Jewish Hungarian immigrant in Côte-des-Neiges struggling to find a way to raise her brilliant son and vegetarian daughter. I hope I'll be forgiven for this cavalier attitude that has probably held back the antiracist struggle in Quebec.

Carefree, I had for a number of years been enjoying the cinema of our little closed-in-on-itself province without complaining or wondering too much about it. To redeem myself, I started going to lots of Quebec films full of diversity, like *Incendies*, and guess what, there are more and more of them… and frankly, it worries me a little.

I fear for the uniqueness of Quebec cinema. I fear that in response to these moralizing critics, our filmmakers will feel increasingly obligated to sprinkle their films with Tamils just to show their openness. A bit like those artists from communist countries who voluntarily set their stories in a factory – thus seeming to be concerned about the fate of the working class – in order to receive their grants and stay in the regime's good graces. Even though their works could be penetrating and remarkable, they ended up sooner or later smelling like old machine oil.

Most of the time, artists produce what they know, their reality, their universe. A child who grew up on rue Fabre in the East End will write the *Chroniques du Plateau-Mont-Royal*, a child from Haiti will talk about *How to Make Love to a Negro Without Getting Tired*, and a spoiled child from the West Island, well, he'll make movies about spoiled children from the West Island. It's kind of normal, and isn't letting artists create in peace the best way to promote diversity?

Guilt plays its role quietly but surely. Filmmaker Denis Villeneuve has directed four movies since this episode, all produced in the U.S. and filmed in English… Same for Jean-Marc Vallée and several others. The same people who criticized Quebec cinema as too white and too French now celebrate the courage and unabashed openness of a new generation of Quebec filmmakers to the world…

Ironically, the danger of this preachy multiculturalism is that it actually takes us farther away from the diversity it preaches.

THE PERFECT FOREIGNER

In the spring of 2011, Immigration Minister Kathleen Weil invited the public to visit YouTube. An act that she thought would bring some perspective to the problems of the integration of immigrants in Quebec. It was to view "a web series that presents the authentic testimonies of people of immigrant origin as well as the testimonies of people who work with them."

I'm not saying this to torture you, but listen to her, she perfectly summarizes the official discourse on immigration: "Diversity is an asset for all modern societies. For generations, people of immigrant background have contributed to the growth and dynamism of society. These women and men are our neighbours, our colleagues, friends, parents, as well as consumers. Together, whatever our origins, we shape today's Quebec and contribute to the collective enrichment of our society."*

These "people" are also our teachers. As a beautiful film directed by Philippe Falardeau released at the same time reminded us. With more efficiency, I must say, than the YouTube clips that have only been viewed two hundred times in four years. I must not be the only one to prefer *cinema d'auteur* to cheap propaganda.

---

* Minister Kathleen Weil read this release, entitled "Toutes nos origines enrichissent le Québec," at the launch of a campaign to promote the contribution of diversity in Quebec, March 22, 2011.

The teacher in the film is named Mr. Lazhar. He is like other teacher heroes who naively arrive in a milieu that is foreign to them, and, by the end of the story, everyone is transformed. In the first place, the audience, which exits the theater with tears in their eyes and the blissful conviction that a barely exceptional individual can by himself change – with the help of some anti-conformism, humanism and authenticity – the fate of the kids despite having to work within a rotten system.

The genre offers a bit of nostalgia, optimism and utopia. Sometimes we imagine ourselves in the role of the hero, sometimes seated in front of him, sometimes he reminds us of the teacher who changed our lives. It's Mr. Nicolas, it's Madame Desruisseaux, it's me teaching fencing classes to children in Ville Émard or French classes to immigrants from Côte-des-Neiges.

In these modern fairy tales, instead of dragons, the hero confronts obtuse bureaucrats, and instead of saving a princess, he goes to the rescue of schoolchildren entombed by a dreadful minister of Education. In this story written by Évelyne de la Chenelière, the brave knight is an immigrant fresh from Algeria, come to free pitiful little Quebecers from the clutches of the school reform and school psychologists.

Mr. Lazhar is the opposite of the beloved Mr. Keating, a big influence on my adolescence, who in the *Dead Poets Society*, tears out the pages containing the introduction to the students' poetry books, because they explained a mathematical formula for rating poetry. Twenty years later, Lazhar no longer says "*carpe diem*," he says "Shut up!" He tries to fix the mess left behind by his predecessor. He is strongly against the whole idea of this school for pampered children that has left classics, discipline and traditions by the wayside, and pupils "at the center of their learning." A school where there are too many managers, too many shrinks and not enough masters.

While Mr. Keating invites the youngsters to stand on their desks in order to rise above the suffocating conformity around them, Mr. Lazhar summons his pupils to sit down quietly behind desks that are finally arranged "in beautiful straight rows." Mr. Keating wishes to put an end to the mechanical learning of classical poets, Mr. Lazhar dictates word for word extracts from Balzac, a writer they have never heard of. While Mr. Lazhar doubts the pedagogical utility of the play his colleague is having his students produce, Keating challenges one of his students to devote himself to the theater. While in the *Dead Poets Society*, it is a student who commits suicide, in *Monsieur Lazhar*, it is a teacher. Before, it was the students who felt stifled by the school; today, it's their teachers.

This critique of our education system would not please the minister of Education, but it's pretty trendy, and the authors do not push their transgression too far. Mr. Lazhar doesn't puff cigarettes in class, doesn't make jokes about Arabs and doesn't poke fun at "intercultural week." I could easily have imagined him serving hot dogs and coke to his students and teaching them, a beer in hand, campfire songs, out of sight of their parents. And, ultimate sacrilege, to tackle the meaning of life with them by inviting Monsignor Ouellet to come to his class in person.

The film's real critique, vehemently aimed at Quebec and, if I may say so, Western civilization, can be summed up by one detail: Lazhar has never taught in his life. But what do you know? His common sense, his life experience – most of all his foreign culture – can produce better results in a few weeks than anything that the Quebec government, its

Ministry of Education, its programs and Quebec's educational institutes of higher learning have been able to produce since the Quiet Revolution.

Mr. Lazhar's greatest asset, which makes him so lucid and prodigious, is that he is not from here. The choice of the authors (both Quebecers) to conceive of a hero who is a foreigner was absolutely essential to making their point. Bashir Lazhar could have been named Basil Lamarre and come from Abitibi, but it wouldn't have been very believable: it's common knowledge today that more cultivated people grow under the shade of palm trees than spruce. Reading Balzac in Rouyn-Noranda... that's a good one!

So they created a fantasy character. Lazhar is the perfect immigrant. Polite, respectful, educated, courageous, soft-spoken, Francophile, phlegmatic towards women, he spends his free time reading Hubert Aquin. Not the type to demand places for prayer at work, to find Bill 101 inhuman or to drown his wife and children in a canal lock.*

Lazhar is the perfect foreigner, the one who is going to save us from all our economic ills, our labour shortages, our demographic challenges and – need I remind you? – who will finally open us to the world. Somewhat like the messaging of the Ministry of Immigration's awareness campaigns, directed to an audience that both intuits and experiences, without daring to say anything, that the reception of foreigners is a little more complicated and less cinematic than they want us to believe.

---

* "Honour" killing—trans.

MONTREAL TANGO

7:30 a.m. in the Montreal metro
it's full of immigrants
up and on the go
at the crack of dawn
maybe the old heart of the city
is still beating
thanks to them

Gérald Godin, *"Tango de Montréal"**

I rarely take the Montreal metro at 7:30 in the morning, but I know like everyone else, thanks to the poem by Gérald Godin engraved in the brick behind the Mont-Royal metro station, that at that precise moment, there are a lot of immigrants moving through the station. I would say that there are many more today than when the poem was written in the seventies, and not just at dawn.

Those were the days when a poet could become minister of Immigration and reach out to the "cultural communities" by saying that "there are one hundred ways to be a Quebecer." Godin wanted to preserve the cultures of new arrivals while promoting their integration in a new Quebec, each one enriching the other. And who knows, maybe even rally them to the sovereigntist cause. A sincere idealism mixed with genuine openness (and obtaining modest

---

* Translated by Casey Roberts.

results). He managed to make many friends in these *milieux*,
but few converts as he himself admitted. This didn't prevent
certain bystanders from criticizing some of his formula-
tions. Saying "full of immigrants" is not acceptable today,
no more for a poet than a minister. Nowadays, it's prefer-
able to speak about the beauty of diversity in the public
transit system. But it might be best to say nothing.

As for myself, I don't say anything, but I do observe. As
a child, it was mostly on the western segment of the orange
line that the number of immigrants was striking. On the
green line, what struck me was how the metro cars gradually became whiter as the train moved eastwards. I even
went on expeditions all the way to the terminal just to
observe the process whereby by the time I got to the end of
the line, I thought I'd fallen asleep and woke up in
Drummondville.

I never lost the habit of anthropological observation of
metro passengers.

Westmount teenagers entering at Vendôme station
appear even more well-off when their peers climb in at the
next station, Place-Saint-Henri. In Côte-Sainte-Catherine,
Filipinos outnumber West Indians, and at the next station
(Plamondon), it is the opposite, and at Namur station,
Indians prevail. At Atwater, I can distinguish quite easily
who's going to McGill University and who's going to
Concordia. At Park, I can see a few older Greek people and
people from Southeast Asia, but that's all. At Saint-Michel,
blacks speak French, at Villa-Maria, English. At Place
d'Armes, the old Chinese women with their full plastic bags
keep their eyes lowered and remain unaware of the tourists
who are avoiding taking snapshots of them. They won't be
going to the same restaurant in Chinatown.

Upon exiting Henri-Bourassa metro, Haitians take the
bus to the east, people from the Maghreb to the west, and

the other Quebecers walk home. At McGill, if it weren't for the posters in French, you'd think you were in Toronto; at Acadie metro, in Bombay and at the Outremont station, with its groups of young collegians coming in from Stanislas College, it's like being in the metro in Lyon, France. The French themselves are partial to Mont-Royal metro, where browsing the farmers' markets and local crafts boutiques is their way of enjoying our great outdoors. When I was a teenager, the most beautiful girls got on at Snowdon, in their private-school uniforms; Later, it was at Berri-UQAM; today, they get on at Jarry, and I help them up the stairs with their strollers.

I'm convinced that I'm invisible, indecipherable; in any case, they are all, without distinction of origin, glued to their portable phones. To the point where I forget – hidden behind my white skin and my newspaper – that I myself am an immigrant.

At least until a couple enters the car with their child. And then when they quickly scan the car, when people jump up from their seats and when I see how quickly the child takes the place he knows to be rightfully his, settling in without saying thank you or even looking the good Samaritan in the eyes, I feel like a *foreigner*, convinced that I will remain so until the end of my days.

Sitting there, I remember when I was a child in the Budapest subway or tramway, how I could never settle into my seat, knowing that at each stop, as the people piled in, my time could be up. A not so old adult would eventually get on, approach my seat and scold me if I didn't get up. Unless my mother had already done so.

Each time I think about it, I am outraged by this scene and I would like to re-write it. I'd like to rerun the tape and this time I'd put in my two cents about little North American princes and princesses who if we ask them to stand up for a couple of stops, it would be called torture. I'd start to rant about how children in Quebec are brought up and all my sentences would begin with "In my country...". I would become the kind of insufferable immigrant who often gets on my nerves because he doesn't understand: other countries, other customs.

I don't actually do anything, I calm myself and sometimes I'm able to regain my sense of hope. On the radio, they are talking about civility. A popular actor is speaking about kids sitting in the metro and explains that he has done things differently with his son, teaching by example. But my sudden rush of hope is precipitous. You see, what he taught his son was to be polite when he asked for "his" place and to say thank you.

At that moment, I suddenly hear the (swear) words of the poet, Gérald Godin in my head:

> *Cinciboires de cincrèmes*
> *de jériboires d'hosties toastées*
> *de sacraments d'étoles*
> *de crucifix de calvaires*
> *de couleuré d'ardent voyage,*
>
> *I'm aching in my own land*
> *ciboriums of chrism,*
> *holy ciboriums of toasted wafers,*
> *sacramental vestments,*
> *Calvary cross,*
> *tarnished remnants of an ardent voyage,*[*]

I violently turn off the radio.

And tell myself that there's really nothing that can be done here. *I'm aching in the land* of Godin.

---

* Gérald Godin, "Mal au pays," 1975; translated by Casey Roberts.

It's no sure thing that my children will speak Hungarian. I would hope that at a minimum they'll be able to recite some poems from my childhood, passed down by my mother and my grandmother. If not, then maybe they'll love Sport chocolate, whose rum flavour will remind them, in the manner of a genetically-transmitted Proustian madeleine, of my experiences as a school kid wandering the streets of Pest's 13th district. I want them to know the broad outline of Hungarian history, and some of my own. And I would like, in a way, that they be proud of this heritage that they combine with the sweets, poems and stories of their mother. I would like that but still, I wouldn't get too worked up. On the other hand, you can be certain of one thing: they will smartly relinquish their seat to an old person in the metro. And please don't dare call me an insufferable immigrant!

People often say that the integration of immigrants is like a tango danced in pairs, each must do their part. This isn't incorrect, but neither does it rule out missteps. Sooner or later, even with the best intentions, we risk stepping on each other's feet. Etiquette dictates that we don't find fault and simply resume the dance as if nothing had happened, paying greater attention to the music and responding in time to the other people's rhythms.

But there's one thing we should always remember: you have to get up early – well before seven in the morning – to leave behind your native culture.

NOUS

"If there is a Quebec tradition to maintain, it's not poutine or xenophobia. If there is a Quebec tradition to maintain, it is the one the students of Quebec are carrying on. A tradition of struggle; of trade union struggle, of student struggle, of popular struggle."[*]

Spring 2012. This is how the intrepid student leader of the *"printemps érable,"* Gabriel Nadeau-Dubois, ended his inspired talk at an event called "Nous?", where well-known personalities representing social causes and Quebec nationalism came together to present their thinking on "how to make visible and operative the freedom that both characterizes us and escapes us."

I spent hours in front of the TV listening to them, one after another; filmmakers, artists, sociologists, politicians, writers. In their remarks, they tried to come to terms with the great question of Quebec nationalism: who are we? And more concretely: what defines the Quebecer, what moves them into solidarity, what makes them progress? Their social struggles or their identity struggles?

To the classical left, grounded in a trade-unionism inherited from Michel Chartrand and others, the two causes are inseparable. Fighting for respect of one's language rights means fighting to be respected on the shop floor. Fighting

---

[*] Gabriel Nadeau-Dubois, at the *"Nous"* event, April 7, 2012, at the Monument-National.

to defend Quebec's natural resources means sharing them with all Quebecers. Fighting for free education means fighting to provide education for all. Fighting for independence means equipping ourselves to ensure our development in the common interest. According to their way of thinking, it was understood that any redistribution of wealth or social gains would benefit all without discrimination. In its essence, this nationalism was "inclusive" despite the pushback from big business and its supporters in Quebec and Ottawa, who accused them of every kind of evil. That's my "*nous.*"

The speech of the young student had echoes of Chartrand. A hyperbolic speech, neatly sliced and uncompromising, on behalf of the people, against the private interests of the "greedy elites" and for the common good. So far, so good; it's a speech to which I'm sensitive, I would almost vote for him. As a student, I helped organize strikes, against neoliberal globalization and a rector who wanted to fund UQAM by selling cans of Coca-Cola. I have neither remorse not regret. Twelve years later, I proudly wore the red square and marched down the street with a sign and a pan in my hands.

The nuance, increasingly present today in the discourse of the left, is that the concept of the people has given way to an effort to break Quebecers into categories: there is a supposedly exclusive "we," and then there's the "others," supposedly rejected by the former. Let's go back to the quote from Nadeau-Dubois: "If there is a Quebecois tradition to maintain, it's not poutine or xenophobia..." What? Xenophobia, a tradition? A Quebec tradition, moreover? A sort of local specialty that we are pleased to cultivate and export alongside our popular singers?

Analyze this joke. Poutine is a Quebec tradition. OK, we died laughing, but xenophobia? I can't deny that there are racists in Quebec, but I do not think we serve as a good example by spreading such clichés and lumping everybody together. You don't fight racism by claiming that it comes from a specific source, a source that smells like little globs of cheese melting under brown gravy, in this case.

So, who are these poutine-eating xenophobes? Surly not our media, business and political elites who, while eating their salmon tartare are almost unanimously in favour of welcoming 55,000 immigrants annually to Quebec, which does not indicate *a priori* an inordinate fear of foreigners, you must agree. Should we search for these poutine-eating xenophobes among Anglophones and immigrants? That would be misguided.

In my view, he was rather thinking, disgusted, of the uncle at the Christmas table who felt moved to say that he didn't see why those black Hassidims should be able to make everybody else eat halal pork.

Somebody should have responded, and it's not always easy; I know from experience. Someone should have taken the time to listen and talk, without preaching, without judgment and without rejecting from a feeling of superiority the cultural insecurities of the members of one's own family. I have already left the table, discouraged, but deep down I know that people's fears tend to dissipate when solutions are offered that address their concerns: we could do more to encourage immigrants to use French, offer better integration services, redefine what is "reasonable accommodation," secularize the schools, better allocate our immigration, reduce it maybe... Obviously, if we disqualify any identity concern – sitting up there with our degrees, our vested interests and research chairs – as being racist and xenophobic, we only serve to reinforce these concerns and the only satisfaction we will have is the validation from both sides of our prejudices.

If you go to war against every manifestation of intolerance – without trying to listen, to discuss – you end up
without realizing it assuming a position of superiority
towards Quebecers, by pointing your finger, by rejecting
these people as ignorant. You can't then hope to also speak
out for those same people.

By the time I got to the last speech, all these visions of
"nous" that were bouncing around in my head no longer
seemed irreconcilable to me. I felt hopeful. I turned off the
TV reflecting on ways I could begin a sentence with "we"
without it ending with "they."

But first of all I had to stand up and enter the stage.

RUSALKA

In Russian mythology, *rusalki* appear in the form of beautiful young girls who live at the bottom of lakes and rivers, in a sumptuous crystal palace. Their main distinguishing trait is their thick green hair that they arrange using magic combs, which they also use to cast spells. The character of the rusalka is particularly ambiguous and, in general, it is better to be careful. Alas, when I encountered a representative of the Russian community in Montreal, I wasn't careful enough.

She was in the category of immigrants labelled "involved," who I often rubbed shoulders with and who – sometimes barely off the plane – diligently work their communities in search of business opportunities. But they don't open restaurants, grocery stores or the (trilingual) child care centres that have materialized up and down the street; their stock-in-trade is actually communitarianism.

Some become immigration consultants, suggesting themselves as (unnecessary) intermediaries between immigrant candidates in their country of origin and Canadian government services. They have a talent for making themselves indispensable, offering their reassuring although expensive advice to a naive and ignorant clientele who are convinced that to get what one wants, one must know the right people. Others organize their community. They start a newspaper, publish a directory, coordinate summer camps, colloquiums, Saturday schools and "ethnocultural" festivals.

Always looking for sponsors, they become experts in finding funding, which usually comes from government programs "for intercultural activities" and the discretionary budgets of elected officials.

To establish their legitimacy, they assume leadership in an organization in whose name they can come before our elected officials as spokespersons of their community, and, *voila*, that's how they become indispensable political intermediaries. In Quebec, one might think this is unnecessary because people from immigrant backgrounds almost automatically vote for the Liberal Party; but in practice, they play an important role in turning out the vote, lining up volunteers and especially raising money. They roll out the red maple-leaf carpet for the elected officials, are appointed to all sorts of committees and work hand in hand with the members of the National Assembly to ensure, on the one hand, that they continue to receive support from the government, and on the other, the sustainability of this communitarian system.

Somewhere down the pike, these representatives become *apparatchiks* and political aides in exchange for their having mobilized voters, and to receive the ultimate recognition, once their community is sufficiently organized and large (when their political and economic weight warrants it), they become in turn (unless it's their daughter, their son, their husband or wife) candidates and elected officials. A rise that might only be thwarted by the ambitions of competing personalities from other cultural communities or star candidates from the majority to which the party leadership has promised a safe riding. (The imposition of candidates "*de souche*" in immigrant constituencies by the Liberal Parties of Quebec and Canada deprives us of better representation of ethnic minorities in our legislatures, but doesn't spare us having to listen to the fine words about the beauty of diversity.)

They hold cocktail parties, organize social events and conferences on immigration issues (the more daring become "experts") and quickly gain enough access to power to get noticed by ministers, mayors, deputies, councillors and even… school commissioners. It was in that capacity that I met this typical specimen, particularly effective, this hyperactive representative of the Russian community.

I was campaigning for re-election as a Montreal School Board commissioner, where I represented for four years the citizens of Westmount and Côte-des-Neiges. Saying "the citizens," when you see how many people voted, is a bit of a stretch. I got a few hundred votes in an election that only interested the parents of kids in school, the very politicized and community groups.

I never turned down an opportunity to participate in an event where I could speak to potential voters during an election campaign, including this invitation from a woman who offered to put me in touch with others at a meeting of the Russian community "to work together on our common goals."

My objective was clear, and she knew what it was: meet Russian parents, who were a growing presence in my territory. On the other hand, her objectives were unclear to me. I knew that the Russians wanted to emulate the Chinese and sought a way to prepare their children to pass the entrance examination to the École internationale de Montréal (the Chinese there now outnumber the French-speaking kids). I also knew that they wanted the teaching of Russian to their children to be funded by the original Heritage Languages Program of the Ministry of Education, as other languages were. Two causes that left me cold, which made me their potential opponent. But that much I kept to myself.

I had prepared a little speech for the small audience of fifty people. In a pale imitation of Denis Coderre,* I started with a few words in Russian, retained from my obligatory two-years of Russian studies in Hungary, and once having gained the sympathy of the room, I pivoted to my experience and my projects. "You know, I developed the intercultural policy of the CSDM, organized the consultations for its adoption. We will make the integration and Francisation of immigrants a priority, we're currently investing a million dollars a year! Here in our district, each school has a community and school liaison who facilitates links between schools, families and the community... *Spasibo damy i gospoda, merci, mesdames et messieurs*, thank you, ladies and gentlemen, I hope you will take the time to vote [for me] next Sunday." I received a round of polite applause, but I doubt that these particular ethnic votes played much of a role in my re-election, contrary to what their representative wished me to believe.

After my presentation, while the room woke up, a woman challenged by my speech on French vindictively accosted me. She had recently moved to Laval and couldn't understand why the school wasn't bilingual like her city, Quebec, and Canada. I was accustomed to hearing this point of view and I had my little speech ready that I deliver on such occasions; that Bill 101 makes French the common language on the collective level but does not prevent individuals from become bilingual. A little speech which I like, even if it's not terribly convincing to such an audience, gaining me mostly pity for my naiveté or, at worst, my narrow-mindedness.

---

* Liberal MP from 1997-2013; elected mayor of Montreal in 2013—trans.

Except that the woman was looking for a fight. I wasn't bothered; anyway, she votes in Laval. The president of the association came to my rescue. She handed the woman her business card, and I learned that she was also the political aide to the Quebec minister of Immigration, "in charge of East European cultural communities." She also had her spiel. "It's not the school board's decision, but the Quebec government's. Before, the PQ wouldn't allow children to be taught English [before third grade – *Ed.*], but with Jean Charest, now it's from the first grade. It's a good start."

Her speech was more convincing than mine. On the spot she sold the person a Quebec Liberal Party membership card and invited her to share her ideas "somewhere where it matters." If my cell hadn't rung, I'd still be standing there, speechless, in the face of such *chutzpah*.

I suddenly became aware of my naivety; that the invitation and the event, the whole pretence was designed to give them a platform and put the spotlight on her and her party, not me. Well, it's not like I had better things to do.

The two ladies, apparently comfortable at various levels of the party, must have been effective advocates within the red *nomenklatura* because the following year, the Liberal Party announced with great fanfare that grade six would henceforth be required to be bilingual for all students in Quebec (except Anglophones).

Life is strange. A few years later, after the return to power of the Parti Québécois, I succeeded this Russian woman as a political aide in the office of the Ministry of Immigration and Cultural Communities.

My new secretary, accustomed to the old ways of doing things, asked me, after seeing my name, if I was going to be taking care of Eastern Europe.

"Uh... no ma'am, I'm going to try and take care of Quebec."

THE SHIT RAINS DOWN ON MY HEAD

Anyone who has inadvertently found themselves in a political discussion with Anglophones knows that it takes only five seconds to get to the question of separatism, ten to Bill 101 and, at the thirty second mark of this fascinating discussion, Jacques Parizeau's remarks on money and ethnic votes. Essentially.

Me, ironic, *Métro Daily*, September 2012

In spring 2013, for an entire week, they discussed my literary works in the majestic Blue Room of the National Assembly, as once they chatted about the pamphlets of Henri Bourassa. The episode will not be recorded in the parliamentary history books, but I will remember it. Especially since during that period I was asked to "go back to my country," a first in thirty years in Quebec.

The liberal opposition called for my resignation for a column I had written in the *Métro* newspaper before being hired as a political aide to the Minister of Immigration, Diane De Courcy. For a week, day after day, I was accused of being the enemy of intercultural harmony in Quebec in a surreal hyper-partisan witch hunt, whose target was the minister and whose victim was me.

The main article causing the ruckus was entitled "*Ils sont fous ces anglos.*" The misunderstanding around the title could illustrate, if necessary, that language and culture are inseparable. Because anyone in the French-speaking world

RHAPSODY IN QUEBEC

would recognize the inoffensive and ironic reference to the character Obelix in the popular *Astérix* comic series. He always tells Astérix "Strange guys, those Romans (*Ils sont fous ces romains*)," while tapping himself on the forehead. Everyone? Apparently not!

In the trenches of West-Islanderium, the French-speaking world seems like a far off land. From there, Liberal diehards and the English media translated "*fous*" as "crazy," though if they had asked my opinion, I would have suggested "nuts." But what do you want, they're the champions of bilingualism.

In a caustic piece (I confess), I put forth – brace yourself – that anglophone public opinion seemed to be its most monolithic and touchy when it came to Quebec politics, and that you would have to search for a long time before you'd find a sincere defender or even moderate supporter of Bill 101 in the pages of *The Gazette* or at the Tim Horton's in the West Island.

It was a sendup of the tired old song. I wrote: "Without exception, Quebecers in general – and separatists in particular – are xenophobic racist chauvinists, bigots on the margins, who cultivate their ignorance by depriving themselves of the inestimable economic and cultural wealth that would come from the English language in general and Anglophones in particular. These provincial "*incultes et bègues*,"* whiny spoiled children, oppressors of Westmounters and torturers of immigrant investors would prefer to live in an underdeveloped Quebec in ruins, transformed into a *joual*-ized version of the Third Reich than to appreciate like everyone else the benefits of Canadian multiculturalism, the most wonderful invention since Athenian democracy."

---

* Uneducated and stuttering, a quote from "Speak White," by Michèle Lalonde—trans.

I would have been delighted to be proven wrong, to be shown that I had been mistaken to speak of the "scornful, abusive and insulting tone taken on call-in shows, adopted by commentators in the anglo press and on social media." The shit rained down on my head in the form of hundreds of hate messages coming from every part of Canada. I especially recall this masterpiece of twitterature: "Buy him one-way ticket back to Hungary. He doesn't deserve to be in Canada." There were more than a few people who sent me this wish, several also suggesting that I go fuck myself on the way back to my native land.

QED. "The proof is in the pudding,"* as they say.

Nobody had seen fit to set the context: my column was written the day after the attack on the Métropolis nightclub by Richard Bain, "the lover of Canada with the troubled soul," as he was neatly described in *La Presse*; this fanatic who shot a man with a semi-automatic rifle and came close to assassinating several of my friends and the two women who were to become my bosses.

Eight months after this had become old news, the English media had all reported on my text, but none believed it important to dig into its subject. Still less to recall its conclusion, which went as follows: "If we want to coexist, in respect, anglos and francos in Quebec, we should start by taking some deep breaths, lighten the atmosphere and recognize – without judging – the legitimate insecurities of the Other. In any case, the way things are at the moment, we would all be crazy not to try."

This extract wasn't mentioned by Liberal MNA Geoffrey Kelley, who claimed without embarrassment to be in the National Assembly to represent Anglophones. He only quoted the beginning of the article: "I'm not a psychiatrist

---

* In English in the original.

like Camille Laurin, the famous anglopologist, but I have always found our anglos a bit crazy – with notable exceptions of course. Not stark raving mad like the infamous Richard Bain, but only suffering from a sort of mild paranoid-obsessive disorder triggered when Quebec is the topic."

In fact, he forgot to read the part where I said "with notable exceptions."

This master of indignation accused me at every turn of wanting to commit all Quebec Anglophones to the Pinel Institute psychiatric hospital, even Christopher Hall* and Jim Corcoran,** without ever mentioning the one person who really belonged there, Richard Bain. Even Kelley, although he cheerfully helped to maintain the climate of hatred that I had denounced, doesn't deserve to be locked up. I know he has his wits about him, he's clever, and this episode had supplied ample proof. He's just one of those pyromaniac firemen who know perfectly well that linguistic peace is not in the interest of those who owe their automatic re-election to the continuing insecurity.

We are compelled to note that the Quebec National Assembly is not a place for intelligent debate and frank discussion, which is perhaps the saddest conclusion to be drawn from the event. The master manipulators of the populist mind, jumping like starving hyenas on any prohibited word or poor use of the language appearing in the media and on the lists of acceptable terms approved by public communication strategists and the guardians of virtue, with the complacency of illiterate people who denounce their neighbours as having read a blacklisted book, go to sleep content for

---

* Anglophone comedian and TV commentator who works mostly in French—trans.
** English-speaking singer-songwriter who sings in French and has long promoted Quebec music—trans.

having contributed to the general dumbing down of the people, thanks to their privileged position.

We're talking about a text with a fair amount of substance, written to get people thinking (I assure you), with disdain, like any *"coquerelle de parlement"** hanging around the sanitized corridors of the National Assembly. Henri Bourassa (and perhaps even Robert Bourassa) would be equally saddened to see the seat of our national debates become no more than a new kind of colonial administration, just the place to send ideas – disturbing to the motherland – to oblivion.

Talking about the motherland, the appeal for calm would actually come from Toronto, a long week later. The editorial in the *Globe and Mail* took the time to explain to its readers the humour of Asterix and replied respectfully, in substance: "Yes, it's true, Anglophones are a bit obsessed and a bit obsessive, but there may be reasons that can be quite sane." I would have liked to have had the freedom to pursue the debate, defend myself, or even better, to be able to discuss the future of a French Quebec with Anglophones who had not fallen into a toxic vat of magic potions when they were little, who didn't think that the vitality of their community would only be ensured through the anglicization of Quebec and its immigrants. I've actually met some.

"It's only politics, don't worry. Take the week off. If you receive concrete threats, we will notify the SQ,"** I was assured by the minister's office.

That's what I did. We had just finished travelling around Quebec. Everywhere people told us they were overwhelmed

---

* Backbenchers and parliamentary staff. From Godin, "J'ai mal à mon pays."—trans.
** Sûreté du Québec, provincial police—trans.

by the work of being hosts, of dealing with the francization and integration of the increasingly numerous immigrants who surely would appreciate if the members of the National Assembly inquired about their fate from time to time. Which I would have appreciated as well.

The balm to the heart came from the Publisher of *Le Devoir,* the newspaper founded by Henri Bourassa. During a radio interview that ridiculed the controversy, he said: "In addition, it was well done, his commentary; he knows how to write." Thank you, sir.

It made me want to write again and to stay in Quebec, finally. *Désolé.* Sorry guys.

THE GRAND SEDUCTION

It seemed like a dream. Was it one? A Parti Quebecois minister standing on a stage under the slogan "A Quebec for Everybody," generously applauded by all those who, from near or far, deal with the integration of immigrants in Quebec.

"It is no longer necessary that the great seduction of immigrants end in a great disappointment," she declared at the end of a long speech in which she explained the measures her ministry would now implement to improve the selection, integration, regionalization, francization and employability of newcomers. Jargon that sounded like a sweet melody to the ears of hundreds of people present at the Bonsecours Market on this radiant autumn day.

It was a few months after I had been tasked to organize a ministerial tour. I had accompanied the minister to all the regions of Quebec, not just in Montreal and its suburbs. We were already far from the time when immigration was confined to a few Montreal neighbourhoods. From the 20,000 to 30,000 immigrants who were welcomed annually by Quebec in the 1980s and 1990s, the number had grown to 55,000 during the last decade of Liberal rule.

These changes were obviously becoming visible, and here and there, there were difficulties of integration which the minister had the good sense to go and see for herself, even though she knew that the opposition and the opinion-makers were going to criticize her for wasting public funds. The obsession with balanced budgets, privatization, tariff increases and cuts in public services had not been without its effects, and they were nowhere as blatant as in the disadvantaged neighbourhoods, which welcome an increasing number of immigrants. Words and deeds have consequences, although some people would rather we didn't notice.

During the tour, thousands of people shook hands with the minister saying that the integration of immigrants is possible and necessary, but – of course – not with the available resources, which do not reflect the increase in immigration: such resources have even been steadily declining for several years. The number of people from immigrant families has increased in schools, daycare centers, factories, and cities, but also at food banks, in social housing, shelters for homeless people, and especially among people looking for work.

But nobody contested the increases in immigration levels. Not the community organizations who are "partners" of the ministry. Not the business community, happy to have new consumers and inexpensive labour. Not immigrant organizations, who could count on new members. Nor of course the Liberal Party, whose electoral support was growing thanks to those who are the most vulnerable to its austerity policies. Nor the other political parties, academics, actors of "civil society," who feared being accused of xenophobia.

Nor did many people question the whys and wherefores of this utilitarian immigration, supposedly destined to save our economy, when in front of their eyes, the social safety net was fraying. It is much more convenient to be alarmed at the sight of those intolerant and lazy Quebecers who don't make enough babies to support their pension plans, than to question the real impact of the immigration system on the economy and on... immigrants.

A seductive idea was gaining ground: that a multiethnic population – in itself – engenders a more open, more dynamic, more prosperous society. The government cannot afford to provide universal quality public services because of its deficit and debt? It is no longer capable of ensuring equal opportunities and reducing inequality? Don't worry, "diversity" will solve these problems for us, or at least, say the pragmatic, let's save what can still be saved.

So we visited a few of these Eldorados such as Parc-Extension and Brossard, but we also went to cities like Trois-Rivières, Gatineau, Rimouski and Joliette, even further from the multiethnic concept, but where more and more people from other countries can be seen as a result of the last ten years of immigration policy. The minister was everywhere politely received. People said they welcomed newcomers, while admitting they felt overwhelmed by the task of integration.

In fact, the representatives of the organizations we met with were all playing the same game. Each was trying to get what they could from the Ministry of Immigration's budgetary share of the declining government revenues. They proposed programs, projects, activities, initiatives for anything that would improve the integration of immigrants and help make intercultural relations more harmonious. New groups were being organized, others adapted to the "new realities." Each offered its recipe "for meeting the challenge of diversity."

They all had their sights set on the mythical manna chests of the Ministry of Immigration and ministerial budgets targeting ethnocultural communities. From the smallest community groups to the largest community organizations, school boards, cities, regions, even institutions such as the *Grande Bibliothèque*; all used the increasing number of

immigrants among their clients or on their territory – and
the great challenge that this represented – to get more funding. Even the Montreal Chamber of Commerce put together
a project to help a few dozen newcomers find an internship
(unpaid) in order to receive hundreds of thousands of dollars from the province – while publically advocating the
acceptance of 65,000 new immigrants each year because of
the economic benefits that would result, and to address the
persistent shortages in the workforce!

The presentation of funding applications inevitably went
down two tracks: first, they emphasized how immigration
is a richness with strong potential, indispensable for Quebec
society; and then, they demanded some of that wealth to
cover the resulting costs and – surprise, surprise – that they
were the best placed to address.

During these visits, we also heard serious criticism of
our incoherent system, too slow and frustrating, that gave
immigrants the impression that their life in Quebec would
be free of bumps, but which was unable to help them or at
least lower their expectations. Nobody wants to admit that
discrimination and lack of resources, although real, are
insufficient explanations for all their problems. It is natural
that the latecomers, those who have been trained abroad,
those who do not master the local cultural codes and languages, those with work experience in another country,
those who have a smaller network in Quebec, have more
trouble finding a job than natives do. No one dared to say
that to offer well-being to newcomers and avoid their going
on welfare, yes, we must fight against discrimination, but
we first we must rebuild the welfare state.

As far as reducing the number of immigrants admitted
per year, the taboo remained, even though the Auditor
General of Quebec had subtly suggested the idea in a damn-
ing report:

Consultation and collaboration mechanisms between the Ministry, its partners and the organizations concerned have led, over the years, to the decision to increase immigration volumes [...]. The consultation process reveals certain integration difficulties. However, the Ministry does not use socio-economic indicators to clearly define Quebec's real capacity to welcome and integrate newcomers [...]. Without an evaluation, the Ministry cannot obtain the assurance that the province is capable of supporting the progressive increases in immigration volumes while optimizing the effects of immigration on Quebec's development.

I was one who would have liked to break this taboo. I found creative ways to support the proposal to make it more presentable and understandable: we would do better with less, everyone would gain, primarily immigrants who are already here. We even commissioned a poll which showed that the majority of Quebecers would agree. Ultimately, fear of the critics and unshakable faith *in the little engine that could* prevailed over my ambitions and I had to accept the sad reality, of which my colleagues reminded me every day at the office: I wasn't the minister, (much less the prime minister*).

My job was mainly to take notes. After each meeting, I drew up the list of grievances and tried to find temporary solutions. I provoked the anticipated retirement of a valiant ministry official in charge of compiling such grievances. The minister, no less valiant but more persevering, got the Ministries of Employment and Immigration to better coordinate their work, to select stronger candidates for potential integration, to see that the candidates were better informed, that they understand they are choosing a French future before they arrive at Dorval Airport, that a better

---

* Premier, in French, "*le premier ministre*"—trans.

knowledge of French be required and that there be more services available upon their arrival. And above all, she obtained the impossible: "new money" from the Treasury Board. In the "hard budget context" of the Marois government, it was worthy of mention. And jealousy.

So It wasn't just a dream. The announcement took place. The applause was real. This action plan had indeed been launched. It wasn't a dream that I was revising the minister's speech for the umpteenth time, that I welcomed the participants in my freshly cleaned suit, that I was nervously playing king of the outhouse with the organizers of the event.

Strangely, I don't have a memory of having sent the press release, greeted the journalists or shared our success on social media. For some absurd reason that I would never have imagined in my worst dreams: the launch of the plan, which was basically the best news for the integration of immigrants there'd been in years, was to remain a secret! In the premier's office, it was explained to me, they had suddenly decided that the announcement should be postponed and made by another minister…

The public announcement never took place. The government wanted to ensure that nothing would distract from an upcoming policy announcement of high importance, which would energize our way of "living together": the Charter of Quebec Values.

So I never dreamed that upon hearing this, I would bombard the wall of my office with every object of little value that had fallen into my hands.

Now I do clearly remember, it did all take place. The grand seduction turned into a great disappointment. It was like a nightmare.

THE BANALITY OF EVIL

What has come to light is neither nihilism nor cynicism, as one might have expected, but a quite extraordinary confusion over elementary questions of morality – as if an instinct in such matters were truly the last thing to be taken for granted in our time.

Hannah Arendt, *Eichmann in Jerusalem.*
Report on the Banality of Evil

"Let's say I wouldn't do it like that, if you really want my opinion." And the crazy thing was they really did want it. For a while now, people had been asking me about the Charter of Values that my party had just announced "in an effort to ensure the neutrality of the state towards religion and to provide a framework for accommodation requests for religious reasons."

Look, I said, even the Bouchard-Taylor commission on reasonable accommodation in its report that popularized the twisted notion of "open secularism" recommended that people in authority – police, judges and prison guards – refrain from wearing religious symbols. The PQ in its Charter should "simply" propose to lengthen the list. Leave out hospital employees, our health system is already going through enough turmoil. Okay for government functionaries, but most important: add teachers. Such a proposal would focus the debate on the importance both of ensuring a neutral state and the role of schools in transmitting the

common values of an increasingly diverse society. And
without further ado, we would have a Charter on the
Secularism of the Quebec State – not a Charter of "Quebec
values," if you'll so permit.

Thus spoke the political aide of the minister of Immigration that I had become.

I feared that the PQ would overly prolong our collective
pleasure, through consultations, navel gazing, and improvised strategies of which it is the past master. The consensus
was broad enough that a more measured bill could be passed
before the next election and we could move on to something
else – for instance, the integration of immigrants. Not only
"economic integration," but also cultural. Hadn't this been
the underlying concern, somewhat obscured by their vehe-
mence, of all those who for some years had been troubled
about the proliferation of conspicuous religious symbols and
not always reasonable accommodations?

But in the PQ, the believers in intransigence had quickly
taken over.

(One could argue against my position that the consensual
approach had not been proven in the case of the other charter, the Charter of the French Language. I was well placed to
know. The changes to strengthen Bill 101, proposed by my
boss at the time, didn't survive long in a National Assembly
led by a minority government. Even if, in the beginning after
it was tabled, Bill 14 was praised for its moderation and time-
liness by people as disparate as Julius Grey and Gérald
Larose. A new linguistic harmony; but too good to be true.

During the following months, the project was little by
little, section by section, indignation after indignation, tor-
pedoed by the historical opponents of Bill 101: the PLQ, the
spokespeople for the English-speaking community and big
business, and all those who believed that people of this ilk
have their interests at heart. Their torpedoes were armed

with the same toxic warheads – racism, nostalgia for the past, economic collapse – as in the 1970s. Just because we knew it was coming didn't mean it left any less of a mess. After some timid resistance, all that was left under the debris was the dust of our modest political ambitions. In the end, after months of consultations and negotiations in good faith (I swear!), the bill we had been working on for a year was abandoned amid general indifference.

In short, intransigence prevailed among proponents of the Charter, now called the "Secular Values Charter," and grew more stubborn as its opponents increasingly bore down, draping themselves in inclusivity in the name of the Holy Trinity of Openness (to the Other, to the world, to differences). In lieu of a healthy debate, and with favourable polls, suddenly, *that* carried more weight than the negligible opinion of a political aide… or even a minister.

My main problem with the Charter was that almost all of my friends were against it. People who closely followed politics and those who were interested from afar and with whom, in normal times, I would be on the same wavelength. My appeal to noble republican principles couldn't prevail over the horror of prohibiting niqab-wearing women educating children in Verdun daycares and Sikh teenagers going to school carrying knives. OK, I was more and more in bad faith, but I was frankly surprised to see the extent to which the principles of the Charter of Rights and Freedoms, the precedence of individual rights over collective rights, and the respect for religious choices ever more wacky and regressive had apparently won over a new generation.

I would have liked to have been able to let go of being right and instead build a consensus before the battle's frontlines set in. Why wait for the ultimate coalition of these young people with the followers of Yahweh, Mohammed,

Vishnu and Pierre Elliott Trudeau? Why wait until even the most secular, most integrated and most favourable to the cause of Quebec among my compatriots of immigrant origin, including Muslims (just saying), begin to feel forever alienated from this cause in general and independence in particular?

All's fair in love and war. Burrowed into my fox hole, I decided to respond to ideology with ideology by taking refuge in my secular values, which have remained for me, whatever they say, the basis of "living together" since the days of the Enlightenment (and, closer to home, the Quiet Revolution). Amidst the turmoil, I also clung to this message from the Charter, which I didn't find terribly shocking and which I think explained its popularity: "We are in Quebec, this is how things work here!" In any case, nuances were no longer possible, compromises neither; the degree of polarization was total. The belligerents promised a humiliating defeat to the opposing party, but it was my humiliation that was to come first.

"You know the situation, if you're not comfortable with it, I'll leave it to your personal discretion. Questions? Next item on the agenda?"

"Your schedule, Madam. You are invited to the commemoration of Kristallnacht at the Holocaust Memorial Centre, an important event in the Jewish community, but they are not inviting you to speak. It's certainly because of the context…"

"It's not a big deal. You've been on the board of directors for years, right? You'll accompany me."

I tried to spit out the words, "But, it's going to be boring as all get out, Madam…"

Despite my efforts, there was no getting out of it.

A violent November storm raged as I waited for the minister's car in the lobby of the building that houses the

Holocaust Museum where I had been a volunteer for the last four years – working alongside some mighty fine people, I hasten to say because of how things turned out. I was responsible for organizing an annual event that sought to draw universal lessons from the Nazi horrors without falling into generalizations. My goal of attracting a wider audience – Francophones, youth, non-Jews – was largely shared, my ideas welcomed with openness and the results of our actions, meaningful. But that evening, the frosty atmosphere put a chill on the modest warming in community relations which I believed, modestly, that I had contributed to.

The minister finally arrived. If she'd have come wearing the uniform of the Waffen SS to mark the seventy-fifth anniversary of the first Nazi atrocities, the people present would not have batted an eye: only to be expected. The cold reception she received contrasted with the general enthusiasm for the contingent of the opposition Liberal Party who arrived like a liberating army, distributing little kisses and handshakes all around, like the GIs had distributed packets of Marlboros to the newly freed Buchenwald survivors.

To respect the solemn nature of the commemoration, the audience was asked to remain silent throughout the ceremony. There were songs from children, short speeches from dignitaries and poems throughout the evening, captivating for those who were not on the receiving end of looks that could kill. The closing word was offered by an influential Montreal rabbi who told the story of a man killed in Berlin on November 9, 1938, during the Night of Broken Glass, after he refused to remove his yarmulke in front of his Nazi murderers. When the grandiloquent rabbi said that like that man, if he would have to choose between the prohibitions of the Charter of the Parti Quebecois and death, he would

choose death, Philippe Couillard* and his associates decided
to break the prescribed silence, leaping to their feet to
applaud this common sense choice. They knew better than
anyone that death's name wouldn't appear on the ballot,
unlike theirs.

Two people remained seated in the room under the gaze
of the triumphant audience, reminding some of when
Eichmann, in Jerusalem, had been sentenced to hang for
crimes against humanity, guilty of the deaths of four hundred thousand Hungarian Jews, including some of my
ancestors.

The next day, the Liberal Jean-Marc Fournier, still delirious,
decided to keep it going and publicly endorsed the rabbi's
subtle analysis in the National Assembly. The comparison
between Hitler's final solution and Premier Marois' ** pre-
carious solution received a mixed response, requiring him
to explain himself for a couple of days.

"Madam Minister, you might remember that his leader
was no less convinced of the correctness of this comparison
at the commemoration; I can prepare some lines for the
press on the banalization of evil."

"Nothing requires us to engage in a game of tit-for-tat
with our opponents, and we're not going to up the ante
now."

This act of Christian charity was like a breath of fresh
air amidst the din; while I had lost my voice along with my
reason, I couldn't see why we should in any event so will-
ingly turn the other cheek.

---

* Leader of the Quebec Liberal Party—trans.
** Pauline Marois, Quebec premier, leader of the Parti Québécois—
trans.

MON PAYS (MY COUNTRY)

From my great solitary country
I shout before holding my tongue
To all the people of the Earth
My home is your home
Between my four walls of ice
I put my time and my space
Build a fire, prepare the place
For all the humans at the horizon
And humans are of my race

Gilles Vigneault, *"Mon pays"*

A few years earlier, not far from here, I volunteered at the Côte-des-Neiges community centre to give French conversation workshops – *free for adults who didn't speak French, regardless of your status in Canada.*

In my classes, I handed out the words to a song from Quebec. As we worked to decipher the words and expressions, they'd talk about the meaning of the song and share personal experiences that related to the music. At the end, I would play the CD, and my students could hear our song for the first time. "Toune d'automne" by the Cowboys Fringant, "L'Étranger" by Pauline Julien, "I Lost My Baby" by Jean Leloup were memorable educational successes. For the last class, I would bring the workshop to a close with Gilles Vigneault. As they listened, I felt that here was at least one time when I had an impact on the integration of immigrants in Quebec.

We didn't know about this community centre when we came to Canada. Or of all the activities going on in the neighbourhood: the sugar shack in the park, the "*Lundis québécois*," the bonfire on Saint-Jean Baptiste Day,* or the welcoming ceremony for newcomers. Which I don't think even existed back then. Not that we would have gone. We had our hearts set on the real deal, the Canadian one.

It took place in 1989. The citizenship ceremony is just as moving as we imagine it will be, this milestone in the journey of the immigrant. A happy culmination of years of efforts, investment, and expected and unexpected changes. For many, a point of no return, arrival at the starting point. For others, it's the opportunity to finally go home with a new passport, this lifelong insurance policy, transmitted from generation to generation.

Otherwise, the precious document doesn't change much for the immigrant. His permanent resident status already accords him the same rights and services as his neighbour whose ancestors were trappers in the Laurentian Forest in the seventeenth century. The difference in his legal status does allow him the pleasing perspective that he can now join – if he wishes – the military, vote (for the Liberal Party, according to local custom) and, if things really go off the rails, serve a criminal sentence in a Canadian prison.

The most profound change for the immigrant who wants it is to be able to consider his future as a Canadian, quietly blending into the culture of his new country.

I remember how happy my family was, at the Guy-Favreau Complex, to become Canadian, to have a new country. I remember solemnly declaring my loyalty and my sincere allegiance to Her Majesty Queen Elizabeth II, her heirs and successors. I remember singing the national

---

* Quebec's national holiday—trans.

anthem and that I was given a little pin in the shape of a maple leaf that I still cherish, in spite of my oath of allegiance to the British Queen.

I remembered all this when, twenty-five years later, I was the "guest of honour" at a welcoming ceremony for newcomers as a representative, not of the queen, but the immigration minister of Quebec. The activity was neither "official" nor "Canadian." Put together by volunteers and community organizations and modestly supported by the Ministry of Immigration, these events are conducted in an attempt to arouse in immigrants a sense of belonging to Quebec.

It reminded me in any event of our citizenship ceremony, the happy faces of the immigrants: the children and parents in their poorly fitting clothes, and with their appealing smiles.

In any case, the event couldn't be more than a pale imitation of the original. In the community hall of Côte-des-Neiges, they weren't handing out passports, just leaflets and sandwiches with the crusts cut off. Or just about. Because this year, thanks to my efforts as a political aide, there would be little Quebec flags too! I mention this because it was no small accomplishment, such purchases not figuring in the ministry's budget. I must have made some kind of face when I was offered the explanation, because a couple of days later I was breathlessly informed that they had found a box of fifty flags in the basement of the building in Old Montreal. "No Union Jacks, I hope!"

So, I thought it prudent not to suggest that we organize such a ceremony for all immigrants who receive their Quebec selection certificate before getting their Canadian citizenship. Every year. With the Premier. At the Olympic Stadium. On Saint-Jean Baptiste Day. They would follow the march and attend the big concert at the Fête Nationale in Maisonneuve Park! Quebec may not have passports, but it does have the Loco Locass rappers.

I held back. Such a pilot project had already been tried, I knew, but had been shelved and soon forgotten upon the Liberals return to power ten years earlier. Big ideas were no longer on the agenda of the Quebec public service since it had been dulled into submission by a barrage of stupefying government discourse on zero deficits and fiscal austerity. I also knew that the Ministry of Immigration no longer dealt directly with immigrants. In a fit of re-engineering, its francization, reception and integration missions had been outsourced to community organizations. From now on, there'd be no officials to meet the new arrivals, they would now be appointed to scrutinize the content of reports, assessments and agreements with "partners," without being able to know whether this way of doing things produces results or generates savings.

In this depressing context, it's a good thing for these kinds of initiatives that these organizations exist. They would like, however, to receive a reasonable share of the famous economic benefits that immigrants are expected to produce in Quebec. Question of being able to give a little hand to get going, an encouraging slap on the back while waiting for the newcomers get down to solving our problems.

Here, no Canadian flags, so no certificate of citizenship, no anthem, no federal ministers who come to have their photos taken in preparation for the next election cycle. However, a welcoming speech was expected, but the minister had an emergency and no other members of the National Assembly were available. As for municipal politicians on the campaign trail, they preferred to shake the hands of voting immigrants. The speech would have to be delivered by me and me alone. I find it insane that the task would have fallen to a political aide, charming though he may have been, and I don't believe I was the only one in the room to think so.

I remember our mistress of ceremonies, twenty-five years earlier, particularly morose, who seemed as if she had just been transferred from the Ministry of Agriculture where she was a slaughterhouse inspector. OK, group. We don't have a national anthem, no official room, no passport in hand, no minister, but we do have some nice little flags and I'll try to do better than a federal civil servant. I delivered an inspired speech, I believe, enough so that the overall impression was above the audience's low expectations.

Thanks to Gilles Vigneault. To conclude my remarks, I read "Mon Pays."

In the moments that followed, the atmosphere around the buffet was warm: children running around with "my" flags, and the guests, increasingly less shy, kept talking once they broke the ice. The neighbourhood volunteers, members of the host committee, community organizers who took the time to organize this ceremony when no one had asked them to. And immigrant families who also were under no obligation to be here on this beautiful autumn Sunday, but out of politeness and motivated by curiosity responded to the invitation they considered generous.

The event gave me hope. I thought that even though they hadn't arrived in a country that sees itself as more than a venial provincial outpost, the new immigrants appreciated the warmth of this great solitary village, the one that I ended up discovering, the one I ended up loving, the one I wanted people to love, this country that had become my country, *this country that is not a country*, this country would indeed be welcoming to, in the words of Vigneault, *"les humains de l'horizon."*

WHERE ARE WE HEADED?

To make a long story short, somewhere along the way I became a Quebecer.

Not overnight, as you have seen. Nothing predestined or forced upon me, nothing I even noticed. There was no specific trigger event, epiphany or moment of truth when I saw the light. It was rather, to think back on it, the result of the combination of a particular political context, some more or less conscious choice, chance encounters, and my personal sensitivities and interests.

But you're right – and thank you for being so attentive all along – my story is unique as is that of the hundreds of thousands of immigrants. Mine demonstrates that cultural integration in a French Quebec is possible (and could be enjoyable – in any case, it is surely no more unpleasant here than elsewhere). That the Charter of the French Language, by requiring the school-aged children of immigrants to study in French, can help us progress towards its ideal: to flourish collectively and individually in French in Quebec.

I also wanted to show you that this is desirable. We cannot live on the same territory, be fragmented into cultural communities, electoral clientele, with our only thing in common our situation as consumers and taxpayers, without strengthening suspicion and intolerance between the host society and its newcomers. Not only must we be able to speak the same language, but we also have to have something to say to each other, to have common points of reference.

A common culture with its literature, music, universities, museums, libraries, cinema, television, but also with its French fry trucks, its western festivals, the annual demonstration against police brutality, its Fringe festivals with its hipsters, lawn bowling tournaments in Town of Mont Royal, chariot racing in Saint-Eustache, bingo in church basements, softball in the park at sunset, discussions about potholes at the *dépanneur*, its obsession with hockey, the vicious radio broadcasts from Quebec City and the virtuous ones from Montreal. I ended up considering a little bit of all of this as part of my Quebec identity, while distrusting those who wished to try pit one part against another or who choose one gang in order to better scorn the others.

I became a Quebecer in my own way, frequently delighted by my discoveries and my encounters over the three decades I've been here. I never felt like the character in *La Grande Seduction* who was given the red carpet treatment, and whose every whim was catered to so that he would want to stay. But neither have I felt like the Outlander,* ill-treated by the village because his difference, his "foreignness," will always make of him an object of their suspicions.

I've heard some stuff, maybe some people made fun of me behind my back, maybe some exploited my "difference" to ease their consciences, maybe my resilience helped me to forget some unfortunate moments, perhaps I managed to avoid or defuse unpleasant situations, but I haven't personally suffered because of intolerance, discrimination or racism. Maybe if I had been a black man named Mohammed, with dreadlocks, who uses English to belly ache about

---

* Reference to the classic novel *Le Survenant* by Germaine Guèvremont.

French Quebec, my experience would have been different. I know that life is not the same for everyone.

Anyway, I am at home here. I've travelled to every region of Quebec. From Chibougamau to the Îles-de-la-Madeleine, from Gaspé to Rouyn, from Gatineau to Sept-Îles. There is a small church in Saint-Narcisse-de-Beaurivage, in Lotbinière, where I've attended baptisms, weddings and funerals. I have my RRSP accounts with Desjardins and the FTQ's Solidarity Fund. I read Quebec literature, and not only Michel Tremblay, I listen to Quebec music (but mostly oldies). I watch Quebec films without having to make an effort and I wouldn't have a problem watching an American movie dubbed by Yves Corbeil. I even saw Celine in Vegas. I read *Le Devoir*, I speak French every day and I've complained to the Office de la langue française. I went to college in French, and then to UQAM. Every Saint-Jean, I hang a small *fleur-de-lis* on my porch railing. I happened to vote PQ and Bloc Québécois. And in the referendum, I voted *Oui*.

It's often been said to me, too often, that I'm the perfect immigrant. An ideal child of Bill 101 such as even René Lévesque and Camille Laurin would never have dared to dream of. It bothers me on two or three counts, but mostly because I do not want them to use me to suggest that all is well in the best of worlds (because isn't he brilliant, the little Hungarian?).

Furthermore, I do not want my example to serve as some kind of a threshold below which we consider any immigrant as a failure of our immigration system. In terms of integration, best to have realistic expectations. We'd better not believe that all it takes is a couple of classes about our culture in a francisation course to see all the students at the *Fête Nationale* next summer, regardless of their origin, singing along with the rappers from Loco Locass, "*Libérez-nous des libéraux*".

Immigrant integration is not an easy task. You know, I could have held on to the first bank account I had at the Bank of Montreal; studied in English as soon as Bill 101 allowed me to; continued reading *The Gazette*; moved out to Chomedey; put my hat over my heart listening to Ginette sing the national anthem before the Canadiens games; gone to Dawson and Concordia; worked bilingually; voted *Non*, for the Quebec Liberals and Justin Trudeau; spoken the impeccable frenglish of Sugar Sammy... and felt the same as hundreds of thousands of immigrants, at home in Quebec.

Between these two possibilities, there are as many nuances as there are immigrants. Integrating immigrants is not like stamping out Beanie Babies, where with the right inputs, the right machines, good stuffing and quality certifications you end up with perfectly satisfactory and identical end products through an automated process, to which you only have to add a card with the child's name on it, question of giving each product a unique identity.

That said, we still should have a number of expectations. A host society has not only the right but also the duty to state them clearly, both to those already here and those who have just arrived. And then it has a responsibility to work to achieve results.

I've avoided using figures and statistics from the beginning, which I hope you appreciate, and I'm not going to start now. Anyway, how can you measure integration, an idea that could not be more subjective? But we can nevertheless recognize certain realities: that an immigrant who speaks French and uses it is more integrated than one who prefers English or his or her mother tongue; an immigrant who "consumes" cultural products from Quebec is more integrated than one who does not even know about them; an immigrant who lives, marries, studies and works in the circle of one community is less integrated than one who lives in a cultural mix.

I'm not saying that people who don't integrate should be thrown into the lions' den and their bones given to those who do as a reward for their integration. I just want it to be possible to state a goal. I think that a majority of Quebecers would like immigrants to learn and use French in their daily lives and adopt some of Quebec's culture as even a small part of their own – and that this minimum program doesn't take three generations to accomplish. True, they also want immigrants to work, pay taxes and be good citizens without having to experience discrimination or racism. Me too.

These goals are actually now not that far from what René Lévesque and company had in mind with the Charter of the French Language...

I say this and yet I've been troubled for a few years now about the possibility of ensuring the French fact going forward. Because just as I'm telling you I have no problem calling myself a Quebecer, it seems that Quebec is thinking that maybe it doesn't really want to be any more. The new idea is to get free of everything that distinguishes us; what's worth it is English and what's happening in Mile End/London/New York, commonly called "the world." And all of a sudden, in this new Quebec, I feel like a foreigner.

When I suggest that the many people who come to Quebec to live, study, work, run a business or carry a squeegee should be minimally required to get along in French, I'm accused of undermining the possibility of a new Quebec, one in which people will be able to live without complexes or insecurities. When I point out that in reality requiring French-speaking people to be bilingual actually aims at and results in enabling the English-speakers to remain unilingual, I'm said to be intolerant.

They're becoming more and more visible, these model citizens of a new world order that would ask the defenders of a French Quebec to lay down their arms and stop resisting, but in an ok way, because we would now be governed by globalization, which have democratically decided, through the choices of its consumers and internet social networks, that the language of international commerce, culture and cool people should be English, not an incomprehensible local dialect.

Well, I seem to have heard that discourse somewhere...

Wait, it's coming back: in the immigrant and English-speaking communities where I grew up. Where they made fun of the villagers, so determined to protect their language and culture, all the more ridiculous because they needed laws to do so. People dreamed of the day when they'd be able to function exclusively in English (in Quebec or elsewhere, individually and collectively) and, in the meantime, they were satisfied with a creole that is now called "franglais" in French, and "frenglish" in English, though not exclusively. French-speaking milieux were regarded as necessarily closed, and their cultural products as mediocre, while the English-speaking world and its culture were considered to be liberators.

In reality, it was perhaps the immigrant and English communities that began to subsume the idea of a French Quebec into their ideal of a Canadianized and anglicized Quebec. This is the normal and foreseeable outcome of the referendum defeat of the sovereigntists and the increase in the number of immigrants in French milieux. One of the effects of Bill 101 is that immigrants can now challenge the laws, plans and orientations of Quebec society in French. This is both a challenge to and success of integration. And this has all the more impact as the defenders of a vision of a French Quebec become more and more ambivalent and less and less numerous.

We must face the facts: the inclusion of the Charter of Rights and Freedom into the Canadian Constitution in 1982 to thwart the purpose of the Charter of the French Language has been largely successful. Ultimately, we were mistaken about the identity of this new generation of Quebecers who are too young to have been alive during the referendum years. They are not, for the most part, children of Bill 101, but rather the products of the other charter: they are children of Trudeau.

People prefer not to think about it, but just in case it's particularly difficult for some to hear this: Quebec is a province in Canada where two competitive models of integration are superimposed that are diametrically opposed in their approach, purpose and vision. One presents itself as multicultural and multilingual, the other as a distinct nation with a common language; one seeks to impose English just by letting it happen, the other, French by law; one sees Quebecers as a minority among others, the other sees Quebecers as a historical majority; one has Canada as a space of reference, the other Quebec; one cultivates a sense of belonging to Canada, the other first and foremost to Quebec.

These models are contradictory in their very essence. The immigrant is tossed between them, offered to the highest bidder, and is inevitably looked at askance by one of the two clans. Ah, if Quebec were independent! or at least recognized in the Constitution as a distinct society… While we await the great day, we are permitted to act, starting with clarifying and choosing our own model.

Reconciling these two models of integration is no easy task. We cannot simply say that we promote "diversity" as much as "integration," although it's a pretty good slogan. We need to understand that the more we encourage immigrants to preserve their culture, to maintain it and pass it on, the less they will be integrated. And conversely, the more immigrants come to resemble their compatriots of different origins, the less the landscape will be diversified over time.

We can sketch out this new landscape together and say what we want it to look like. The key is that everyone would have to agree that the final portrait will be different than the sketch. Immigrants would need to be prepared to mount this canvas on an existing frame, one that can be expanded. They must accept that their identity – and that of their children – will change, and that it will have to be superimposed on a backdrop that already has colour and depth.

Immigration diversifies the population, something everybody understands, and I believe that the majority sees this as something positive from which to draw pleasure and profit. People welcome demographic changes if they are not worried that they will be at the expense of the originality and essence of their own identity. For Quebecers, it is their language, the recognition of a Quebec that is evolving in its own way, having expressed itself in its own language in North America for four hundred years. When diversity allows Quebec to remain distinct, it is historically well received, but when it seems to lead towards the disappearance of Quebec's specificity, or worse, its assimilation into Canada as a whole, it arouses suspicion and frustration. Similarly, if the vast majority of Canada's immigrants were to adopt French as their spoken language and almost all of them become sovereigntists, you can be certain that the powers that be would quickly lose their enthusiasm for immigration.

Immigration is accepted as long as it doesn't push too fast or too hard, as long as it doesn't alter too profoundly the image that people have of their neighbourhood, their city, their *pays* or country. It's not only "ignorance" that provokes reactions of intolerance towards foreigners (as opposed to what is often simplistically repeated), but also the fear of finding ourselves in an environment that no longer resembles us.

We need to bring our model up to date. Quebec has changed since I arrived. What seemed obvious before is often criticized today as being out-dated. We must say: we are not going to always agree with everyone else, there are conflicting interests and visions, but there will always be strong opposition to a project that would turn immigrants into Quebecers more than anything else. Which should not stop Quebec from dropping the pious pronouncements and magical thinking and determine exactly how the Quebec state should integrate the immigrants it is accepting.

Integration can't be forced, but neither can we be satisfied with laissez-faire indifference. A carrot doesn't grow faster if you pull on it, but it won't grow at all if you don't give it water. Not only must we define and clarify the expectations of the host society, but we also need to work to achieve results. Problems related to the cultural integration of immigrants are not just the result of poorly allocated resources and a weak consensus in Quebec on what is expected of them. It is also the consequence of a timid attitude, a refusal to act, even though it still might be possible to intervene in the current political context.

We can't just say that French is the official language and then offer all our government services in English to immigrants for the rest of their lives; there is no reason to have control over the immigration selection process if we don't have the courage to tighten the criteria and reduce the number of immigrants we will accept in relation to our capacity. Why control our own education system if we are going to cut university budgets, if we don't try to teach more about the people who have made our literature and our history? Why praise our culture if we only offer minimal support to artists, bookstores, libraries, publishers and writers from Quebec? What purpose is served in producing relevant and original artistic works if we hesitate to share them with all Quebecers when they're not "representative of diversity"? What purpose is served by having international diplomatic rights if it is only to maintain practically invisible service desks in Canadian embassies?

When we invite people over, we share about our lives, we put out our finest, we invite them to sit down at the table with all of us, everyone is served out of the same yummy pot. We also believe that everybody will enjoy it too.

Integration is a complex process that will vary according to the goals; the values; the political, psychological, family, and community sensitivities of each immigrant. But I am convinced that immigrants share a common desire to feel at home in their new *pays*. A desire also shared by those who long ago felt that way. For that to become reality, it's not enough to open the door, you also have to set the table. You must, as the poet said, *between your four walls of ice, put your time and your space, build a fire, prepare the place.*

That means more people around the table. Once seated, we will, I hope, be able to let go of our fears and speak openly. And maybe while we're talking to each other, sharing our stories, discussing what moves and shakes us, our multiple voices will start to resonate and we'll be able to tell our tales in all our accents in a harmonious Quebec rhapsody, and we would wish each other enough days to see our hopes become reality and we would finally stop asking "Where are you from?" and instead, ask "Where are we headed?"

The Question of Separatism
Quebec and the Struggle over Sovereignty
Jane Jacobs

Songs Upon the Rivers
The Buried History of the French-speaking Canadiens and Métis
From the Great Lakes and the Mississippi across to the Pacific
Robert Foxcurran, Michel Bouchard, and Sébastien Malette

The Prophetic Anti-Gallic Letters
Adam Thom and the Hidden Roots of the Dominion of Canada
François Deschamps

Rebel Priest in the Time of Tyrants
Mission to Haiti, Ecuador and Chile
Claude Lacaille

Scandinavian Common Sense
Policies to Tackle Social Inequalities in Health
Marie-France Raynault & Dominique Côté

America's Gift
What the World Owes to the America's and their First Inhabitants
Käthe Roth & Denis Vaugeois

The History of Montréal
The Story of a Great North American City
Paul-André Linteau

A People's History of Quebec
Jacques Lacoursière and Robin Philpot

The First Jews in North America
The Extraordinary Story of the Hart Family, 1760-1860
Denis Vaugeois

Iron Bars & Bookshelves
A History of the Morrin Centre
Louisa Blair, Patrick Donovan, and Donald Fyson

Printed in March 2017
by Gauvin Press,
Gatineau, Québec

Real
Gwynedd

Other Titles in the series:

Real Aberystwyth – Niall Griffiths
Real Barnsley – Ian McMillan
Real Bloomsbury – Nicholas Murray
Real Cambridge – Grahame Davies
Real Cardiff – Peter Finch
Real Cardiff #2 – Peter Finch
Real Cardiff #3 – Peter Finch
Real Cardiff #4 – Peter Finch
Real Chester – Clare Dudman
Real Glasgow – Ian Spring
Real Gower – Nigel Jenkins
Real Hay On Wye – Kate Noakes
Real Liverpool – Niall Griffiths
Real Llanelli – Jon Gower
Real Merthyr – Mario Basini
Real Newport – Ann Drysdale
Real Oxford – Patrick McGuinness
Real Port Talbot – Lynne Rees
Real Powys – Mike Parker
Real Preseli – John Osmond
Real South Pembrokeshire – Tony Curtis
Real South Bank – Chris McCabe
Real Swansea – Nigel Jenkins
Real Swansea #2 – Nigel Jenkins
Real Wales – Peter Finch
Real Wrexham – Grahame Davies

Real
Gwynedd

Rhys Mwyn

SERIES EDITOR: PETER FINCH

Seren is the book imprint of
Poetry Wales Press Ltd.
Suite 6, 4 Derwen Road, Bridgend,
Wales, CF31 1LH

www.serenbooks.com
facebook.com/SerenBooks
Twitter: @SerenBooks

© Rhys Mwyn, 2021
Photographs © Rhys Mwyn

The right of Rhys Mwyn to be identified
as the Author of this Work has been asserted
in accordance with the Copyright, Designs
and Patents Act, 1988.

ISBN 978-1-78172-569-6

A CIP record for this title is available from
the British Library

The publisher works with the financial assistance
of the Books Council of Wales.

Cover photograph: Adrian Evans Photography
adrianevansphotography.wordpress.com

Printed by 4Edge Ltd.

CONTENTS

Series Editor's Introduction   8

INTRODUCTION   13

NORTH

Abergwyngregyn   19
Bethesda   24
Castell Penrhyn   28
Bangor   31
The Bridges / Menai Strait   43
Y Felinheli (Port Dinorwic)   45
Caernarfon   48
Llanrug   56
Penygroes   58

SOUTH

Harlech   62
Roman Steps   68
Capel Salem   69
Y Bermo   71
Friog / Fairbourne   75
Tywyn   77
Cwm Maethlon   81
Aberdyfi   82
Corris   83
Dinas Mawddwy   84
Bwlch y Groes   84
Gwylliaid Cochion   88
Mallwyd   88
Dolgellau   90
Brithdir   92
A470 Detours   94

EAST

Arenig 100
Frongoch 104
Bala 106
Llanuwchllyn 109
Glan-llyn 111
Llyn Tegid 113
Tryweryn 115
Carndochan 116
Eastern Boundary 119
Y Berwyn 120

WEST

Llŷn Peninsula 124
Nant Gwrtheyrn 125
Tre'r Ceiri 131
Pistyll 134
Nefyn 136
Aberdaron 139
Ynys Enlli 142
Plas yn Rhiw 145
Abersoch 146
Llanbedrog 150
Penyberth 151
Pwllheli 153
Llanystumdwy 156
Cricieth 158
Pentrefelin 160
Tremadog 162
Porthmadog 167
Eifionydd 170
Pant Glas 173
Bryncir 175

CENTRAL

Llanberis 178
Glynrhonwy 182
Craig yr Undeb 183

Pen y Gwryd   185
Yr Wyddfa   187
Rhyd Ddu   191
Beddgelert   194
Dinas Emrys   195
Blaenau Ffestiniog   196
Ffestiniog Railway   198
Bwlch (Y Slaters), Manod, Cwt y Bugail   201
Crimea   205
Portmeirion   206
Penrhyndeudraeth   210
Trawsfynydd   212

Works Consulted   216
The Photographs   220
Acknowledgements   223
The Author   225
Index   226

SERIES EDITOR'S INTRODUCTION

Back in May, 1999 when HMQ came to south east Wales to ceremonially open the brand new National Assembly the media had a bright idea. Giant public screens would be erected at locations right across the soon to be slightly more self-governing principality. The royal ceremonials would be beamed out to all. Through simple geography no one would be denied a glimpse of the spectacle. In the event there was rain. In Wales there always is. On the news a shot showed the scene live from Caernarfon where a screen stood in the corner of a car park. The camera panned out across the thronging crowds. A man with a dog. A couple of kids in hoodies. A woman with a pushchair. A Ford Escort badly parked. Gwynedd, the Welsh heartland.

The county is huge. It is made up of the former historic counties of Merionethshire and Caernarfonshire which, under local government reorganisation, were merged into one administrative authority in 1974. Gwynedd, the return of the kingdom from before the time of the Romans. Wales back on its feet again.

I reach it by car, roaring up the A470 south of Mallwyd. There ought to be a marker here, an Angel of the North West: a one hundred and twenty foot slate miner, a huge climber in crampons, the faces of Dafydd Iwan, Max Boyce, Llywelyn ab Iorwerth, Myrddin ap Dafydd and Bethan Gwanas carved into the hillside like US presidents. But there's nothing like that.

In the days before speed cameras there were those who claimed to cross the country in three and a half hours making Wales as traversable as it should be. But it's always been a four and half hour slog for me. Gear changing. Slowing. Failing to overtake. The great plan of the Institute of Welsh Affairs to have money spent on fixing the A470's bottlenecks, building passing places, smoothing bends and all for 10 per cent of the cost of a motorway, still languishes. It is kept in the same bucket as the M4 extension around Newport and the Severn Barrage. Won't happen in our lifetimes.

I could have taken the train, the one from the south that dodges back and forth along the English border to finally unseat its determined passengers quite a few hours later at Bangor. Failing that I might have taken Transport for Wales' zip across the heart of Wales from Shrewsbury to Criccieth in just under six hours. The south and the north can talk to each other but they're not really friends.

When I had regular business in this part of Wales most of my time was spent not in the conurbations of Bangor or Caernarfon (although we should use the term conurbation here with care), nor on the crags and outcrops that attract thousands of visitors, nor even the vaguely Pembrokeshire-like beaches and greenery of magical Llŷn. But instead in the village of Llanystumdwy which lies hiding behind the hedges which line the coast-hugging A497. Resolutely hard to pronounce for incomers this is the place where Lloyd George made his home and, indeed, where he lies buried. His grave is beside the Dwyfor marked with a simple boulder.

His house up the hill is Tŷ Newydd. There's a shaky 1945 black and white film of his horse-drawn cortege leaving the gates on its way downhill to his final resting place. You can view it in the small local Lloyd George Museum where it's offered along with copies of the great man's letters, dozens of jars, mugs, plaques and plates bearing his likeness, and the nameplate of the London Midland and Scottish steam railway engine that once bore his name.

If you go down to the eighteenth century Afon Dwyfor bridge nearby you can find his initials carved into the stone of the parapet by penknife. DLlG MP.

But it's that house which draws me. The Tŷ Newydd Writing Centre, a place of creativity and residential literary wonder set out in the non-metropolitan distance. Courses, readings, creative writing weekends, festivals and shows have been presented here by some of the leading lights of the literary world.

I taught a course on performance poetry once in the nineties. My fellow tutor Ifor Thomas and I wanted to get the students used to the bash and bang of real world performance where poetry readings get regularly interrupted and there are always noises off. We got Elis, the groundsman and building bricoleur, to cut the lawn while our students performed. This he did, ear protectors on, beard flying. Back and forth before the window he went with his roaring machine. How the students managed I can't now remember. By giving up, I think. The right answer. Elis told me that he owned twenty-one sheds scattered across the local district. In one he kept a boat.

Fish caught in the waters of Llanystumdwy: macrall, cimwch, cath fôr, lleden, lleden goch, cranc heglog, ci môr, draenogyn, mingrwn, morlas, gwrach, môr nodwydd, gwyniad, chwyrnwr, tyrbotsan cranc.

Llanystumdwy's eminence extends well beyond the residence of the former War leader. Up the hill lived the great Jan Morris, historian, travel writer, (*The Times* correspondent who was first up Everest after Hillary and Tenzing topped it) and author, in her pre sex change days of the defining history of the British Empire. Jan, with as large a Gwynedd heart as it is possible to have, was simultaneously a recipient of the CBE, accepted 'out of polite respect' and a deep and caring Welsh nationalist republican. With such credentials where else could she live?

She has read her work in a bi-lingual duo with her son, the chaired bard and singer, Twm Morys, at a literary festival held on Ty Newydd's lawns. This is part of the Welsh national obsession for standing around wearing wellingtons at events held in muddy fields. If it isn't the National Eisteddfod or the Urdd then it's an agricultural show or a food or music festival. In Tŷ Newydd's case for once it fails to rain.

Down the road from Llanystumdwy is the former slate port of Porthmadog. Tourist centre, coach park and place where two of north Wales' great narrow gauge railways, the West Highland and the Ffestiniog meet. On its southern outskirts is another major attraction – the premises of Cob Records. Named after the 1810 sea wall, the Cob, that William Maddocks built in order to reclaim part of the estuary for agriculture Cob Records is a vinyl collector's heaven, a Shangri La out on the fringes of the Western world.

I completed my collection of Magic Band albums here, located the elusive Beefheart and Zappa collaboration *Bongo Fury*, added some choice Phil Ochs and a long-missing Dion and the Belmonts set from their New York heyday. Gwynedd distorted my sense of place. These cult items belong in stores located in city basements rather than in racks from which you can clearly see the Irish sea.

Llŷn, the peninsula the Porthmadog road rolls on into, is also the land of R.S. Thomas, Wales' greatest poet and promotor of the linguistic cause. One of his cottages was the unheated Plas-y-Rhiw out towards Aberdaron where the winter chill would regularly penetrate the four hundred year old and several foot thick walls. His poetry was an uncompromising mix of spirituality and nationalism. The place of the Welsh as a conquered people was never far from the surface. He would be seen, on occasion, walking the Gwynedd hills and ducking behind walls to avoid meeting people. A private man but a powerful poet. He died in 2000.

Inland from here the land rises and keeps on doing that. The hard Cambrian rocks have been buckled upwards and refuse to wear away. This is Eryri, Snowdonia, the highest place in England and Wales. It's a massive tourist attraction. In summer thousands attempt the climb, most ascending the four and a half mile Llanberis Path with the faint hearted taking the steam train up the rack and pinion railway. My first experience of a steam whistle up there in the swirling 3560 feet mists was completely surreal. As was the sight of a woman with handbag and high heels standing next to me in the mountain top café.

Most guide books report at length on just how old Gwynedd actually is. Its rock strata are more than aged. The kingdom's Cambrian and pre-Cambrian rocks are some of the earliest in the UK. It has more castles, both those of the conqueror and the conquered, than anywhere else. It is also rich in standing stones, hut circles, hillforts, cairns, and other menhir-powered ancient memorials. Because this is land that has not been overdeveloped the older surface features remain.

Real Gwynedd's author is the perfect reporter for all of this. A qualified and practising archaeologist, Rhys Mwyn is no stranger to muddy trenches, lecture halls and academic research. But making him a lot more reader-friendly he is also an aficionado of pop culture. In pioneering style he formed the punk band Anhrefn in the 1980s and rode a wave which saw him as performer, band promoter, record label owner, broadcaster and all-round alternative champion. Today he is as much at ease with the Welshness of John Cale as he is with the Roman Steps of Cwm Bychan.

He shares with me an obsession with the locating of dance halls and clubs gone by. The places where the cult and celebrated of the music world once performed leave a sort of shimmering rip in the fabric of space time. That these places then go on to be redeveloped as homes for the elderly or black-surfaced car parks only adds to their mystique. Finding them can be triumphant.

He also has a healthy interest in what we end up actually calling places. History all too often gets lost to commerce. If it is pronounceable by non-Welsh speakers then it will sell. Cwm Maethlon in the county's southern reaches gets itself rebranded as Happy Valley. More marketable, I guess, than Nutritious Cwm.

Everyone's psychogeography is different, not least that of Rhys Mwyn. There's no climbing the peaks of Eryri in alphabetical order, catching every bus, nor hunting for evidence of Martian visitation in the rock formations around Nant Gwrtheyrn. He does, however, test out Iwan Huws, lead singer of Cowbois Rhos Bottwnnog's, song suggestion that the River Soch is jumpable, but only at its source near Carn Fadryn. Rhys does an eight mile road trip and proves that it clearly is.

There's something about the nature of this distant land that keeps it a place apart. Its location and its history are irrevocably entwined. Its myths, dragons, war warriors, giants and bards differ from those elsewhere in Wales. Its people are unmistakable. Rhys is the perfect demystifier, explaining and taming, as far as it ever can be explained and tamed, this essential Celtic world.

Peter Finch

INTRODUCTION

Real Cardiff, *Real Aberystwyth*, *Real Liverpool*, *Real Llanelli*, *Real Merthyr*, *Real Newport*, *Real Swansea*, *Real Wrexham* all urban areas, towns or cities. *Real Powys* breaks the mould. Does psychogeography work in the rural landscape? Following in the footsteps of Mike Parker, I aimed for just that with rural, craggy, mountainous, coastal, small town Gwynedd. A new perspective. Slightly anarchic. I'm honoured to write alongside the Real series writers. This is an opportunity to spend time with Gwynedd. To renew the friendship and to make new acquaintances with this most ancient of kingdoms.

When asked where I come from, or where do I live? I have a standard answer. I was born in Montgomeryshire but I live in Caernarfon. My own roots are firmly Sir Drefaldwyn, rural, green rolling hills, river valleys, small towns near the English border and right on the linguistic border. With parents from Gwynedd, I managed to avoid inheriting either of the two strange and distinctive Montgomeryshire accents. The Welsh one, where they hold and stretch their E's and the English one, where they dip slightly into Shropshire Oarrr. To this day my accent often confuses people. Lacking a distinct accent, I am broadly recognised as a 'Gog' (north Walian) but not a 'Cofi' (Caernarfon) and certainly not from Montgomeryshire. I like to imagine my accent as being 'cultured' in a north Welsh kind of way.

Having parents from up north, we were always seen as incomers. Everybody else in our primary school in Llanfair Caereinion seemed to be related. Moving to Gwynedd as an adult I once again became an incomer. No change then. Not belonging has its upside, a positive – not fitting in is the first step for any rebel or non-conformist worth his or her salt.

Being raised on or near the political and linguistic border has given me a deeper understanding of the complexities, the contradictions, the comedy, the irrationality and the often claustrophobic, infuriating and frustrating nature of Wales, Welshness, Cymreictod and its people. We are 'Pobl y Ffin', Border folk. For that I am grateful. But I will never return. I am, for the rest of my days, a Gwynedd citizen.

Caernarfon, my adopted home town, and the home of my adopted boys, has a distinct character. Maybe there are few real cultural parallels with cities such as Liverpool – agreed we do not have the same number of great bands and our port was much smaller. But there is a sense of Caernarfon doing things in its own way and not worrying too much as to what others think. I'm happy here. The Republic of Cofiland has a ring to it.

From my house in Twthill, I can have two feet at the starting point of the Rhyd Ddu path up Snowdon within 30 minutes on a good day. This makes me happy. I collect seaweed from the beach (Y Foryd) just outside Caernarfon for my allotment up in Carmel above the Nantlle Valley. This also makes me happy. Both mountains and sea are within spitting distance. Liverpool is only 1 hour 30 away. We are connected in all senses. Nature. Landscape. Rock'n Roll.

Gardening may well be a metaphor for re-discovering my family roots in Gwynedd and Dyffryn Nantlle specifically. On my father's side, quarrymen at Cilgwyn and Pen yr Orsedd. On my mother's side railway men from Pant Glas. Gardening and eating the produce has become the new Rock'n Roll for many of us. Homegrown food on the plate just as my grandparents would have done – out of necessity rather than pleasure for them of course.

Cerys Matthews published a history book doubling up a as a cookbook. A fellow musician and kindred spirit we now talk about vegetables from the garden as much as we do about music and records for our respective radio shows. My admiration for Cerys, from making those early records with Catatonia, has only grown – she has moved on, refused to stand still, embarked on new adventures. My whole creative and cultural life and work has been driven by a constant desire to move on.

This journey of re-discovery is akin to a road trip. The writing of this book was a bit like an extended road trip. Somewhere in the back of my mind was Kerouac and *On The Road*, a constant sense of adventure and of new discoveries. Less desserts and doughnuts, less jazz and beat poets, less 'hobos' jumping on the roofs of trains but Gwynedd still provides strange twists and turns, dark corners and the unexpected.

Some road trips around Gwynedd evoked a sense of déjà vu. My Montgomeryshire youth had already made me familiar with Manafon and the R.S. Thomas connection. R.S. was to re-appear several times on my various trips, popping up in Aberdaron, Rhiw, Llanfaelrhys, Plas yn Rhiw and finally coming to rest at Porthmadog

Gwynedd has produced many Rock'n Roll bands, musicians

and artists. Some are featured in this book. Others are not. For what is mainly a rural area Gwynedd has punched way above its weight. There has always been a vibrant music scene; sure bands and venues come and go, but Gwynedd can stand proud in the Welsh Rock'n Roll Hall of Fame.

Bangor produced New Wave act Fay Ray. Bethesda is the home town of Gruff Rhys (Super Furry Animals) and John Gwyn who went on to produce *The Tube* for Channel 4. Caernarfon's finest blues singer Rhiannon Tomos is worthy of re-appraisal and her songs can now be found on digital platforms. Just over the Strait, Anglesey born musician David Wrench is now an internationally sought-after award-winning producer. Wrench was engineer at Bryn Derwen Studio at Tregarth for many years and produced records for pre-fame Amy Wadge and Georgia Ruth. John Lawrence of Gorky's Zygotic Mynci has re-located to Eryri. No shortage of talent. Young bands continue to spew out of the Snowdonia heartlands like gushing streams after a storm. New songs, uploaded to Bandcamp, new band in town, next gig.

A whole Gwynedd roadtrip or circuit is impossible to complete within the county boundary. Eryri (Snowdonia) edges into the county of Conwy. No through roads. A circular route of Snowdonia involves the A470 and A5 through Conwy and Denbighshire. A narrow strip of coastal lowlands to the north, dominated by the A55 dual carriageway gives great views over Anglesey and the mountains on the opposite side, but it's hard to get much sense of Gwynedd on this road. Llŷn, the peninsula jutting out into the Irish Sea is the anomaly in some ways. Away from the mountains, outside the National Park – this is a different landscape all together. Eryri and its mountains dominate the rest of Gwynedd. Roads follow the passes. Towns are on valley floors or on the coast. Mountains tower above in most directions. Montgomeryshire I always described as green. Gwynedd is pretty well grey. The landscape is sharp and defined.

A land of 'myths and legends'. During the Iron Age this was the land of the Ordovices tribe. North west Wales was already defined as a 'political' entity. Once the Romans up and left around 393AD, Gwynedd was given free rein to fight it out amongst the various warlords for dominance. Maelgwn Gwynedd, described by Gildas as a 'drunken tyrant' won the day. Partly by deception. Maelgwn organised a competition at Aberdyfi, where the next king would be the candidate who could sit on his throne longest in the face of the incoming tide. While all the other prospective leaders turned up with jewel encrusted thrones, Maelgwn turned up with a wooden chair. Bobbing afloat on the sea while the others sunk, Maelgwn was promptly crowned as King of Gwynedd. In many ways it all starts here in the sixth century.

Maelgwn's citadel was up on the twin crags of Deganwy Castle. It was from here that the first Welsh Eisteddfod was organised. A fact that must irritate the citizens of Aberteifi. The Lord Rhys held his eisteddfod at Cardigan Castle in 1176. Favouring the bards over the harpists, the ever deceptive and conniving Maelgwn is said to have re-located the eisteddfod to the opposite western shore of the Conwy river. Contestants were forced to swim across the river with the inevitable consequence that the harps went out of tune. The Bards and Poets won it on the day.

A land that was never fully captured, never fully conquered. Edward I may have built his 'ring of steel' at Harlech, Caernarfon, Conwy and Biwmares but the Welsh population hung in there. A hundred years later, Glyndŵr's Revolt of 1400 was supported in Gwynedd. Capturing and occupying Harlech Castle, the Welsh regained control of the very symbol of English conquest. Owain held court here for over four years and his second parliament was held at Harlech during August of 1405. Never betrayed or captured, one of Owain's many hiding places is said to be Ogof Glyndŵr high up in the crags above Beddgelert. Owain was also said to be seen wandering the lonely Berwyn mountains. Gwynedd makes its claims. Herefordshire probably wins on this count.

Gwynedd remains a Welsh speaking heartland. No amount of Welsh Not or Blue Books managed to disrupt the course of the language. Mallwyd played its role in Biblical translations which in turn contributed to the very survival of the native spoken tongue. During my travels and road trips while writing this book it was remarkably few, if any, English conversations that took place. Long informative chats on hillsides and at churchyards, on winding back lanes waiting for the cows to cross and in Llŷn pubs were mainly Cymraeg.

Croeso i Wynedd.
Rhys Mwyn 2019.

NORTH

To the north and east, Gwynedd is bounded by the Menai Strait[1] and the Carneddau Mountains respectively. On the opposite, northern shore of the Strait lies Ynys Môn, the island of Anglesey, then beyond and around Anglesey the Irish Sea. Just to the north of Bangor the Menai Strait flows into the Irish Sea. There is only one strait. Therefore, it's the Menai Strait not Straits (sic), no 's' at the end. Many insist on referring to the Strait as the Straits, in print, on radio and TV and of course locally in everyday conversations. But there's only one Strait.

Before the construction of Thomas Telford's 1826 suspension bridge linking the mainland of Wales to Anglesey, people crossed the Strait at various points on small ferries. Following an Act of parliament 1815, Telford was responsible for the construction of the London to Holyhead road and associated bridge as the route for the mail to Dublin, Ireland. Robert Stephenson's railway bridge was to follow in 1850. Anglesey became fully connected.

Pre-bridges, travellers often made the treacherous four and a half mile crossing across the Lavan Sands from the east, somewhere between Bangor and Llanfairfechan, over to Beaumaris. At low tide, that meant four miles of wet sand under foot and a boat for the final half mile to Beaumaris. To miss-time such a crossing was to risk an incoming tide with potentially fatal consequences.

Inland the Carneddau mountain range dominates. Slightly more rounded than the rugged peaks of the Glyderau to the west and crowned with Bronze Age cairns hence the name 'Carneddau', the Welsh for cairns. At the eastern extremity of Gwynedd and Snowdonia, the Carneddau drop down to the Conwy Valley. Somewhere up in the hills an invisible, unmarked border is crossed from Gwynedd to Conwy. Road signage marks the spot on both the A55 and A5 heading out east from Gwynedd.

The boundary shifted back and forth with various treaties during the thirteenth century as the princes of Gwynedd, Llywelyn ab Iorwerth and Llywelyn ap Gruffudd gained and lost territory. With the Treaty of Montgomery, 1267, Gwynedd extended right up to the Dee Estuary. Ten years later, with the Treaty of Aberconwy, 1277, and Gwynedd is pretty well where it is today – west of the River Conwy. Llywelyn ap Gruffudd built a castle at Ewloe near Chester which would have marked the eastern front of Gwynedd right up to that defeat in 1277 at the hands of Edward I.

For the reader, NORTH will broadly consist of the area within Arfon parliamentary constituency.

ABERGWYNGREGYN

Over the years, I have written a column for the *Herald Gymraeg* which is an insert in the Liverpool and north Wales newspaper *Daily Post*. I mainly wrote about Welsh culture and Welsh History / Archaeology. It was a popular column with the readership which attracted many letters but rather fewer emails, which gives a good indication of the demographic. Most of the letters were enquiries for more information on various archaeological sites or objects. The demographic is obvious. I never, or very rarely, got responses to my articles on Welsh Pop Culture. I suspect they were 'tolerated' by the readership but they'd much rather have the history and archaeology.

One such letter enquired about stories of Rhen Eglwys, high above Abergwyngregyn in the Anafon Valley near an old farmstead called Hafod y Gelyn (Hafod Gelyn / Hafod y Celyn). Rhen Eglwys translates as 'old church'. The Welsh in this case is spelt as you'd say it, 'ar lafar', not correctly and it's not the 'real' name for the site.

A quick search of *Archwilio* website[2] reveals that nearby Hafod y Gelyn is a post medieval farmhouse and the surrounding area is littered with Bronze Age and Iron Age sites: burnt mounds, enclosures, hut circles and hut groups, cairns, platform houses and hollow ways but there is nothing at all on the ruined building located about 100 yards to the west of Hafod y Gelyn.

I am fortunate in two ways on my first visit up here at the beginning of the search. I am looking to provide some answers to a letter by a gentleman called R.A. Jones. Firstly, having driven up the steep and narrow lane up Cwm Anafon there is space at the 'end of the road' carpark. A full carpark spells trouble. That would mean nowhere to leave the car and turning around to get out of there would be a challenge. Good news! I can get on with the job in hand.

Secondly, the first person I meet is Wyn 'Aber' the farmer-landowner, and he's seen me on telly (S4C) so introductions are un-necessary. Once I've explained the nature of my mission and sought his advice, I'm invited to hop on the back of his 4x4 quadbike. We go hurtling along medieval hollow-ways, through gates (hopping on and off to open and close) and descend the rather steep slope down towards the river Anafon.

This is an adventure. I am not terrified as I am distracted by

Wyn's stories of Luftwaffe plane crashes and a German spy executed during World War II. Wyn delights in recounting stories that relate to this upland area high above Abergwyngregyn. I am delighted that I am distracted. My hands grip the rear bars of the quad bike as tightly as possible.

Wyn of course knows the building that I am looking for and with a firm handshake leaves me at the appropriate gate before bouncing off with a roar along the fields back up towards Hafod y Gelyn to tend to his sheep. I give him the thumbs up, and am quietly relieved to be back on terra-firma. (Note: the ruin/building is on private land and permission should be sought from Wyn for any visits.)

My archaeology colleague 'Beaver' from Llanfairfechan has already told me that the building is featured in Hughes & North *The Old Churches of Snowdonia* and with photocopies in hand it's quite obvious that I am in the right place. The building is aligned north-south rather than the east-west one might expect for a church. In all honesty it looks and feels more like an old tithe barn (gut archaeological instinct). Could the old chapel / church theory have come from the rather intriguing north window with lintels and a splayed window slot? It is a window, of that I have no doubt. This really does not look like a recess or space for a *piscina*, which is a bowl often found in a chancel wall near the altar within churches.

The alignment is wrong. Unless it's a barn that has been re-used as a chapel at some point? The Unitarians did this around the eighteenth century. An example would be Capel Pen-Rhiw now at St Fagans[3]. But there is no Unitarian connection up here to my knowledge. The early non-Conformists had secret meeting places (Tai Cwrdd), this would certainly be remote enough – but again there is no evidence for this.

Interestingly the aforementioned letter by R.A. Jones bears the same name as the credit for the photograph reproduced in *The Old Churches* of Snowdonia. Is my letter writer and the photographer one and the same? Unlikely as the book was published in 1924 but I am left wondering if this is some sort of test? Or does R.A. Jones just want to find out more? I reply by letter. But the trail goes cold. I've found the building and photographed the north window. Old church or not old church – that remains the question.

Wyn 'Aber' had also mentioned the 'Arrow Stone' (SH 6925 7097) up alongside the track towards Llyn Anafon. As it is mentioned in both *Archwilio* and *An Inventory of the Ancient Monuments in Caernarvonshire Volume I East*, I decide to brisk-walk the thirty minute climb to take a photograph. It's stunning and peaceful up here and the stone is easy enough to find – just off the track on the righthand side as the track begins to turn and climb up and a short distance past the impressive flower-shaped sheep folds lower down the track on the valley floor.

On the track I meet an ornithologist photographing wheatears. He was very impressed that I'd found the Arrow Stone – he'd never succeeded. We chatted and I told him the Welsh name for wheatear, *tinwen y cerrig*. Translated as 'white arse of the stones', there is a more polite version *cynffonwen* or 'white tail' but the *tinwen* version is the grittier. Another hour or so climbing would get you to the reservoir Llyn Anafon. I leave that for another day. I have no drinking water or packed lunch and am focused, for this visit at least, on the old church and the Arrow Stone.

The name Hafod y Gelyn in itself is interesting. A 'hafod' is a summer dwelling in the uplands while the 'hendre' is the lowland winter dwelling and usually the main farm. This dates back to the Medieval period and the practise of transhumance – a seasonal movement to the uplands. Some of the farmhands or family would have spent the summer in the uplands tending the livestock.

Hafod y Gelyn translates as 'Summer dwelling of the Enemy'. Celyn or celynnen on the other hand means holly as in the bush or tree. We also call holly leaves 'celyn' when we put up our Christmas decorations. Are we getting confused here? Are we really talking about ancient battles and historical links with the princes of Gwynedd with this area? Mutated could Hafod Gelyn or Hafod y Celyn actually refer to the summer dwelling near the holly trees?

Aber was one of the courts (a 'llys') of the princes of Gwynedd during the thirteenth century. Archaeologist Neil Johnstone, working for Gwynedd Archaeological Trust, excavated the hall building at Ty'n y Mwd (sometimes referred to as Pen y Mwd) during the early 1990s. Ty'n y Mwd in the centre of Aber village is most likely a Norman motte and bailey castle belonging to Hugh of Avranches, Earl of Chester and Robert of Rhuddlan, built during their campaigns into north Wales around 1093.

Although there is no documentary proof, it is probably the most likely explanation. Along with the motte at Rhuddlan and the one that's slightly hidden underneath Edward I's castle at Caernarfon, these are surely early Norman castles. The bailey, that would have been alongside the motte, has never been conclusively identified at Aber but the field to the east by the river is the most likely location. It is here that rectangular structures showed up as parch marks in aerial photographs, which led to the excavations by Johnstone and subsequent excavations by David Hopewell and John Roberts during 2010 and 2011[4].

In form and plan, the structures excavated were very similar to the foundations excavated at Llys Rhosyr, Newborough on Anglesey (Johnstone, 1999). Question: if these are not the foundations of the hall building of the court of the princes of Gwynedd then what are they? Answer: we really do run out of options. What else could they be? High status pottery and metal finds from the thirteenth century support this interpretation. By re-occupying the site of the castle of their Norman oppressors the princes of Gwynedd were making a statement. They were taking back lost territory, winning the psychological battle. Gruffudd ap Cynan had already booted out the Norman oppressors on his return from exile in Ireland at the end of the eleventh century. His son Owain Gwynedd, grandfather of Llywelyn Fawr, had begun the process of re-establishing Gwynedd as a kingdom. If I were Llywelyn ab Iorwerth this is exactly where I would build my 'llys'. Two fingers duly raised to the Normans!

Of course, I can't prove that psychological warfare was a factor, but surely regaining control of a Norman castle would have been of great political capital. It isn't known if any use was made of the mound during the time of the princes of Gwynedd it seems very likely that the llys and associated buildings would have occupied the bailey area of the castle.

I'd graduated with a degree in Archaeology at the University of Wales, Cardiff in 1983 and then worked with Clwyd Powys Archaeological Trust for two years. A career detour was to take place. Our punk band Anhrefn became a full-time job – John Peel sessions, recording deals and European tours. I gave up archaeology and jumped in a transit van with my bass guitar. There was never a plan and I had no idea how long it was to last.

It wasn't until Ty'n y Mwd with Hopewell and Roberts in 2010 that my trowel was to next see the light of day. Like riding a bike – it all came back. If archaeology was my first love, Punk Rock had been my teenage political awakening. The political activism has continued uninterrupted from 1977 but fortunately I'd never thrown away the trowel from Clwyd-Powys days. There is no better day than out excavating in the open air, in the dirt with colleagues. I loved it and within twelve months I'd pretty well re-structured my work and business to be a fulltime lecturer, tour guide and archaeologist with a bit of writing thrown in. I still managed bands but it paid very little. By the late 1990s we were on the cusp of the download generation – it was time to move on and I knew it. The decision was easy. Archaeoleg yn Gymraeg became my next mission.

The great debate around Abergwyngregyn of course relates to Pen y Bryn House built sometime after 1616. Wrongly attributed as the site of the llys or court and sometimes referred to as Garth Celyn, it has been the subject of much heated debate. Johnstone's excavations at Pen y Bryn and at Ty'n y Mwd would suggest that the llys was at Ty'n y Mwd but the 'propaganda machine' at Pen y Bryn has never accepted this interpretation. Various Americans, gullible visitors, Celtic freaks, un-informed Nationalists, the easily led, the want-to-believers have all fallen for stories about Llywelyn's tower and tunnels underneath the Menai Strait. At its earliest the building is seventeenth century – the pebble-dashed tower at Pen y Bryn could not have belonged to the princes of Gwynedd. The advocates of Pen y Bryn being the site of Llywelyn's llys do themselves no favours by assigning seventeenth century building to thirteenth century princes. Talk of tunnels under the Strait further undermine the credibility of the Pen y Bryn advocates.

BETHESDA

I was on my way to take a picture. I'm walking up Bethesda High Street and am stopped by two ladies waiting for the bus to Bangor. "Ti'n cerdded heddiw, ddim sgwennu" one of them welcomes me with a broad smile (tells me that I'm "walking today, not writing then"). She must read my column in the *Herald Gymraeg*. She can't remember which band I was in. She must be in her late seventies if not in her eighties but that's north Wales for you – they know that you have been in a band even if the name escapes them.

A guess then, "You were in Maffia Mr Huws weren't you". No, it was Anhrefn, but I am good friends with Maffia. Funny she should mention Maffia – I explained that I was on my way up to take a picture of their old home, Bwthyn. She comes out with a story, that could only come from a post-industrial slate town like Bethesda. The Bethesda-based rock band Maffia Mr Huws used to rehearse in Bwthyn most days. Sunday rehearsals would upset all the chapel-goers in the Adwy'r Nant area of the town. She however, thought it was nice to hear some music – any day of the week.

Maffia Mr Huws, named after school teacher and Caradog Pritchard expert, J. Elwyn Hughes, lived at Bwthyn during the 1980s without any apparent parental supervision. We thought that was very cool. They were a full time Rock'n Roll band. That's all they did, played gigs, rehearsed, recorded, slept, and I guess they must have eaten beans on toast from time to time. Maffia Mr Huws were (arguably) the first full-time non-student Welsh language Rock'n Roll band. They, and various other Rock'n Roll mavericks and associates crashed at Bwthyn. No parents. No Rules. Cool. We never asked.

Always more Rory Gallagher than Joe Strummer, punk seemed to have by-passed Maffia and most of Bethesda. It was always a denim sort of place – but Maffia sculpted some mighty fine tunes. There was a character called Mickey Punk who hung out with Maffia and was a member of another great Bethesda band, Offspring[5]. Check out their single 'One More Night', a great power-pop slice of vinyl. The Goddard brothers also hung out with Maffia. Word was that their uncle was Stuart Goddard aka Adam Ant – so maybe punk did sneak through the slate gateposts of Bethesda after all.

Punk or not, Maffia are an important band, culturally and in the great scheme of Welsh language pop songs. Maybe there should be one of those Ivor Novello, here lived musician(s) / composer(s) style blue plaque on the outer wall of Bwthyn. Or a Caerffili style Tommy Cooper statue of the band on Bethesda High Street, just outside Spar. That might be over doing it. On the reverse sleeve of Maffia'r debut LP 'Yr Ochr Arall', (Sain 1286M) from 1983 is a photograph of a wall planner with all their gigs and recording dates filling in most days of that particular year. Maffia played over a hundred gigs a year at their peak in the early 1980s and that became the benchmark for the next generation of Welsh low-slung loud guitar bands like Anhrefn and Cyrff. We too had to clock up over a hundred gigs a year if we were to reach the same giddy heights of Welsh language pop stardom. No doubt a very young impressionable local drummer called Gruff Rhys was inspired by the hometown heroes. Over the years Gruff has acknowledged the musical lineage of Bethesda as he tours the world with the Super Furry Animals and as a solo artist.

Clues are to be found on the High Street that allude to this musical lineage. I spotted a 7" record sleeve by Côr Meibion Y Penrhyn stuck to the inside of a shop window. Faded and sellotaped but prominent. It's their single 'O! Na Byddai'n Haf o Hyd!', probably collectable. Proud. Male voice choir. Neuadd Ogwen on the High Street provides a venue for touring and local bands alike.

An independent venue still in business today, this is remarkable in many ways and especially so in a small town like Bethesda.

Artist Catrin Williams has a mural just off the High Street, on the River Ogwen side, down a side alley. Multicoloured guitars and banjos twist and shout out from the mural. Produced with the help of local school kids but distinctly 'Catrin Williams' in style. Multicoloured, vibrant and cartoon-like. Amongst the throng of pink faces, resembling a sunburnt male voice choir, I count at least five guitars and one saxophone. Bethesda bands did have sax players. I remember a sax player with Jecsyn 5, and also Maffia contemporaries, Proffwyd. (In Punk Rock terms the only cool bands ever to include a saxophone were X-Ray Spex and then Essential Logic – with sax player Laura Logic being the common thread).

The Bethesda landscape is dominated to the south by Penrhyn Quarry. Historically Bethesda is dominated by the Great Strike 1900-1903, Streic Fawr y Penrhyn. The longest dispute in British Industrial History. 'Arglwydd Penrhyn' is still a dirty word. 'Does Dim Bradwyr yn y Tŷ' (no traitors in the house) refers to those who broke the strike, who are still talked about to this day. Or are they? Is it just a myth that descendants of strike-breaking families are still regarded with a degree of contempt and mistrust? I talked to someone during a guided tour that I was giving around Bethesda and he thought this whole myth around 'bradwyr' (traitors) was all a bit of nonsense by now. He must have been late thirties or early forties and he reckoned that this was never discussed as a real 'issue' during his school days.

Penrhyn Quarry was the largest quarry in the world at the end of the nineteenth century – roofing the world with its slate. Parts are still worked. Other parts of the quarry have become an outdoor adventure playground for thrill seekers. You can zip it these days. Zip World offers a 100mph zip wire experience over the mile-long open cast Penrhyn Quarry. I wonder what the 1900-1903 striking quarrymen would make of it?

Mike Peters from The Alarm has held two open air charity concerts at Zip World, right at the edge of Penrhyn open cast. The stage overlooks the blue waters that have filled the disused part of the quarry below. Local bands perform alongside well-known acts such as Slade and Cast. Love Hope Strength is the world's leading Rock'n Roll cancer charity. Dramatic backdrops, sheer cliffs of heather blue coloured slate and then the zip wire directly overhead. During Zip World Rocks adrenaline junkies on the zip wire fly right over the stage – a bird's eye view of musicians below, strutting the stage, doing their stuff. At 100pmh the music is drowned out by the wind. Trying to make sense of the political history, culture and context and the current re-use of the quarry landscape is an intriguing concept. Things change, simple as that.

Another story or 'urban myth' about Bethesda is that the pubs on the High Street are all on the same side of the street. This would appear to be true. The Llangollen (closed), The Victoria (open), The King's Head (For Sale), Y Tarw (open) and the Douglas Hotel (For Sale) are indeed all located on the south side, the Ogwen side.

On the day I wander up the High Street in search of Bethesda pubs, Wales are playing rugby. Both the 'Vic' and the 'Tarw', the only pubs open at the time of writing, overflow with red rugby shirted smokers on the pavement. By the time I pass, the match has finished, but the sound of clanking glasses and beer fuelled laughter spills out, almost amplified, on to the street to join the smokers.

Most of the chapels are on the other side. Historian and archaeologist John Llywelyn Williams has documented the Bethesda pubs in the excellent blog *Hanes Dyffryn Ogwen* which can be easily found on-line. Williams goes some way to clarify the myth. It is true that two different landowners or estates, Penrhyn and Cenfaes, controlled Bethesda. Lord Penrhyn less inclined to support pubs initially refused the demon drink on his land. Hence the concentration on the River Ogwen side.

Of seventeen public houses or hotels recorded on Bethesda High Street in 1874, four were on Penrhyn land. The 'myth' has grown over the years and the remaining pubs are indeed all on the Ogwen side. It's just that pubs like the Cenfaes Vaults and the Castle on the north side have long gone. Intriguingly, the Douglas, on the Ogwen side, is obviously named after Douglas Pennant, Second Baron Penrhyn. Bethesda has great stories, ingrained within its cultural fabric.

CASTELL PENRHYN

"You will be hung for stealing a sheep from the mountain, but for stealing the mountain you will be made a Lord."

Thomas Hopper's mock/folly/ever so slightly OTT, neo-Norman Castle dominates the landscape. At least from certain viewpoints. Even the National Trust guidebook describes the castle as a 'forbidding fortress'. 'Foreboding' would be an easy substitute. For Castell Penrhyn is forever tainted by the Streic Fawr (Great Strike) of 1900-1903, tainted by sugar and slate, slavery in other words. No need to mince them.

Foreboding is a feeling that bad things might happen. Well, here they did. The Pennant family's first million came from sugar plantations in Jamaica. That's a definite yes for slavery. The second million came as Richard Pennant developed Penrhyn Quarry in the eighteenth century. And that's another yes for slavery. Different kind, but the prevailing and continuing attitudes of the Pennants resulted in the Great Strike. At the time, this was the longest prolonged strike in British industrial history. All the quarrymen wanted and asked for was better pay and better working conditions. Reasonable.

Even today, as the tweed set enjoy the National Trust property and hope for a glimpse of his Lordship, there are many who (still) won't step inside Castell Penrhyn on principle. My father (a son of a quarryman from the Nantlle Valley) being one of them. No argument can be made. I understand that. I won't attempt. As an archaeologist and historian, things are a bit more complicated. I have my political opinions, of course I do, but my firm view is that history has to be dealt with not ignored and certainly not erased.

Many a time I have heard the argument that Penrhyn Castle should be levelled to the ground. And I do get that. But we need Penrhyn to understand and debate the history. In the same way that you need the castles of the princes of Gwynedd and the four mighty castles, Harlech, Caernarfon, Conwy and Beaumaris built by Edward I. Both sides of the argument, both sides of the history, enable us to understand and debate the whole. Politics, opinions and taking sides really does not come into it – although we all know in reality that they do. But we have to deal with the history.

Take for example a tour guide at Kilmainham Goal, Dublin – they obviously don't agree or support what happened there – executions of the leaders of the 1916 Easter Uprising. They are there to provide information and context – which allows the rest of us to learn the lessons of History. It is the same argument with Castell Penrhyn. Objectionable in many ways to Welsh quarrymen stock – we do nevertheless have to deal with it. Castell Penrhyn is a great learning tool. Reclaim!

Politics aside, Thomas Hopper's architecture is a sweet shop experience for anyone interested in Norman / Romanesque (folly) arches and columns. The main entrance being a fine example of a Norman arch. Decorated with chevrons, a perfect semi-circle arch stood on two pairs of Corinthian columns. Beneath this, another inner decorated arch with leaves and strange little medieval characters. A coat of arms stands above the door. An impression is certainly made. Welcome to Castell Penrhyn.

Underneath this whole mock Norman forbidding and foreboding display of wealth is an earlier medieval Welsh hall belonging to the

Griffiths family. The foundations of the hall survive beneath the library, the drawing room and the Ebony Room. Glimpses of an old staircase can be caught between the library and the Ebony Room behind a National Trust cordon. The Griffiths family are descended from Ednyfed Fechan (d. 1246), seneschal or steward to Llywelyn ab Iorwerth. This is where history gets complicated. Ednyfed Fechan is part of the dynasty of Penmynydd on Ynys Môn which in time gives rise to the Tudors of Penmynydd[6].

Despite all the justifiable cries of 'slavery' and 'exploitation' we have on-site the remains of an earlier medieval hall. A Welsh Hall with direct family lineage connections to the princes of Gwynedd. Either ignored or not really known, this history, this Welsh connection, distorts the usual narrative.

And as hard as it may be for some, if we can suspend the politics, there is no doubt that the Slate Bed is a remarkable object. Built for Queen Victoria during her 1859 visit the story goes that she refused to spend the night because it looked too much like a tombstone. Great story. Probably true, the foot of the bed does look like two tombstones lined up next to each other. The William Morris 'Pomegranate' design for the cotton hanging around the four poster is later and dated to 1877. Victoria's visit took place before the Arts & Crafts movement kicked in.

Castell Penrhyn is both a fascinating and uncomfortable visit. There are culture clashes and contradictions around every corner.

BANGOR

Regional colloquialism certainly exists within Gwynedd. Bangor locals end their sentences with "aye". As in yes, affirmative, "I come from Bangor aye". Statement. Heading west, the 'Cofis'[7] in Caernarfon end sentences with a 'cont', "Dwi'n dod o Gaernarfon cont" (I come from Caernarfon cont). Statement. To the east in Llanrwst it's an "an-aye". "We live in Llanrwst an-aye". Statement. Not usually affirmed in the Welsh language mind, apart from Caernarfon folk who manage the 'c-word' fluently bi-lingual. This is a very peculiar Welsh-English phrasing, a poor English really, endearing possibly – raw material for stand-up comedians.

Bangor, a city since 1886, cathedral town, university town. The population increases dramatically during the academic term. Bangor population just over 18,000 (2011 census). Students 10,000 plus. Even the old Three Crowns pub on Stryd y Ffynnon, once the 'gay pub', recently burnt down, is being renovated as student accommodation. It's big business the university. Students are attracted not by Welsh culture, from which they remain largely un-engaged and insulated, but by the surrounding crags of Eryri and the marine life of the Menai Strait. They scramble, climb and dive (and traditionally drink too). The landlords dominate. To Let.

As I stood outside the new construction and scaffolding at the site of the Three Crowns, there was just a hint at ground level that this had once been a pub. I asked a passing grandmother and daughter pushing a pram, definitely Bangor 'ayes', and just popped the question. What's happening with the old Three Crowns? "Student Flats. It's all student flats 'round here." The economy of Bangor depends on the student population. The old community is changing if not disappearing on streets like Stryd y Ffynnon. No political answers on a postcard just a nagging feeling of displacement. Ironically, it's this kind of community uncertainty that contributed to the Brexit vote thereby damaging the very economy that Bangor depends on.

HIGH STREET

It feels long. It is long. At a mile long, Bangor High Street makes and wins the claim to be Britain's longest High Street. It runs roughly parallel with the Menai Strait half a mile to the north and west and below and alongside Bangor Mountain to its south and east. 'Lower East Side' to 'Upper West Side', not that anyone locally refers to the High Street in that way, but it does broadly run downhill to the north-east and climbs up to the south-west. It's also a tad more run down on the lower side, as the shops give up the fight, give up their last breath and give way to a mish-mash of residential. From Georgian to modern bricked and pebble dashed housing – twentieth century infill between the Georgian splendour.

Pedestrianised High Street runs from opposite the Cathedral as far as the junction with Dean Street and Mount Street. A slate and brass engraved historical timeline of Bangor implanted in the pavement leads us from the Neolithic c3000BC at the Cathedral to 2012 and the Olympic Flame at the Dean Street junction. Depending on your direction of travel you can walk towards the present day or walk back in time. I head forward in time.

Follow your footsteps and follow the complete history of Bangor, look up at your peril for you may miss one of the myriad of interesting facts. The seagulls shit, chewing gum sticks, the shoppers ignore, the traders spill coffee but it is there underfoot, to follow, to educate, to guide, to suggests places of pilgrimage, to remind. I get strange looks from passing shoppers as I stop-start and take a picture of each date. Not many bother I suspect.

As I've decided to do the Dylan Thomas thing and begin at the beginning my first point is a rough date given for Neolithic flint arrow heads found locally. Early Neolithic farmers would have farmed and hunted in this area during the fourth and third millennium BC. There was no Bangor then of course, but a few miles south east at Llandegai was a vast ritual landscape with a double henge monument and cursus. Our very own north Walian Stonehenge. A Neolitihic / Bronze Age landscape without the standing stones of Salisbury Plain. Excavated by archaeologists and then left re-buried under Parc Gegin, a half-completed industrial estate[8]. Industrially ambitious in its un-necessary destruction of significant archaeology.

Slate plaque 546AD signifies the Christian clas or early Christian establishment that was founded by Saint Deiniol. Bangor actually gets its name from a 'bangor', the wooden wattle fence that would have surrounded this early Christian establishment. A vast array of interesting dates are provided by the timeline. Some make me laugh. Some provide historical anchor points. Some are just interesting. Some are important in their own little way – cspccially for the locals at the time.

1786 Porth Penrhyn. 1848 Museum & Reading Room. 1848 Chester & Holyhead Railway. 1876 Bangor Football Club Established. 1884 Bangor University. 1896 Garth Pier Opened. 1907 Library Opened. 1912 First Bus Service. 1935 BBC Bryn Meirion. 1937 Social Housing Maesgeirchen. 1953 HMS Conwy runs aground. 1965 Swimming Baths Opened. 2012 The Olympic Flame comes to Bangor. End.

Just off High Street, near the town clock in the centre of Bangor, I take a quick detour, a musical detour, and head up the steep hill of Caellepa, under the shadow of Bangor Mountain. I head towards 31 Caellepa to be specific. A nondescript rather small terrace house. Go up the slate steps and just to the right of the door is the plaque commemorating the birth place of Harry Parry, jazz musician.

My producer at BBC Radio Cymru, Bangor, Dylan Wyn had given me the heads-up that I should investigate Harry Parry and I duly found a CD on eBay for under £5: *Crazy Rhythm* by Harry Parry's Radio Rhythm Club Sextet. Bangor-born then London-based, Parry and his sextet were pioneers and early advocates of swing. This is terrific stuff indeed.

As a child, Harry Owen Parry (1912-1956) was obviously some kind of prodigy. A multi-instrumentalist, being proficient on the cornet, tenor horn, flugelhorn, violin and drums. He added clarinet and saxophone in 1927 before his move to London in 1932, where he played with various dance bands. Parry performed worldwide and also developed a career as a radio presenter. His profile is not what it should be in Bangor, but as is too often the case, jazz is the stuff of specialist interest.

Back on High Street, Cob Records is now closed. Sister shop to the world-famous mail order record shop of the same name in Porthmadog, Cob finally shut its doors after thirty-three years of trading in 2012. Always more than a 'record shop', Cob was a focal point for musicians and the local music scene. Owner, Owen 'Cob' Hughes is still active as a promoter of roots and blues gigs in the Gwynedd area.

At the north-eastern tip of High Street, on a grassy knoll and slightly obscured by trees, is the entrance arch of the Penrhyn Arms. All that remains of the original location of the University as established in 1884, built by quarrymen and used as such until 1926. Six Doric columns in total stand proud as part of the arch, but the building is long demolished. Considering that the Welsh at this time were strict non-Conformists and probably tee-total it does raise a smile that the first University was held in a pub.

The salty sea breeze gives flavour to the air here – blowing in from the port area, Porth Penrhyn on the mouth of the river Cegin. Aber Cegin to give it the correct Welsh name, Porth Penrhyn being the English version of the name despite its Welsh wordage.

On the hill in the distance to the west, overlooking Bangor, stands the Main Arts Building of the University. Known in Welsh as 'Coleg ar y Bryn', stonework stained dark – the college on the hill is a Bangor landmark. This is Upper Bangor, university and student territory. Not visible is the Adda river, culverted under Deiniol and Garth Roads and flowing towards the Menai Strait at the port.

Beaumaris is visible across the Strait to the north. Tan-y-Coed, once the Caernarvonshire and Anglesey Dispensary, still has a notice within the slate porch stating that the building should be *'visible from Beaumaris, so that the loyal and charitable inhabitants of Anglesey could always see it'*.

A few hundred metres walk up the old narrow gauge Penrhyn Railway line (later the Penrhyn Quarry Railway) along the Cegin river and we find the spectacular Cegin Viaduct. Still standing and maintained by Cadw. This three-arched bridge built between 1798 and 1800 is the oldest surviving multi arched railroad bridge in Wales, if not the world. At this point the Cegin wide and brown flows under all the arches. A broken wooden gate enables those with real interest to walk the bridge.

Slate was brought along this line from Penrhyn Quarry to the port for export. Most of the line can be followed on what is now a cycle path and footpath known as Lon Las Ogwen. Dog walkers, afternoon strollers, joggers and cyclists compete for a straight course of travel on the path. Dogs on extendable leads criss-cross oncoming joggers and cyclists alike. Lush tree cover gives Lon Las Ogwen the feel of one long railway tunnel, but not too dark. Various bridges cross the Cegin. Modern roads cross above our heads. Next stop heading south would be Tregarth, then Bethesda.

CATHEDRAL

Owain Gwynedd (1100-1170), prince of Gwynedd, does not lie under the cracked slate slab which bears his name in the nave of Bangor Cathedral. He'd married his first cousin Cristin, as his second wife, much to the displeasure of both the Pope and the Archbishop of Canterbury, Thomas Becket. Owain had already argued with Becket over the choice of Bishop of Bangor, appointing his own man Arthur of Bardsey. Neither Arthur or Cristin were acceptable to Archbishop or Pope. They just went ahead and excommunicated the stroppy prince of Gwynedd.

Excommunicated or not, Owain still managed to get buried here, somewhere, just probably not beneath the commemorative slab. I'm no fan of royalty, Welsh or otherwise, but someone who is excommunicated and still ends up buried within the cathedral walls has to be a bit of a dude. Another 'dude' and Gwynedd prince, Gruffudd ap Cynan, Owain's father, is also here somewhere. Both await discovery Richard III style, when the cathedral requires a new car park.

As children we had visited the Robert (Mouseman) Thompson museum in Kilburn, North Yorkshire. Thompson, a 1920s furniture maker and craftsman in the tradition of William Morris / Arts & Crafts, used carvings of mice as his signature on various pieces of furniture. Some of Thompson's mice got out of Yorkshire and grace various fittings in the Cathedral. The challenge is to discover them. Some are fairly easy to find but I must confess, I ended up asking a cathedral volunteer when one mouse proved too elusive. It's in the chancel – slightly hidden behind the pews. The mouse scurrying around the base of the font is the easiest to find. As part of my 'other day job' as tour guide finding the Mouseman mice has provided the challenge for many a group of over-active school kids and adult Welsh learners who come with me on a Cathedral tour. 'Ble mae llygod Mouseman?'.

Hidden in the shop, obscured by books and gifts is the Eva Stone, a fourteenth century carved gravestone effigy. A *Vogue* front cover c AD1380. Eva, a member of north Wales gentry, is described in relief by archaeologist Frances Lynch as "wearing a wimple and a square fourteenth century head dress. She has a tight-fitting dress with a finely pleated-skirt. Eighty-five buttons and buttonholes are worked down the front". What was that about a *Vogue* front cover? Fashionistas back in the day. Wealth and privilege worn and displayed and subsequently carved to last for ever. Shame about the bookstands, but the cathedral has running costs to cover.

STORIEL

Museums are places that should encourage a sense of adventure and discovery. Derived from and meaning a combination of 'story', the story of Gwynedd that's the museum role, and 'oriel', the art gallery component, the name 'Storiel' was created by local graphic designer Tim Albin. It has meaning, it has a ring, it's not too obvious. It need not be too obvious. We are in the Welsh-speaking heartlands, over forty per cent of the locals speak Welsh in Bangor. A much higher percentage understand, "I don't speak Welsh ond dwi'n dallt". There is no demand for the name to be bi-lingual. It works.

Storiel occupies the former Bishop's Palace, a Grade II listed building traditionally ascribed to Bishops Deane and Skevington c. 1500. Skevington's inscription can be seen above the west door of Bangor Cathedral. Returning to the Timeline on the High Street another connection is made. 1884, Bangor University. The university collections form the basis of much that is displayed and stored at Storiel which is administered by Gwynedd Council.

Objects dominate Storiel rather than the ubiquitous touch screen displays of modern museums, but careful curation here also means that the objects have space to tell their story. Author Caradog Pritchard's hat is given space within a case[9]. Not obvious to the non-literary types maybe, but here lies the encouragement to discover, to learn more, to read *Un Nos Ola Leuad* in any of the twelve languages into which it has been translated.

A reminder of less enlightened times is provided by the 'Welsh Not', a piece of wood with the letters 'W.N.', hung around the neck of school children caught speaking Welsh in the classroom and repeatedly handed over to the next culprit. The last unfortunate culprit of the day was punished further with a beating. Dating from the 1840s onwards and in use throughout the nineteenth century, the 'Welsh Not' spectacularly failed in its mission to dissuade people from speaking Welsh. Enlightened times indeed. The 'Welsh Not' was barbaric, but also a brilliant symbol appropriated as a weapon of counter-propaganda by language campaigners from the 1960s onwards. Just like the drowning of Tryweryn in 1965 and the Investiture of 1969, the 'Welsh Not' gets the blood to boiling point. The Welsh language has survived and thrived.

Carved slate, mostly associated with the Bethesda and Dyffryn Ogwen area, is another unique feature of the quarrying tradition here in Gwynedd. Fireplaces were decorated with concentric circles and figures. After a long hard day's work at the quarry extracting, shifting and cutting huge slabs of slate, leisure time was spent making intricate carvings on household fittings or making slate models for the mantlepiece. One would have thought the quarrymen had seen enough slate for one day.

Gwenno Caffell's excellent book *The Carved Slates of Dyffryn Ogwen* sets the tone in many ways. Her extensive research of carved slate and fireplaces specifically in the Bethesda area provides the starting point for further research. I have met people from Nant Peris who have found carved slate in rubbish dumps behind cottages. During the summer of 2019 Gwynedd Archaeological Trust excavated at Pen y Bryn quarry cottages at Dorothea, Nantlle Valley, and a carved fireplace lintel was uncovered. There is more to the carved slate story than Dyffryn Ogwen, it's just that all the other areas are playing catch up with Caffell.

PONTIO

Pontio, meaning 'to bridge', presumably between the locals – 'aye' – and the students. Challenging. Replacing the old, now demolished Theatr Gwynedd and Student's Union building, Pontio sits next to the Memorial Arch and below the main arts building of the university on top of the hill, the 'Coleg ar y Bryn'. It's a strange juxtaposition of architectural styles. Pontio is Modern, Brutalist almost. Obviously not 1970s Brutalist as it's a twenty-first century building, but a lot of concrete and a lot of glass. The coffee drinkers are on public view in the second floor café.

Bangor and the wider Gwynedd area and indeed all of north Wales needs its theatres and spaces for the arts. However challenging the actual bridging process at Pontio may seem, – Bangor is a university town – it would be strange not to have a theatre and gallery. Caernarfon is served by the slightly smaller capacity Galeri. Bala has a new theatre at the high school 'Theatr Derec Williams' (2019) and Neuadd Dwyfor, Pwllheli, a Victorian building, provides a stage for theatre and a cinema on Llŷn. There are other smaller spaces scattered around Gwynedd but the main towns of Bangor, Caernarfon, Pwllheli and Bala can now hold their own with touring theatre and gigs.

Public art should provoke. A tender was given out for a public work of art next to the Pontio building. Dutch artist, Joseph van Lieshout won the commission and set out to make the connection between his art and the traditions and culture of the slate quarries. The public art was to have a sense of place and a sense of tradition. Traditionally the caban (hut) was a place where quarrymen met at breaktime in the slate quarries and mines to eat their lunch, drink their stewed tea, debate politics and matters of the day, sing and even hold mini eisteddfods. Interestingly the caban had its own hierarchy, where the elders sat closest to the fire and the youngest boys caught the draught by the door.

Joseph van Lieshout's lime green, fibreglass 'Caban' set on the hill next to Pontio and below the university provokes. Predictably the local north Wales newspaper *Daily Post*'s headline screamed 'Golden nugget or monstrosity? The Pontio commissioned artwork had cost a whopping £109,000'.

According to the *Daily Post* on 14 January 2016, an online poll by the 'Bangor Aye' blogger on Twitter found that fourteen per cent of people surveyed liked it while sixteen per cent said it was 'not for me' whilst the vast majority, seventy per cent, said they had no idea what it was. That's pretty tame stuff actually. More predictably it has been compared to a huge piece of lime green snot. Not surprisingly its now locked overnight because people sleep or pee in it. The original intention was a space to be used by whoever for whatever (artistically speaking).

Artistically speaking, north Wales artist Bedwyr Williams put all this into context, "Pontio's Caban was selected because it was challenging. This is not meant to be a literal representation of a traditional caban, but rather something unique that celebrates the way the workers transformed what was basically a hut into a myriad of different uses – a space to perform, to argue, to discuss and to dream."

VENUES

Alan Holmes, bass player with The Fflaps and Ectogram and head honcho of the Central Slate record label and I meet up in Pontio artist's car park. We are searching for the space once occupied by the 1980s and early 90s music venue – the Jazz Room (aka Jock's Bar). Back in the day, the venue, most often referred to as the Jazz Room, was actually located underneath Bangor University Students' Union, next to the ground floor carpark and just off Deiniol Road (the A5). Pontio now largely occupies this site. The Jazz Room just like the Menai Strait often became the Jazz Rooms (sic) but there was only ever one space.

My memory serves me poorly, Alan is an excellent guide and slowly but surely we work out that the Jazz Room was situated right alongside the main road. An old tree still stands next to the road and therefore the venue would have been just next to this tree and just off the Memorial Arch which still stands. Everything else has been built up with the construction of Pontio, slightly further up Glanrafon Hill. The Jazz Room was on ground level, road level and we realise that the bank leading up to the Pontio piazza covers the site of our venue.

Staff at Pontio suggest that the current steps up towards the main entrance roughly follow the line of the old access road to the underground carpark. Lines on the map are being drawn. Just north and east of Pontio the grassy slope was originally the site of Theatr Gwynedd. The iron railings along the kerb define the northern and eastern extent of the demolished theatre.

Our conclusion is that the site of the Jazz Room is now buried underneath the bank leading up to Pontio. Landscaped. What was once culturally an 'underground venue' has literally been demolished and buried underground. 'Always an underground venue' I joke with Alan. I still have some of Alan's hand drawn posters for gigs here. As a member of Third Spain and responsible for releasing records by Cut Tunes via Central Slate he was the go-to guy for posters and record sleeves for during the late 1980s and early 1990s. Alan also designed some of the early record sleeves for Gorky's Zygotic Mynci.

The Jazz Room was always a great venue. A venue where the non-Welsh speaking hipsters, goths and post-punk casualties got up close and personal to post-Punk Welsh language bands that were much supported by the late John Peel on his late-night Radio One show. Y Cyrff, Tynal Tywyll, Fflaps, Anhrefn all strummed and strutted their stuff here in the mid to late 1980s. Catatonia played an early gig in 1993 before graduating to the larger venue upstairs known as the 'Curved Lounge' which stood next to the 'Main Hall'. That's three different venues all within one building. Ahhh, the 1980s (or even the 1970s-1990s). Good times for live music in Bangor.

Catatonia's early show here was during my time acting as their first manager. Mark (guitar) and Paul (bass) had already played here as members of Y Cyrff. Cerys was a newcomer, the next upstart, the future princess of Welsh pop, treading the boards of a non-existent stage. She held her own. Even in the early days of low-key semi-secret gigs the Media were present. I gave a BBC Radio Cymru journalist soundbites and throwaway quotes about 'Cerys having cheekbones to Dai for', 'if Nico had been born in Wales', 'glamorous, sexy, young'.

In Peter Finch's *The Roots of Rock from Cardiff to Mississippi and Back* there is a great reference to "car parks that once had famous buildings on them". Finch was talking Rock'n Roll venues and recording studios on his Roots music road trip across the US[10]. It's a thread that we can play with in this book. A common theme. An all too common theme of lost venues, changing landscapes, building developments, carparks, good times, bad times, a lack of venues, new venues, new trends, new promoters and more carparks.

Venues come and go, that's just the way it is and Bangor is no exception. Alan Holmes remembers promoting gigs upstairs at the Glanrafon pub in the early 1980s. This was a small upstairs room, a local bands type venue. Glanrafon became the Old Glan, served food for a while then finally closed its doors before re-opening as a Chinese restaurant.

I certainly promoted Datblygu at the Albion pub in the mid-80s. This was just up High Street from the cathedral. Not enough room for amps and a drum kit, the bands squeezed into a corner of the room, this was never a suitable venue. But the search for new venues was constant. Bands wanted to play gigs. This would have been the first Bangor gig for a then unknown Datblygu. At least three people turned up.

Trax, a cellar bar near the station, was a venue for a short time in the 80s. Downstairs and prone to flooding. Floods from the toilet rather than the nearby river Adda. I remember this as more of a Goth-style venue, slightly later than the more punk and post-punk gigs at the Jazz Room. Satz in Upper Bangor held gigs in the later 1980s and then became Rascals and still has occasional gigs in an upstairs room. As venues go, the upper room at Rascals is actually quite suitable. At the time of writing (2019) I saw Libertino Records acts Los Blancos and Papur Wal perform here in front of a capacity crowd of 150.

Now demolished, Theatr Gwynedd provided a stage for touring folk bands. A sit-down venue for concerts and listening rather than the drinking and dancing that took place in the pub venues. Theatr Gwynedd has been replaced by the larger capacity and much more modern Theatr Bryn Terfel at Pontio.

The Octagon nightclub on Dean Street was another larger venue used occasionally for gigs. Sticky carpets and dodgy beer. The Octagon was a proper old-skool night club. Handbag disco style venue. I can only imagine it was hired because there was a stage, and its larger capacity provided a suitable venue for bands with a more substantial following.

The Crosville Club in the downtown Hirael area hosts bands once in a while. Clwb Blewyn Glas, Bangor City FC social club, has been demolished, as has the Railway Institute. More lost venues. Undeveloped plots of land, not even graced with a carpark. The Normandie lower down the High Street has changed names many times — I don't know if it's still in use.

Within the university, concerts and gigs were held and are held at PJ Hall and JP Hall while other in-house venues such as the Main Hall, the Curved Lounge, Ffriddoedd Refectory have gone – demolished along with the much-loved Jazz Room.

Bangor Pulse / Curiad Bangor is a current annual festival that showcases local bands at The Skerries, Rascals, Y Menai and the Belle Vue. In many ways the organisers of Bangor Pulse keep the tradition of the Jazz Room alive and kicking. Band names have changed, young musicians have emerged but some of those who performed at the Jazz Room can still be spotted gracing the stage at Pulse events.

THE BRIDGES / MENAI STRAIT

Just to reiterate my statement (rant) in the Introduction section. There is only one, only one Strait, but so many, far too many, insist on calling this stretch of sea water between Ynys Môn and mainland Gwynedd the Menai Straits (sic) even those in the Media who should know better. There is only one, only one strait, ending with a t not an s. Strait.

Standing beneath Robert Stephenson's Britannia Bridge (1850) on the Gwynedd side, cars and HGVs thunder above me like repetitive beats at a primitive rave. The Holyhead to London railway runs on the original deck, below the 1972 road double-decker built after some kids with a box of matches accidently put Stephenson's tubular bridge on fire in 1970. 'Looking for bats' was one of their better excuses but up in flames it went. Just as well in some ways because we would have needed that double-decker anyway as road traffic volume was soon to increase.

From Treborth a path leads down to the Strait, right past one of the four huge limestone lions that guard the railway. John Thomas's sculptures were later immortalised by Porthaethwy poet John Evans

(1826-1888). The four fat furless lions he called them, two each side of the bridge.

Pedwar llew tew
Heb ddim blew
Dau 'ochr yma
A dau 'ochr drew
(Two fat lions, furless
Two this side and two on the other)

Passengers in vehicles on the top road cannot view the lions and you have to be pretty sharp to catch a glimpse on the Holyhead London train as it hurtles past. Best to walk down from Treborth and look up. £1000 fine if you step on the railway. Even below the lions, it's difficult to get a decent view or a decent photograph. Necks are strained and the lions too often appear as a silhouette against either the bright or dull Anglesey skies depending on the day.

Every now and again a third bridge across the Strait is mentioned and then forgotten about for a couple of years. Funding – challenging. First Minister, Carwyn Jones hinted at a preferred route between the two existing bridges as recently as October 2018. In government speak this option was referred to as the 'purple route' and was to include provision for pedestrians and cyclists. The

A55 reduces to a single lane at the Stephenson bridge with additional feeder routes merging each side of the bridge approach. At rush hour the congestion is obvious.

Alongside the Strait, just west of Stephenson's bridge, directly on the opposite Anglesey shore, Nelson stands proud. 'England expects every man to do his duty.' A folly sculpture by Clarence Paget (1811-1895) fourth son of the Marquis of Anglesey. Most likely a navigational aid for ships. There is to my knowledge no historic connection between Nelson and the Menai Strait beyond his comments of the challenges of navigating this stretch of water. Clarence Paget was a naval man who served on or commanded HMS *Asia, Pearl, Howe, Aigle* and *Princess Royal*. In the absence of any further evidence, I'm guessing his interest as an amateur sculptor and his seafaring life accounts for Nelson as the subject matter of his statue. The family home and country seat of the Marquis, Plas Newydd, is a mile or so to the west on the Menai shore, Anglesey side. Open to the public and cared for by the National Trust.

Thomas Telford's 1826 suspension bridge crosses from Bangor to the village of Porthaethwy on the line of his London to Holyhead road. A walk across Telford's bridge is a thrill. Not recommended for vertigo sufferers. The open metal grid and railing fences add to the sense of exposure. At times of high wind there are severe gusts at both bridges. Traffic is often restricted or slowed down to 30mph on the Stephenson bridge. A firm walking posture is required to cross the Telford bridge at times like this.

Towering thirty metres (ninety-eight feet) above the fast-flowing strait below and known locally as Pont Borth or Pont y Borth, the walk affords excellent views towards the Stephenson bridge to the west and the town of Beaumaris to the east. On a fine day it's a place to enjoy the scenery, savour the atmosphere and take a bit of time to cross.

Telford's iron gates can still be seen on the mainland, Treborth side of the bridge. Modelled on the rays of the sun splaying out from one corner of the gate. Distinctive of Telford's design.

FELINHELI (PORT DINORWIC)

Literally meaning the mill of brine /sea / salt-water, Felinheli acquired a new (additional) name with the development of the port to serve the Dinorwic slate quarry, which exported from here, and thus Felinheli became Port Dinorwic. As a place name this is quite interesting as the English is not a translation of the original Welsh name. In the same way Porth Penrhyn is not a translation of Aber Cegin.

One of the great features of north Wales industrial archaeology can be found behind the closed Halfway pub, now developed as flats. Or rather I should qualify, quite is difficult to find and even more difficult to follow. The Penscoins Incline is an impressive rock cut incline that brought slates down to the port. On arriving at the top of the hill, where the current Felinheli by-pass runs, the Dinorwic Railway (later Padarn Railway) was faced with a substantial drop down to the port. Victorian engineers, not put off by any obstacles, simply cut into the rock.

Walking down the incline, thousands of slate pieces crunch underfoot. Sunlight becomes restricted as the cut is over ten feet deep in places. A canopy of trees further restricts sunlight and adds to the whole otherworldly feel of the experience. On arriving at Felinheli, the incline gave way to a tunnel underneath the present road and popped out where the kitchen is now situated at the La Marina restaurant.

A marina now occupies the site of the old slate quay. Boats named 'Seren y Môr', 'Keoki' and 'Miles Aweigh' serve only to confuse. Not all these boats are locally owned with such exotic names. More boats sit in dry dock alongside the Menai Strait. An elderly couple, flask in hand, enjoy a cup of tea on deck despite the boat being on land. Like gardeners with sheds and allotments, the flask is crucial, as is the deck chair. Others in wellingtons, hands in pockets, stand dockside pointing towards boats – deep in maritime discussions.

Transformed completely from industrial to leisure, the marina is remarkably quiet. Without wind there is no rustling of sails. There is no hustle and bustle, no exports and imports. No ballast and no wagons, just retired folks with boats. A café and restaurant stand alongside the dock. At the far end of the dock boat repair sheds are still in operation. Along the main part of the dock, wooden fronted, Scandinavian-looking, block flats have taken up the space previously occupied by warehouses and weigh sheds.

Beyond the docks are modern housing estates. Gated avenues. Manicured lawns. All very neat, prim and proper. There is barely a hint of an industrial past. On the Strait, someone is sure to be out there sailing, most days of the year.

CAERNARFON

Caernarfon's history is well known, a town situated next to where the river, Afon Saint / Seiont (we still argue about the correct version of the river name) flows into the Menai Strait. Caer refers to the Roman fort not the Norman castle. Arfon literally translated means next to Môn (Anglesey). It's the fort near Anglesey then.

In AD77 the Romans set up a fort here, Segontium, about 150 feet above sea level on a ridge bounded by the rivers Cadnant to the east, the Saint / Seiont to the west and the Menai Strait to the north. What a posting for those poor soldiers – often wet and windy and at least for some periods surrounded by hostile Celts.

Arriving around 1093, the Normans opted for the low rocky strip of land right at the mouth of the Afon Saint with the River Cadnant a short distance to the east. Both flowing into the Menai Strait. Effectively an island defended by water on three sides, Robert of Rhuddlan's motte and bailey castle was later partially obliterated and built over by Edward I for his 'palace-fortress'. The careful eye of the archaeologist or psychogeographer can still see the outlines of the motte and bailey in places. The levelled motte is visible inside the castle where the Investiture slate lies, while the outline of the motte ditch is followed by the castle walls under Queen Eleanor's Gate.

Designed by genius architect Master James of St George in 1283, the castle is arguably modelled on and inspired by the banded walls of Roman Constantinople. From the west the different coloured bands of limestone are clearly visible on the castle walls. Edward was building to impress as well as defend.

Demand for Welsh slate during the nineteenth resulted in the eastern banks of Afon Saint developing as Caernarfon's industrial area. Lime kilns, timber stores, copper and iron ore yards, ironworks and various buildings and offices associated with the slate trade lined the river bank. Immediately below the southern and western defences of Edward's castle the quay known as Cei Llechi (Slate Quay) was built up, possibly using earth from the remnants of Robert's motte and bailey and more likely waste ballast from the slate ships.

Acts of Parliament in 1793 and 1809 had paved the way for harbour improvements at Caernarfon. Henry Paget, First Marquess of Anglesey, used unemployed soldiers recently returned from the battle of Waterloo (1815) for much of the construction work during the 1820s. Paget had famously fought alongside Wellington at Waterloo and was shot in the right leg by a cannon during the battle. Wellington and Paget were not close as Paget was having liaisons with Wellington's sister-in-law. On realising that he had been shot, Paget is said to have exclaimed "By God Sir, I've lost my leg!" to which Wellington unsympathetically replied "By God Sir, so you have!". Paget's artificial limb can still be seen at Plas Newydd.

Welsh slate roofed the world. Ships docked at the quay, loaded up with dressed slate and sailed to all corners of the globe. In order for the export trade to work efficiently slate was brought down to Caernarfon from the Nantlle quarries via a horse drawn tramway. Parts of the line are now used by the North Wales Highland Railway – a major tourist attraction, a close second to the 176,000 who visit the castle annually. Whatever the politics of Edward I's castle, the death of Llywelyn ap Gruffudd in 1282 and the Investiture of 1969, Caernarfon's economy relies heavily on the castle and visitors.

The Investiture of Charles as Prince of Wales in 1969 was a huge media event. It is also an event that is ingrained within the present-day political landscape. Following the death of Llywelyn ap Gruffudd in 1282, Edward cunningly offered his son, the future

Edward II as a replacement. Edward of Carnarvon as he was sometimes known was born in the castle on the 25th April 1284 thus sealing the royal connection with Caernarfon (Royal Borough / Royal Town). MP Lloyd George, seeking re-election instigated the Investiture of Edward VIII in 1911 and this became a blueprint for the 1969 event.

Lord Snowdon, photographer and husband of Princes Margaret, played a key role in the organisation of the 1969 Investiture. In many ways the whole affair bordered on the 'camp'. Pomp and pageantry were in plentiful supply. The smallest details were attended to by Lord Snowdon. Invitees were presented with a red chair bearing the three ostrich feather heraldic badge of the Prince. Even the black cast iron waste bins were designed by him. The black bins still stand along the paths around the castle. Few realise their origin.

Over fifty years have passed since the Investiture, but there were no anniversary events at Caernarfon Castle. In fact, the fiftieth anniversary was very much a non-event. Charles did not return to Caernarfon. S4C and the Welsh media discussed the events of fifty years ago. Documentaries were broadcast about M.A.C bomber John Jenkins[11] and a film was made of the meeting of Charles and pop singer Dafydd Iwan. Remarkably, or possibly not that unexpectedly at all, Charles and Dafydd got on well. They have a shared interest in architecture and the environment. Charles must have known of Dafydd's recordings during the 1960s. The conversation was not filmed but Charles's welcoming smile and body language suggested two men at ease, fifty years on.

Dafydd Iwan released two singles during 1969 which specifically commented on the events around the Investiture. Both were released on the Telidisc label, 'Carlo' and 'Croeso Chwedeg Nain' lightheartedly poked fun at the absurdity of an English prince of Wales. An edgier and very much more underground song was recorded by folk singer Tecwyn Ifan on the MAC record label. Tecwyn Ifan was never credited although his voice is unmistakable. This record tacitly supported the bombing campaigns of the Free Wales Army and MAC. The recording is poor, with more crackles and hiss than actual music, but this is a very collectable item. Of its time.

Wandering along the present-day car park on Cei Llechi, rusting rails bubble out from under the tarmac. The clues are always there if you look carefully enough. 5ft 6" gauge suggest it's not the original Nantlle Tramway (Railway) track which was 3ft 6". A mile out of Caernarfon the Coed Helen tunnel built as part of the Nantlle Tramway has been fenced off to stop the local youth from using it as a beer drinking den. A cycle path now follows parts of the Nantlle line and the previous main railway line to Afon Wen (closed by Beeching in 1964).

Demolition and re-use of buildings means that interpretation of Caernarfon's industrial archaeology can be quite challenging but it may be worth having a look at *Ports and Harbours of Gwynedd* a report by archaeologists Andrew Davidson and John Roberts.

Culturally, Caernarfon is a very Welsh speaking town, the locals are known colloquially as 'Cofis'[7] and they use the C*** word a lot mid-sentence albeit in its Welsh form with an o not a u. The definition of a local is always difficult to pinpoint. Cofis should be born and bred in Caernarfon. They should also probably speak 'Cofi'. Maes Barcer housing estate, usually referred to as 'Sgubor Goch' o'r 'Sgubs', has the greatest concentration of Cofis and Cymraeg speakers in the world with one thousand houses and a population of two thousand all within a square mile.

I live in Caernarfon. I am an incomer, as are so many of the Culture-istas here. Maybe I'm over generalising but there seems to be two Welsh language communities in Caernarfon – the local Cofi community and the middle-class professional, self-employed, entrepreneurs, media types. We may like to think we are as one but events such as Investiture, royal weddings and more recently Brexit expose the cultural fissures. At the risk of over simplifying, many of the older Cofis would be sympathetic to the royal family and the royal connection with Caernarfon.

Let's detour. Let's look for the hidden history, the less obvious, the forgotten, the obscure and obscured but nevertheless important. Forget for a moment the events of July 1st 1969, the Investiture of Charles as Prince of Wales, that scar on the collective Welsh / nationalist psyche (I'm an anarchist but am still slightly damaged).

There's always more to find if we detour. Caernarfon Pavilion, demolished in 1962, has left an imprint on the landscape. Street names and road layouts reveal clues as to the history of the place. Historical buildings often inherit a greater cultural importance. Caernarfon Pavilion is no exception. Paul Robeson sang here in September1934. Part of his performance fee was donated by Robeson to the Gresford Mining Disaster Fund[12]. Just the fact that the great Paul Robeson performed in Caernarfon is remarkable. Robeson had a political conscience and an empathy with the Welsh. Donating part of his fee to the miners is testament to that strong bond.

A little bit of psychogeography and map reading (or map research) has to kick in if we are to locate the site of the pavilion. Ffordd Pafiliwn (Pavilion Road) runs off Bangor Street, uphill past the library on the right and Theatr Seilo on the left and onwards towards the Arfon Council offices. Turning right at the top of the hill, Ffordd Pafiliwn continues between the Arfon Council staff multistorey car park and the job centre and Welsh Government buildings.

But the absence of any street names or signage here means that it's the map research that tells me I'm on Ffordd Pafiliwn. This road is joined to the west by North Penrallt, another offshoot from Bangor Street. Parallel to North Penrallt is Allt Pafiliwn or 'Pavilion Hill' which comes uphill alongside the Institute from Bangor Street. The pavilion would have stood between these roads.

Sandwiched between the Government buildings, Bangor Street, the Institute and the Library is Cwrt Pafiliwn (Pavilion Court). Another clue. New red brick buildings / residential flats have replaced an iconic building. Could be worse – could have been a car park. I see no signage at Cwrt Pafiliwn. For postal addresses, 'Pavilion Hill' seems to be used for both Ffordd Pafiliwn and Allt

Pafiliwn. Both the Institute and Library give their address as Pavilion Hill. Confusing. Even the local postman is not sure which is 'Ffordd' and which is 'Allt', but as long as the letters reach their destination this minutiae of detail is surplus baggage for our mail man.

A slate plaque on the wall of the library confirms that we are in the right place – the Pavilion was here. Built in 1877 and demolished in 1962 with a capacity of 7000 it must have been a wonderful building. The two slate plaques on the library wall confirm two facts. Firstly, that we are indeed on the site of the Pavilion and secondly, that Lloyd George 'thrilled' people here. He certainly did – the great orator – it would have been a 'hometown-gig' for Lloyd George, capacity crowd. There is no third, corresponding plaque for Paul Robeson who sang here, which is a pity.

Looking at old photographs of Caernarfon before the building of the town bypass (which you can easily find on Google), the pavilion is clearly visible. Other nearby landmarks are Capel Pendref (1791) and the now demolished Majestic nightclub, the site of which is currently in use as an overflow carpark for the Celtic Royal Hotel. The BBC recorded the final concert at the Pavilion on the 21st October 1961. A vinyl copy of this recording was found in one of Caernarfon's many charity shops by my good wife. For a record collector, for an archaeologist, for a psychogeographer – this is a great discovery. £1 for 4000 Voices.

As an archaeologist and 'tour guide' I have done many 'Roman Caernarfon' walking tours. I have done countless tours of the castle and dealt with the 1969 Investiture in my most professional non-political way. Recently I have developed 'pop culture' tours of Caernarfon –to give my regulars some variety, an idea that came about from a request by the annual literary and music festival Gŵyl Arall.

Ed Povey's 'Helter Skelter' mural on Bangor Street counts as 'pop culture'. Painted in 1979 to celebrate the National Eisteddfod at Caernarfon the mural is half obscured by the library extension of 1982. Culture destroys culture. 'Libraries Gave Us Power' sang the Manic Street Preachers via Aneurin Bevan. There is a sad, predictable, irony here that Povey's mural should be half obscured so soon by another cultural building. Sad also that the paint flakes on the remaining visible half.

Painted on the original mural, a bus departing y Maes is now obscured by the library wall. In reality, buses no longer depart from the Maes (town square). Maybe the builders foresaw the future?

Saunders Lewis and his two Penyberth protesting buddies, Lewis Valentine and D.J. Williams are featured (page 152). They are not of Caernarfon. Lloyd George features prominently, as do various 'local characters' – known only to fellow local characters. Once offered on sale, but never sold, to Americans for £2.5 million, it does need some care and attention.

In search of pop culture, I stumbled upon Llew Llwyfo, the first Welsh singer to tour coast to coast in the USA. A Victorian era popstar. Good looking, elegant, a distinctive poster-boy before the era of pop posters that followed Elvis and the Beatles. Researching, I later discover he once lived next door to our house, at 'Rock Cottage' now known only as No 4 Twthill Terrace. What happened to 'Rock Cottage'? The slate name plaque lost to pebble-dash, I suspect.

During my research someone mentioned a portrait of Llew Llwyfo at Caernarfon Institute, so I search it out. Vernon Pearce, the clerk at the time, had no memory of it and I am turned away slightly disappointed. As my hand reaches the door handle, Vernon remembers that "there is something up in the attic". "Do we have time for a quick look?" I quickly suggest, and at the far end of an empty, dusty attic is a dusty frame leaning against a dusty wall. We pull it back gently – there is Llew Llwyfo faded, dusty, lost.

Caernarfon has a good side, a cultural awareness. Portrait cleaned and restored, Llew Llwyfo now hangs in one of the committee rooms. But it gets better, Vernon remembered something else: Llew Llwyfo's crown from the 1895 Llanelli Eisteddfod is still kept in the Institute safe. It is brought out and photographed.

Christopher Williams's 'Deffroad Cymru' can also be found in the Institute. Williams is Wales's forgotten artist. He was War Artist for Lloyd George, and too nice and normal according to some – certainly when compared to his contemporaries Augustus John and J.D. Innes. Maybe Williams was 'normal' by comparison but his work deserves a re-appraisal. Art historian Peter Lord has done much to address this as has Robert Meyrick in his book *Christopher Williams '...an artist and nothing else'*.

Meanwhile, Williams's painting of Archdruid Hwfa Mon, dressed in druidic robes, long mane of white hair, held at the National Library of Wales collections is powerful indeed. Acknowledging on canvass the Welsh bardic tradition and lineage, Williams paints a man with authority. Hwfa Mon (real name Rowland Williams)'s day job was as an independent minister. Had Hwfa Mon been a Celtic period druid rather than a nineteenth century minister he would no doubt have resisted the Roman invasion of Anglesey in AD60. I imagine chapel services of fire and brimstone.

Another of Williams's powerful paintings is 'The Charge of the Welsh Division at Mametz Wood on 11th July 1916'. Blood splattered, mud covered, Welsh and German soldiers clamber over

each other, fall over each other, many to their deaths. Bayonets at
the ready. This is war at its most brutal. This is painting at its most
brutal. Brutal in its honesty. Once it hung at Caernarfon Castle but
is now held at the National Library.

Too much is obscured in Caernarfon. Tanybont, the local music
venue during late 1970s and early 1980s once stood on the site of
a present-day car park, just outside the east gate of the town walls.
This is a recurring theme. I have already mentioned that a car park
occupies the space where the Majestic nightclub once stood. For
years it has been a familiar story – venue lost to car park – not even
a multi-storey – just a plain ground floor car park. A new venue
always springs up somewhere else, becomes a cultural central
gathering point then goes out of fashion and is destined in time to
cultural oblivion as a car park.

On the subject of oblivion, Llew Llwyfo, our Victorian popstar
poster-boy is buried at Llanbeblig Church, in the old part of the
cemetery. The church is out on the Beddgelert Road, on the line of
the Roman road heading south out of Segontium, a quarter of a
mile from the Maes, the castle and the town centre, and uphill.

The older section of the cemetery is overgrown with Japanese
knotweed (*Polygonum cuspidatum*). 'Cwlwm cythraul' we say in
Welsh but I have also read 'canclwm Japan' and 'llysiau'r dial' being
used for this plant. A non-indigenous weed and growing tall like
bamboo – it is indeed the Devil's knot weed. In this part of the

cemetery, alongside the brambles and small trees it has created an otherworldly labyrinth of tunnels for the urban explorer.

So overgrown is the cemetery that graves can be difficult to find, but Post Office engineer and Marconi sponsor William Henry Preece[13] and sailing instructor Ellen Edwards[14] both lie here.

LLANRUG

Llanrug, four miles to the east of Caernarfon, boasts the highest percentage of Welsh speakers in Arfon at eighty-eight per cent. From a population of roughly 2900 that would make 2552 Welsh speakers, excluding babies. And as to the 'dysgwyr' currently learning – where do they fit in statistically? Each learner increases the number of Welsh speakers, Llanrug feels distinctly Welsh.

Llanfihangel yn Rug, the old, original name, became shortened to Llanrug with the passage of time. Not so much a corruption or a mutation but a linguistic evolution and shortening. There is no Saint Grug, as grug means heather. This place was the church of St Michael in the heather.

Llanrug is not alone in Gwynedd as a 'Llan' placename not dedicated to a saint. Usually 'Llan', meaning church, is associated with the patron saint. However, there are exceptions. Llanuwchllyn would be a good example, meaning the church at the top end of the lake. Just west of Caernarfon, Llanllyfni is the church on the river Llyfni. There are plenty more examples nationally – just think Llandaf, the Church on the Taf or Llanrheadr (Montgomeryshire's Llanrhaeadr-ym-Mochnant or Dyffryn Clwyd's Llanrhaeadr-yng-Nghinmeirch). Another example is Llantrisant, Rhondda Cynon Taf, (home of Dr William Price) referring to the three saints but not naming them. There is another Llantrisant in northern Anglesey.

The church of Sant Mihangel (St Michael) lies half a mile to the west of the village. It stands apart. Not the village centre. In some ways this is quite unusual, medieval villages tended to grow up around the church. Llanrug grew up along the Caernarfon to Llanberis road, its development boosted by the slate quarries of Dinorwic and Llanberis during the nineteenth century.

At the eastern end of Llanrug on the A4086 (Caernarfon to

Capel Curig road) just at the crossroads known locally as 'Groeslon Marc' stands the corrugated and rusty abandoned garage once belonging to J. Parry-Jones and subsequently his son Milwyn. Still called Garej Milwyn, three battered and silent petrol pumps stand guard on the minimal forecourt like old soldiers turned metallic scarecrows.

The pumps have seen better days but they are photogenic. It's comforting somehow to see old things still standing, still there. A link to the past. Not cleared or landscaped, not replaced or erased. Tyres are piled up high alongside the garage. Cars stand silent, flat-tyred, not moving or going on a road trip anywhere or anytime soon. Could be a scene in the mid-west of the USA but we are on the western edge of Snowdonia, Wales.

Another 'placename' anomaly occurs with the name of the river. The river Rhythallt (Rhuddallt) flows as the Rhythallt from Llyn Padarn but becomes the Seiont or Saint at Pont Rhythallt in Llanrug. The Seiont flows into the sea (the Menai Strait) near Caernarfon castle. At Caernarfon, the bridge Pont Saint crosses Afon Seiont – the debate rages on as to whether it's the Saint o'r Seiont. For the locals – its Seiont. No one seems to care that it started life as the Rhythallt.

PENYGROES

At the crossroads, the Victoria Hotel is boarded up. One of the boards is the recipient of 'Cofiwch Dryweryn' graffiti, a phenomenon that sprung up throughout Wales during the late Spring / early Summer of 2019 following the partial destruction and vandalism of the original 'Cofiwch Dryweryn' mural near Llanrhystud. One act of vandalism at the Llanrhystud site was to cover 'Cofiwch Dryweryn' with 'Elvis' – how very Rock'n Roll!

My visit on a Friday afternoon coincides with lunch being served for the elderly at Penygroes Memorial Hall. £6 for a three course meal. Tables laid out regimentally. Tableclothed. It's a chance for the retired to socialise and chat, to have some company. A sense of community prevails. I'd put my head round the door to see if it was suitable for my elderly father who lives at nearby Carmel up on Mynydd Cilgwyn. I never did persuade him despite the ladies' offer that I could join them on one of the tables.

On the outer western gable wall of the hall, the clock stands still at 4'o clock. From the ruined condition of the clock, it looks like it's been stuck at 4 o'clock for quite a few years. Time stands still here. Nothing about this hall shouts twenty-first century. I'm trying to figure out if this is an Art Deco façade? Easily could be as the War Memorial outside is for the Great War of 1914-1918. A memorial hall built in the 1920s would be of the right period for an Art Deco frontage. This is a building with faded charm. It could do with a coat of paint, some new stained glass in the arch windows below the clock and obviously repair the clock!

Above the doorway is a plaque commemorating the 1926 Peace March. Two thousand women marched for peace under the banner 'Women's Peace Pilgrimage' from this very spot. That's an impressive number and more impressive still is that this was fifty-five years before the Welsh-based 'Women For Life on Earth' marched from Cardiff to Greenham Common in 1981 and from Cardiff to RAF Brawdy, in Pembrokeshire, the following year.

The 'Women's Peace Pilgrimage' marched to London from the four corners of Britain. Pathé News footage show the Penygroes march passing the castle walls in Caernarfon. 2,000 ladies is more than the local population. According to the 2011 Census, the population of Penygroes was 1,793. The march was organised by a lady called Mary Silyn. Along with husband R. Silyn Roberts, a minister, crowned bard and one-time associate of Lenin, the husband and wife team were also responsible for setting up a north Wales branch of the Workers Education Association in 1925.

Yma y daeth 2,000 o ferched
ar y 27 Mai 1926
i gychwyn y
Bererindod Heddwch
dan y faner
"HEDD NID CLEDD"

This is almost a hidden history. A Peace March starting from Penygroes is not the first thing that comes to mind. Penygroes developed during the nineteenth century along with the development of the slate quarries at nearby Talysarn and Nantlle. The slate had to come out this way from the Nantlle Valley to the harbour at Caernarfon for export. Parts of the 1828 Nantlle Railway (or Tramway) can still be traced.

Built and designed by father and son George and Robert Stephenson, this was a horse drawn narrow gauge railway running from Pen-yr-Orsedd quarry at the eastern end through the Nantlle and Dorothea quarries onwards through Penygroes, and north towards Caernarfon. Between 1856 and 1865 the line operated as the first public railway in north Wales before substantial parts of the route were replaced by the Caernarfon to Afon Wen LNWR standard gauge mainline.

Notes

1. Menai Strait: a narrow stretch of shallow tidal water about 25 km long, which separates the island of Ynys Môn (Anglesey) from the mainland of Wales.

2. *Archwilio.org.uk* the online Historic Environment Record database for the four Welsh Archaeological Trusts. This is a resource that the public can use for free.
3. Pen-Rhiw Unitarian Chapel at St Fagans, National Museum of Wales. Opened in 1777, re-erected in 1956. Originally located at Dre-fach Felindre in Carmarthenshire.
4. Ty'n y Mwd also known as Pen y Mwd. PDF Excavation Reports by Johnstone and also Roberts can be found on *Archwilio* website under Motte, Pen y Mwd, Abergwyngregyn.
5. Offspring were a Bethesda based New Wave band formed by Les Morrison (full name Les Paul Morrison, named after the guitar) who released two singles, 'Doctors and Nurses' (1983) and 'One More Night' (1984) and on the Cottage Records and Offspring Promotions labels respectively. Lead vocals were provided by Hefin Hughes of Maffia Mr Huws.
6. Owain Tudur of Penmynydd was to secretly marry Katherine de Valois, widow of Henry V. Their grandson Henry Tudor became Henry VII, which is the Tudor link with Anglesey.
7. 'Cofi', plural 'Cofis', the nickname given to local people born and bred in Caernarfon. Sometimes known as 'Cofis Dre'. 'Dre' meaning Caernarfon.
8. Llandegai Industrial Estate excavation reports are listed on *Archwilio* under Henge, Cursus and Settlement, Llandegai.
9. Caradog Pritchard (1904-1980), Welsh author and journalist born in the slate quarrying town of Bethesda. He worked as a journalist in London for much of his life. Best known for his novel *Un Nos Ola Leuad,* translated into twelve different languages.
10. Peter Finch, Cardiff based poet, author, editor of the 'Real' Series.
11. John Barnard Jenkins, Cardiff born. During the 1960 Jenkins and Mudiad Amddiffyn Cymru (MAC) led the bombing campaign against the drowning of Capel Celyn and the Investiture of Prince Charles.
12. Gresford Disaster, 22 September 1934, 266 deaths following an underground explosion and fire at Gresford Colliery near Wrexham.
13. William Henry Preece (1834-1913) Electrical engineer and inventor born in Caernarfon. A commemorative plaque can be found on the Post Office wall at Y Maes, Caernarfon.
14. Ellen Edwards (1810-1899) Established a school of navigation in Caernarfon and over the course of 60 years trained over 1000 mariners.

SOUTH

HARLECH

We don't really have enough anarchy in the archaeological world. A lecture given by Andrew Davidson, Chief Archaeologist at Gwynedd Archaeological Trust, titled *'Anarchists and Artists: Their impact on the architecture of Harlech in the early 20th century'* alerted me to the possibility that there may be more to Harlech than Edward I's castle and the medieval town. Of course there is! but the word 'anarchist' in the title of Andrew's talk was enough to spark further interest. Who were these anarchists and artists? Why is this story not better known outside the various circles of Harlech's local historians? Why have I not heard of all this stuff before? This set me thinking about bigger questions and concepts.

Indeed, something else was thrown up from this. There is a hidden history of anarchy, art, culture, photography, Arts & Craft architecture, bohemianism, happenings and gatherings in Harlech at the turn of the twentieth century, but it has little if any 'Welshness' about it. A parallel history. A parallel universe. Native versus Incomer. It is out of character, alien, introduced. Introduced to Non-Conformist Welsh-speaking Ardudwy. I can only imagine what the chapel-goers, must have made of it all.

This is what interests me most, this editing or selective hearing/viewing of Welsh History. Anything that is not particularly Welsh in character, especially in terms of the language, is ignored or overlooked, dismissed as non-Welsh and therefore of no interest. By-passed. One only has to think of the difficult relationship that Welsh speakers often have with Dylan Thomas. Thomas accused by some of being anti-Welsh, dismissive of y Gymraeg, is consequently far too often whitewashed out of the cultural landscape or left for others to deal with in the 'Anglo-Welsh' section.

John Cale, a Welshman who has not worn his Cymreictod prominently enough (for some), is another case in point. Cale from Garnant near Ammanford is a Welsh speaker but his crime was to pack his bags, leave, join the Velvet Underground and spend more time in New York than in Garnant. Not that there is any real antipathy towards Cale that I have ever come across, more a cultural apathy towards his obvious cultural significance and influence. Within Welsh Rock'n Roll circles however there is a humorous suggestion bandied around that Cale is the coolest Welsh speaker of all time. An invite for Cale to join the Gorsedd[1] would put this debate to rest once and for all.

Harlech in the early years of the twentieth century was a hotbed of culture and happening but not really dealt with properly in terms of Welsh History until Andrew Davidson's research, certainly not nationally. Certainly not dealt with at all 'yn y Gymraeg' – none of them spoke Welsh, so what interest could it possibly have to Welsh speakers? This is good stuff – let's deal with it now!

The central character in this story is George Davison, photographer and millionaire, anarchist / socialist sympathiser. He'd made his millions investing in Eastman Kodak[2], indeed he had worked as general manager for Kodak UK but his support for social reform brought him into conflict with Eastman. Can't have the general manager hanging out with anarchists. Davison moved to Harlech, firstly to Plas Amherst and then he had Plas Wernfawr built for him in an Arts & Crafts style with classical façade.

Built of blocks of local grey stone and designed by radical Scottish architect George Walton,[3] Plas Wernfawr is a Grade II Listed Building. It was later to become Coleg Harlech, the 'Second-Chance' College, established by Thomas Jones[4] (aka T.J.) in 1927 to educate workers who had missed out on formal education first time round. A noble aim. The Workers Education Association known to all as the WEA not only ran courses at Coleg Harlech but just as importantly ran courses out in the community.

As a young and newly qualified teacher and having just finished a stint working as an archaeologist for Clwyd Powys Archaeological Trust in the mid-1980s, I was to run a WEA archaeology class at Trefeglwys near Caersws, Montgomeryshire. In more recent years I was to tutor archaeology classes / courses at Abersoch, Bryncroes, Golan and Brynsiencyn for the WEA. I was also involved with WEA mentoring and confidence building workshops at Caernarfon, Dolgellau and Pwllheli for single mums, the longer term unemployed and members of the community with various learning difficulties. It was indeed a privilege to be part of the WEA team. I always enjoyed our get-together days when we were reminded of the socialist roots of the WEA. I would just substitute 'anarchist' for 'socialist'.

During the early Coleg Harlech days in the 1930s, artist Robert Baker was to paint a series of murals in one of the west-facing rooms. Depicting scenes of both rural and industrial Wales we catch glimpses of both coalminers and slate quarrymen at work. North and South. Baker paints Gorsedd y Beirdd, robed, white, green and blue with seated accompanist on harp. An agricultural scene balances the landscape. Valleys are sharpened, peaks stretched high, crags accentuated, rivers froth in an almost J.M.W. Turner-like exaggeration. Wonderful. But since the closure of Coleg Harlech in 2017 and the turning off of the heating the plasterwork has begun to bubble and flake from the dampness.

Despite being a Grade II Listed Building, Baker's masterpiece is slowly but most surely deteriorating. I was there in 2018 during a guided walk with Andrew Davidson. It was a sad thing to see and a real sense of powerlessness that the mural crumbles and seemingly nothing can be done about it.

Nearby St David's Hotel is also falling into disrepair, beyond repair and no chance now that it will ever be a top-notch hotel for all the golfers descending on Harlech unless its bulldozed and a new one built. Harlech is well known for its golf course. For Harlech to compete on an international level a locally situated 'high end' hotel is an essential component of the package. Looking over the security fence, with multiple keep out warnings, at the broken windows, the flaking paint, the small trees growing from the chimney pots and the overgrown car park, this is a sad image of shattered dreams.

During the mid/late 1980s the basement bar of the St David's was a music venue for Welsh bands. Llanrwst-based Y Cyrff played here (featuring guitarist and singer Mark Roberts and bassist Paul Jones later of Catatonia fame), I'm pretty sure Cardigan's finest and John Peel favourites, electro-minimalists Datblygu played here, as did my own band Anhrefn. Promoter Gorwel Roberts (guitarist with Camelod Fflat and later of folk band Bob Delyn with poet Twm Morys) reminded me that Plant Bach Ofnus (electro), Elfyn Presli (punk), Steve Eaves (blues) and Gwrtheyrn (blues) also performed here.

Handmade posters were the order of the day. Discount for the unemployed who showed their UB40 card. That was a common consideration at gigs in the 1980s. Unemployment was political and very real. Most of the small number in the audience must have been unemployed, students or plain unemployable. UB40 card and admittance for a quid.

George Davison's circle of friends were also to contribute to the transformation of the cultural landscape of early twentieth century Harlech. Architecturally this is still visible today. The clues are there to be found on closer inspection. In many ways the buildings have outlasted the ideas. The anarchists and artists created and then passed on. There is nothing remotely anarchic about present day Harlech.

'Alvin Langdon Coburn Photographer (1882-1966) Lived Here'. A small blue plaque on the lawn of Bryn Bugeilydd just south of the town centre confirms the fact. The B4537 that passes through the centre of Harlech starts off as Stryd Fawr (High Street) and just beyond the centre of town becomes Ffordd Isaf (lower road). Ffordd Uchaf, (top road) runs parallel about half a mile up the hill and runs south towards Llanfair. The coastal road that passes the school, the railway, Theatr Harlech, Plas Wernfawr and the St David's Hotel is the new road 'Ffordd Newydd', the Harlech by-pass in effect.

Coburn also lived at Cae Besi, just on the junction of Ffordd Newydd and Ffordd Isaf. Visiting Harlech for the first time in 1916 at the invitation of George Davison, Coburn was to settle here, join the circle of friends and have Cae Besi built for him sometime after 1918, possibly by local architect Moses Griffith but certainly in an Arts and Crafts style.

Born in Boston, Massachusetts and buried at Rhos-on-Sea, north Wales. Coburn spent some twenty-nine years at Harlech with Davison and his circle of friends. Almost half his adult life. His final days were lived out near Conwy. Best remembered as a pioneer of abstract photography and the use of elevated positions or viewpoints for landscape photographs Coburn was increasingly drawn towards mysticism, Druidism and Freemasonry. Following these new interests, he was to turn his back on photography, destroying many of his original glass negatives in the summer of 1930. This could be interpreted as an iconoclastic act of rejection of his past activities. Coburn was made an Honorary Ovate of the Gorsedd in 1927.

His acceptance to the Gorsedd in itself is quite interesting. Maybe I'm being a bit harsh on the Welsh establishment's lack of acknowledgement for these Harlech anarcho-artistic-maverick incomers. This creative bohemian community is so out of place it borders on genius (or the bizarre). It may well be that it's only by reading the buildings, specifically the Arts and Crafts architecture, that one gets any hint today that something else was going on in early twentieth century Harlech. If you didn't know you wouldn't know. Architectural clues suggesting artists and anarchists at work. I see no other present-day evidence or any tangible cultural legacy beyond the buildings.

Wandering the streets of Harlech, a persistent thought is that all this seems to be too much of a hidden history. This is all far too interesting to be lost in the Celtic mist of Ceredigion Bay. There's probably a book to be written here. Imaginary titles such as The Hidden History of Harlech. Hidden Harlech more to the point. As a basic introduction, Andrew Davidson's archaeological assessment report on Coleg Harlech (2018) is a good starting point. This is readily available as a PDF online. Many of these characters are also covered in the 2015 publication *100 Facts about Harlech* written and compiled by the local branch of the Women's Institute.

Druidism and the Celtic twilight come to the fore with another central character in Harlech society. Alfred Percival Graves (1846-1931) is buried in the churchyard. A writer and a collector of Celtic songs, Graves was born in Dublin and lived at Harlech from 1899 onwards. Graves would have looked westwards over the sea towards his place of birth. Harlech would have been 'Celtic' enough for Graves. Alfred was the father of Robert Graves, poet, critic, classicist and author of books such as *Goodbye to All That* (1929) and *The White Goddess* (1948).

Harlech gets a mention too in Martin Scorsese's film *Living in the Material World* (2011) about the life of George Harrison. Pre-Beatles and pre-fame, teenage friends George and Paul (McCartney) holidayed at Harlech in 1956/57, guitars and sleeping bags on their backs hitch-hiking into town – or so the story goes. I've heard different versions.

An accepted tale is that young Liverpudlians jammed with a local band called The Vikings. The Vikings were Bernard Lee, John Brierley, Aneurin Thomas and Glyn 'Gwndwo' Williams. Bernard has confirmed that the two young Liverpudlians did guest with The Viking Skiffle Band on stage at the Queens Hotel in 1958.

ROMAN STEPS

One of the more dramatic and more remote walks in Snowdonia is up the so-called Roman Steps from Cwm Bychan[5] over the pass below the very wild and very rugged Rhinog Fawr. But they are not Roman at all. It was very common at one time (the nineteenth century) to describe all sorts of things as being 'Roman', Roman bridges, Roman roads. All this before we actually knew what they really were. According to *Archwilio* the steps are most likely of medieval date used by drovers or merchants. This would have been a route from the west coast along Cwm Bychan and then Bwlch Tyddiad before heading east along the course of the Crawcwellt river towards Trawsfynydd and Bronaber. From here it's only a short distance south to the market town of Dolgellau.

Roman or not, the steps in places are pretty dramatic, occasionally disappearing beneath the peat, but mostly there, solid underfoot. As a walk along the northern edge of Rhinog Fawr this is a good one. The pass at the top is known as Bwlch Tyddiad. I have asked many an authority on Welsh place names about the meaning of *Tyddiad*. Dr Rhian Price of Cymdeithas Enwau Lleoedd Cymru (the Welsh Place Name Society), managed to track down a possible explanation from Hywel Wyn Owen who suggested that 'tyddiad' may be derived from tyddfiad meaning a jutting or projection. Does part of craggy Rhinog Fawr jut out at the pass? A pass is a pass, in between higher mountains. I can't really see the pass as something that projects outwards. The name does not seem to appear in use much before the first decades of the nineteenth century. Not conclusive therefore. Maybe it's nice to have a bit of mystery as to the origin of the name'.

From the pass at Bwlch Tyddiad the ascent up Rhinog Fawr past Llyn Du involves meandering past boulders and diverting away from the Roman Steps. Not so easy from now on. Following tracks that are more akin to sheep tracks than the kind of manicured and maintained paths that you see in mainstream Snowdonia and on Snowdon specifically. No trainers here. Not many ramblers either. Summiting Rhinog Fawr with no other hikers present is a pleasure indeed. Remote and wonderfully so. Views in all directions, westwards over the sea, towards Rhinog Fach to the south, eastwards towards the A470 and back towards more 'accessible' Snowdonia National Park to the north.

Consult Hopewell, D., *Roman Roads in North-West Wales* if you are in any doubt or still cling on to a remote hope that the Romans were here.

CAPEL SALEM

At one time I imagine every other Welsh household had a copy of Sidney Curnow Vosper's 'Salem' painting hanging proud in their living room. Our family did not and this was something I rectified recently. It cost me £40 in an antiques shop in Penmaenmawr, battered gold frame, faded, measuring 40x48cm. It now hangs proudly in my living room at home in Caernarfon. Kitsch value alone it was worth the £40. As a talking point, a conversational tool it's priceless.

Salem (built 1850 and extended 1860) is the Baptist chapel at Cefncymerau, Llanbedr near Harlech. The chapel building has the feel of time and memories hanging on, lingering in mid-air. Quiet. Secluded. Wooded. The road past Salem leads up Cwm Nantcol and ends at Maes y Garnedd, home of Col. John Jones one of the signatories of Charles I's death warrant. Salem is a place for quiet contemplation (or a picnic). 'Quiet' is something that's getting increasingly hard to find – even in our mainly 'rural' Gwynedd.

Vosper's picture was used to advertise soap (rather successfully) by entrepreneur Lord Leverhulme, making it one of the better known pieces of art alongside the Mona Lisa, even by people who don't like or don't 'do' art. Careful examination of central character Siân Owen's traditional Welsh costume reveals a side profile of the Devil's face on her shawl – long beard, narrow mouth, narrow eyes – evil and threatening.

Today the original Salem watercolour hangs behind a small curtain for protection against sunlight at the Lady Lever Art Gallery at Port Sunlight on the Wirral. This is a pilgrimage for many a Welsh art lover, a stop off before the Mersey Tunnel and a day out shopping in Liverpool. Sadly, many of the Welsh art fellow travellers are on a 'Salem mission' and don't allow enough time to appreciate the Pre-Raphaelite collection at Lady Lever.

Edward Burne-Jones's 'The Beguiling of Merlin' (1872-7), Dante Gabriel Rosetti's 'The Blessed Damozel' (1875-9), Ford Madox Brown's 'Cromwell on his farm' (1873-4), William Holman-Hunt's 'The Scapegoat' (1854) and John Everett Millais's 'Spring (Apple Blossoms)' (1859) all hang here. You can do both. Do Salem for sure. But definitely do some Pre-Raphaelites. Let the shopping wait awhile. Make time.

Sidney Curnow Vosper (1866-1942) married Constance James from Merthyr Tydfil. There are further Vosper works on display at Cyfarthfa Castle, including a second, slightly different version of

Salem – as verified by art historian Peter Lord.

I mentioned that Capel Salem has the air of the past hanging on. The interior is largely unchanged since the time of Vosper's painting. To be honest if Siân Owen, the central character of the artwork, was to pop up from behind one of the pews I don't think anybody would be that surprised. You almost expect Edwardian / Victorian costumes here on a Sunday. A battered print of Salem hangs on the north wall of the chapel. Maybe it hangs there to confirm – yes this is the right place – this is the chapel where Siân and other locals modelled for Vosper for a princely sum of 6d each.

Siân Owen is often referred to as 'Siân Tyn-y-fawnog' because she ended up living in Tyn-y-fawnog, but she was actually born at Maes-y-Garnedd. She was brought in by Vosper as a model and paid to pose. Interestingly, she was not even a member of this congregation. She must have suited Vosper's vision. There is fakery and trickery to Vosper's masterpiece.

Does the Devil in the shawl represent Siân's vanity? And what about the clock at almost ten? Siân is late for 'oedfa'r bore', late for service, deliberately so perhaps in her posh shawl just to draw attention to herself. The other 'characters' in Salem are also real people, real local characters; we have Robert Williams (deacon), Laura Williams, Ty'n y Buarth, and Owen Sion, Garleg Goch. But none of the others flaunt their fashion.

On one of my many visits to the Lady Lever Art Gallery one of the custodians asked if I'd ever seen the 'cherub' in the window? Indeed, if you look carefully – lower right pane – there is a green unearthly face – two eyes and a mouth just peeking in through the window, just behind the curtain. Of course, this could be accidental. Just tree leaves outside the chapel. Our possible cherub looks a bit like the character from Edvard Munch, 'The Scream' (1893) – but in green. My two boys spotted it immediately, as kids do. There is not much discussion about the little green cherub in the window. Siân and the Devil shawl get all the attention – but once seen it does make you wonder. Was Vosper playing with us?

Y BERMO (ABERMAW /BARMOUTH)

Y Bermo (Barmouth) owes its origins to shipbuilding on the mouth of the River Mawddach but it's as a Victorian seaside resort that the town really developed. With the coming of the railway in the 1860s, the tourists flocked here to 'take the air'. Pwllheli becomes connected to Aberystwyth via the Aberystwyth and Welsh Coast Railway. A spectacular railway bridge crosses the River Mawddach. Bermo is in business. The west coast and Cardigan Bay accessible.

Poet William Wordsworth described Barmouth during a visit in 1824 thus "With a fine sea view in front, the mountains behind, the glorious estuary running eight miles inland, and Cader Idris within compass of a day's walk, Barmouth can always hold its own against any rival." His words were inspired by the views from a boat trip along the Mawddach.

I have arrived early in Bermo on a cold but dry morning in February, with the intention of finding a free parking space somewhere on the edge of town and then grabbing a breakfast before beginning my wanderings. I have left home without eating, driven for just under an hour and find a space for the car near the football ground. No parking meter, no time limit, I'm free to relax and walk.

It's still before 10am. Most of the cafés are shut – for the winter, rather than just late opening on a cold February morning. Mind you, most of the other shops here seem to be opening the curtains just as the tenth hour approaches. I end up in the only open café I can find, the Milk Bar. As children in the 1960s, National Milk Bars were a treat on Saturday shopping days. As I sit down and order tea and a fried egg butty there's just a hint of nostalgia in the whole experience. They don't change much do they, Milk Bars? You could film a 1960s style pop video in here without the need for props – no one would notice the difference, just go B&W and polka dot.

Milk Bar refreshed I'm heading out for Dinas Oleu. The internet (advance research) suggested that it was well signposted from the centre of town but I don't spot any of the signs. No problem. I follow my nose and walk up the very steep Dinas Oleu road. Soon I'm looking down on Bermo, the narrow strip of development each side of High Street. Clearly in view is the local theatre, Theatr y Ddraig. Below me is the roof and tower of the magnificent, imposing and dominating Victorian splendour of St John's Church[6]. Over and beyond the dunes, Fairbourne and Y Friog to the south, the Irish Sea in front and to the west, Llŷn on the distant horizon.

Dinas Oleu was the first area of land donated to the National

Trust[7] and in that sense it is an important piece of history. It's just one hell of a climb up there but absolutely, no cliché intended, the views are stunning. The word 'dinas' is often associated with an Iron Age fort or settlement and a quick search of online archaeological database Archwilio suggests that there may have been an enclosure or defensive stonework around the actual crest of Dinas Oleu itself.

The footpath allows for a circular walk around the hill, but does not lead directly to the 'possible hillfort'. It took me an hour's brisk walking to do the circuit. My feet got very wet in places, and once away from the cliff edge overlooking Bermo, we are really in the uplands. Heading north, east, south and finally back west the circular walk is completed with the vista of the railway bridge and the Mawddach estuary before Bermo comes back into view.

Most of my hour wandering was spent imagining the story behind the 'Frenchman's Grave' which is up here on the side of the hill. I will not reach the spot of the grave until the end of my walk going in this direction – plenty of time for imaginary stories. Ship building, sailing, coast and more ships, I thought shipwreck most likely. Just as the circuit around Dinas Oleu completes I pass the wooden gate 'Frenchman's Grave Only' – this is literally a dead end. Paved in stone the path leads us tantalisingly downhill and at each turn I'm thinking is this it? A few twists and turns later, the final gate, some steps and a narrow dry-stone walled enclosure that leads to the cliff edge. Bare rock exposed in places but I see no 'grave'.

Slightly disappointed I read the small plaque on the north wall. My theories of shipwrecks and finding true love in Bermo with a local Welsh girl were way off the mark. The Frenchman was a sower.

> Here lodged a sower who,
> To his grave, sowed the seeds,
> Of truth, of right, of beauty,
> With obsession.
> In a thousand struggles,
> With pen and body,
> Such labours are not rewarded,
> In this world.

There is a touch of 'glamour' to our story I later discover, and that is not to say there is no glamour in hillside terrace gardening, but the Frenchman Auguste Guyard settled here in 1871 after fleeing the siege of Paris during the Franco-Prussian War. Guyard spent the rest of his life planting herbs, flowers and vegetables on these steep slopes to the east of Barmouth. His wish to be buried here, high on the slopes, were fulfilled – it's just that I can't see a grave or gravestone and given the proximity of the bedrock to the surface one is left wondering how they managed a burial at such a spot?

As little adventures go, this is a worthwhile trek. Maybe there is no actual grave but there is plenty of scope for imagination. 'The Frenchman' was here. Planting flowers. I retrace my steps downhill and back into town. After the giddy heights of Dinas Oleu downtown Bermo, sea level, definitely feels a bit more terra firma. Time for a cup of tea, but the reading room at the Sailor's Institute is closed, I would have gone in and gathered my thoughts and notes, just for the experience of sitting inside the wonderful tin-shed building.

With the coming of the railways, Barmouth's importance as a maritime town was in decline. Seamen sought work on deep sea ships sailing out of the larger ports like Liverpool, Hull and Cardiff while the families remained at home. Sailor's Institutes came into being as places where the family could access the *Lloyds List and Shipping Gazette* and thereby track the voyage of ships. A billiard room provided for some entertainment and relaxation. Barmouth's Sailing Institute was set up in 1890 by Canon Edward Hughes, the Rector of Barmouth, for the benefit of the local maritime community. No doubt the Rector was also concerned about their spiritual wellbeing of his maritime flock.

Restored and open to the public, the Institute still offers the service of a 'Reading Room' daily between 9am and 6pm. I've just timed things a bit wrong in February. I keep on the move.

Around the corner from the Sailor's Institute is Ty Crwn, the nineteenth century lock up. Diplomatically the notice hints there was bad behaviour occurring but it's worded so as not to cause too much offence to the good people of Barmouth. The disorderly were detained until sober. Acknowledging the fact that Barmouth was a seaport, the notice board suggests that some seafarers and some locals, male and female, did not always conduct themselves in the manner expected. Half the round lockup was given to hold the ladies and the other half the men – they misbehaved equally one assumes in nineteenth century Barmouth.

"Barmouth in the 18th and early 19th century was a flourishing seaport, used by foreign as well as British ships. It is therefore safe to assume that at times that there were elements in the town whose conduct was not all that it could be."

FRIOG AND FAIRBOURNE

Friog and Fairbourne are not the same place. I have proof. There are two place name signs. Agreed they are very, very close. Literally a stone's throw, but the two signs make the case. The scatter of houses along the A493, that's Friog. Situated between Arthog and Llwyngwril opposite the Fairbourne junction, if it qualifies as a village, then it's definitely a 'small village'. Slate was quarried at the nearby quarries of Henddol, Goleuwen and Cyfanedd Fawr[8]. The 'small village' of Friog developed along with the nineteenth century quarries providing homes for some of the quarrymen.

There is a dis-used garage on the junction, not much else. 'Friog' probably means 'tir uchel' (higher land), at least that's the suggestion by the University of Wales dictionary, but this explanation is qualified with a question mark. Far too many Welsh speakers claim that Friog is the Welsh for Fairbourne. This is not the case.

Just off the A493, follow Beach Road and we arrive at Fairbourne. This place is of a totally different construct to its neighbour. Established in the early twentieth century as a seaside resort by Arthur McDougall of flour-making fame, or rather self-raising flour fame to be precise. There is nothing old about Fairbourne. St Cynon's church dates to 1926-27. The brickworks and tramway that McDougall developed in order to build

Fairbourne date to the 1890s. Traces of the brickworks and tramway remain in some of the fields near the railway line. Fairbourne is firmly twentieth century.

Built on the costal lands south of Barmouth and the Mawddach Estuary on land once known as Morfa Henddol just to the west of the rocky outcrop known as Ynys-y-Bugail. I have also heard that Rowen or Ro'wen was the Welsh name for the area where Fairbourne was built. There is a street named Heol Rowen just off Beach Road – that may be a clue.

At the time of building it was McDougall who came up with the name 'Fairbourne', some had suggested South Barmouth while the locals suggested Ynys Faig after a local farm. McDougall wielded the most clout. Fairbourne it was to be.

Some of the best-preserved World War II defences in Wales are to be found on the beach. As the threat of German invasion from Ireland during 1940-41 loomed on the horizon, several hundred concrete anti-tank blocks, known as dragon's teeth, were built along the shingle beach. It was too much effort to remove them after the war and they still stand here in magnificent glory today. One of the pillboxes has also survived while another was destroyed by recent storms. Local graffiti artists have forced Cadw to block off the pillbox entrance for safe keeping. It may not have seen action against invading forces but the graffiti artists have managed to get it blocked off.

Gwynedd Council regard Fairbourne as a location of managed retreat. Global warming and climate change will eventually lead to Fairbourne joining Cantre'r Gwaelod[9] under the sea. No amount of dragon's teeth can stop the waves. Fairbourne may not last that long. It's a strange thought, but buying a house here I guess you need to calculate how long you've got until the battle is lost?

Fairbourne Railway is a legacy of the Edwardian vision. Tourism always the aim, and the narrow-gauge miniature railway that runs along the beach towards the end of the peninsula, provides today's tourists with a tangible thing to do. One for the tick list if the dragon's teeth don't rock your boat. Originally, the line was used to transport material for the building of Fairbourne. Like the rest of Fairbourne, the railway is on borrowed time.

I've never taken a ride on the railway. It looks too much like a kiddie's railway. Adults bulge from the seats and tower above the locomotive. Far too embarrassing for a punk rocker. If I was going to do it, then I should have taken advantage when my kids were younger. Maybe I could have justified a ride as part of my research for the book. The World War II dragon teeth win every time I visit Fairbourne.

TYWYN

Approaching Tywyn from the east, as one travels along the A493 Dolgellau road, the large square tower of St Cadfan's Church dominates the view above the rooflines. Tywyn is on the coast, almost invisible from a distance, and the tower is the first feature that stands out on this flat land.

Dating to the twelfth century the nave is the oldest part of the church, which probably stands on earlier Christian 'clas' foundations – hence the Sant Cadfan associations. Most stone churches that we see in the landscape today have Norman or medieval origins. Not all of course, some may be as recent as the nineteenth or even the twentieth century but generally speaking stone-built churches tend to date from the Norman period onwards. The Welsh, Celtic and sometimes Irish saints associated with churches belong to the Early Christian Period, around the fifth and sixth centuries. It is around this time that native Celtic Christian sites are established and probably had a wooden building

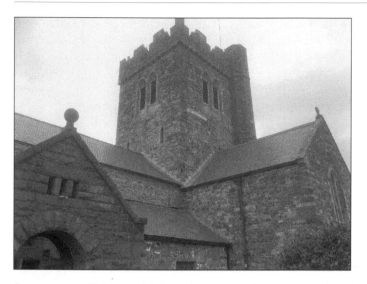

for prayer. This would be what we refer to as a 'clas', an early Christian establishment as opposed to the later Norman churches which may well occupy the same site.

The tower is modern (1884) and solid. Cadfan, a Breton, was the first abbot of Bardsey (Enlli) in the sixth century and also established a church at Llangadfan in northern Montgomeryshire. As 'Welsh' saints go he's one of the main dudes, up there with Dewi Sant and Illtud. Establishing the monastery on Enlli around 516AD (see West) secures Cadfan's place in history. 20,000 saints. Boat trip across Swnt Enlli. Cadfan cannot be ignored.

However, Cadfan is not commemorated on the Early Christian memorial to be found within the church. Although the stone is sometimes referred to as 'Cadfan's Stone', it dates to at least a century later than Cadfan's time. The inscriptions however are important. Academics have argued about the interpretation. New interpretations are offered. In reality few people are even aware of the stone.

Eminent archaeologist Frances Lynch describes the memorial now standing in the north aisle of St Cadfan's church as a 'vitally important stone'. This may well be the earliest inscription in Welsh that we know of, and dates to sometime in the period seventh to ninth century. The inscriptions on the narrow, rough pillar of volcanic tuff are almost impossible to read and there are two differing historical interpretations by academics Sir John Morris-Jones and Sir Ifor Williams.

Inscriptions are to be seen on all four sides of the pillar stone and record the names of *Cingen* (the body of Cingen) on the right-hand side according to Morris-Jones and *Ceinrwy wife of Gwaddian* on the front according to Williams. Both the front and right-hand side have rough crosses pecked into the surface. Williams however interprets the right-hand side inscription as *Cun wife of Celyn.* Other names featured may be lineages or family connections, *Egryn, Mallten,* and the aforementioned *Gwaddian* appear. Egryn for example could be the patron saint of nearby Llanegryn. Williams has suggested that the stone commemorates the *memorial of four* based on the inscriptions at the bottom of the rear of the memorial.

The interpretation debate will no doubt continue to rage, change and evolve within academia – the rest of us will simply struggle to read any of the inscriptions. Looking closely at the mottled surface, I'm reminded of the spotted dolerite found in Pembrokeshire and often used for Early Christian and Ogham gravestones during the fifth and sixth centuries. The Ogham script was an early Irish alphabet and the fact that there are so many Ogham stones in the south west of Wales, especially Pembrokeshire, suggests Irish migration in the post Roman / Early Medieval period. The only known Ogham stone in Gwynedd is at Llystyn Gwyn, Bryncir, (page 175).

Whoever is commemorated, what is not debatable is that this is an early example of Old Welsh and this is based on the fact that the inscribed names do not have genitive case endings, thus Cingen is not recorded as CUNOGENI as would be usual in the British / Latin variant. Sometime around this point in history the Welsh language develops and evolves from its British and Latin form.

Standing next to the Early Christian stone is a sundial made of the same volcanic tuff. Although the sundial is of a more recent date one has to ask whether there is any significance to the use of this particular stone? Rocks that naturally form 'pillars' are often chosen for use as memorials or gravestones. But the Tywyn volcanic tuffs make any inscriptions difficult to read. A smoother pillar stone would be more suitable. Why use a stone with an uneven or mottled surface?

This is the irony of the 'Cadfan Stone'. It's the first recognised or acknowledged Welsh inscription in Gwynedd but it's difficult to read or make out. We have to take the academics' word that it is Old Welsh. Even the pecking of the inscription is crude. A drawing of the inscription provided in the church helps or a copy of Frances Lynch's book Gwynedd. Otherwise, you'd never really figure out the inscription.

Much of Tywyn is nineteenth century Victorian seaside development attributed to Worcestershire industrialist John Corbett[10], 'the Salt King'. Corbett wanted a Torquay for the Cardigan coast. Tywyn never quite matched this but the High Street and Promenade retain that Victorian seaside feel. The promenade development cost £30,000, a pier was built and promptly fell. Corbett's grand vision was thwarted. Only Pier Road leading from town to the seafront gives us a clue that the pier once existed.

At the southern end of the promenade fish and chips are on sale at the Golden Sands. A caravan park hugs the coast to the south of Tywyn and is bounded by the culverted Afon Dyffryn Gwyn which flows into the sea via a sluice gate. Despite improvements to the promenade it's difficult to avoid the conclusion that Tywyn will never quite be Torquay. There's not much to do here on the promenade. Maybe it's a good thing.

Corbett provided funding for the Assembly Rooms (1893), later Tywyn Cinema. Recently renamed, given a coat of paint and relaunched as Magic Lantern, the cinema and arts space is run by a small group of enthusiasts. I attended a spoken word gig by DJ and broadcaster Andy Kershaw here. A full house at the Magic

Lantern. Kershaw was superb, a live-wire, energetic, no-pause 100mph raconteur who told stories of his travels on the African continent as a war correspondent. Tales of Tuareg and Mali musicians were interspersed with songs played over the PA. A spoken word / DJ set on speed.

I'd met Kershaw several years ago on the BBC 2 music show, *The Old Grey Whistle Test*, with my band Anhrefn. At Tywyn we caught up at the Salt Marsh Kitchen, a small café opposite the Magic Lantern. Meal and chat before the gig. Kershaw kept talking. Non-stop. I was worried he'd be exhausted before hitting the stage. Or get indigestion. He does not stop. His is autobiography is appropriately titled *No Off Switch*.

A recurring theme in this book is lost venues, or car parks on the sites of demolished buildings. Tywyn does not contribute to this narrative. At the time of writing the Magic Lantern is alive and kicking. A refreshing story, like Neuadd Ogwen in Bethesdsa, Tŷ Siamas in Dolgellau and Theatr y Ddraig, Barmouth. Family films probably pay the bills while live music events just about break-even if lucky. Without venues and live music, these areas could easily become cultural deserts.

CWM MAETHLON

Place names are another recurring theme in this book. Wonderfully named in Welsh, Cwm Maethlon is rather insulted in English as Happy Valley. Sounds like a caravan park. Maethlon, meaning 'nutritious' in the sense that this is a rich, fertile valley which has been farmed over the centuries. This is a perfect example where the English name does no justice to the original Welsh.

Another recurring theme of this book are detours and Cwm Maethlon provides a wonderfully wild, remote and narrow lane escape from the coastal A493 between Tywyn and Cwrt. Recognised as a potential route for invading Germans during World War II, the pass at the highest point of the valley is defended by anti-tank walls. An unexpected location for Second World War defences perhaps, or testament to the thoroughness of the local Home Guard.

On the eastern side of Cwm Maethlon, a mountain track leads up to the Bronze Age cairn circle known as Eglwys y Gwyddelod

(SH 662 001). Carefully positioned alongside an even more ancient track through these hills, the cairn circle is built on a small platform with maximum visual effect as one climbs up the slope. A similar effect can be seen at Bryn Cader Faner near Talsarnau (SH 648 353) where the cairn is not actually on the crest of the hill but is obviously positioned for maximum visual drama on approach. Aspect has been taken into consideration by our Bronze Age forefathers. Monuments were placed within the landscape with positioning and visual effect prominent in their planning. Upright stones give the impression of a crown.

ABERDYFI

Aberdyfi is at the southern tip of Gwynedd, the last town before we enter Powys. South of Aberdyfi the main road hugs the Dyfi Estuary – this is quite a spectacular route. Winding road, wide estuary. A dramatic drive, before heading inland and re-joining the Dyfi at the bridge just north of Machynlleth. This is the border between Gwynedd and Powys.

Wales is at its narrowest east to west at Aberdyfi. Sometimes described as a 'wasp waist' and along with the fact that the Dyfi estuary is pretty well mid-way between north and south on the Cardigan coast, the port here has always been important for its geographical location. Industries including copper, silver, slate and timber as well as ship-building once gave the port life with both imports for local consumption and exports fulfilling essential economic roles for the surrounding area.

Industry and shipping have long given way to tourism. As with many Gwynedd towns, the coming of the railway transformed things. Nineteenth century houses in bright pink, blues and pastel colours, B&Bs, hotels, cafés and bars line up in east west rows, neatly parallel to the railway. Cafés and tearooms invite the sea front strollers in for afternoon tea. Sea air, gentle walks and Welsh Cakes.

In all my years working within the music scene in Wales, I've never promoted a gig at Aberdyfi, never trodden the boards of any Aberdyfi stage or attended a gig in any shape or form here. Could this be the least Rock'n Roll place in Gwynedd?

CORRIS

CAT, the Centre For Alternative Technology, may seem like an unlikely setting as a location for S4C's Welsh version of *Question Time, Pawb a'i Farn*. I have sat on the panel alongside Welsh politicians several times over the years. Invited to voice an alternative viewpoint to the party line-toeing politicians, I have always enjoyed the thrill of an invited audience and the chance to spout some anarcho-punk theories on live TV.

Pawb a'i Farn is filmed at different locations around Wales. We are at CAT during winter-time and the chance to wander around the site is lost as it's around 6pm when I arrive for makeup, sandwiches and a chance to shake hands and exchange niceties with the other guests.

This would have been my most recent visit to CAT. We would often stop here with the family when the boys were young on one of those long north south hauls. CAT always seemed like a suitable place to use the café and let the kids out of the car. As you'd expect from young boys, they were fascinated with the compost toilets.

Established on an abandoned quarry site in the 1970s CAT was set up with noble aims. At that time 'alternative' meant 'hippy'. Growing concerns about the environmental impact of fossil fuels and questions of longer-term sustainability had instigated a worldwide process of re-thinking and re-appraisal. Eco-activism had taken root and was about to bloom.

During our youth in neighbouring Montgomeryshire, CAT visits always seemed to be about composting the land with human manure and using windmills for power. Things have evolved, developed and moved on. Climate change is real. We are all concerned, Welsh included. Since many, many years, this is no longer the preserve of Beetle-driving, tepee-dwelling incomer English hippies. Still, there is a sense that CAT has some way to go to fully integrate with Welsh-speaking Corris.

Mike Parker deals with this issue in his book *Neighbours From Hell*. As an English incomer to Wales, Parker is not only entitled to his view but he is able to say what we would probably not get away with saying. I have no sympathy for anti-English rantings, but Parker makes some points that are at least worthy of discussion. At the time of publication his book was deemed quite 'controversial'. People were upset. Some have not forgiven. Not often do we hear criticism of the attitudes of English incomers by an English incomer.

DINAS MAWDDWY

George Borrow[11] may have been slightly unkind to Dinas Mawddwy when he described the village as "little more than a collection of filthy huts…. A dirty and squalid place" on his journey around Wales in 1854. Indeed en-route to Mallwyd he moves on from Dinas Mawddwy with the parting shot "I was glad to leave it behind me".

Dinas Mawddwy nestles on the valley floor beneath the A470 almost obscured from the road. You have to come off the A470 to get in to the village. As a teenager, Dinas Mawddwy Village Hall was a venue for Welsh rock and pop bands. Derec Brown (ex-Hergest) the Carmarthen born, country-blues singer performed here in the early 1980s with his blues band, the Racaracwyr – it was Derec Brown a'r Racaracwyr. The blues rack and racked musically speaking. I DJ'ed before the band on that particular evening – playing vinyl. This was a decade before CDs.

Nothing of Borrow's dirt and squalor is apparent today. Apart from the pub, Y Llew Coch, the streets are mostly quiet, the café in the centre of the village has closed. Life speeds past Dinas Mawddwy on the A470 above, that is until there is an event at the Village Hall.

On the notice board near the pub, I'm informed that citizens of Dinas Mawddwy still enjoy grazing rights on the Common Land. Whether many or any of the citizens practise their right is another matter. Good question! The noticeboard also states that "Three things come from Mawddwy. Hateful men, blue ear-marks and rain". This is the stuff of George Borrow of course, but his 'dirty and squalid place' and his visit get no mention.

BWLCH Y GROES

A detour, a single track, minor back road version of a road-trip from Dinas Mawddwy takes us up to Bwlch y Groes, 545 metres above sea level. It was once a drover's route through the mountains leading over to Llanuwchllyn to the north or Lake Vyrnwy to the east. From all directions this route starts as a gentle narrow country road ambling along a wooded valley floor, mountain stream running parallel, but as it climbs the trees give way to open mountain. At the final approach to the summit, concentration is required as the hill falls steeply on one side and rises just as steeply on the other. There are no barriers for the whole route. A momentary lack of concentration could lead to your vehicle bouncing down to the valley floor. Some stretches are white knuckle rides, hang on to the steering wheel and keep your eyes out front on the road ahead.

Abercywarch is the first hamlet, situated right on the confluence of the Cywarch and Dyfi rivers. You can actually see the rivers meeting, colliding and frothing just off the side of the road. Another detour, a dead-end detour, takes you up the Cywarch valley. I'm struck by the beauty of the placename, Abercywarch (the mouth of the river Cywarch). Great sounding address – but too remote for many. The nearest shopping towns would be Dolgellau or Machynlleth and maybe essentials like milk or daily newspaper from the garage at Mallwyd.

I keep alongside the Dyfi river, heading towards Llanymawddwy and its thirteenth century church dedicated to St Tydecho. Very little remains of the original building first mentioned in the Norwich Taxation of 1254. Annual payments (annates) were made by churches to the Archbishop of Canterbury or the ordaining authority and were recorded in the Norwich Taxation. This is often the first documentary evidence of the existence of a church building.

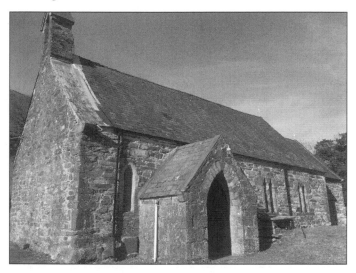

Although the church was largely rebuilt in the nineteenth century, that does not detract from the peace and beauty of this place. Let's settle for the fact that it feels older than it actually is – at least factually and historically. Away from the roar of traffic, four miles from the A470, surrounded by mountains, this is not a place of hustle and bustle.

Our direction of travel not only follows the route of the drovers but also the footsteps of giants. Legend has it that two were buried here at the churchyard. Most churchyards struggle to claim a single giant. Llanymawddwy, this tiniest village in southern Gwynedd has two. Maybe there was something in the pure waters of the Cywarch and the upper Dyfi. One of the giants was called Llywelyn Fawr o Fawddwy, very definitely not to be confused with Llywelyn Fawr the thirteenth century prince of Gwynedd.

This giant who was obviously a large fellow (mawr) was named Llywelyn, maybe even after the prince, though it's a common enough Welsh name. But there's a difference between 'large' and 'great'. Someone referred to as 'mawr' would be physically big or large. It is only through achievement, most likely political, that one would be known as 'Fawr' (Great). Noted, thereby avoiding any confusion.

Llywelyn o'r 'Llowelyn' as he was referred to in an article in *Y Negesydd* by a Mr R. Evans of Dinas Mawddwy in 1896 was a person within living memory of the publication of the article. So no confusion with any medieval princes of Gwynedd there, and the account mentions Llywelyn as wearing his hair in the same style as Samson, having slightly innocent looking eyes and often being an arbitrator in local arguments. He was real then, a nineteenth century big fella. Not a real giant.

Cawr Mawddwy is our second giant, the Giant of Mawddwy whose bones were supposedly twice the size of those of a normal man and were said to be found within the churchyard. Intriguingly there is a large mound beneath the yew tree on the southern side of the churchyard. To my eyes as an archaeologist, it looks typically like the remains of a Bronze Age tumulus. Ancient monuments were often incorporated and 'Christianised' within churchyards. Could this be the burial place of Cawr Mawddwy? Nothing on the *Archwilio* website suggests that there was a Bronze Age tumulus or Medieval mound or motte here at Llanymawddwy. Nothing to suggest that the mound was the burial place of the giant.

Onwards and upwards towards Bwlch y Groes. The road continues. A modern cross greets the intrepid motorist / cyclist / walker on arrival at the summit. Consecrated by the Bishop of Bangor in 1989, the recent cross is probably very similar to many a medieval cross that would have stood near the same spot over the centuries comforting and guiding pilgrims from north Wales en route for St David's. It adds to the atmosphere – modern or not. The view back down the steep sided Dyfi valley as it twists and turns towards the coast is breath-taking from Bwlch y Groes.

At the carpark, on the Llanuwchllyn side of the pass, the information board informs that an English gentleman once named the pass 'Hellfire Pass'. First I've heard of this name – it hasn't stuck. Did it ever? This is Welsh hill farm country – the name was and is Bwlch y Groes. Two other facts on the information board are that this is the highest pass in north Wales and that during the 1920s these back roads leading up to Bwlch y Groes were used as a testing ground for Austin cars.

GWYLLIAD COCHION MAWDDWY (RED BANDITS OF MAWDDWY)

The Red-Haired Bandits were sixteenth century highwaymen or bandits who operated in the area around Bwlch yr Oerddrws, the pass between Dolgellau and Dinas Mawddwy and along the Dolgellau to Welshpool road in the Dugoed area. Whether red hair was a requirement to join the gang or whether they were all inter-related locals does not really detract from the mythology. Travellers feared the 'Gwylliad Cochion' as they ventured along the lonely winding roads from the Marches towards Snowdonia. Borderlands. Between the Marches and Meironnydd. Lawless. Bandit territory.

Few historical facts survive regarding our red-haired bandits. It is acknowledged that they murdered the local baron, Lewis ap Owen in 1555 and several of the bandits were subsequently captured and hung. Tales and myths abound that Lewis ap Owen's murder was an act of revenge for earlier cruelty by the baron. During my Primary School days in neighbouring Montgomeryshire, afternoon stories of the red bandits evoked crystal clear images of blood-stained woods and corpses, of muddy tracks and galloping horses.

What is believed to be the earliest colour film in Wales was made here in 1938 when the locals of Mallwyd dressed up as Gwylliad Cochion and did their very best Oscar performance attempts at depicting these bloody events of the sixteenth century.

MALLWYD

On arrival at St Tydecho's Church, Mallwyd we are greeted by a huge rib bone arching over the south porch. Could this be that last remaining bit of evidence of some ancient pagan ritual practised in Mallwyd that has long disappeared in the mists of time? Striking if not a little unusual, it does not obviously chime the Christian bell but nor does it chime any obvious pagan bells either – there has to be some other explanation for its presence.

In fact, there are two bones above the porch entrance – the obvious large rib bone and another more rounded bone. All sorts of theories have been wildly thrown around. Dinosaur bones – but these are not fossils and this is not dinosaur territory. We are told that the bones were found in the vicinity of the church – but they do not originate from this area. The bones are too modern looking to be from prehistoric animals. Woolly Mammoth bones they are not either.

It seems most likely that they belong to a whale, brought here by a sailor or seafarer. Modern day biologists suggest a whale rib and possibly a piece of limb bone – the bit connecting to the flipper. Modern whale. Nothing actually prehistoric, I'm disappointed but no amount of wishful thinking or fanciful imagination gets us even remotely close to a Tyrannosaurus Rex.

Perhaps the rib was once used as a garden feature and later dug up and placed above the porch of the church. 'Re-found' locally is far more probable than 'found locally' in the sense that the bones are not of this place. If we accept the whale rib theory, we immediately discard any possibility that one of the two Giant of Mawddwy's ribs ended up here above the porch. To my knowledge no one has ever made the connection with the 'giants' buried at Llanymawddwy and the large bones here at Mallwyd.

Being a sister church to the main church at Llanymawddwy, Mallwyd church is also dedicated to St Tydecho. Most of what we see here is seventeenth century. The porch for example has a 1641 date on the cross beam. A Grade II Listed building – this is a good example of a medieval church which perhaps shows more architectural similarities with Montgomeryshire churches rather than the Meirionnydd churches. We are in border country after all.

Inside and just in front of the pews near the chancel is a commemorative slab for Dr John Davies, Mallwyd. Rector here from 1604 until his death in 1644, Davies is best known as an editor and translator of Biblical texts. He assisted William Morgan on some translations, but it is as editor of the 1620 Welsh Bible and the 1621 Book of Common Prayer that Davies is perhaps best known.

William Morgan's translation of the Bible in 1588 is widely credited, and widely accepted, as being a major factor in the preservation of the Welsh language. Unintentionally, Elizabeth I helped save the language even though her aim was to secure better Christians by providing Bibles the Welsh could actually read. 1588 is a date ingrained in the Welsh psyche, along with the death of Llywelyn ap Gruffudd in 1282 and the Investiture of Charles at Caernarfon in 1969. Dr John Davies played his part in this great story – how the Bible saved the language.

Whether it's the Dr John Davies connection or the whale rib that attracts people to St Tydecho's this is a worthwhile visit. Lying just off the A470, Mallwyd is a handy north-south coffee stop on the long haul between Caernarfon and Cardiff. The Brigand's Inn or the café at the garage serve that purpose. From either, it's just a few minutes walk to the church.

DOLGELLAU

Marion Eames's 1969 novel *Y Stafell Ddirgel* (The Hidden Room) paints a dark, gritty and brutal picture of Dolgellau and the surrounding area in the seventeenth century. Quakers. Charles II. Intolerance. It may be earthy, raw and violent but it's gripping stuff, a classic novel. Witches were 'tried' and drowned under Y Bont Fawr. Strapped into 'y gadair goch' (the red chair) and into the Wnion river they went. Betsan Prys was one such 'witch', innocent of course as were all the witches, but Eames hits hard with her line, "there is no one more cruel than frightened and ignorant ordinary folk".

Baying mob more like! For the ordinary, frightened, ignorant werin bobl (folk) this was just entertainment at the end of Fair Day. They don't really care if she's a witch or not, she's going to drown anyway. For the witches this was a lose-lose situation. After ducking in the gushing waters of the Wnion, anybody floating back to the surface was deemed a witch and executed. If they drowned, well too late and tough luck – they must have been a witch anyway.

During 2018, I caught punk poet Patti Smith in concert at The Apollo, Manchester. She came on stage and spat on the floor, claiming her space. She dedicated the set to the misfits, outcasts and misunderstood, or words to that effect. At a youthful seventy-one years of age, bouncing with energy and humour – she would definitely have been drowned in seventeenth century Dolgellau. That wasn't a great time for punk poets, or anyone outside the 'norm' of society, anyone vulnerable, lonely, old or un-married. Chilling.

There are quite a few 'trials' and drownings in *Y Stafell Dirgel* and there is no happy ending possible beyond emigration for the Quakers. Bryn Mawr was the home of Rowland Ellis, a Quaker, and after years of persecution and a period of imprisonment in Dolgellau he emigrates to the USA giving Bryn Mawr, Pennsylvania its Welsh name. It is with emigration to the US that the novel ends – ready for the sequel *Y Rhandir Mwyn*.

Dolgellau itself is a labyrinth of grey dolerite buildings and narrow streets, almost claustrophobic. Beyond the centrally located Eldon Square you could almost get lost wandering but for the fact that you inevitably return soon enough to the square if you keep going around corners. Chapels with classical facades tower above the narrow streets. Dominating like overbearing parents. Mostly dis-used today but the one-time dominance of non-conformism is unavoidable here in Dolgellau.

Above the modern shop fronts, the architecture remains unchanged here. Grey is the only colour. Everything here is very consistent. Dolgellau shouts loud and clear – traditional, vernacular, Meirionnydd town.

The Quakers left their mark on this area. Up the hill at nearby Tabor is the site of the Quaker cemetery at the farm of Tyddyn y Garreg (SH 755 177), although no stones survive. At Dolgun (SH 750 187), another farm that was a secret Quaker meeting place, Abraham Darby of Coalbrookdale built a blast furnace between 1717 and 1719. Charcoal or coke fired blast furnaces were developed by Darby for the smelting of iron. The remains can be seen at the entrance to Dolgun caravan park.

BRITHDIR

To the south of Dolgellau is the village of Brithdir. Just off the A470. I am all for detours, unplanned, random, psychogeographical (even by car). Anyone traveling along the A470 north-south, south-north, should detour. I imagine for anybody local criss-crossing the old Sir Feirionnydd, they may be slightly bemused at my calls for detours. The road through Brithdir is a shortcut from the Dinas Mawddwy side of the A470 on the south side of Dolgellau, towards Rhydymain and the A494 eastwards towards Bala.

There is a Roman fort here, barely visible, only a few bumps suggesting the line of the banks and ditches, under one of the fields at the edge of the village. The Romans often got here first. Didn't stay too long – out at the time of Hadrian in the 120s. Few stop to stare at the field. I do and am more than happy to stare at a field, looking for bumps, traces of banks and ditches. Ploughed out. The faintest trace, a shadow of a bank and I'm a happy man.

St Mark's Church[12] also has as an air of invisibility. Today its shielded by trees. Abandoned as a place of worship. Cared for by 'Friends'. Easily done, we've all done it – you drive in to Brithdir and miss the church, turn around and in fact its slightly more visible heading south.

Architect Henry Wilson conceived the church as something that would grow from the rock almost naturally. Grey stone. Stark. Arts & Crafts. Very Arts & Crafts. A few years ago, my work brought me to the church. I'd been commissioned to write a report by Cadw on accessibility, wheel chair access, nearest public lavatory, nearest bus stop, nearest cycle track, nearest train station for over 150 historical sites in Gwynedd.

St Mark's took me by surprise. Wilson's vision was for a church built of local stone growing naturally from the bed rock. The stone was to be as undressed and raw as possible. Stone masons having pride in their work disagreed with Wilson and proceeded to ignore his instructions and to cut and dress the stone to their usual high standard. Missing the point. Artists and craftsmen no doubt but not quite getting Arts & Crafts.

A young architect called Herbert Luck North[13] was sent by Wilson to oversee the construction work. By all accounts it was all too much for the young North struggling to convince the hardened

stone masons not to be too precise and tidy. Even if the stonework is overworked and over precise it's still a stark and grey church from the outside. I don't think Wilson's vision was completely lost but a rougher stone would have added to the 'natural' effect. I'm sure Wilson's vision was correct but it's only apparent if you hear this story – otherwise you'd still stand here, outside the church, and just think this is one of the starkest, greyest building I have ever seen.

Inside is a different matter. Once through the doors a fantastic splash of terracotta red and a turquoise blue engulfs the visitor. An apsidal east side with arched interior giving the impression of a dome, this is a truly remarkable building. Totally unexpected. I might have just landed in the south of Spain rather than the south side of Dolgellau. I'm thinking Cadiz not Brithdir. But there is discipline in the Arts & Crafts. There is a sparseness and a sense of space here – nothing is overcrowded. The art and the craft can breathe – it has its own space just to be.

On the west side the lead font modelled by Arthur Grove. Carpentry by Charles Quennell, Wilson's beaten copper pulpit and his copper altar in the chancel. And then the little animals, hare and tortoise perched on the edge of the stalls carved by Grove. Attention to detail is evident on the oak doors with teak chevrons crowned by little mother of pearl crowns.

'A hidden gem' is often over-used and thrown around far too casually. At St Mark's the detour is destination hidden gem. Herbert

Luck North, became a successful architect and designed the
Cottage Hospital in Dolgellau (1929). Stress free, or at least to his
own design, no pressure to be 'rough and ready and naturalistic'.

A470 DETOURS

Heading south from Trawsfynydd the A470 trundles towards its
final destination, the sea front at Cardiff, passing through the south
Gwynedd villages and towns of Bronaber, Ganllwyd, Llanelltyd,
Dolgellau (the only town), Dinas Mawddwy (bypassing) and finally
Mallwyd before entering Powys. Much straightened and improved
over the last thirty to forty years but it's still single carriageway as
far south as Merthyr Tydfil with only the final southern twenty-six
miles operating as dual carriageway.

Officially known as the Cardiff to Glan Conway Trunk Road and
at 186 miles long, the A470 is the main north-south artery linking
Llandudno with Cardiff. Many still prefer to take the English route,
via the A49 south of Shrewsbury towards Ross on Wye and then
heading 'back' into Wales.

The A470 enters Gwynedd, and the old county of Meirionnydd,
just west of the Crimea Pass, then passes through Blaenau
Ffestiniog and Llanffestiniog before doing a sharp turn just south
of Maentwrog and just north of Trawsfynydd at the junction with

the A487. Many of us refer to the journey south to Cardiff as the 'A470' but depending on our starting point it can vary as to when we actually join the route proper. Heading from Bangor to Cardiff, for example. involves almost forty miles on the A487 before hitting the A470 proper.

Songs have been written about the A470. Folk-jazz-funk singer Fflur Dafydd has a song called 'A47Dim' which has a suitable thumping Motown beat for those embarking on the long haul north or south. Geraint Lovgreen a'r Enw Daw on the other hand have a laid-back jazz feel to their song 'A470' probably more suited to sunny Summer Sunday afternoon drives. Blues singer Steve Eaves touches indirectly on the A470 with his song about a young lady taking a journey of the 'Traws Cambria' bus which would inevitably lead to the bus being on the A470 for part of the journey if you went Bangor to Aberystwyth for example.

During our gigging days with Anhrefn in the late 1980s we'd often play gigs in Cardiff or Swansea and face the prospect of an overnight transit van journey back home. Van loaded up with gear, on a good night we'd be out of Cardiff by 1am and hope to be back home north safe in bed before daybreak. This was never first choice. Crashing down on somebody's floor was always the preferred option but inevitably one member of the band would have work in the morning. It was always the drummers (I half joke).

These four-hour cross-country dashes through the night usually meant foot down and get home having filled the tank before leaving the big city. If there were no on-coming headlights we could safely hog the white lines and skim corners keeping the van firmly on the centre of the road.

We did this overnight journey so often that we knew each bend, each bridge, each bit of straight road. So familiar were we with every single gear change on the A470 we could almost have done the journey on automatic. With no 24-hour garages in those days it was best to stock up with snacks. Every unlocked public convenience was familiar, as was each layby.

Over recent years the A470 has become much straightened and improved but little bits of overgrown road or abandoned bridges still make the odd appearance alongside the newly built sections. Glimpses of the past. "I remember that turning, down to second gear". Some of them were sharp, second gear if not first gear.

As we enter Coed y Brenin Forest Park, just south of Bronaber, one such reminder is the crossing over the Afon Eden. Pont

Dolgefeiliau is a nineteenth century Grade II Listed bridge, on the old 'Dolgellau road'. So narrow was the bridge that two cars could not pass at the same time. This was definitely one of those first gear sections. The bridge still stands, nestling below the straight and wider modern A470.

Walkers and cyclists can cross but concrete bollards stand guard like soldiers turned to stone to prevent any joyriding ambitions across the bridge. This was once a popular picnic spot just off the A470 but the road improvements mean that few now notice the turning for the old bridge. This might be a good thing. Picnic in peace on the river's edge – the edge of Eden.

Afon Eden, a tributary of the Mawddach, does not flow from the Garden of Eden but rather from the boggy foothills around Crawcwellt just south of Llyn Trawsfynydd. I am informed that the Eden River is notable for the fact that it is one of the few breeding grounds for freshwater pearl mussels. Crawcwellt is an area that was farmed during the Iron Age and excavations by archaeologist Peter Crew of the Snowdonia National Park revealed use of local bog ore for making iron objects during this period. Resourceful people the local Celts. Lumps of bog ore were to be found in the surrounding peaty bogs. One imagines daily Iron Age chores as the youngsters were sent out with a large stick to find and collect ore under the peaty waters.

Just south of Ganllwyd, another detour takes us over the Mawddach and along the opposite side of the valley on a narrow forestry road. Half a mile along and the George V Memorial, celebrating the twenty-fifth anniversary of George's accession to the throne gives us that vital clue as to the origin of the Coed y Brenin name (The King's Woods).

On the outskirts of Dolgellau, at Llanelltyd, the remains of the Cistercian Abbey of Cymer still stand. Under the patronage of the princes of Gwynedd, the Cistercians (white monks) were given lands to farm and an abbey to pray. What was during the thirteenth century a remote and peaceful site on the banks of the Mawddach is now slightly spoilt by a neighbouring caravan park. The curse of Snowdonia, beautiful locations next to a caravan park. Ball games and barbecues and very little interest in history. Juxtaposed – the spiritual and medieval versus the modern and twenty-first century caravans.

Notes

1. The Gorsedd of the Bards is an association made up of poets, writers, musicians, artists and other people who have made a distinguished contribution to the Welsh nation, the language, and its culture. Gorsedd y Beirdd members are present on stage during three of the main National Eisteddfod ceremonies dressed in their white, blue and green robes, led by the Archdruid.

2. Kodak, a US-based camera-product company founded by George Eastman and Alfred H. Strong in 1888. Originally specialising in mass produced and cheaply priced cameras and associated products such as film and printing paper. Its headquarters is at Rochester, New York.

3. George Walton architect, see Andrew Davidson GAT report available as PDF on *Archwilio*: Berks, T & Davidson, A., 2008, 'Coleg Harlech Archaeological Assessment'.

4. Thomas Jones founder of Coleg Harlech. Educationalist, Civil Servant and Deputy Secretary to the Cabinet under four Prime Ministers including David Lloyd George.

5. Cwm Bychan, Llanbedr, carpark near lake. Grid Ref SH 645315

6. St John's Church, Barmouth, built between 1889 and 1895, designed by the Chester architects Douglas and Fordham. The foundation stone was laid by Princess Beatrice, daughter of Queen Victoria.

7. The National Trust. Founded in 1895 by Octavia Hill, Robert Hunter and Hardwicke Rawnsley.

8. Slate Quarries at Friog (ref Richards, 1991, *A Gazetteer of the Welsh Slate Industry*) Henddol Quarry (SH 619122), Goleuwern Quarry (SH 621 122) and Friog possible evidence of quarrying (SH 621 127).

9. Cantre'r Gwaelod, a mythical ancient kingdom submerged under Cardigan Bay. An early version of the myth appears in the *Black Book of Carmarthen*. A drunken Seithenyn is often blamed for leaving the sluice gates open resulting in the drowning of his kingdom.

10. John Corbett, an industrialist from the English Midlands who wanted to develop Tywyn as a major seaside resort during the 1870s.

11. George Borrow undertook a tour around Wales in 1854 and published an account of his adventures in *Wild Wales* (1862).

12. St Mark's, Brithdir. Architect Henry Wilson (1864-1934). Built for Mrs Louisa Tooth in memory of her second husband Revd Charles Tooth, chaplain and founder of St Mark's English Church in Florence. Opened in 1898. This is a Grade I Listed Building.

13. For Herbert Luck North see: Voelcker, A., 2011, *Herbert Luck North, Arts and Crafts Architecture for Wales* (RCAHMW).

EAST

ARENIG

Rather brilliantly titled, *The Mountain That Had To Be Painted* was a BBC 4 Documentary first broadcast in 2011. Artist Iwan Gwyn Parry is featured. It tells the story of artists Augustus John and J.D. Innes slumming it and painting in the wild landscape around Arenig Fawr in 1911. They also drank and met girls in Bala. Rough pubs. Drunk farmers. It's certainly a great title for a film. The declaration of 'has to be painted' confirms that there is no choice with creativity, it's something that has to be done. Passions burn, paint to canvas – choice does not come into it.

Iwan is arguably, probably and certainly in my opinion, one of the greatest living Welsh landscape artists. He painted the Bronze Age cairn at Bryn Cader Faner high above Llandecwyn (near Harlech) for the cover of my first book on Welsh archaeology *Cam i'r Gorffennol*. He is a fragile Innes-like character in many ways. Iwan and myself decide to retrace the footsteps of Augustus John and J.D. Innes on the slopes of Arenig Fawr and the Migneint uplands to the west to see where that takes us. Lying within the parish of Llanycil, this is a remote boggy upland area to the west of Bala. Empty and barren but for sheep.

I first met Iwan in a flat in Cardiff sometime in the early 1990s. I'd played a gig in town with my band Anhrefn and ended up crashing on the floor of a flat that was full of Welsh speaking art students. They had all been at the gig and had kindly offered us a 'hotel' for the night. No actual art was seen from my recollection but I was distinctly impressed by how 'cool' they all looked.

To my twenty something eyes, these young arty kids looked the part. Iwan had quite long hair thrown back almost in a quiff. At that point in time I was unaware of the adventures of Augustus John and Innes, the politics of punk rock being my one and only focus (anti-racism, animal rights, the Peace Movement, Class War). Looking back, I now realise Iwan was already self-conscious, carefully dressed, cravat-ed. I was an admirer before I saw any art.

Punk politics involved constant protesting. It may have been great fun doing anti-racism gigs, animal rights benefits and talking through the night about the rights and wrongs of all this but there was culture to discover. Class War borrowed heavily from Situationist tactics as used during the period around the May 1968 Paris Riots[1]. Malcolm McLaren, manager of the Sex Pistols, and his art director Jamie Reid claimed to have been in Paris during '68. It dawned on me that the revolution within the Welsh cultural landscape had to go beyond Punk Rock. It needed a parallel injection of art, poetry, design, film, photography, literature – a culture with no boundaries. Rules to be broken.

Back to the present. Picking Iwan up outside Tesco Express in Bethesda, we head down Thomas Telford's 1820s masterpiece, the A5 London to Holyhead road and before we know it we are on the outskirts of Bala. The first hour of our journey was, to put it quite simply, spent putting the world to rights. Art, culture, music, broadcasting, Wales and Welsh attitudes are covered but also much of our conversation was spent responding to the scenery.

We leave Bethesda and climb up Nant Ffrancon. Hanging valleys Cwm Ceunant, Cwm Perfedd and Cwm Coch carved by glacial action hover below the peaks of Carnedd y Filiast, Mynydd Perfedd and Foel Goch. Hanging valleys indeed. Cwm Idwal looms high to our south. Darwin was here in 1831 with Adam Sedgwick looking for fossils of sea creatures in the rocks. Some years later on a return visit he realised that the valleys were made by glaciers with evidential markings on every rock. Our hanging valleys were truncated, nose bitten off, by the main glacier pushing and carving its way westwards. Looking down this glaciated valley, this is textbook stuff. Flat floored and steep sided. U-shaped for sure.

On the Origin of Species is realised here in a way. Adam Sedgwick, Darwin's tutor and mentor struggled with Darwin's theory, a crucial milestone towards the end the road for the Creationist version of life. Even today, over 150 years later, some literally and stubbornly cling on to their Bibles. There is a wonderful line in a letter from Sedgwick to his former pupil after publication in 1859, "I have read your book with more pain than pleasure. Parts of it I admired greatly, parts I laughed at till my sides were almost sore; other parts I read with absolute sorrow, because I think them utterly false and grievously mischievous."

Iwan's role as a Coleg Menai tutor in Art involves inspiring the young art students to 'see'. This leads us on to a long discussion – you can look – but do you see? Can you teach someone to see – or does that have to come from within? I comment that archaeology is a similar discipline – you have to be able to see – to see and ask the right questions. Some will never get it. Some will never see. It's both a passion and a learning process but we agree that they are not mutually exclusive. Without passion you will never truly see.

As we pass through Betws y Coed we rather guiltily ignore David Cox and Clarence Whaite who founded and were active members of the Artist Colony[2] based at the Royal Oak. There can be no detours on this road trip – we need to get to Arenig and deal with Augustus John and J.D. Innes. Cox and Whaite will have to wait, for another book maybe, as by now we have crossed over (temporarily) into the county of Conwy before we re-enter Gwynedd further south.

I'd planned to stop at the café at Frongoch near Bala and treat Iwan to breakfast but it seems that they have closed down. Pity, these little cafés along the backroads of north Wales are the oases in the mountains for Gwynedd explorers and travellers. Locals and visitors alike. We get to know our cafés. First name terms with a lot of them. We end up in Bala, two strangers in town. A bit like Augustus John and Innes but we are very sober and not looking for booze or a good night out. We just want some breakfast before wandering around Arenig.

One fried egg butty and a mug of tea later we are on our way through Rhyd Uchaf and Llidiardau towards Arenig. My attention is drawn to the funny little tin shed buildings in Arenig and the old station house, red bricked and looking distinctly early twentieth century. Iwan is interrupted mid-flow as I jump out of the car for a quick picture, or two, or three. Photographers Pete Davies and more recently Antonia Dewhurst have been photographing tin sheds[3]. It's reassuring to know that artists and photographers are documenting these little tin sheds of Wales. This is archaeology the archaeologists might not get around to.

Pictures taken, Iwan directs us towards the track for Llyn Arenig Fawr. The area where John and Innes had painted and where Iwan had filmed for the BBC 4 documentary is rough underfoot and probably very wet. I happily go along with his suggestion that we follow the track towards the lake rather than trudge through the bog.

J.D. Innes had a definite style. His paintings of Tour Madeloc in Collioure, painted during the same period (1912-13) are almost interchangeable with his paintings of Arenig. The same use of deep purple and lilacs, the similar unearthly quality, strange colours and the brushstrokes creating the folded rocks. His peaks are exaggerated. Iwan suggests he is painting breasts. He has a point. Arenig's twin peaks in reality are low and rounded. In his paintings J.D. Innes goes all Madonna-conical-bra[4] at the mountain tops.

It's always good to have a knowledgeable companion on trips like this. Iwan knows his J.D. Innes and I listen and learn. On our arrival at Llyn Arenig we sit on a bench and stare. No words. Two pairs of migrant Canada Geese descend and we are distracted. Iwan, a keen ornithologist explains that these must be migrant birds to arrive at such a remote spot. Native geese would have found a more popular lake with more geese for company and a nearby tea room for breadcrumbs perhaps.

Innes collapsed and nearly died on the Migneint moors. He was dying at this time anyway and the Migneint could have accelerated things but for the fact that he was found and saved by a passing shepherd. It's bleak at the best of times crossing from the Trawsfynydd road (A4212) over towards Llanffestiniog (B4391). Hard to imagine Innes in a coat, no tent, no sleeping bag. We agree that they must have painted in summer or both artists might well have died of hypothermia Migneint style.

Bleak but good for painting. Open and wild. There are too few spaces like this left. Often there are no houses in sight. I wonder if Augustus or Innes painted the little stone bridge, Pont Tai-hirion, over Afon Taihirion. Probably built in the sixteenth century, the single pointed arch bridge was mentioned in 1698 by Edward Lhuyd and referred to as Pont Rhyd y Porthmyn which would translate as the Bridge of the Drover's Ford. Drovers would be en-route to and from places like Ysbyty Ifan to the north of the Migneint.

This was not a 'Roman' bridge as some locals have called it, any more than the Roman Steps at Cwm Bychan. So many sites have been wrongly associated with the Romans over the years. People often referred to things as 'Roman' before their actual dates were known. So many myths and misrepresentation to disentangle.

As a name, Taihirion probably relates to medieval longhouses or platform houses which are to be found in this area. During the medieval period, people lived and farmed in the uplands during the summer months. Climate fluctuations may well have resulted in more favourable weather at certain periods. In agricultural terms they adopted the practise of transhumance, the movement of livestock and people from the main farm and winter dwelling known as the 'hendre' up to the summer dwelling or 'hafod' for upland grazing during the summer months.

The Welsh Archaeological Trust's online database *Archwilio* records Medieval landscapes, peat stacks, sheepfolds, Victorian manganese mines, Bronze Age cairns and prehistoric hut circles and enclosures in the area around the bridge. The same pattern is recorded for most of the Migneint area[5]. Few live here today in what is one of the largest areas of blanket bog in Wales.

The café owners at Pont yr Afon Gam are an exception. They are situated at the junction of the B4391 and the B4407 right at the top of the Migneint, before descending down (high above Cwm Cynfal) to Llanffestiniog. A windswept, rain-lashed, whitewashed stone building with a great choice in home-made gluten-free cake. Iwan and myself end up here, having skipped lunch, and reward ourselves with tea and cake and a huge pot of tea for two. Enough for four.

FRONGOCH

Whisky Galore, the 1949 Ealing comedy, tells the story of the inhabitants of a fictional Scottish island becoming increasingly depressed when the whisky runs out. This dramatic event occurs at both the beginning and the end of the film. Respite comes in the form of a shipwreck carrying 50,000 crates of whisky. The closing statement of the film, with whisky all gone, is that the inhabitants lived "unhappily ever after". Comedy (Ealing style) at its best.

No such problems of island isolation or comedy occur at Frongoch which once had its own whisky distillery. Trading as the 'Welsh Whisky Distillery Co. Ltd' from 1889 until 1899 and under the ownership of local brothers and landowners Richard and John Lloyd Price. The Price family still occupy Rhiwlas, the current house designed by architect Clough Williams-Ellis, just on the outskirts of Bala on the banks of Afon Tryweryn.

No real comedy here for this whisky distillery, but after only ten years of trading the company was wound up and despite a transfer of ownership the whisky business did not survive. The drama occurs later, after the closure. By 1914 the site of the disused distillery was utilised as a World War I internment camp for German prisoners of war. Following the 1916 Easter Rising in Dublin the Germans are replaced by 1800 Irish prisoners.

Amongst the Irish prisoners was Michael Collins, one of the leaders of the struggle for Irish independence. An aspect of Ealing comedy then occurs at Frongoch as Collins and his fellow inmates turn the internment camp into a 'university' in Republicanism and guerrilla warfare tactics. A hotbed of Irish nationalism on the outskirts of Bala. The British State really did not think this one through.

On the hundredth anniversary of establishing the Irish internment camp, commemorative public events were held at Frongoch primary school which now occupies the site of the former distillery. Nothing of note remains of the internment camp above ground but a geophysical survey by Bangor University Archaeology Dept carried out during 2015 confirmed that foundations for some of the huts remain beneath the field.

A collapsed tin shed by the side of the A4212 road is a more recent Women's Institute building and not a surviving shed from the internment camp despite all sorts of local myths. A commemorative plaque fixed to a boulder stands in the layby. The Irish tricolour flaps in the wind alongside the Welsh Draig Goch. Wreaths lay beside the boulder, flowers wilting with the passage of time. The field itself yields no visible remains.

BALA

Thomas Charles's statue stands proud outside Capel Tegid down one of Bala's side streets, Heol Tegid. Charles famously proclaimed 'Beibl i Bawb o Bobl y Byd' (A Bible for all the people of the World). Converted to Methodism during the eighteenth century, Charles's main concern was the lack of education amongst the young people of Wales. Reading the Bible was the key to changing this and his method were traveling schools. Visiting villages for six weeks at a time – the aim was to teach children basic reading skills and then move on. In many ways Thomas Charles is typical of the early Methodists, God-fearing but with a social conscience.

As school children in north and mid Wales, we were taught Charles's mantra of 'Beibl i Bawb o Bobl y Byd'. It rolled off our young tongues. I also distinctly remember being taught the story of fifteen year old Mary Jones who walked barefoot over twenty-five miles from Llanfihangel-y-pennant near Abergynolwyn to buy a Bible from Thomas Charles at Bala.

Accounts vary. Charles had sold out of Bibles. He gave her a copy promised for another. Or she had to wait two days for a new supply. Whatever the truth Mary's barefoot efforts inspired Charles to set up the British and Foreign Bible Society. He really did want to get the whole world reading the Bible. I suspect that in today's world the 'Word' would be spread via the internet. Charles would proclaim 'Broadband for all the people of the World'.

Capel Tegid and the statue stand at one end of a small square incorporated into the grid pattern of Bala, just set back slightly off the street. A place for quiet Methodist contemplation perhaps. Hikers staying overnight at Bala Backpackers on the corner of Heol Tegid and the square probably have no clue as to who the statue

commemorates or its Biblical implications. They just require effective broadband during their overnight stay, rather than the traditional Bible in the drawer of the bedside table.

Bala was a planned Norman town and the original regular grid pattern has become fossilised in the current street plan. Arenig Street, High Street and Heol y Domen run parallel from the Norman motte, Tomen y Bala, which stands on the eastern edge of town. Side streets intersect in Manhattan style, but with no skyscrapers just predominantly Victorian housing.

Tomen y Bala, most likely a keep for a Norman lord, has been somewhat altered. Today it feels more like a landscaped garden than a medieval castle. A footpath spirals up the mound to the summit where the visitor is greeted by a planted tree with surrounding bench. Nice for a picnic – but a medieval castle is not what comes to mind.

This is the Dee Valley, the main route in to Wales from the Norman stronghold of Shrewsbury. There are so many Norman mottes in this valley that one is forced to conclude that during the eleventh and twelfth centuries this was tough territory. The Welsh resisted. The Normans built more and more castles. I'm tempted to say that in some ways things have not changed that much. Bala is still wild and agricultural, still Welsh and rowdy. Augustus John and

J.D. Innes were right to be fearful (if ever they were?) and pobl Penllyn (Penllyn locals) remain un-conquered and independent. No amount of Norman Castles could defeat the Berwyn tribes.

Llywelyn Fawr is known to have attacked the castle around 1202 during one of his power grabs against the princes of Powys. History complicated, as it is – this castle could have a Norman origin and a subsequent Welsh history. No documentation exists regarding the building work, but a Norman origin would make sense. By 1310 there was an English borough at Bala – again this was not to last. Today, Bala is definitely a Welsh town, nothing English about it beyond the street plan.

Returning to the theme of abandoned venues, at the western end of the High Street the brightly painted (blue and yellow) Neuadd Buddug has finally given up the fight to remain open. Mostly used as a cinema but occasionally doubling up as a concert venue it has been replaced by the new Theatr Derec Williams. This is based at the High School, Ysgol y Berwyn. State of the art, new technology, better equipped. Things (and venues) move on. Neuadd Buddug, Art Deco fronted, will need to find a new function. Sold off by Gwynedd Council. Demolished to make way for a carpark – I certainly hope not.

Gorky's Zygotic Mynci have graced the stage here during Gŵyl y Gwyniaid, a local festival named after the 'gwyniaid' (*Coregonus pennantii*) a freshwater whitefish that inhabits Llyn Tegid. Due to

declining numbers the fish are now bred at neighbouring Llyn Arenig as a safety measure to secure a healthy fish population. Increasing costs and decreasing attendance led to Gŵyl y Gwyniaid falling silent but they left a legacy of attracting successful bands such as Gorky's to a small town like Bala.

Gŵyl y Gwyniaid brought Rock'n Roll to Bala, Welsh style, Welsh bands. It is missed. Some of the organisers are involved with the successful T-Shirt company Cowbois based at the industrial estate. A best seller is 'Jones'. Another organiser runs the local bookshop Awen Meirion. They have not given up being cultural activists.

Beyond the medieval planned town, Bala has sprawled outwards. The aforementioned industrial estate a case in point. The coming of the railway in the mid-nineteenth century, as is so often the case in north Wales, gave people access to these remote parts. Tourists arrived for the Berwyn mountains and Llyn Tegid. People could also get out easier. A solitary signal stands in the carpark near the site of the station – the only clue left today. On the 18th January, 1965, the last train passed through Bala on the Ruabon to Barmouth line.

LLANUWCHLLYN

The Bala Lake Railway runs along the southern shore of Llyn Tegid. The station at Llanuwchllyn, with small tea room, is like a throwback to the 1950s. Reminiscent of a scene from *The Railway Children* film (1970) or maybe better still Arthur Askey's *The Ghost Train* (1941). Time has stood still here as it can only do on railway station platforms and with steam trains. Arthur Askey pulled the emergency brake in *The Ghost Train* and the train stopped in rural Cornwall. Passengers wishing to change trains were forced to stay on the platform overnight and thus witnessed the passing of the ghost train – a result of a train crash some years earlier with substantial loss of life. There are no ghost trains at Llanuwchllyn.

At the Bala station at the eastern end of the lake, weathered and much faded Free Wales Army (FWA) graffiti graces the rusting footbridge over the track. Painted alongside the letters 'FWA' is the symbol of the white eagle of Snowdon. This is the same symbol used by the FWA on their peaked caps as part of their uniform. The story of the Free Wales Army is well documented in Roy Clews's often hilarious accounts of their 'rebellion against the British Crown' during the 1960s, in his 1980 book *To Dream of Freedom*.

Tourists and visitors today may have no idea about the story of the FWA. I have long argued that an information board giving context and background would be an interesting addition to the railway platform. That the graffiti should be preserved. Context – Llyn Celyn, Tryweryn, the drowning of Capel Celyn to provide water for the City of Liverpool – it's only a few miles up the road (page 115). This is all the stuff of Welsh Nationalism 1965-1969.

The graffiti may not be that old, probably far more recent than the 1960s. Just a modern reminder.

The Free Wales Army made one of their first public appearances at Capel Celyn in 1965. Uniformed and organised, the story goes that they led a charge by protestors down the hill towards the dam construction undertaken by Liverpool Corporation. Formed by the enigmatic Cayo Evans, a horse breeder from Lampeter and Dennis Coslett from Llanelli, the Free Wales Army excelled at creating PR and media events. They even appeared on the Frost show on TV.

Such visibility was not really conducive to actual subversive military activities which were undertaken by the far more underground and secretive M.A.C. (Mudiad Amddiffyn Cymru / Movement for the Defence of Wales). John Jenkins, ex-army, was the man behind M.A.C. who were organized as cells or small groups and a very much a need to know basis. Most of the bombs that went off between the drowning of Capel Celyn and the Investiture of Charles at Caernarfon were organized by M.A.C.

GLAN-LLYN

David R. Edwards RIP (aka Dave Datblygu) was the lead singer of Cardigan based Welsh Post-Punk band Datblygu. He was also a poet and has published several books, and of course released dozens of records with his band. *Al, Mae'n Urdd Camp*, his first collection of poems was published in 1992. The title is a play on words. Literally translated he's announcing to someone called Al, that this is an Urdd Camp. His play on words is that the Welsh for Germany is Almaen. Split into two Almaen becomes Al (the person) and 'mae'n' (it's). Clever. Poetic. Very Funny. This does not work well in English.

Dave Datblygu was also arguably a stand-up comic who has never done stand-up comedy. In the real world he was a songwriter, pop singer and bard. He reflected on Wales and Welshness in a similar fashion to Dylan Thomas and R.S. Thomas. No mincing of words. Punches hit their target. Always poetic, Dave's reflections of Wales come via a broken mirror. Thrown to the floor and then replaced on the wall. Hanging, just. Glass cracked. Fragile. Hilariously accurate and hilariously funny because of the accuracy of his poetic punches. Distorted because of the cracked mirror he employs, but his lyrics benefit from the broken pieces of glass. This is barbed wire poetry often accompanied by a post-punk beat. One of his more profound lines is that 'living in Wales is like watching paint dry' from a song called 'Gwlad ar Fy Nghefn' from the 1988 LP *Wyau*.

Dave plays with the reader / listener. *Mein Kampf* is not named explicitly but you know what he's getting at. Conceived as a Welsh language version of a Boy Scouts camp, the first gwersyll (Urdd camp) was established at Llangrannog in 1932 and Glan-llyn followed in 1950. At Llangrannog beach, lines were formed and dozens of swimming-costumed young Welsh speakers would charge into the sea screaming in Cymraeg. Folk dances were also part of the experience. Along with rows of white teepee tents.

Glan-llyn is geared towards outdoor activities. Youngsters get the opportunity to canoe on Llyn Tegid and scale the climbing wall. Less of the dancing and more adventure. As a youngster I got to go to Llangrannog and hated every second. Homesickness. I was only nine years old. But, old and wise enough to hide behind one of the sheds when somebody announced 'Dawnsio Gwerin'. Folk dancing at such a young age can have lifelong effects – possibly traumatic – it probably accounts for the surge of Welsh punk rockers a few years later. Somebody had to say sod this and start up a new battle cry. Not sure if Dave ever folk danced but he absolutely captured the trauma that too many of us had felt as youngsters.

Urdd Eisteddfods were equally traumatic. On stage reciting and singing. Stage fright. Words inevitably forgotten. Too young to be embarrassed but old enough to want to be anywhere else but on that damned stage. Of course, thousands and thousands have benefited from these early performance experiences and have gone on to grace the stages of the world – just think Bryn Terfel. Two sides to the Eisteddfod coin.

Llanuwchllyn-born O.M. Edwards (1858-1920) established the first Welsh language children's periodical or magazine *Cymru'r Plant* in 1892 with the specific aim of arousing an interest in Welsh History and the language. His son Ifan ab Owen Edwards (1895-1970) published an article in *Cymru'r Plant* in 1922 which led to the founding of the Urdd – often wrongly translated as the Welsh League of Youth. Urdd Gobaith Cymru actually means Welsh League of Hope.

A triangular logo in white, red and green symbolises Wales (green), fellow man (red) and Christ (white). Dave Datblygu's play on words with 'Urdd camp' do not suggest any fascistic connections with the Urdd. It's just a broad shot at mainstream Welsh culture, the Establishment if you like. Christians not fascists.

Owen and Ifan greet the visitor and locals alike on arrival at Llanuwchllyn. Standing next to the school and opposite the garage, just off the main road (A494). The 1972 statue is by Jonah Jones[6]. Ifan is the taller of the two, both have neat haircuts, are suited, with books and papers in hand. Men on a mission.

Llanuwchllyn retains an air of cultural awareness to this day. In Welsh we'd refer to Llanuwchllyn as 'diwylliedig' (cultured). Maybe it's the legacy of O.M and Ifan? Llanuwchllyn people are proud, The Welsh language thrives here. Young families return post university or remain full stop and have never left at all.

LLYN TEGID

The Dee River flows through the village of Llanuwchllyn. Heading east into Llyn Tegid. Bala lies on the eastern shore. 'Bala', meaning an outflow from a lake. The valley is wide. Roads run both sides of the lake. By car, cycle or even long distance running it's perfectly possible to do a lap of the lake. The southern route via Llangower being the quieter route, but a narrow, undulating, single lane for much of the way.

Llyn Tegid has its own monster, 'Teggie'. A distant cousin to 'Nessie', the Loch Ness Monster. The last reports of a 'Teggie' sighting I could find in local newspapers were from 2016, but accounts date back to the 1920s. Retired warden Dewi Bowen had experienced a sighting in the 1970s. Like 'Nessie' some accounts mention a dinosaur or a *plesiosaurus*-like creature while other accounts mention an animal more akin to a crocodile. Hiding. Lurking somewhere in the murky 40foot depths of this deep glacial lake.

At Bala, a canoe stands at the ready on the shore. Paddle provided. But no canoeist to be seen anywhere. It would be too obvious to remark that 'Teggie' as got him. The canoeist has probably just popped to the loo before venturing onto the lake. Thefts of canoes or rather 'borrowing' a canoe and heading off for a spin across Llyn Tegid must be an unusual occurrence. Still, leaving the paddles is a bit of a leaving the keys in the car syndrome.

Twenty minutes of 'Teggie' watch and I see no monster and no sign of the canoeist either. The waters ripple but are relatively calm. There is no turbulence, bubbles or frothing resulting from the passing of a prehistoric beast. In the distance the mountains of Aran Benllyn and Aran Mawddwy dominate the skyline. Llyn Tegid is surrounded by mountains.

Llyn Tegid is long, over three miles in length. This is Wales's largest lake and it actually looks quite cold. At the height of the Industrial Revolution, Thomas Telford raised the level in order to improve the flow of water to the Ellesmere Canal. His plan here at Llyn Tegid was for a water feeder running into the canal system intended to link the Mersey and the port of Liverpool with the Severn and the industrial areas of the Midlands. The Ellesmere Canal was never fully completed and never connected to either the Mersey or the Severn, falling short of both destinations. But even before Telford's intervention, this was Wales's largest natural body of water.

TRYWERYN

To the north west of Bala, on the Trawsfynydd road, is Llyn Celyn. One of the most significant events of twentieth century Welsh History occurred here in 1965 when the village of Capel Celyn was flooded to provide a reservoir to supply water for Liverpool and the Wirral. In terms of its lasting effect on the Welsh psyche, the drowning of Capel Celyn has remained a bitter and painful event. Cofiwch Dryweryn (Remember Tryweryn). Not forgotten. The tragedy of the Aberfan[7] disaster, 1966, is another event that has remained raw and emotional to this day. Once again ingrained on the Welsh psyche.

One hundred and sixteen school children lost their lives at Aberfan. A whole community saw their homes and village drowned at Capel Celyn. There is no comparison in terms of loss of life and it is wrong to compare. However, the devastating effect on both communities lives on.

Welsh pop singers Huw Jones and Meic Stevens have commented on Tryweryn with their songs 'Dŵr' and 'Tryweryn' respectively. Huw Jones also references Aberfan in 'Sut Fedrw'chi Anghofio', another of his singles. Many lyrics allude to the politics of these events on records released during the 1970s. Pop singer Gwenno covered Meic Stevens's 'Tryweryn' on her *Vodya* EP (Crai CD089, 2003).

The damaging of the iconic 'Cofiwch Dryweryn' graffiti on the Llanrhystud wall just south of Aberystwyth early 2019 sparked a spontaneous and nationwide graffiti campaign. Cofiwch Dryweryn appeared on walls across Wales. As a slogan, political and emotional, 2019 saw a revival of interest and awareness. The events of 1965 were given a new leave of life and introduced to a new generation.

At the western end of Llyn Celyn a memorial chapel and a small graveyard stand as silent as the waters. The gravestones were removed and replaced before the drowning of Capel Celyn. Decaying fallen leaves dancing in the breeze betray a feeling of inevitable loss here. Peering into the chapel there is a sense that it's not used that often. Only sadness is reflected on the Llyn Celyn waters. It's a strange place to stop and reflect. Emotional. Haunting. Raw.

At the eastern end of the lake stands the dam. It's possible to park here and walk across. An unintentional irony is highlighted in the warning signs provided by Welsh Water. Swimming here is not recommended. Welsh Water warn 'Danger of drowning'. How very accurate – a whole village was drowned. A faux pas of signage. It's not really funny but it does make for a great photograph. The issue remains highlighted!

CARNDOCHAN

Dolbadarn, Dolwyddelan and Castell y Bere, all castles of the princes of Gwynedd, are tangible. Of stone. Visible. Dolbadarn round towered, Dolwyddelan square towered and Castell y Bere, although much ruined, are still very much identifiable as medieval castles. Carn Dochan near Llanuwchllyn is almost invisible, a pile of stones, the castle here is not obvious.

During the thirteenth century the princes of Gwynedd under the leadership of the two Llywelyn's, the Great and the Last, were to build several castles in stone. Of these castles, Carndochan is the least known and least visible. Both these facts complement each other. There is little to see on the ground. Little is known historically about the castle.

Sitting at an altitude of 332m above sea level, it's definitely a steep climb up to Carndochan from the Lliw Valley below. Unlike Dolbadarn, Dolwyddelan and Castell y Bere which have carparks, signage and footpaths, the walk up to Carndochan is a rough and at times wet mountain path. Perhaps this lack of accessibility accounts partially for the lack of awareness of this castle.

Having climbed the 332 metres it's 'just a pile of stones on top of a crag'. From a distance this does not look like a castle. Only by climbing up to the stones themselves do the foundations, the remains of walls and the plan of the castle become apparent. In mist, walkers could easily walk past, and have no idea that they are passing a castle. That may be another reason for the lack of public awareness – only close inspection enables an appreciation that this is a medieval castle rather than a natural outcrop.

Several courses of walling are apparent. There is a castle here but the architecture has to be read and interpreted. A challenge perhaps but a rewarding site to visit. Overlooking Llyn Tegid and the Dee Valley, this must have been a strategically important location. If the English were to attack, they would come from the east up the Dee Valley towards Snowdonia. From Carndochan it is possible to look right along Llyn Tegid. This is the eastern boundary of Gwynedd. Next stop land controlled by the princes of Powys, and beyond that England.

Archaeological excavations at Carndochan by David Hopewell of Gwynedd Archaeological Trust were undertaken over three seasons (2015-2017). There were two components to Hopewell's work. Firstly, to evaluate the state of preservation of the castle and of the remaining archaeology on site, and secondly to attempt to learn more about the design and construction of the castle. And just maybe, with a bit of good luck, find some dating evidence at Carndochan.

Dating evidence can come from objects such as coins or pottery or from the radiocarbon dating process. Due to an almost total lack of historical documentary sources about Carndochan, only archaeological excavation can provide further information. It seems that the construction of the castle was poor. Lime mortar was used on some of the towers though not throughout the entire castle. Disappointingly it would appear that parts of the D-shaped tower fell into disrepair and collapsed on to the castle entrance rather than being burnt down as a result of an English attack as some local myths would have it.

A poorly built castle, possibly not in use for long. Falling into disrepair, collapsing in on itself. A lonely castle on the edge of Gwynedd. Radiocarbon dates secured during the excavations fell between the reign of the two Llywelyns. Were they both here building at different times? Was the castle built by one of Llywelyn's sons – sent to guard the eastern frontier? Radiocarbon dates are not always precise. More questions than answers. Even after the excavations Carndochan still retains a shroud of mystery.

Archaeological excavations inevitably lead to more knowledge even if accompanied by more questions. It's the questions that really matter. Ask the right questions. During the excavations I helped out with guided tours. Most of our visitors were locals – interested in finding out about the castle. I calculated a 50/50 rate of those who had been up here before and those who had never set foot on Carndochan.

EASTERN BOUNDARY

Heading east towards the boundary with Denbighshire the B4401 follows the southern side of the Dee Valley while A494 takes a course a short distance to the north. Both roads head out towards Thomas Telford's Holyhead to London road. Next stop the market town of Corwen, Denbighshire.

Llandderfel is the last village in Gwynedd on the B4401. Quaint with a stream flowing through the centre, a small tributary of the Dee, it could be the Cotswolds but for the grey stone architecture. I hear Cockney accents as I wander around the village centre. Incomers looking for the quiet life and they seem to have found it.

St Derfel's church is what has really brought me here. Within the porch, (always open), is the 'Llandderfel Horse'. A wooden object that is actually a metre-long carving of a stag. Somehow and at some point, the wooden stag got decapitated and then mistaken for a horse. Everybody refers to the stag as the 'Llandderfel Horse'. In religious terms, this is a 'relic'. An ancient object used in obscure rituals in less formal Christian times. Almost pagan and not Christian at all. *Wicker Man* springs to mind.

The 'Horse' occupies the porch. A tail is still visible as are two folded legs beneath the stag's belly. He's resting rather than galloping and a box like cut on the upper surface (the stag's back) gives the whole thing the impression of a Victorian wooden horse designed for children to sit on.

Sheep graze in the churchyard. Avoids the need for lawnmowing. Notices warn visitors to 'Keep the Gate Shut – Sheep Grazing'. Saves on costs maybe, but the footpaths through the churchyard are littered with sheep droppings.

Almost on the Gwynedd / Denbighshire border, 'Get Wet' offers paintballing, raft building and high energy adventures. Travelling in towards Gwynedd from the Corwen side of the B4401 this is really the first visible tourist attraction. Part of the Crogen Estate, corporate events and team building – this is the new 'high'. On the northern A494 route Glassblobbery studios at Glanrafon offers handmade glass art sculptures and gifts. High energy adventure on the south side of the Dee. Glass art on the north. Both are Welcome to Gwynedd notices in their own way.

The real sense at this eastern boundary, the edge of Gwynedd, the final gasp of Snowdonia is of the meandering, slow flowing Dee. Wide valley floor. Flood plains. Often floods. We are leaving the Gwynedd heartlands. Out through Denbighshire and Powys – heading out for England and the A5. This is a place of coming and going. Historically and currently a main artery to and from the north west.

Y BERWYN

Another border occurs on the B4391 road from Bala to Llangynnog, over the Berwyn mountains. The boundary between Gwynedd and Denbighshire is marked by a road-sign but a differentiation in the tarmac is testament to the maintenance work of two different councils. I've heard this tale so many times, that there is a line in the tarmac between the two counties, that I have decided to drive up to check it out for myself.

In fact, there are three boundaries on this road, Gwynedd to Denbighshire and a little further south, Denbighshire to Powys. Clear lines are to be seen in the tarmac. The lines betray different composition of tarmac, colour differentiation and the effects of weathering and road use. Each council team tarmacs up to the line. Each line perfectly straight.

This is a lonely road. No cafés or garages and only the faintest hint of very distant houses. Care is needed as sheep randomly and casually cross the road. At night there are no lights up here. This is moorland.

Just within the Powys border, guarding the eastern approach to the Berwyn is the Iron Age hillfort of Craig Rhiwarth (SJ 055268). During the 1970s a hill fire exposed the approximately 170 hut circles enclosed within the dry-stone walls of the fort. The heather has reclaimed the hilltop and the house platforms are once again obscured.

Lead mines litter the eastern slopes of the Berwyn. Bronze Age burial cairns cap many of the peaks. Despite its rather bleak and exposed feel today, the whole Berwyn range is covered in archaeological remains. Medieval and Post-Medieval sheepfolds and field boundaries confirm that this landscape has been grazed and farmed as best as possible by hardened hill farmers over the centuries.

At the foot of the Berwyn, on the Bala side, a large boulder marks the spot of the first known sheep dog trial. Taking place on the 9th October 1873, on land belonging to the Rhiwlas Estate, a slate plaque confirms this as the first recorded sheep dog trail. I assume that this is the first in the world? Since 2002, the International Sheep Dog Society has held the World Trial at Bala. An event that takes place every three years, the World Trial sits comfortably at the 'spiritual' home of sheep dog trials.

Notes

1. Paris May 1968. A period of unrest with student occupations and demonstrations and strikes by workers which almost brought down the government and French economy. Student demonstrations at the Nanterre campus of Paris University were integral, as were the artistic slogans and actions of the Situationists International. The SI were a major influence on the theories of Punk.
2. Following the coming of the railway to Betws y Coed, Britain's first Artist Colony was established in the 1850s. Based at the Royal Oak Hotel the colony was established by landscape artist David Cox. Another prominent member of the colony, Clarence Whaite, went on to establish the Royal Cambrian Academy of Art in Conwy. Augustus John would be president of the RCA from 1934-1939.
3. Davies, P., 1984, *Great Little Tin Sheds of Wales*.
4. Madonna's conical bra was worn during the 1990 Blind Ambition Tour. Designed by Jean-Paul Gaultier. Sold recently at auction at Christies for $52,000.
5. See *Archwilio.org.uk* Pont Tai-hirion is within Gwynedd unitary authority and the Conwy area covers much of the Migneint.
6. Jonah Jones (1919-2004). Born in County Durham. Real name Leonard Jones. Welsh-based sculptor, writer and artist-craftsman.
7. Aberfan Disaster, 1966. A coal tip collapsed on to the village killing 116 children and 28 adults on the morning of 21 October.

WEST

LLŶN PENINSULA

Extending thirty miles out into the Irish Sea, Penrhyn Llŷn (Llŷn Peninsula) is the sum of many parts. Boundaries dating back to medieval times still exert a cultural influence. Pen Llŷn is the western tip of the peninsula, while the south eastern part is known as Eifionydd. East of Pwllheli, the river Afon Erch, forms the boundary between Llŷn and Eifionydd. Somewhere west of Llanaelhaearn the invisible border with Arfon is crossed and, on reaching Llithfaen, your feet are firmly on Llŷn soil. Llŷn itself is sub-divided into Llŷn and Pen Llŷn proper.

People know if they live in Llŷn or Eifionydd. They are well aware and will soon tell you whether it's Llŷn, Pen Llŷn or Eifionydd. People wear this fact as a badge of honour and proudly so. There may be occasional discussions about the exact line of the 'border', but mainly they just know from growing up there. Technically the northern part of the peninsula starts in Arfon, a local government area, but this does not have the same resonance or cultural significance for its inhabitants as those of Llŷn and Eifionydd.

Singer and funk guitarist Endaf Emlyn gave the Llŷn v Eifionydd debate a subtle acknowledgement on his wonderfully titled 1976 LP *Syrffio Mewn Cariad*. Translating as 'Surfing in Love' (rather than falling) and released on the Sain Label (Sain 1051M) one of Endaf's better known songs 'Macrall (Wedi Ffrio)' describes fried mackerel cooked with Llŷn cheese and Eifionydd butter. The South Caernarfon Creameries is based at Chwilog, close to the very border.

Passing Pontllyfni, Aberdesach, Clynnog Fawr and Trefor on the A499 there is a definite feeling of heading 'down' the peninsula. My feeling is that this journey starts from the junction for Dinas Dinlle. Straight road. Caernarfon and Snowdonia left behind. Destination Llŷn. Whether Pontllyfni is actually on the peninsula may well be the subject of debate but at this point the north coast makes a distinct turn towards the south west.

My mother was born in Station House, Pant Glas, on the old Afon Wen railway line (LNWR Bangor to Pwllheli). She was an Eifionydd girl, with family members in places like Chwilog. Just before my birth, she was a school teacher at Cricieth for a while. Her school notebooks are full of Eifionydd characters and

Eifionydd historical and archaeological sites – lesson preparations for the Cricieth youngsters. Pant Glas to Cricieth is distinctly Eifionydd.

Llŷn can work very well as a day trip. Starting at the northern end, on the Caernarfon to Pwllheli road, at Llanaelhaearn take the B4417 (off the A499) and head for Aberdaron, almost at the south-westerly tip. Returning via Pwllheli on the A499 and A497, head back for Cricieth and Eifionydd. Both roads broadly follow the northern and southern routes taken by the early medieval Christian pilgrims heading to Enlli (Bardsey Island). At Capel Uchaf (SH 430 498) near Clynnog Fawr and Pistyll (SH 319418) two eighth or ninth century incised cross-stones can still be found on the roadside marking the northern pilgrim route.

Tre'r Ceiri, Garn Boduan and Carn Fadryn, the three large and very impressive Iron Age hillforts, form a spine like line on the landscape. Running right down the middle, each hillfort conspicuous, like protruding vertebrae, guiding the traveller. Heading south-westerly, down towards the tip of Llŷn, Pen Llŷn, the end of the world, pen draw'r byd, The sea is often visible to the south, west and north.

A Welsh music festival takes place in the summer at Aberdaron. It's known as Gŵyl Pen Draw'r Byd (End of the World Festival). There is a Facebook page and in 2018 the event featured artists such as folk singer Gwilym Bowen Rhys and jazz influenced singer songwriter Geraint Lovgreen. Being held at 'the end of the world' has served the marketing campaign well. The festival is just one example of a vibrant cultural scene on Llŷn.

There is a sense of place here with the Welsh language very much at the centre of things. Things are done in a Llŷn way. More relaxed. A fact that is betrayed by the Llŷn accent. Words are drawn out almost in slow motion. There is no urgency to finish the sentence. Conversations are conducted with a smile rather than a hurried expression to get a move on. The clock really does tick a little slower here and that's a rare thing these days.

NANT GWRTHEYRN

Situated on the north coast of Llŷn, the drive down the 'modern' road that twists and winds its way steeply, precariously, slowly and surely down to Nant Gwrtheyrn is nothing short of spectacular. On approach towards the first major hairpin bend the sea is a few hundred feet below, with sheer cliffs just the other side of the retaining wall. This is the stuff of white-knuckle riding. Holyhead Mountain, Anglesey, appears on the horizon to the north. Otherwise, its wide-open sea in front. A real sense of vertigo.

Each cliff hugging hairpin bend is navigated in low gear with hands held tightly on the steering wheel. Praying that no other car approaches from the opposite direction, forward vision is lost momentarily at each bend before regaining a sense of the road ahead. Long thin evergreen fir trees shoot upwards above and below the road in search of the light. Passing places along the single track are committed to memory just in case. Reversing would be treacherous. Stopping would be nerve-wracking.

A sense of relief on arrival at the bottom. This is Nant Gwrtheyrn, National Welsh Language and Heritage Centre. Residential option for those on courses learning the language who wish to stay. 'Immersive' is a description often used for Welsh learning courses here at Nant. No escape and very little distraction. The success rate is high.

For visitors and the public there is a café and a path to the beach. Without doubt a very special place historically and culturally. Scenery nothing short of dramatic on this section of coast. Those arriving are often greeted by choughs. Y frân goesgoch (the chough) has returned in numbers. Once rare, dozens can now be seen hopping over the green and perched on the stone walls around the centre of the village. A black crow lookalike but with a red beak and red legs. Unmistakable.

Musician Cian Ciaran[1] from the Super Furry Animals has produced a classical CD based on the tragic tale of childhood sweethearts and Nant Gwrtheyrn residents, Rhys and Meinir. Playing hide and seek, (a local tradition known as the Wedding Quest) on the morning of their marriage day, Meinir was not found by husband to be, Rhys. Naturally his heart is broken and it is several years later after a terrible thunder storm that an old oak tree at 'Nant' is split open only for Rhys to discover the skeleton of his true love. Mystery solved. Tragic. Absolutely – it does not get any more tragic than that.

It's enough to put anybody off playing hide and seek for life. During primary school, both my sons went on school trips to Nant Gwrtheyrn and studied this story. In terms of a non-happy ending, it ranks up there with the tale of Llywelyn killing his own dog Gelert by mistake. Rhys and Meinir lived at Nant Gwrtheyrn during the eighteenth century when it was a small farming community on the lower slopes of Yr Eifl. A modern sculpture commemorates Meinir's Oak next to the path leading to Café Meinir.

The growth of the northern industrial towns of Liverpool and Manchester during the Industrial Revolution required vast amounts of building material. Granite occurs in the hills around Nant Gwrtheyrn and quarrying operations began around 1850 to produce square blocks of granite known as 'setts' for road surfacing. Export was via the sea. The remains of the jetty at Porth y Nant can be seen at low tide.

A solitary wagon, stacked with setts, stands silent next to the path for the beach. This load never left Nant. Cut by hand by settsmen who worked standing up. Measured accurately with an iron gauge called a 'meidrydd'. The heaviest tool in the armoury was a sledge hammer known as a 'moli mawr'.

The village as we know it today with associated school and Methodist chapel (Seilo) was built for the quarry workers at Nant. Agriculture gave way to the industrial revolution. Nant Gwrtheyrn was transformed and the population was recorded as two hundred according to the census returns during the 1880s. Previously Nant had composed of three farms.

Nant Gwrtheyrn overflows with legends. There is an association with Gwrtheyrn (Vortigern) the sixth century native British leader who fled the Saxons. Gwrtheyrn is often blamed for inviting Hengist and Horsa, the Saxon leaders, here to the British Isles in the first place. After the departure of the Romans around 393AD Britain was descending into anarchy. That is according to the 'Imperialist' historical narrative.

Brothers Hengist and Horsa were invited over as mercenaries to help defend the British against the threat from the Picts in the north and invaders from across the sea during the fifth century. Eventually they turned on their British hosts and thus began the Anglo-Saxon conquest of eastern Britain. England eventually becomes the Saxon / English area. Offa finally defines things with his dyke in the late eighth century between the Welsh and English lands. This is pretty well the border today. Wales remained Celtic in origin. As the Saxons took over in the east, Gwrtheyrn and his men head out west.

Gwrtheyrn, the historical character, is also associated with the post-Roman occupation of Dinas Emrys hillfort near Beddgelert. The archaeological evidence would seem to confirm post-Roman activity up at the fort but it's the stuff of legend to make the association with Vortigern and Emrys / Merlin. Never ruin a good story they say – but the archaeologist in me is sceptical. Unlikely then that Gwrtheyrn actually ever came down to Nant in the sixth century.

The hippies did though, in the early 1970s. Following the Second World War the demand for setts was in rapid decline. Nant Gwrtheyrn was winding down. 1959, the last family moved out. It's pretty remote here. The road down then was little more than a track. Similar to those experiencing island life – economic pressures, daily hardships and the allure of town / city life seeps over the inhabitants like thick sea mist. The old want to remain – the young just want to get out.

'New Atlantis Commune' says it all – the hippies who occupied Nant in the early 1970s, without electricity, sewage facilities or running water, managed to further the decline. Surely they should have cultivated gardens and given the place a coat of paint? By all accounts they burned floor boards for heat and cooking, and left the place trashed.

Communal living, a life free from the constraints of society, became part of the hippy philosophy during the 1970s. Activists such as Sid Rawle, 'King of The Hippies' had been active with the

Free Festivals movement and the London squatting scene. Communes had been set up at old china works in Cornwall and abandoned open cast coal works in the north east. Communes were all the rage. Someone on the hippy scene must have come across the disused quarry at Nant. Isolated, quiet and ideal.

Jamie Reid, Sex Pistol graphics designer in-chief's iconoclastic slogan declared 'Never Trust a Hippy', but one suspects that was more to do with is aversion to Virgin Records MD Richard Branson rather than an opposition to actual hippies. Any pop historian will tell you that many of Reid's ideals were hippy but to admit that in the punk heyday would have been tantamount to betrayal. Nothing less.

As my teenage years coincided with Punk Rock, Reid's various slogans became the battle cry. I probably subscribed too heavily to Jamie Reid's anti hippy slogan. But even today that 'aversion' to hippies is never far away. The Nant Gwrtheyrn 'trashing' episode does little to pacify my contempt for 'peace and love'. Without respect for the place and culture that's an empty slogan. Blood boils.

Punk Rock or not, I am fascinated with this hippy commune at Nant. It's not widely documented. All traces of the commune have disappeared today. Nant has been fully restored as the Language Centre. Carl Clowes hints in his book *Nant Gwrtheyrn* that ex-Beatle John Lennon played a part in moving the hippies on from Nant. He bought an island for them at Clew Bay in Ireland. John Lennon therefore inadvertently played a (small) part in paving the way for Nant Gwrtheyrn becoming the Welsh Language Centre soon afterwards.

Musical and especially Super Furry Animal connections are unavoidable here. Dreaming of turning the abandoned quarry village into a centre for the learning of the Welsh language, local GP, Dr Carl Clowes turned his dream into reality during the late 1970s. Carl Clowes is the father of Dafydd Ieuan, drummer, and Cian Ciaran, keyboard player, with the SFAs. I have interviewed Clowes on my BBC Radio Cymru show about the New Atlantis Commune and what the language centre campaigners were to inherit as a result of the hippy occupation.

Welsh folk-rock band Ac Eraill[2] recorded a song called 'Cwm Nant Gwrtheyrn' in 1974 way before Clowes's dream was realised. Close enough to remember the hippies. But Ac Eraill's anthemic wistful yearnings for better days at Nant, hope for a future, 'parhad' for y Gymraeg and for the Welsh tradition on Llŷn is indication of another ideology. Mudiad Adfer were a political group in the 1970s who advocated that the only way the Welsh language would survive would be by moving west to the Welsh heartlands.

Translated loosely as 'Restoration Movement', Adfer were a splinter group of Cymdeithas yr Iaith (Welsh Language Society). Following a more purist ideology of Welsh-only speaking areas and communities, Adfer in many ways were just as naïve as the hippies. Form a commune, drop out, create an ideal paradise. They also advocated restoring old buildings and keeping Welsh community life vibrant. Not all bad, but totally divorced from reality. Maybe it was of its time. A time where dreams could at least be dreamt. Thatcher put an end to all that.

From 1979 onwards there was no more dreaming – politics got real. Dropping out was no longer an option. Rock Against Racism. The Miner's Strike. Gay Rights. The Feminist Movement. Anti-Apartheid. Everything stepped up a gear. It was time to fight back, not drop out.

As a Montgomeryshire born and bred Cymro, that's mid-east-Wales, border country – the Adfer philosophy was anathema. Citizens of Newport, Cardiff, Swansea, anywhere south of the Landsker Line in the south west, Flint, Deeside, Broughton, Yr Wyddgrug, Ruthin, Denbigh, Newtown, Welshpool, Rhaeadr, Llanidloes, Builth, Brecon were excluded, not west enough, non-Welsh. What were we to do – move to live in Ceredigion?

Still 'Cwm Nant Gwrtheyrn' is a great anthemic record. Hard to listen too without being emotionally drawn in. An area such as Llŷn has to survive as a natural Welsh-speaking area and Nant Gwrtheyrn is a truly special place. Sit there by the sea if you want proof. But in the future, it's the Welsh language schools in the industrial south that will create the numbers. Adfer as a philosophy is redundant, left behind as Cardiff gained confidence post-devolution as a Welsh city – of that I have no doubt.

'Tua'r Gorllewin', the 1973 first release, 7" single, by Ac Eraill advocated moving west. These boys wrote anthems. Tecwyn Ifan, Cleif Harpwood, Iestyn Garlick and Phil Edwards all have long hair on the cover. They look like clean hippies, a bit west coast Eagles. Cardigan Coast rather than California. I have had the privilege of knowing all four. They are good guys. Total respect by the old punk. Culturally and in terms of twentieth century Welsh History this is all interesting stuff. Who cares where we agree and disagree? There is no copyright on 'Welshness'.

TRE'R CEIRI

One of the best-preserved Iron Age hillforts in Britain, Tre'r Ceiri
is certainly worth a visit. Depending on the path taken, the walk to
the summit will take between forty-five minutes and an hour or so.
Just west of Llanaelhaearn a signposted footpath leads up the
southern slopes towards the south western entrance of the fort.
Another track over open moorland starts at the top car park for
Nant Gwrtheyrn near Llithfaen. Both are equally good walks.

From the summit, the views north and south are equally
spectacular. To the north, across Caernarfon Bay, is the south west
coast of Anglesey, Llanddwyn, Aberffraw and then Holyhead
Mountain further west. Looking down the peninsula in a broadly
south westerly direction are the hillforts of Garn Boduan and Carn
Fadryn

Debate has raged about the actual meaning of 'Tre'r Ceiri'.
Thomas Pennant, writing in the 1770s, may well have mis-spelt the
name as Tre's Caeri in his book *A Tour in Wales*:

> On the Eifl is the most perfect and magnificent, as well as the most
> artful, of any British post I ever beheld. It is called Tre'r Caeri, or,
> Town of the Fortresses.

But in the 1883 edition, this interpretation is challenged by editor
John Rhys MA:

> This explanation is the usual one, but it will not stand examination,
> for the place is called not Tre'r Caeri but Tre'r Ceiri, or Tre Ceiri
> which is pronounced differently, and means in Carnarvonshire
> dialect the Town of the Giants – ceiri being plural of cawr, giant in
> that county.

Caer is the Welsh word for fort but the plural of caer would be
caerau not ceiri or caeri and the translation 'Town of the Fortresses'
does not really make sense. If we accept that John Rhys is correct
and that 'ceiri' is indeed the plural of 'giants' in Caernarfonshire
dialect then the naming of the fort dates back to a time when such
magnificent and monumental building was attributed to a superior
people. In the same way as Stonehenge in Welsh is known as 'Côr y
Cewri' (henge of the giants), these 'superior' people who lived in
the past, must have been 'giants'. An understandable assumption or

explanation, albeit factually incorrect.

What is agreed on is that there are approximately one hundred and forty-six structures within the hillfort of which around twenty-six are round houses or hut circles in which people lived. Accounting for the fact that not all the buildings would have been in use at the same time, that suggests around a hundred structures would have been workshops or storage buildings. As a general rule during the Iron Age, people lived in round houses and the rectangular or sub-rectangular buildings served other more practical functions.

It is also accepted that there are two distinct phases to the fort at Tre'r Ceiri. The earlier phase of occupation during the later Iron Age which includes the substantial stone rampart and the later phase during the Roman period probably includes the northern annexe and the subdivision of many of the roundhouses. There may even have been a period of abandonment between the two phases.

Another archaeological debate rages as to the actual function of hillforts during the Iron Age. Whether they were permanent settlements or seasonal. Whether some of them were tribal centres, or sites for other activities such as trade, or just in use as a refuge at times of threat? Toby Driver outlines all the current arguments in his book *The Hillforts of Cardigan Bay*. Driver discusses the obvious defensive aspects of hillforts but he also suggests that some entrances were more about display of power and the status of those living within, rather than actual defence. As is often the case, things may be more complicated, but Driver's book is well worth a read and is a very good and accurate outline of current discussions.

David Hopewell of Gwynedd Archaeological Trust (GAT) spent three years (1989-1992) restoring many of the walls at Tre'r Ceiri. Partly due to increasing number of visitors, sections of the rampart had become perilously close to collapsing. Many of the round house walls had become displaced or dislodged. The restoration project sought to preserve the site for future generations, to make the hillfort safe to visit and to help with interpretation on the ground. Fallen or dislodged stones replaced within the walls were marked with a small drill hole to distinguish between original Iron Age walling and the modern restoration.

Hopewell recognised that many of the huts had been subdivided during the second phase of the fort. In fact, some had even been rebuilt within the collapsed walls of the earlier roundhouses. This strongly suggests a period of abandonment or disuse between the two phases. Pottery finds would suggest that this phase occurred during the Roman period.

What event brought people back to the hillfort? Was there a period of political instability or external threat? I've heard Hopewell describe this second phase of rebuilding as being more akin to a 'refugee camp' than what would be expected in a normal Iron Age village? Yet despite all this, there is no evidence of any attack on the hillfort. Charcoal would be present in the archaeological record if the fort had been burnt down. Despite the Romans being based at Segontium, barely fifteen miles to the east, there is no suggestion that the fort was attacked by the Romans during its first phase.

It's always possible that the first phase was over before the Roman Conquest of AD77. Perhaps Phase II occurs at a time of political instability as the Romans loosen their grip on north Wales from the second century onwards? Recent archaeological excavations by GAT at Tai Cochion near Brynsiencyn on Anglesey have uncovered an undefended Roman trading settlement on the banks of the Menai Strait.

Dating to the second and third centuries AD, Tai Cochion throws more light on our understanding of Romano-British politics. Perhaps relations between the native Celts and the Romans were more stable than we thought. Maybe the native farmers realised it was better to trade with the Romans than fight them.

I've always joked that the Romans were too frightened to venture

down the Llŷn peninsula. New evidence suggests a possible small
Roman fortlet at Abersoch dating to the Agricolan campaign of
77AD. Did they venture down there, build a fort and then promptly
return to base at Segontium? No other Roman occupation on Llŷn
has been discovered.

PISTYLL

If you ask the locals where Rupert Davies is buried, they'll give you
a blank look. You need to ask where 'Maigret' is buried and you will
get a direct answer. Top right-hand side of the cemetery, downside
of the footpath that follows the wall (that'll be the south east side of
St Beuno's church). I'm too young to remember the original
1960-1963 TV Maigret series. Based on the novels by Georges
Simenon about a fictional French detective, actor Rupert Davies
was the first Maigret, followed by Michael Gambon in the
1992-1993 series and more recently by Rowan Atkinson.

Appearing in films such as *The Spy Who Came in from the Cold*
(1965), *The Brides of Fu Manchu* (1966) and *Dracula Has Risen
from the Grave* (1968) I would have seen Rupert Davies on the telly.
An avid pipe smoker he became, in 1965, the first recipient of the
Pipe Smoker of the Year Award. There is in fact a 45rpm record by
Rupert called 'Smoking my Pipe' released on Parlophone (1963)
which has a very Maigret / Parisian accordion accompaniment feel
to the whole thing. He was to die of cancer in London in 1976.

Having a film star living locally generated interest. A retired policeman remembers Davies driving around Nefyn on a tractor in the late 1960s. On one occasion, around this time, the police were called to investigate a break-in at Davies's cottage – off filming for long periods I'm guessing that burglars would have identified an empty house.

Another piece of information is recalled by a former Llŷn archdruid who told me Davies was pretty dismissive of the Welsh language – who knows? Looking at Davies's grave, I'm left wondering how on earth Maigret ended up in Pistyll? Davies was of Welsh descent and by all accounts, holidayed up at Pistyll. On retirement he settled here.

He is related to Archdruid T. James Jones of Parc Cilie, Ceredigion. My appeals for more information on social media for this book were always productive although difficult to verify. Many tales are second hand. Faded distant memories. But there is no shortage of Maigret stories around Pistyll. His son Hoagie (Hogan), I'm informed by another source, played keyboards with a rap crew based at Blaen-y-Cae recording studios in Garndolbenmaen. Later this crew evolved to become the Porthmadog based rap band Pep le Pew. Another family connection is early twentieth century opera singer Dame Ethel Gomer-Lewis.

St Beuno's church lies on the northern coast pilgrim route to Enlli. This would have been via Clynnog Fawr and onwards through Penllech and Llangwnnadl towards Aberdaron. Dating back as early as the twelfth century the church feels old despite extensive restoration over the centuries. This feeling of 'ancient' is enhanced by the rushes and herbs which are strewn on the floor. On opening the door, the smell of rushes is noticeable before one's eyes adapt to the darkness and actually see what's on the floor. There is no electricity here.

A much faded – barely visible – red ochre mural depicting St Christopher, the patron saint of travellers, is framed within the last bits of medieval plaster clinging to the walls. Making the connection, a reminder of the pilgrims on their travels. Scallop motifs surround the circular gritstone font. Dating to the twelfth century, the font is probably the oldest thing here beyond a few large stones in the lower courses of the church walls. A leper window high up on the north wall allowed the ill to look in on church services from the nearby field known as Cae Hosbis (Hospice Field).

Everything here suggests peace and calm. A place of rest. It's still some distance to Enlli. This must have been a welcome stop for the pilgrims. Next to the church is 'Natural Retreats', rebranded as 'Natures Point', which offers luxury accommodation for pilgrims of a different kind. Modern tourists who don't want to rough it. The sign on the road is missing a to bach on Llŷn and spelt incorrectly as 'Llyn'.

NEFYN

Tyddyn Gwêr on Mynydd Nefyn became the first holiday home set on fire in the early hours of 13th December 1979. Another arson attack occurred within a few hours at Swn-y-Môr, Llanbedrog, together with two other holiday homes at Pennal near Machynlleth and a further two near Porth Gain in Pembrokeshire (Gruffydd, 2004). Meibion Glyndŵr had appeared on the scene.

The 'Arson Campaign' carried out by unknown activists 'Meibion Glyndŵr' attacked second or holiday homes. No loss of life occurred and as a result there was a degree of support amongst many Welsh people for the campaign. Many locals and young families could not afford to buy a home due to inflated prices as a result of others selling property in England and buying much cheaper in Wales.

Places such as Abersoch became overwhelmed by holiday homes, locals priced out. Homes occupied for a few weeks in summer by non-residents. Closed down for the winter. Welsh communities under threat. Of course, this problem is not peculiarly Welsh in nature – the same loss of community and traditional way of life has occurred in Cornwall and the Lake District. Same story – loss of local community and house prices pushed up by selling in London or the south east of England. Just that in Wales the language is dis-placed as well as the people.

Situated on the northern slopes of Mynydd Nefyn, the fire at Tyddyn Gwêr could be seen from Nefyn below. One local story is that the fire brigade just followed the flames without need of an address. Not that anyone would have been around the cottage to make the call. There is something quite strange about driving up here as research for this book. After all, this is Welsh History – but recent and still relevant. It's not quite the same as visiting one of Llywelyn's castles or a battle site. Might my interest and research be mis-construed as tacit approval of the arson campaign? I'm slightly uneasy. This feels edgy. Subversive. Tyddyn Gwêr remains a holiday cottage. Rebuilt.

I've driven up here before. But that was for research of a different kind. Carreg Lefain (the wailing rock) is a cliff face where an echo can be heard, but only from a certain point on the approaching path. In order to hear the echo, the trick is to walk up the footpath and keep shouting. Starting at the end of the road (and at the junction for Tyddyn Gwêr) the footpath leads uphill towards the quarry on Mynydd Gwylwyr. Eventually the echo comes back. This is the spot. Walk on and the echo stops.

Research completed, I retreat to the Bryn Cynan pub, just west of Nefyn, for a bite to eat and a pot of tea. I chat to a few local lads enjoying a post-work beer at the bar and explain the purpose of my visit. They all laugh. There is no disgust or opposition. Holiday homes are still the subject of jokes not sympathy.

A few arrests were made but the arson campaign ended as quickly as it had begun. Meibion Glyndŵr simply evaporated into the Celtic mist. Like their hero Owain Glyndwr who led the revolt against English rule during the first decade of the fifteenth century, never captured, never found out, never betrayed. There is a saying that 'somebody knows'.

Nefyn's early nineteenth century Watch Tower stands on top of a very much damaged Norman period motte. Modern public lavatories have cut into the western corner of the motte. Not much is known about the origins of the castle here at Nefyn. Motte and bailey castles were typically Norman and often part of military campaigns against the Welsh during the eleventh and twelfth centuries. This would make sense, there are other examples of mottes on the peninsula at Ty Newydd, Llannor and also at Abersoch.

Steps lead to the top of the watchtower. Modern buildings spoil the view and indeed obscure what Nefyn's fishermen were seeking – herring shoals at sea. Still, it's worth a visit. Tyddyn Gwêr is visible to the east, Garn Boduan to the south. A panoramic view. Ignore the modern housing developments.

On Nefyn's industrial estate, Cwrw Llŷn is a craft beer brewery. Employing up to six people over the summer months and distributing their beers widely, this is a superb example of how to revitalise the economy in rural areas. Beers labelled 'Seithenyn', 'Neigwl' and 'Enlli' highlight local places. A sense of place is the marketing campaign. No compromise. The beers are good. Reputation and word of mouth will win the day. I've taken American visitors here for beer tasting evenings. Stating the obvious – they loved it.

Opposite on the Industrial Estate is Dwyfor Coffee Co, next door is the Police Station. Depending on how much Cwrw Llŷn beer is sampled there are convenient options of a coffee to sober up or calling the police if too much has been consumed.

ABERDARON

Continuing our journey towards the tip of Llŷn we pass through the village of Llangwnnadl. Approaching from the east, the sign reads Llangwnadl, one 'n'. From the west the village sign has two 'n's, Llangwnnadl. Probably a spelling mistake. The signs differ, suggesting that they were not printed at the same time. Someone pointed this anomaly out to me. I'm encouraged that the people of Llŷn notice spelling mistakes.

Llangwnnadl parish church is dedicated to St Gwynhoedl. Various legends suggest that Gwynhoedl was a son of Seithenyn. The very same Seithenyn often blamed for the drowning of Cantre'r Gwaelod[3] in Cardigan Bay. Restored by Victorian architect Henry Kennedy, the church had seen an expansion in the sixteenth century. Two aisles were added hinting that there was money in the area and there must have been a substantial congregation at that time. This is something that is quite noticeable on Llŷn, large churches, small villages. Llanengan church is similar in many ways – a church seemingly far too large for the village population. Hard to imagine much of a congregation these days. Quiet villages. I hardly saw a living soul when visiting most of these churches for the writing of this book.

Situated on the northern pilgrim trail from Clynnog Fawr, the main route to Enlli, the church of St Gwynhoedl would have been one of the last major stops before Aberdaron. Incorporated in the south wall of the nave is a seventh to ninth century cross stone. Another marker for the pilgrims and presumably placed here for safe keeping during Kennedy's restoration work. Interestingly the cross is painted red. Why and by whom remains a good question.

Iron Age roundhouses have been recreated at Canolfan Felin Uchaf, Rhoshirwaun. Take a quick detour off the Aberdaron road and several thatched roofs become visible in the valley. Felin Uchaf is a centre for keeping traditional carpentry and thatching skills alive. Volunteers from all over the world contribute and work here for their keep. Sleeping in roundhouses, learning their craft by day. Higher up on the slopes of Mynydd Rhiw, actual Late Bronze Age – Early Iron Age roundhouses have been excavated by Bangor University at Meillionydd. The tradition continues. There is nothing out of place about Felin Uchaf.

Mynydd Ystym is the last hill before we reach the sea at Aberdaron. It is crowned by Castell Odo a Late Bronze Age or Early Iron Age fort which was excavated by Leslie Alcock during the 1960s. Like Meillionydd, this is a 'double-ringwork'. Peculiar to Llŷn, these small forts were defended by a double bank and ditch. A local tradition. Excavation suggests a sequence of development at these forts from open hut groups to enclosure and then double enclosure. Probably more to do with status and marking boundaries than defences.

During my University days at Cardiff, Castell Odo was standard text book stuff. Annoyingly pronounced 'O-doow' by lecturers. Later in life I was to lead guided tours of Castell Odo. Those lectures in 1980 still come back to haunt me.

St Hywyn's church at Aberdaron has one of the best examples of a Romanesque (Norman) arch that I have seen in north Wales. Surrounding the west door, this semi-circular arch dates to the twelfth century. 'Romanesque' means something derived from the Romans but in Britain this architectural term is synonymous with Norman architecture.

Three badly weathered sandstone clustered columns stand on each side of the doorway. These provide the base for three arches which spring from cushion capitals. A hint of carvings around the capitals would suggest columns of the classical Corinthian Order. So weathered is the sandstone that I hesitate to suggest acanthus leaves for the decorations. Covering the arches is a hood mould with stops. Overriding, defining and framing things neatly.

Within the church two early Christian gravestones throw some confusion on the theory that 20,000 saints were buried on Enlli. Veracius and Senacus were both priests. The stones date to the early sixth century, But the stones were found nearby on Mynydd Anelog. On the mainland. Not on Enlli. Maybe they missed the boat?

Veracius and Senacus are acknowledged as priests, 'PBR' and 'PRSB' (presbyter) respectively on the stones. Could Anelog be the site of an earlier monastery before the same monastic community established churches at Aberdaron and Enlli? At present we have no answer.

Reading *Gwynedd* by Frances Lynch (1995), there is a suggestion that both stones were carved by the same sculptor. The inscriptions bear stylistic similarities and the two rounded pillar stones bear a remarkable resemblance in form. Like many other early Christian gravestones they have been placed within the church for safekeeping. We shall never know the site of the original burials.

Aberdaron becomes grid-locked during the summer months. The two pubs, the cafés and the National Trust car park overflow with beach-destined visitors. Two vehicles cannot pass at the same time over the single arched bridge over the river Daron. So small is the bridge that it's often damaged by inappropriately large delivery lorries. Ironically the bridge is named Pont Fawr (Large Bridge).

A long sandy beach is the obvious attraction, sheltered slightly from the south-westerlies by the Uwchmynydd tip of the peninsula. Coastal erosion saw large tracts of the graveyard falling on to the beach. St Hywyn's is now protected by a large and rather unsightly sea wall. Still, the views over Ynys Gwylan Fawr and Ynys Gwylan Bach just out to sea remain dramatic and unspoilt.

YNYS ENLLI

Bardsey Island (or Ynys Enlli under its lovelier, more alliterative Welsh form) rises out of the western sea off Braich-y-pwll like a humped-back whale. – Jonah Jones

Twenty thousand saints are buried on Ynys Enlli. Bardsey in Norse. There is no English word for Enlli. Like Swansea and Anglesey, Bardsey is a Norse name. The Vikings must have passed through. It may be Iolo Morganwg[4] who first made the Arthurian connection with Enlli. Iolo has a lot to answer for. Stone mason, forger and poet. And, if we are honest, we should emphasise, talented forger of poetry. Maybe include fantasist and proto-situationist albeit unintentionally. To this day, historians and archaeologists alike are still untangling the web of historical mischief making by Iolo.

Many still believe that Enlli is Avalon, Ynys Afallon. This is where Excalibur, Arthur's sword was forged. I have met many on Llŷn who claim Arthur is buried on Enlli. Argue with them at your peril. Maybe King Arthur is all Iolo fantasy but the citizens of Enlli did have their own king, at least four of them.

The earliest king is unnamed but the subsequent John Williams I and John Williams II are well documented. King John Williams II was even photographed in 1899 wearing his crown. Coron Enlli, (the Bardsey Crown) as worn by John Williams is on display at STORIEL, Bangor. Enlli was part of the Newborough Estate. The Wynnes of Glynllifon may well have been patrons of sorts for the king and may have had a hand in the making of the slightly comical crown. It does resemble something from a school play.

Love Pritchard, the final king, was rejected for the army during the Great War due to being too old to serve. This event provides Enlli with one of its more bizarre stories. Love Pritchard, deeply unhappy and annoyed by the decision, is said to have declared Enlli neutral. Other stories have him declaring his support for Kaiser Wilhelm II. By 1920 the King of Enlli was living on the mainland. His death in 1926, sadly brought an end to this tradition.

During the summer of 2017, I had to make one of the most 'difficult' professional decisions of my life. I was offered work as a tour guide doing archaeological tours of Enlli every Tuesday over the summer months. Hmmmm, let me think about this for a minute. No-brainer. What a wonderful opportunity. How could I, or anybody, refuse such an offer?

With small groups of interested visitors, this work involved catching the boat from Porth Meudwy early morning in the wonderful company of Colin the boat operator. Colin is born and bred Enlli. Island life seeps out of his every pore, from his very soul. To describe Colin as inspirational is an under-statement.

In the event of choppy waters as we crossed the 1.9 mile Swnt Enlli (Bardsey Sound), the stretch of sea between the mainland and the island, I'd often stand with Colin in the cabin. Looking ahead over the rough seas helped with any motion sickness. Chatting with

Colin was a pure learning experience. Both knowledgeable and opinionated Colin would inevitably supply me with new information on each trip. This became a weekly routine, up front with Colin, I'd have plenty of time with my visitors later.

On arrival with my intrepid visitors, we would walk as far as the remains of the thirteenth century tower of St Mary's Abbey. Stopping off at the school house and exhibition and the chapel en-route. Mentioning Bardsey apples near Plas Bach and Bangor-born artist Brenda Chamberlain[5] my aim was to give context and background. The apple tree at Plas Bach is said to be the only remaining tree from an orchard planted by the monks all those centuries ago.

St Cadfan, one of the early Christian saints, is said to have established the monastery on Enlli. The myth of this being the Island of 20,000 Saints remains very much alive. Walking the footpath near the abbey, long narrow slabs of stone can be seen underfoot. These may well be the remains of medieval cist graves, just some of the twenty thousand.

As an island, Enlli has seen activity since Neolithic times. Rich in archaeological remains, Enlli is also a destination for bird watchers. On a good day the chough may be spotted and the island has a large population of Manx Shearwaters which burrow into the ground, often under the archaeology. Approaching the slipway at Cafn Enlli we were more often than not greeted by the barking and hissing of grey seals.

Little grey and white mottled smooth watery faces with distinctive whiskers bobbing in the sea or full bodies basking on the rocks.

Always a retreat from the pressures of 'everyday life', for the medieval pilgrims as well as modern day week-long abstainers who rent cottages here, it was highly unusual on my Tuesday tours not to meet someone whom I knew while wandering the island. Poets, writers, bird-watchers, Welsh literary types, media execs, culture-freaks, all passed my group on the path as we made our way for the abbey. "Hello Rhys – what are you doing here?"

PLAS YN RHIW

Eileen, Lorna and Mary Honora (Honor) were the Keating sisters of Plas yn Rhiw. Eileen ran a language school in Nottingham and campaigned for rural protection. Lorna assisted Eileen at her Nottingham school and was a supporter of animal charities. Honor worked in child welfare and was a skilled amateur artist. No surprises therefore that within their circle of friends and associates that one R.S. Thomas would make an appearance.

Plas yn Rhiw is now under the guardianship of the National Trust. Overlooking Porth Neigwl (Hell's Mouth) the café with outdoor sitting area commands what must be one of the most impressive views in Wales. A mile downslope, the beach curves ever so gently over its four-mile stretch, yellow sand meets white frothy waves. Bae Ceredigion forms the background. The wind is gentle at Plas yn Rhiw, it's too distant here to hear the crashing of the waves.

I'm told to look out for the twin seated outside-toilet (tŷ bach) at Plas yn Rhiw. A tip off from one of my many cultural contacts on Llŷn. Placed discreetly at the bottom of the garden, the tŷ bach is indeed twin seated and housed within a stone building. A small stream flows below. The seats sit directly above the stream, No need to flush.

I'm intrigued. I'd imagined the three sisters having cultural discussions on the loo. Two seats only and this rules out that possibility. More than likely it was a tŷ bach for garden staff.

Nearby is the small Neolithic burial chamber of Bron Heulog (SH 231 281). An attempt was made to blast the chamber in order to re-use the stones. The drill holes intended for the black powder can still be seen on the capstone. According to local tradition, the burial chamber was saved from destruction by one of the Keating sisters passing in their horse-drawn cab. Enlightened ladies indeed, and the archaeology was allowed to remain.

ABERSOCH

There's a great story by Iwan Huws, lead singer of Llŷn based alt-country band, Cowbois Rhos Botwnnog, in the road movie *Anorac*. In the film, presented by BBC Radio Cymru and BBC 6

Music DJ Huw Stephens, Iwan contemplates the size and scale of Llŷn. Despite Llŷn extending over a distance of thirty miles in length it's not really very wide. From the hillforts of Carn Fadryn and Garn Boduan the coast is visible both south and north. Llŷn is Iwan's muse. This is where he's from and where he will certainly 'spiritually' remain. His songs are from and of Llŷn.

But to get back to Iwan's point in the film, everything here is on a small scale and as a case in point he suggests that near its source it's possible to jump across the river Soch. I decide to follow the Soch back from Abersoch towards its source near Carn Fadryn, and test Iwan's theory. Following the eight-mile course of the river will also create another 'mini road trip'.

Flowing into the Irish Sea at Abersoch, the Soch is at its widest here. Boats stand silent on its muddy banks. Anyone approaching Abersoch from the east on the A499 has to cross the river via a low-lying unremarkable road bridge. Look over the wall and the Soch is wide on the harbour side but to the west it's surrounded by reed beds and looks still.

OS map in hand and a pot of tea on the terrace of Zinc Café Bar & Grill, with glorious views over the harbour, I plot my route. Even out of season Abersoch overflows with tourists. Miraculously I find a free parking spot for 1 hour. Enough time to study the map, enjoy the tea and wander back to the bridge for a photograph.

Researched and refreshed, I follow the valley to the south of

Llangian and to the north of Llanengan. Here the valley is visible, carved into the landscape. The road runs alongside but higher up the slope. One and half miles later, Llangian has an almost Cotswold-like feel with its quaint houses opposite St Cian's church. A post office red Giles Gilbert Scott K6 phone box stands at the junction. A village shop still open on the Llanengan road, but Llangian is silent, still, peaceful.

Melus was a fifth or sixth century doctor at Llangian. His gravestone reads: MELI MEDICI / FILI MARTINI /IACIT, (*Melus the Doctor, son of Martinus lies here*). A simple granite pillar stone stands in the graveyard, possibly even in its original position. Only archaeological excavation could prove or dis-prove that one. As with many of these early Christian gravestones, they are not now the easiest to read but this stone is unusual in that the profession of the person buried is acknowledged. 'Fili', 'Son of' is common enough but a Doctor in that time at Llangian – that's valuable information.

Much later a sun dial was placed on top of Melus's gravestone. I'm pretty convinced that the gravestone saw some alterations during this time. The west and south face of the stone look dressed or shaped and the notch below the flattened platform for the sundial again suggests the hand of man. Melus's inscription reads downwards on the east face of the pillar stone. Notches on the side of the stone above the inscription have been suggested by some as being remains of an Ogham (Irish) inscription but this is doubtful, unproven and probably just the effect of the rough granite. Anyone familiar with the Ogham stones of Pembrokeshire would probably spot the notches and at least ask the same question.

Heading south along the valley, Llanengan was a lead mining area. A solitary ventilation chimney built around 1878 is the only clue today, standing on the hillside above the village. Dedicated to Einion Frenin (King Einion), the church at Llanengan, or it's site at least, is thought to be one of the earliest on Llŷn. When Henry VIII started to trash monasteries some of the fittings from St Mary's Abbey on Enlli ended up here for safe keeping. Here they remain, Llanegan being too remote even for Henry VIII to complete his monastic vandalism.

A debate, possibly not a raging one, but a debate nonetheless exists as to whether the rood screen came from Enlli. St Engan's is unusually large and grew over time. The south aisle is an extension as is the western tower. But where did the congregation come from? Who were these people who populated such a large church? A similar scenario is discussed in the section on Llangwnnadl church (page 139).

At Llanengan, we are just north of the four mile long beach at Porth Neigwl or 'Hell's Mouth'. Hells Mouth because once sailing ships were blown in by storm winds there was only one conclusion – shipwrecks. Porth Neigwl is a much more pleasant name than Hell's Mouth. The beach and the Soch run parallel briefly. A farm called Glan Soch stands on the bank of the river. Surfers do their thing here today. During World War II the RAF trained here at the suitably named RAF Hell's Mouth.

Turing west I follow the river towards Llandegwning, just south of the village of Botwnnog. It's here that the waters of the River Horon merge with the Soch. A small bridge crosses the river at the road junction for the National Trust property Plas yn Rhiw. I can jump the river at this point. Iwan's theory is correct.

Continuing towards its source I follow the Soch to the village of Sarn Mellteyrn at which point the valley takes a distinct turn north between the hills of Cefn Amwlch and Carn Fadryn. A quick detour here to take in the wonderful Neolithic burial chamber at Cefn Amwlch before continuing the climb up towards the farm of Pwllcoed. Over the fields, in a wooded area near Tregarnedd I can see the source point. I make it Grid Reference SH248353. There is no public footpath.

My journey ends tantalisingly close. Two fields away. The road crosses the river but dense undergrowth obscures any view of water. I can hear the river flowing below on each side of the road. Knocking on farm doors to get permission to cross the fields feels like too much of an effort. There's no guarantee that the nearest farm is actually the landowner. I'm close enough. Despite the anti-climax, I am content with my river following adventure.

LLANBEDROG

Plas Glyn y Weddw boasts the distinction of being Wales's oldest private art gallery. Established by Cardiff businessman Solomon Andrews in 1896, he opened a gallery within the mansion that once belonged to the Love Jones Parry family of Madryn, and the gardens and grounds to the public. However, the Second World War saw the closure of the art gallery and part of the mansion was used by the Women's Land Army (Land Girls). Sold off by the Andrews family in 1945, it was not until the 1990s that a charitable trust re-established Glyn y Weddw as an art gallery. This followed purchase of the Plas and intervention to prevent the whole place falling into decay, by artist Gwyneth ap Tomos and her husband Dafydd.

Solomon Andrews is best known as an entrepreneur who developed horse drawn bus and tram businesses as far afield as Belfast, Manchester and Plymouth, as well as his native Cardiff. He was also responsible for the development of the West End Hotel and promenade at Pwllheli. Within Gwynedd, as a developer, he built houses at Arthog and had hoped to develop property on land in Aberdyfi. He connected Llanbedrog and Pwllheli via the Pwllheli and Llanbedrog Tramway and also built the short lived Barmouth Junction and Arthog Tramway (1899-1903). Parts of the Pwllheli to Llanbedrog tramway route can still be followed.

With an ever-increasing reputation as an excellent art gallery and destination over recent years, the café at Glyn y Weddw has to be one of the best in Gwynedd. The views over Llanbedrog beach and Bae Ceredigion make this is a great spot for lunch or mid-afternoon tea. Upstairs, the Andrews Room holds one of the best collections of Swansea and Nantgarw ceramics in the country. Downstairs art and exhibitions are on rotation

Gwynedd is well represented with galleries that showcase

modern Welsh art. Along with STORIEL in Bangor and Plas Brondanw, Llanfrothen, contemporary and up and coming Welsh artists have several suitable venues for exhibitions. Glyn y Weddw is no exception. Modern art is shown. New Welsh artists are showcased. Works are discussed, debated, hated or loved and hopefully sold. Art should always provoke a response.

Another debate often rages as to the source of the contents of museums. The Elgin Marbles being one of the more obvious examples. Should artefacts be returned to their place or country of origin? Many museums would be severely depleted of content if this were to happen. The British Empire of course has a lot to answer for. On each side of the doorway at Glyn y Weddw, two pillar stones stand guard. These are known as 'Meini Pemprys', (Penprys) found at Pemprys Farm near Llannor.

The stones are early Christian gravestones (fifth or sixth century) and commemorate Gwynhoedl and Iovenalis son of Eternus respectively. Gwynhoedl is the patron saint of Llangwnnadl on the north coast of Llŷn. Eternus is arguably an early form of Edern, another Llŷn village on the north side of the peninsula. Early nineteenth century accounts of the stones lining the side of a grave and of an associated skeleton may suggest that the earlier Christian gravestones had been re-used as slabs for a later cist burial. We may never be sure, but what is certain is that the stones were taken to the Ashmolean Museum in Oxford. Firstly, for display and then hidden in storage – far away from home.

Not surprisingly, Llŷn activists and nationalists like R.S. Thomas and other took up the campaign for the return of the Pemprys stones. Remarkably they succeeded. Objects are rarely given back. Maybe they won the argument because the stones were in storage anyway. Or maybe it was the sheer force of R.S. Thomas that buckled the Oxford keepers of antiquities. I once visited the stones in the company of Archdruid Robyn Lewis, one of the campaigners, who delighted in telling stories of their fight for the return of the stones on to Welsh soil.

PENYBERTH

One of the great acts of twentieth century Welsh nationalism took place at Penyberth. Once home to generations of patrons of poetry, the old house of Penyberth had been demolished in 1936 to make way for RAF Penrhos. In itself, this act of cultural vandalism was hardly going to gain much support in this most Welsh speaking of areas. But the fact that RAF Penrhos was to be used as a training and bombing school was of great concern to many in non-conformist Welsh-speaking Wales. Leaning heavily towards pacifism, activists within Plaid Cymru and the emerging nationalist movement were faced with a dilemma. Objections were raised and promptly ignored by the Westminster Government.

Prominent nationalists and Plaid Cymru members Saunders Lewis, D.J. Williams and Lewis Valentine decided on a course of direct action. A symbolic non-violent protest to show opposition to the bombing school. In the early evening of the 8th September 1936, some of the tool sheds were set alight and the subversive threesome promptly walked into Pwllheli police station in true Gandhi fashion and claimed responsibility for their actions.

Over the years the mythology about this protest has taken a life of its own. Undoubtedly this was an important and historic act of resistance. In reality they had damp matches, not much caught fire. Tool sheds were targeted. The bombing school itself was not set alight or destroyed. Symbolism outweighs any actual damage. I researched this event for a BBC radio programme and it was slightly disappointing but not entirely surprising to get closer to the truth. Rather than a crack team of subversives, the threesome composed of a dramatist and lecturer, a minister and a novelist. Pillars of society, in fact. The image of a damp box of matches has stayed with me. They just needed something, anything to go up in flames so they could claim responsibility. Following a nine month stretch at Wormwood Scrubs, the trio were welcomed home by a crowd of fifteen thousand at the Pavilion in Caernarfon. Modern Welsh nationalism had been kick started.

In recent years, Penyberth has been the site of a rock festival called Wakestock, linked to wakeboarding events at Pwllheli marina. I saw the Undertones there. The festival has moved on. Penyberth is mostly silent, no bombs or loud guitars.

At the end of World War II, RAF Penrhos was selected as a site for the demobilization of Polish servicemen. The Polish Village was established in 1949 as the ideal place to provide homes and care for Polish families who chose to stay and settle in the UK after the war. Approaching the village from the main road, the tarmac has a feel of an airfield or military base. The buildings are painted bright white. Houses numbered and arranged neatly. Lawns are well kept. There is a church, library and common room.

Parts are of the village are in use as a care and nursing home. Driving around the village always manifests a sense of guilt, of being a voyeur. I always think of that line in 'Holidays in the Sun' by the Sex Pistols, "looking over the wall and they're looking back at me". There is nothing else quite like this in Gwynedd. A throwback to World War II yet still hanging in there. The population must be ageing by now. I'm not even sure how Polish the Polish Village is anymore. I see no one to ask or chat with so I drive out quietly, leave them in peace.

PWLLHELI

Pwll heli, literally the pool of salt water. Pwllheli is a bustling market town. The main shopping town for Llŷn residents. The main drinking town for Llŷn youth on the weekend. Always busy, always gridlocked with cars. Much of the eastern side reclaimed from the sea, much of the western side developed as a seaside resort by Solomon Andrews. Cardiff Road betrays delusions of grandeur and of being connected, as well as the more obvious Solomon connections. It is Victorian and Edwardian grandeur displayed.

Non-conformist chapels dominate. Standing proud on street corners, sometimes hiding down narrow alleyways. At other times standing alone in the rural landscape, they are such imposing buildings when they come in to view. Salem, on the corner of Church Place, is no exception. A burglar searching for some ready cash broke in to Salem in 1913 and promptly set fire to the chapel when he found no money on the premises.

The re-built Salem dominates, with its impressive overriding arch above lesser arches and Doric columns. As an example of big and bold Non-Conformist chapel building, this is as good as it gets. Classical façade in all its glory.

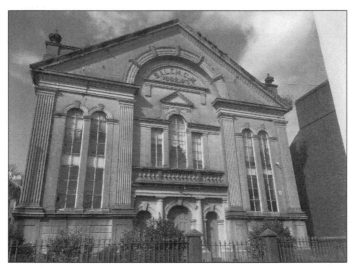

Pwllheli boasts a famous son and a famous daughter. Twice Archdruid, Cynan (Albert Evans-Jones 1895-1970) was born here on Penlan Street. Cynan famously brought some order to the druidic fantasies of Iolo Morgannwg's Gorsedd ceremonies. Or maybe he just gave authority to the myths and fantasies that we still witness today. He is often credited as a 'moderniser'.

Cynan's interest in fishing had brought him into contact with my grandfather, Moses Price. As schoolchildren, asked to bring something of interest or value to school, we would oblige with a baking tray as used for Sunday roast potatoes. Our tray had long been in use as the water bowl for our Dalmatian dog. However, this dog's bowl / baking tray was a wedding present given to my parents by non-other than Cynan. Such disrespect for the most 'valuable' or 'interesting'object that we had at home.

As is the case of so many born and bred on Llŷn, Cynan's wish to spend his last days here, close to the sea are captured in his poetry.

> When I am old and reverend
> With money to my name,
> With all my judgments over
> Yet basking in my fame:
> I'll buy a lonely cottage
> With nothing 'fore its door,
> But the rocks of Aberdaron
> And the ocean's maddened roar.
>
> Cynan (translated by Robin ap Cynan)

A plaque commemorating opera singer Leila Megane (1891-1960) is to be found on the yellow bricked Police Station on Yr Ala (Ala Road) on the western end of town. She is credited, rather endearingly, as 'Cantores Byd Enwog' (World Famous Singer). She was indeed, and performed in Milan, Rome, Paris, New York and London. Before her farewell concert at Pwllheli Town Hall in 1945 her career included recording with Elgar on his *Sea Pictures*. Some of her works have now been released on CD by Sain Records *Leila Megane* (Sain SCD2316).

'Butlins', Pwllheli has long morphed into 'Hafan y Môr'. Out on the Abererch road, the holiday camp established by Billy Butlin as part of his country wide chain may have a new name but it functions in pretty much the same way as it always did. Cheap holidays, rows upon rows of chalets, amusement arcades, swimming pools, go-karts, high-ropes, cycle hire, crazy golf, donkeys, pizza, burgers, traditional fish and chips, pink fluffy souvenirs, picture postcards. From the accents, the holidaymakers have travelled from north east Wales or the north west of England.

Out of season, Hafan y Môr hosts specialist weekenders. Entertainment and accommodation for a reasonable package price. On one occasion, Wil an old friend of mine who works security, invited me over to a SciFi weekender. Adults dressed up as Darth Vader and Superman. Not really my thing, but fascinating to stroll amongst them. Entertainment was provided by headliner, Rick Wakeman – all very Prog Rock. I made my excuses and headed off home.

LLANYSTUMDWY

In an age before spray paint and graffiti tags, people would often carve their initials and dates on stone. By all accounts, Llanystumdwy's most famous son, David Lloyd George, was a youthful proponent of such activity. Built during the seventeenth century and widened in 1780, the bridge over the afon Dwyfor is composed of two main arches with two subsidiary arches. Following heavy rain, the Dwyfor can be fast flowing, water gushing from its source in Cwm Pennant some twelve miles away.

Not exactly easy to find, but at the western end of the bridge, left hand side as one looks away from the village, are the initials 'D. LL. G', carved on the capping stones of the bridge. These are the initials of David Lloyd George. I enquired at the Lloyd George Museum in the centre of the village as to the exact location of the graffiti. Interestingly, on becoming elected as Liberal MP for Caernarfonshire in 1890, I'm told by the museum staff that a local blacksmith added the letters MP to the initials of Lloyd George. Thus, our Lloyd George bridge graffiti shows the hand of two different carvers.

Born in Manchester in 1863, but following the death of his father, raised with his uncle Richard in Llanystumdwy, David Lloyd George's career progression was quite amazing. Chancellor of the

Exchequer 1908-15, Prime Minister 1916-1922. Uncle Richard was a shoemaker living at Highgate cottage in the centre of Llanystumdwy. The young Lloyd George was raised in a Welsh speaking home making him the only British Prime Minister who could speak Welsh.

His friendship with Winston Churchill is another remarkable fact. One raised in a humble cottage, the other born into privilege at Blenheim Palace. It's hard to imagine a more polar opposite in terms of background and upbringing. Lloyd George in many ways remains a 'controversial figure'. One could argue that he would have fitted in quite nicely with our current crop of politicians. His contribution and foresight in relation to the development of the Welfare State however outweighs much of the often-repeated narrative of his failings.

Lloyd George arguably failed to find a long-term political solution for both Ireland and Israel. Lands are still contested. For any politician of any political persuasion these were difficult issues. They remain so. Steering Britain through the final years of World War I was also no easy task. A pacifist at heart it would seem that Lloyd George accepted that the best course was to get things done as soon as possible. Just get the war over. These are toxic issues. Not easy.

Often accused of abandoning the idea of Welsh Independence on becoming Prime Minister – again, this is too easy a narrative, too easy a criticism. He did employ many Welsh speakers during his tenure at 10 Downing Street. Votes For Women, National Insurance and the pension must count for something. He also advocated and promoted the daffodil as a symbol of Wales. He is of this place, I remain objective.

The Lloyd George Museum is full of objects and Highgate Cottage, his boyhood home, has been faithfully recreated and furnished as it would have been. For many, Llanystumdwy is Lloyd George and Lloyd George is certainly of Llanystumdwy. Y Plu, the community pub has re-opened in the centre of the village. A pint and Lloyd George it is then!

CRICIETH

How many 'C's in Cricieth? The answer to the question is there for all to see on the railway station platform. There are two consecutive 'C's in Criccieth, which makes the sum total of three 'C's of course. W.R.P. George, prominent local solicitor and Lloyd George's nephew always argued for two 'C's, Criccieth. Yn Gymraeg you don't really get two 'C's next to each other and therefore the Welsh spelling Cricieth has been adopted and accepted as being the correct spelling – but are we correct here? Gwynedd Council maintain it's Cricieth – one 'c'.

I have seen one theory that the two 'C's were introduced in order to stop non-Welsh speakers pronouncing 'Cricieth' as 'Crisieth'. Surely this is nonsense.

Welsh pop group, Y Dyniadon Ynfyd Hirfelyn Tesog summed up the whole debate with their 1972 song 'Sawl 'C' sydd yng Nghricieth' (Sain 23). A great slice of Dixieland / New Orleans style jazz – fused with Welsh humour. This is a great song. Dyniadon are now a 'cult' band. As far as I know their records have not been transferred to CD – you have to be a vinyl record collector, to seek, find and spin on a record deck.

Criccieth as a word may actually have its origin in two words *Crug-geith* with crug meaning a hillock, cairn or barrow and *ceith* or *caeth* referring to land that was owned or an enclosed area[6]. *Caeth* could also possibly refer to a prisoner or a bondsman. Could this possibly be the site of the capture of the Welsh king Gruffydd ap Llywelyn[7] who died at the hands of the Anglo-Saxons in 1063?

Another myth? Absolutely no way of knowing.

Gruffydd ap Llywelyn's death in 1063 would rule out the motte at nearby Dolbenmaen as belonging to him, as motte and bailey castles were not introduced to Britain until the Norman invasion of 1066. It is accepted that the current Cricieth castle would have been built sometime in the 1220s to 1230s during the reign of Llywelyn ab Iorwerth when the administrative centre of Eifionydd moved from Dolbenmaen to Cricieth. Closer to the sea. Dolbenmaen motte is more than likely an early castle belonging to the princes of Gwynedd.

If the original name is Crug Gaeth with caeth mutated to gaeth then that would explain the two consecutive G's. Surely Cricieth is two words not one. Two 'g's would adopt the sound of 'c' in Welsh? The debate / controversy continues. Lloyd-Jones may well be right, the two words have morphed or corrupted over time to Cricieth / Criccieth.

Another piece of the jigsaw, an additional twist to the story, is the appearance of a 'Cofiwch Dryweryn' mural near the train station, (see also NORTH, Penygroes). This lends further support for supporters of one 'c'. A sense of place is displayed by this particular graffiti artist. Although conforming with the recent upsurge in 'Cofiwch Dryweryn' murals all over Wales, this particular painting has been tagged. 'Cricieth' with one 'c' appears at the bottom right-hand corner of the mural.

PENTREFELIN

A relocated tall and narrow Bronze Age standing stone lies alongside the A497 Cricieth road. Otherwise the main point of interest at Pentrefelin is Ynyscynhaearn Church. It's hard to find. Through the narrow stone posts. Open the gate that drags painfully over the tarmac and follow the single-track road for about a mile. There it is, Ynyscynhaearn Church. Just enough room to turn a car around. Muddy and rural. The cows and sheep have been here.

Jack Black or John Ystumllyn is an interesting character. John Ystumllyn more commonly known as 'Jack Black' lies in the churchyard under the epitaph "I was born in India – and then in Wales I was christened; Here in this dark, cold place I lie under a grey slate." India probably means Africa. Presumably brought over as a slave from West Africa in the mid-eighteenth century. He may be lying in a dark, cold place but this is potentially a dark story indeed.

If you didn't know the location of 'Jack Black's gravestone, the inscription is getting so weather worn that it's very hard to read and making it even harder to find the grave. It's halfway down along the path on the left hand side as you walk towards the church. A greenish tint to the rectangular gravestone helps to locate 'Jack'. His gravestone leans against another box grave.

An ink drawing copied from a painting of Jack in 1754 suggests a young man of African origin? But what's the real story? It seems likely that this story alludes to Britain's colonial past. Wealthy landowning Welsh were guilty participants. Alltud Eifion published a pamphlet in 1888, *John Ystumllyn Neu "Jack Black"* which tells part of the story how this young black boy arrived at the Wynne family home at Ystumllyn, between Cricieth and Pentrefelin sometime in the mid-eighteenth century. Its only part of the story because no-one really knows how Jack arrived here. Some accounts mention that he came from London as a gift from the sister of Ellis Wynne. Other more dramatic accounts describe his 'capture' in Africa.

Alltud Eifion's booklet is of its time. Few in this part of north Wales had seen a black coloured boy before. You can imagine the slightly comical accounts almost a century later. But interestingly John becomes a proficient gardener, a dashing and desirable young man. The love of his life was Margaret Gruffydd the maid. When

JOHN YSTUMLLYN
'JACK BLACK'
1754

she moved elsewhere to work, John eventually absconded from Ystumllyn, following Margaret to Dolgellau, where they married.

According to Alltud Eifion there is a (fairly) happy ending. John returns to Ystumllyn for a time and on retirement is given property and land by Ellis Wynne. It was jaundice that did for him in the end. He died at the age of forty-six. The parish register records his death in 1786. His gravestone records 1791. A small mysterious discrepancy. There are descendants by all accounts. We really should seek them out.

The grave of James Spooner just to the right of the church porch directs my thoughts to Spooner's café at the NWHR train station in Porthmadog. Today the café is probably better known than Spooner, who actually built the Ffestiniog Railway. Nearby, are graves belonging to the Greaves family. Llechwedd quarry owners Greaves I presume, and right by the cemetery entrance is the grave of Alltud Eifion who wrote the pamphlet on John Ystumllyn.

St Cynhaearn is also the resting place of Dafydd Owen (1712-1741) who lived at Y Garreg Wen, Morfa Bychan near Porthmadog. He composed 'Dafydd y Garreg Wen', a well-known and much performed traditional Welsh folk song. His grave is unmistakable, with a huge harp on its slab.

TREMADOG (IN SEARCH OF GOTHIC)

Welcome to Tremadog – the birthplace of Lawrence of Arabia, town and country planning and quite possibly – Frankenstein
Town Square. Information Board.

As someone who has worked in the music industry and completely 'gets' the value of 'hype' this is a pretty good statement (of invitation). Come and discover Tremadog! Those who come to discover may visit the birthplace of T.E. Lawrence, they may remark on the 'planned town square' and may even have a vague awareness of the Percy Shelly connection. Few will take note of the three points on the town information board and actually go out and search for the truth, some truth, any truth. I accept the challenge! A simple task, but there is more to this than meets the eye, I end up on a quest – in search of the Gothic.

I've returned through the iron gate of Gorphwysfa, into the tiny front garden, and not for the first time, and not for the last time either, to take a photograph. 'Lawrence of Arabia was born in this house 1888'. As kids we loved that little plaque above the window.

Born out of wedlock in 1888, to Sir Thomas Chapman and his governess Sarah Junner, Lawrence was an assumed name. Further explanation not required. By the time he found out he was illegitimate the young Thomas Edward had already left Tremadog.

Firstly, for Scotland, then Brittany, Jersey, the New Forest and finally to Oxford, making him barely Welsh at all. He lived in Tremadog for just over a year. At the time of his birth the house on Church Street was known as Gorphwysfa. Later it became The Woodlands, before reverting to Gorffwysfa (with an ff – more Cymraeg). 'Lawrence House' has also been used and finally, replaced today by the unimaginative 'Snowdon Lodge', a hostel used mainly by walkers and climbers. 'Snowdon Lodge' – we are in Snowdonia but outside the National Park. Just.

T.E. Lawrence wrote *The Seven Pillars of Wisdom*, based on his experiences during the Arab Revolt against the Ottoman Empire during World War I. The book became the basis for the 1962 David Lean film, *Lawrence of Arabia* starring Peter O'Toole. Without the film it's questionable if T.E. Lawrence would be as well known today. The Tremadog locals have a more 'take him or leave him' attitude when it comes to Lawrence of Arabia. He wasn't here for very long is a common response. In true rock'n roll fashion T.E. Lawrence was killed as a result of a motorcycle accident in 1935 aged only 46. Welsh or not. Whatever they say. It's still a cool little plaque. Lawrence of Arabia was indeed born here. I suspect that I'll be back soon.

Opera singer Rhys Meirion lived in Tremadog as a child, and world-famous climber Eric Jones has a café here (at the time of writing he's attempting to sell). Eric Jones is probably best known for the first British solo ascent of the north face of the Eiger in 1981. Both are equally loved and acknowledged locally, maybe more than Lawrence. Jones's café serves proper mugs of tea – the kind of large mugs of tea that climbers require to fuel the next ascent of the Tremadog rocks directly across the road from Eric's café. I share just such a mug of tea with Eric. We chat.

Pictures of his many climbing adventures adorn the café walls. There are also pictures of Eric, parachutes and skyscrapers. I have to ask him a 'stupid question' and it's the obvious question. Why jump off skyscrapers in the USA risking arrest as well as life and limb with a single parachute? He smiles kindly, obviously many others have asked the same 'stupid question'. He must be used to it. "For the kicks". I knew the answer all along of course. I just wanted to hear him say it.

Returning to, so as not to undermine or underestimate the importance of, T.E. Lawrence. At the centenary of his birth in 1988, the T.E. Lawrence Society planted a Whitebeam tree in the tiny front garden of Gorphwysfa / Snowdon Lodge. A bench was provided to sit and contemplate the place of his birth. An accompanying centenary plaque was placed above the opposite front window to the original plaque.

Tremadog itself is a relatively rare thing in north Wales, a planned town. Conceived, designed and built in Georgian and Regency style by William Madocks, the MP for Lincolnshire, on buying the land in 1798 and completed by 1811. Hence the large square and mock cross-base at its centre, wide streets and the Town Hall with its five-arch frontage.

Nothing within the centre of Tremadog suggests random or organic development. Everything is regular, ordered, consistent. Grey stone buildings, all uniform. Wide streets that require a more purposeful stride to cross in the face of oncoming traffic. Cars can double park on the square (illegally) without causing a blockage. It's calmer since the opening of the by-pass.

Built on 'reclaimed' land from Traeth Mawr (wide sands) on the western side of Afon Glaslyn, it still gets a bit wet underfoot once you leave the tarmac. Follow any footpath or deviate off the roads and this area is very susceptible to flooding. Motor vehicles using the new bypass (deviated A487) regularly drive past what looks like an extended lake once the Glaslyn gets a bit full and water once again reclaims the reclaimed land.

A quick inspection of the OS map allows for an appreciation of the wider landscape. Afon Dwyryd flows in from the Vale of Ffestiniog past Penrhyndeudraeth and to the north of Traeth Bach joining the Glaslyn at Borth-y-Gest. This wide coastal flat land extends as far south as Morfa Harlech, on the craggy edge of which Edward I built his castle in 1283. There is a lot of sandy colour shading on the OS map.

Before the contract was awarded to Holyhead in 1811, there were two contenders for the site of the north Wales port that would serve as the connection with Dublin, Ireland. The second contender was Porth Dinllaen on the north coast of Llŷn. In anticipation that Telford's road from London would come out west, Madocks built The Cob across the Glaslyn estuary. Completed in 1811 The Cob became a roadway connecting the counties of 'Caernarvonshire' with 'Meironeth'. Within three weeks of completion it was breached by a great storm and took three years to be fully repaired. Today the Cob is a three-way affair: heritage railway, motor vehicles and cycles/pedestrians.

Right up to my twenties the Toll House charged motor vehicles 5p to cross the Cob. The trick was to hold on to your tickets and just wave them at the attendant, who would then assume you'd crossed earlier that day. Day tickets were colour co-ordinated but if you held them up quick enough and smiled you were through. We used to cross regularly in Transit vans with Welsh rock'n roll bands heading for a gig down south, heading down for the A470. This trick always got a laugh. A confidence-trick. Funny how I always felt slightly guilty.

Holyhead won the tender. In Tremadog, 'London Road' and 'Dublin Road' immediately became anachronisms. 'Dublin Road' still exists. London Road became Church Road.

Madocks, almost bankrupted and more than slightly disappointed died on his European travels and is buried in Paris. The story may have a tragic ending but Tremadog remains endearing and quaint if slightly overshadowed by its big brother Porthmadog in terms of hustle and bustle and shops. Tremadog wins though for its open space and a rich concentration of nineteenth century history in such a small area. I can't help but feel slightly sorry for Madocks, a man of vision – crushed by a re-routing of road and port. In the twentieth century Clough Williams-Ellis, responsible for nearby Portmeirion (page 206) advocated a similar vision for town and country planning.

Wandering around Tremadog, the Gothic Revival church of St Mary's stands out. Literally. Built by Madocks in 1811. Before he built The Cob, the tidal Glaslyn would have often washed up to and around the rocky outcrop on which St Mary's now stands. No religious services there before the Cob unless the Druids passed this way and no services now. Currently in use as offices and not open to the public the interior has been converted and adapted. I peered in through the glass door and saw the usual open plan office space divided by boards and housing non-descript furniture.

The outer Gothic archway is worth studying. Climbing up on to the wall for a closer look I'm confronted by scowling cherubs, funny if slightly frightening little Gothic characters that surround the arch. This is almost out of character. There is nothing else vaguely Gothic about Tremadog. Tremadog is clean. Nice. Pleasant. Plain Georgian / Regency. There are no burials at St Mary's, burials took place on drier land at neighbouring cemeteries. Tremadog remains part of Ynyscynhaearn Parish.

Tan-yr-Allt, the home of William Madocks, lies just outside the village on the Beddgelert road and is now a luxury boutique B&B. Stay the night and you may end up in the same bedroom as poet Percy Bysshe Shelley who stayed here in 1812-13. Apart from the architecture of St Mary's, the only other Gothic connection at Tremadog is hinted at on the information board in the town square. A question is posed: *"Could the greatest monster story ever told have its roots here in Tremadog?"*

Whether any of *Frankenstein* (1818) was conceived at Tan-yr-allt by Mary Shelley is unlikely. In fact, what is written on the town information board opposite the Town Hall may be as much fantasy as Mary's Gothic novel. The accepted view is that *Frankenstein* was written following Shelley's stay with Byron near Lake Geneva in 1816. Mary and Percy having become lovers in 1814 would rule out Tremadog as location for either passion between the two or the conception of *Frankenstein*. But, Shelley's *Queen Mab* was contemplated here by all accounts. Shelley shot at by a local for either his unspoken views or for owing money (gambling?) is said to have never returned to Wales after this incident.

Tan-yr-Allt boasts sightings of Shelly's ghost. Given that it is now a high-end B&B one could argue that this is as good a marketing tool as the Frankenstein reference on the town noticeboard. But you have to dig deep at Tremadog, to stumble across the stuff of Gothic novels. None of this is visible. None of this is obvious. Tan-yr-Allt looks welcoming rather than the scene of historical shootings.

My quest for the gothic has been an enjoyable wander around Tremadog. I have seen in plain sight the result of Madocks' town and country planning. The only Gothic in Tremadog is the Gothic Revival Church and its cherub arch. No Gothic novels.

PORTHMADOG

> There is no present in Wales,
> And no future;
> There is only the past,
> Brittle with relics,
> Wind-bitten towers and castles
> With sham ghosts;
> Mouldering quarries and mines;
> And an impotent people,
> Sick with inbreeding,
> Worrying the carcase of an old song.
>
> R.S. Thomas

Harsh words. Perhaps. There are of course many ways of looking at Wales. I am of the opinion, to paraphrase the Sex Pistols, 'that blind acceptance is the same as stupid fools that stand in line'. Where I disagree with R.S. is that Wales is all those things, past, present and future. There is a present and a future. But I agree it should not be viewed uncritically. I am no nationalist, I do not love Wales unconditionally as I would my wife or children. It is political being here, working here, creating here, existing here – therefore if at times it (Wales) needs a good kicking, then give it a good kicking.

If I am no nationalist, what am I? A failed anarchist possibly, but Wales and its language, y Gymraeg, has been central to my life's work in terms of music, writing, broadcasting, archaeology, lecturing, but never uncritically. Somewhere on the 'spectrum of Welshness' we need the Thomases, R.S. and Dylan. We need a critical 'other' voice.

Ronald Stuart Thomas's ashes were scattered on a patch of grass near the north wall of the Grade II listed St John's Church (Sant Ioan) in Porthmadog. Almost nondescript for one of Wales's foremost poets. There is no evidence of pilgrimages to this place. No poems on cards next to the plot. Here there is only the past.

R.S. is not buried with his first wife, Elsie Eldridge (1909-1991). Elsi is buried at Llanfaelrhys churchyard near Aberdaron. Her grave lies very close to those of the Keating sisters. Llŷn dialect pronounces Llanfarlys, incorrectly with the r and l swopped. But it's the same place. Elsi's slate plaque reads 'M.E. ELDRIDGE 1909-1991 AC YN EI YSBRYD R.S. THOMAS 1913-2000'.

'Yn ei ysbryd' translates as here in spirit. R.S. is there in spirit. Elsi was a mural artist and book illustrator. Examples of her work are held by the V&A and the National Museum of Wales. Alongside her slate plaque is a solitary beach pebble with a golden 'G' painted on the surface. The 'G' is for Gwydion, their only son who passed away at the age of 71 in 2016. Gwydion had been an active promoter of both his father and mother's works.

Upstairs, in a small loft at Llanfaelrhys church is what I can only describe as an R.S. Thomas shrine. A kettle and tea making facilities sit on a plain bench. Poetry books lie non-vertically in bookshelves. A Persian rug covers a dusty floor. Pictures of R.S., Elsi and Gwydion grace all other surfaces. I'm not tempted to read or partake in some tea. From the upper window the barren windswept Llŷn coastline is visible. A view from a poem.

Returning down the creaky stairs, the church is cold, stark, ancient. Wealthy landowning families are commemorated on brass plaques. It must be a rare occasion now that would see the pews fully occupied.

Byron Rogers' epic biography of R.S. Thomas *The Man Who Went Into the West* literally maps out his life's journey. Born in Cardiff, then at the age of five the family moved to Holyhead. As an adult, vicar of Chirk for four years, Manafon for twelve years and the final eleven years at Aberdaron. Rogers also draws a map, 'The Lifelong Journey into the West' in which the journey is shown as an arc. From Holyhead, heading along the north coast of Wales, down the Marches, along the Severn and Dyfi rivers and finally up the Cambrian Coast to the south western tip of Llŷn. It almost looks planned.

Porthmadog is usually referred to as 'Port' by the locals. Throughout the year this is a busy shopping town. Tourists buy inflatable beach beds, buckets and spades during the summer months before heading out to Black Rock Sands or Morfa Bychan beach. Locals shop for essentials. The newly built Tesco supermarket always busy. On the other side of the road, the Art Deco cinema tragically demolished for future building. Plot for Sale. Available brown field site but as yet – no takers.

During the 1987 National Eisteddfod, gigs were held at the cinema evoking memories of the Sex Pistols at the Castle Cinema, Caerffili. Abertridwr born Gareth Potter appeared here with his band Traddodiad Ofnus. I was in the audience. Traddodiad Ofnus were having an ongoing dispute with the soundman and Potter promptly emptied the contents of his pint glass into one of the PA monitors.

Abertridwr is next to Caerffili. Potter may have been too young to attend the Pistols gig in 1976 but he's read their textbook on provoking outrage. Great gig – we still talk about the monitor incident!

Port gigs were always good during the 1980s. One of those places where Punk had taken hold and had a lasting effect. Maybe it was all down to the local record shop Cob. Mail Order and thousands of vinyl. Cob was a Sunday afternoon pilgrimage for record collectors from all over the UK and still is. Cob stands on the town side of Madocks' cob embankment.

Even today, Port is a place of music fans. Glen Matlock from the Sex Pistols played at the Football Club in 2018. I've never seen so many 'Never Mind the Bollocks' T-shirts in one place. Ninety per cent locals. They know their stuff musically. Proper fans.

Local punk band Elfyn Presli gained John Peel support. Singer Bern was a visionary. Opinionated and charismatic. Holding court at the Ship & Castle. Bern was guaranteed to talk records, bands with a one hundred per cent certainty of who should be dismissed instantly and who was musical genius. Bern is much missed. The demon drink got to him but his legacy is a great record 'Jackboots Maggie Thatcher' (Anhrefn 04) one of the greatest Punk Rock anthems of all time.

Just up the road, the now closed Glaslyn pub at Prenteg hosted gigs by pre-fame Catatonia and Super Furry Animals. I once saw Irish folk band Altan play there. Our recurring theme of lost venues would include the Ship & Castle. Queen's is still open but the stage is silent. Neville Staple (ex-Specials) performed at Y Ganolfan recently. Port is still a musically happening place.

EIFIONYDD

Books have been written about the 'characters' of Eifionydd and the old county of Sir Gaernarfon. I have two such books, Cybi's *Cymeriadau Hynod Sir Gaernarfon* and William Rowland's *Gwŷr Eifionydd*. Published in 1923 and 1953 respectively the characters are largely forgotten today. Poets feature prominently, Eifionydd's finest wordsmiths such as Robert ap Gwilym Ddu (1767-1850), Pedr Fardd (1775-1845), Dewi Wyn o Eifion (1784-1841), Ellis Owen, Cefn-y-meysydd (1789-1868), Nicander (1809-1874) and possibly most known, heard-of or remembered today, Eben Fardd (1802-1863).

Eifionydd is less wild than Llŷn proper, the hills are much lower, the grass greener, the landscape more wooded. Y Lôn Goed is a tree lined avenue running from Afon Wen on the south coast right across Eifionydd to Hendre Cennin in the north. Constructed during the early nineteenth century to transport lime to the surrounding farms and fields that were part of the estate belonging to Sir Thomas Mostyn, Plas Talhenbont.

Estate manager John Maughan oversaw the work. The 'road' is always twelve feet across and tree lined – they must have planted hundreds of trees. Too many to count. Large boulders moved for the construction remain at the edge of the road even today. Out of the way but too heavy to be moved any further. In archaeological terms the road surface would be described as a 'metalled road', which means it is made up of compacted stones underfoot, almost like cobbling but just utilising small stones that were available.

Maughan would be pronounced 'Môn' in Welsh and Y Lôn Goed is still occasionally referred to as 'Lôn Môn' by some locals when they actually mean 'Lôn Maughan'. There was and there is no Anglesey connection here. Maughan was from Northumberland.

Walking along the course of this tree-lined road various junctions to the surrounding fields become apparent. Almost like little bridges, stone lined, which obviously gave the waggons carrying agricultural lime access to individual fields. In these upland areas of north Wales the calcium carbonate reduced the acidity of the soil. Today reeds have reclaimed many of the fields, the acidity has returned. No horse or carts have passed this way for a good few years. Grass grows underfoot on Y Lôn Goed.

Running in bursts of straight lines with the occasional turn, this is not the track of local hill farmers. Along with the fact that the whole thing is tree lined, this is a product of nineteenth century landowners and estate management. A testament to Maughan's construction and planning skills.

A llonydd gorffenedig
Yw llonydd y Lôn Goed
R. Williams Parry

Poet R. Williams Parry referred to the 'perfect peace' here. He was right. Secluded and covered by a canopy of trees. I've run (jogged) the length of it in the past. For the purpose of researching this book I took a gentle stroll and attempted to listen to the 'perfect peace'. It's a rather cold day in June, a storm is brewing and the only sound apart from the occasional bleating of sheep is the rustling of leaves high above my head. A constant rustle, like running water, in the background.

But I hear no cars. No background noise as a result of human activity. I do smell a distant fire – someone burning rubbish on one of the farms. Birds sing. On my journey here along the back roads of Eifionydd a heron glided high above, long legs positioned backwards. Probably fishing in the Dwyfach river. Goldfinches (Nico in Welsh) skimmed the hedgerows in that particular up and down way that they do. A swallow skimmed to close for comfort and I caught a glimpse of a couple of great tits. Under the canopy of Y Lôn Goed I could hear them sing but I saw no birds at all.

An Englishman walking his dogs was chatting to a local farmer leaning on the gate as farmers do. Just like a character from an R.S. Thomas poem, the farmer looked the real deal Welsh hill farmer. Research for the book I thought – let's say hello and see where the conversation goes. I had just passed the old railway crossing near Maes Gwyn and just let slip that my grandfather, Moses Price, was station master at Pant Glas – a few miles north.

A wooden railway gate with a circular rusted metal plate which once would have been bright red for STOP! still stands at the junction of the grassed over abandoned railway line. The little railway cottage, half cottage – half signal station in form is still there. Silent.

Our farmer, well into his 80s, remembered my grandfather well, by all accounts he was skilled at repairing watches – something I was not aware of. Once he'd figured out the family tree, he commented that my mother, Sydney, had died young. He was quite right, cancer got her at 51. Grammar and County probably meant that they did not attend the same school, but our farmer friend knew of my mother and many other family members that I had to confess of having no real knowledge of or connection with.

Our conversation served only to confirm the dog walker's impression that everybody knows everybody in north Wales. We are all inter-related. He made some excuse and wandered off with his dogs to let us continue with family recollections.

There is a saying within countryside etiquette and certainly within the world of archaeological landscapes and environment that nothing should be left other than a footprint and that nothing should be taken other than a photograph. No litter left and no artefacts or stones 'stolen' and moved. Along Y Lôn Goed someone has been leaving little stone sculptures by the way side. Not of this place. Out of character. Some of the sculptures included slate. Definitely out of context, there's no slate here geologically on the peninsula. Wrestling with this ideological dilemma I ponder on the right and wrongs of these little pieces of art littering Y Lôn Goed.

It's not real litter, it's just natural stone after all. It does no harm. It's just that it does not belong. Context is everything. This is the stuff of beaches given an arty skyscraper of stones by a creative and steady hand. Maybe the sculptures were constructed by members of the nearby Buddhist retreat? Arguably there is no better place for contemplation than strolling along Y Lôn Goed away from the noise pollution, protected and shielded by the trees.

Maybe others have joined in the fun. There were numerous sculptures that probably involved a basket full of stones. Preparation. Concept. Not spur of the moment random guerrilla art. Would R. Williams Parry have been inspired to write an extra verse for his eulogy of the 'perfect peace'. Confused and bemused. Irritated and yet not. I return to my parked transit van at the top of Y Lôn Goed and head for home – before that storm.

PANT GLAS

In the introduction to this section, I mentioned that my mother was born at Station House, Pant Glas, 1932. My grandfather was Station

Master here. On the Bangor - Pwllheli line. Parts of the track, certainly from Felinheli as far south as Bryncir can now be followed as a cycle track. At Pant Glas this part of the cycle path is known as Lôn Eifion.

In the 1930s and early 1940s it was a two-mile uphill walk for my mother and her sister to the school at Bwlch Derwin. Now a B&B and known as the Old School – Hen Ysgol Guest House. At least on the way home it was two miles downhill. There would have been very few road vehicles here in the 1930s. Road safety was less of an issue. In summer the walk would have been glorious. When it rained and blew gales the two sisters must have been soaked to the skin. I'm trying hard to find positives.

Although the school closed in the 1970s the bell is still hanging by the door. Ring a ding – breaktime over. Form a line. Back to lessons. Pant Glas-born opera singer Bryn Terfel would have attended primary school here.

Still very much a rural area, Bryn Derwin borders the upland hills of Bwlch Mawr to the west and Mynydd Cennin to the south. Somewhere on this hillside a crucial battle was fought in June 1255 between Llywelyn ap Gruffudd and his troublesome brothers Owain and Dafydd. Victory for Llywelyn secured his control over Gwynedd and eventually much of Wales. Owain Goch ap Gruffudd was later imprisoned for over twenty years at Dolbadarn Castle and Dafydd was to side with the forces of Edward I in 1277 once again in opposition to his brother.

There is nothing to see of the battlefield today. Mostly given to upland pasture and a smattering of forestry. Y Foel, a small hill standing at an altitude of 218 metres above sea level may well have provided a vantage point to view the battle or as a suitable place to raise a banner. We can only imagine.

BRYNCIR

Icorix's stone at Llystyn Gwyn is what is known as a fifth to sixth century bilingual Early Christian gravestone in that it has both Latin and Ogham inscriptions. Commemorating Icorix the stone reads 'ICORIX FILUS POTENTINI', Icorix son of Potentinus.

As Ogham is an early form of Irish and the fact that Icorix has a bilingual inscription, this suggests he (or his family) is of Irish descent. Perhaps an Irish immigrant. Settled and buried in Gwynedd.

Pembrokeshire and southern Ceredigion overflow with these bilingual Ogham stones. In Gwynedd this is our only certain or confirmed example. I have argued in my book *Cam i'r Deheubarth* (2019) that Dyfed experienced many more Irish incomers than Gwynedd in this early Medieval period. My argument is based on the possibility that Irish immigration to south west Wales followed that of a leader called Voteporix. His stone can now be seen on display at the Carmarthenshire Museum at Abergwili.

Let's just explore the possibility of Voteporix, an Irish 'leader' settling in the south west. His presence would the attract others to follow, certainly family members or followers. Could this explain the numbers in the south west as compared to north west Wales? There was more incentive to head to the south west? As Eurwyn William wrote:

> "… in Wales, there are no 'natives': we are all incomers, and it is only the degree that differs".

This quote is from the Foreword of *Discovered in Time, Treasures From Early Wales* (2011). 12-10,000BP, at the time of the last Ice Age, Wales was pretty well covered by ice sheets. No one lived here, no one could live here. During warm periods of the Ice Ages, man had lived here, but sometime around 8000 BC man returned permanently, crossing over from Europe, hunting and gathering. Probably heading up north and west to the area we know as Wales today in the warmer summer months. This is the beginning of the Mesolithic period. Wales has been populated ever since.

Any debate about migration and 'natives' starts at this point. From now on it's possible to argue that there is human activity in Wales that has continued to the present day. Whether any of us have Mesolithic DNA I have no idea, but this is Eurwyn's point if I have understood – it's only a matter of when we arrived here. We are all immigrants. This could be a slogan on a T-Shirt. People have always moved.

Notes

1. Cian Ciaran is a member of the Super Furry Animals and founder member of Aros Mae, WwzZ and Acid Casuals. Cian Ciaran CD: *Rhys a Meinir* (Strange Town Records).
2. Ac Eraill, *Addewid* EP, 1974 (Sain 43) featuring 'Cwm Nant Gwrtheyrn'.
3. Cantre'r Gwaelod, a mythical ancient kingdom submerged under Cardigan Bay. An early version of the myth appears in the *Black Book of Carmarthen*. A drunken Seithenyn is often blamed for leaving the sluice gates open resulting in the drowning of his kingdom.
4. Iolo Morganwg (Edward Williams, 1747-1826) influential Welsh antiquarian, poet, collector and literary forger.
5. Brenda Chamberlain's account of her time on Enlli is told in the book *Tide-race* (Seren, 1987).
6. Gruffydd ap Llywelyn. King of Gwynedd and Powys and eventually all of Wales in the period 1055-1063. Gruffydd was the great-great grandson of Hywel Dda. J. Lloyd-Williams suggests the explanation of *Crug-geith* for Criccieth, (1928) which may coincide with the story relating to Gruffydd ap Llywelyn.

CENTRAL

LLANBERIS

Llanberis is located at the western foot of Yr Wyddfa / Snowdon (1085metres). Today it's hard to avoid the mountaineering, climbing, walking, hiking, outdoor connection here. An hour's journey on the Snowdon Mountain Railway[1] will get you to the summit café with barely a foot placed on the mountain. Certainly, no feet on real rocks – just ten metres of concrete at the summit station from train to café and back again. A good couple of hours walk on the 'Llanberis Path' more or less follows the same route as the rack and pinion railway and arrives at the same destination.

On the Llanberis Path to the summit it's not uncommon to see young couples, badly equipped, trainers not hiking boots, no kit, no supplies, painfully unaware of the distance ahead. They'll get away with it on a nice day; if the weather turns there could be trouble. With so many other quieter paths on offer, the Llanberis route is probably best avoided if peace and tranquillity are the aim for the day. It can and does get very busy. Too busy.

Llanberis overflows with semi-hippy mountaineering types with £30,000-plus campervans. They stand out dreadlocked, sun tanned, super fit. They have settled here in the mountains. Visitors visit all year around but once again overflow during Bank Holiday weekends and the summer months. Where once it was quarries for roofing slate it is now purely a tourist economy. B&Bs throng the High Street interspersed with outdoor equipment shops.

Llanberis has a new sword, a rust-red/rust-orange weathered twenty-foot sword stuck firmly into a concrete base at the eastern edge of the car park by the shore of the glacial lake, Llyn Padarn. Created by blacksmith Gerallt Evans and commissioned by Welsh Government as part of the 'Year of Legends' (2017). Typically, word associations especially in connection with titles that includes 'Legends' lead to false trails in search of the Arthurian connection. Arthur the sixth century British leader probably never set foot in Llanberis. Excalibur, King Arthur's sword, is not celebrated here but rather the thirteenth century princes of Gwynedd.

It's a lone voice that argues against the Arthurian connection. Llyn Llydaw on Snowdon's eastern flank is often cited as the lake holding Excalibur, awaiting the call for the Welsh to rise again. Snowdon's summit cairn is often associated with Rhita (sometimes Rhitta or Rhudda) the Giant, allegedly slain by Arthur himself. It

does not stop. Arthur here. Arthur there. Arthur everywhere. But most likely no Arthur here.

Whether any of this is clear to the thousands of visitors who pass through Llanberis, I have no idea. Whether it needs to be clear is another matter. The sword stands as a piece of public art – open to interpretation as art should be. I doubt that it attracts any more visitors to Llanberis. It's just there if you want it.

There is no associated plaque or information board to direct people away from Arthurian connotations and to focus firmly on the princes of Gwynedd. A slightly battered and weathered information board nearby informs us that the lake last froze over in 1963 allowing people to walk across, and that the it is also home to the Arctic Char, *Salvelinus alpinus* (Welsh: *torgoch*) one of Britain's rarest species of fish which inhabits deep, cold glacial waters.

At the eastern edge of Llyn Padarn on a low rocky knoll (much exaggerated in paintings by J.M.W. Turner[2]) stands Castell Dolbadarn. Built by Llywelyn ab Iorwerth (Llywelyn the Great) in the 1220s and occupied later by his grandson Llywelyn ap Gruffudd (Llywelyn the Last). This is the real connection with the twenty-foot sword. The princes of Gwynedd ruled most of Wales at various times during the thirteenth century before making the big

mistake of picking a fight with the far stronger Edward I, resulting
in the native princes losing the whole lot in 1282-83.

For a time then, during the mid-thirteenth century, Dolbadarn
was a 'Royal Palace', a home for princes and indeed home, with
associated garden, to Joan (Siwan of Saunders Lewis fame[3]) an
illegitimate daughter of King John. Illegitimate or not, this means
that Gwynedd's Llywelyn ab Iorwerth had pulled off the ultimate in
political marriage trickery – and managed to marry a daughter of
the King of England. Politically shrewd for sure, but was there love?

From certain angles in the carpark the castle stands proud with
the round keep visible in the distance behind the towering sword.
Juxtaposed. Controversy followed the erection of the sword.
Councillors, letters, local press, the usual stuff – the controversy
raged. For a while – then the sword just got rusty.

Just up the road, in the centre of Llanberis, past the legendary
walker's / climber's café 'Pete's Eats' is Goodman Street.
Unassuming, but once home to Welsh literary giant T. Rowland
Hughes.

Keep your bloody chips! "Cadw dy blydi chips", arguably the
first time we come across swearing in Welsh Literature, that is if we
ignore medieval poet Dafydd ap Gwilym[4]. Dafydd ap Gwilym is
known for his often sexual, rather crude and racy poems of lust and
wanting. OK let's argue in Modern Welsh literature then. 'Bloody'
in its Cymraeg form 'blydi'. The swearing quote comes from

William Jones (1944) by T. Rowland Hughes and the novel tells the story of a local quarryman who travels to the south Wales coalfield to look for work when hard times fall upon the slate quarries up north.

It's a common story here in Gwynedd and elsewhere. This happened to my great uncle, Dafydd Thomas, the brother of my grandfather. He was sent to live and work with family in the south Wales Valleys during the 1930s when work was in short supply in the Nantlle Valley slate quarries. T. Rowland Hughes's novels were merely reflecting a reality for many of the quarrymen and their families.

20 Goodman Street is an unassuming terrace house a short way along unassuming Goodman Street. That T. Rowland Hughes lived here is confirmed by a slate plaque high up on the pebble-dashed wall. 'Llenor a Bardd'. Author and Poet – they always multi-tasked these giants of Welsh culture. Novels and poetry.

Opposite the house is a children's playground. I spot no empty discarded chip cones or indeed any litter at all. The park is spotless. The Llanberis kids at the playground either don't eat chips or are well behaved and put all their litter in the bin. Inspired by T. Rowland Hughes's most famous quote, I go in search of a chip shop walking the length of the High Street.

Heading east to west on the south side of the High Street I count seven B&Bs, two convenience stores, a church, a garage, a bike hire shop, an ice cream parlour, a signage shop and two takeaways – one Indian and one Chinese. Chips are served at the Chinese.

Returning from west to east on the north side of High Street the B&B count drops to two and the café count is up to five. I pass a hairdressers, a chapel, two outdoor activity shops, one pub, a bric-a-brac shop, a Community Enterprise shop, a laundrette, a pharmacy, a martial arts academy, an undertakers, a farm shop, three pubs, two restaurants one of which is attached to one of the pubs, an Indian takeaway and finally a proper old fashioned 'English' chippy. I also pass two defunct phone boxes re-used as community spaces / very small exhibition spaces. The re-use is commendable. The fact that they are not the post office red Giles Gilbert Scott, K6 design is disappointing. Just modern glass.

GLYNRHONWY

Just west of Llanberis, Glynrhonwy Quarry was once part of the Newborough Estate. These were the lands of the Wynnes of Glynllifon near Caernarfon. Around 150 men were employed here in the later part of the nineteenth century and although this was a substantial quarry it appears small compared to the workings at nearby Dinorwic. Situated on the northern side of Llyn Padarn and Llyn Peris, and owned by the Assheton Smith family of Vaenol near Bangor, 2710 men were recorded as working there in 1883.

Following the closure of Glynrhonwy in the 1930s the lower pit was taken over by the Ministry of Supply in 1940 for the purpose of bomb storage. This use continued until 1961. Parts of the storage structures survive to this day. Iron gates and fencing prevent public access. Urban adventurers get through anyway.

You Tube has many a video featuring intrepid underground explorers whose raison d'etre is to get into places where there is no public access. GoPro cameras and torches in hand, their adventures are uploaded online. Mission accomplished. Raves have been held here – underground. Hard to imagine with the echo effect of the tunnels. Local kids have played and explored here for years. Fences merely provide an extra challenge.

At some point most of the roof collapsed burying much of the munitions. In order to hide the site from the Luftwaffe, a series of concrete tunnels were concealed by slate debris within the lower pit workings. From the air this would have looked like any other disused quarry. Following extensive clearance, it is now assumed that all the munitions have been taken away from the site. All that remains is around one third of the original tunnels on two levels. Railway tracks and service lifts still remain and a few bits of electrics. But mostly these are empty tunnels. Echo chambers occupied by the ghosts of World War II.

Beyond the activities of urban explorers this is not that well known a site. Access is prohibited and difficult, if not dangerous. Trees line the fence and the pit and tunnels are not visible from the passing roads. Various ambitious plans to develop Glynrhonwy come and go. One of the more fanciful was for an outdoor artificial ski slope.

CRAIG YR UNDEB

Whatever is written about the slate quarrymen, whichever version of history you read there has to be one conclusion. The landowners and quarry owners exploited the workforce. At Dinorwic the quarry hospital was more concerned with getting injured quarrymen back to work than their actual health. The quarry owners blamed tea drinking for silicosis rather than slate dust. Holders of the title Lord Penrhyn retain their bad reputation even to this day. Sugar and slate lingers like a foul odour.

An attempt to form a workers' union took place in November 1865 when over a thousand men gathered at Bethesda. Failing before it had really started, this event had at least sown a seed. Workers' rights were on the agenda. In 1874 they became a reality with the formation of the North Wales Quarrymen's Union.

One of the most interesting things about the 1874 gathering which took place on the shore of Llyn Padarn was that it was on Newborough land. Conspiracy theories abound as to why the meeting was allowed to take place. Disputes between workers and managers had taken place at Glynrhonwy. Some allude to a rivalry between Newborough and Assheton Smith? Was Newborough slightly more liberal than other landowners? The quarrymen's union was established. History was made.

A huge natural rock outcrop formed the podium for the speakers. Known to this day as Craig yr Undeb (Union Rock) the old

Llanberis road passes by on the lake side. Now closed off and used by cows, walkers, cyclist and joggers. Central white lines are still visible but moss and cow dung slowly encroaches on the tarmac.

Jack Jones, General Secretary of the Transport and General Workers Union, unveiled a plaque here in 1974 on the one hundredth anniversary of the union. The new road passes to the south of Craig yr Undeb. Cars zoom by, blissfully unaware of the cultural significance and historical importance of this rock.

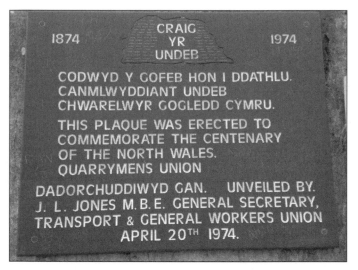

R. Merfyn Jones's account of the quarrymen's struggle against their unforgiving and uncompromising masters is emotionally captured in his epic 1982 publication *The North Wales Quarrymen 1874-1922*. This is not light reading. I must have cried dozens of times as I poured over accounts of instant dismissals for strike organisers and the repercussions for their families. They asked for basic worker's rights and lost their jobs. It's quite understandable how resentment has lingered on towards Lord Penrhyn and his like, even to the present day.

An obvious omission from the whole history of the north Wales slate quarries is the role of women. The traditional 'Welsh Mam' may be a bit of a cliché and is certainly a figure prominent in the novels of authors like Kate Roberts who write about the quarries of the Rhosgadfan area. But it appears that any historical narrative about the quarryman on the rock face, the hardships and culture have by-passed the role of women completely. To the best of my knowledge this was a male dominated industry. Men only in the pits, mills and cutting sheds.

'Merched Chwarel' a collective of female artists[5] based around the Llanberis and Nant Peris area have embarked on a process of re-evaluating this narrative through art and creativity. This is a most welcomed injection of female perspective in an over-romanticised male landscape. Even family stories that I grew up with created an uneasy narrative. My grandmother 'kept the house'. But in reality, she kept the finances in order. Held the purse strings and argued with my grandfather whether it would be food on the table or his next packet of fags.

The stories and drama captured so raw and explicitly by Kate Roberts serve only to feed into the established narrative. Women struggled on. Research and projects by artists such as Merched Chwarel may uncover a new narrative, create new truths. Whatever the outcome, the female can no longer be ignored and written out of the story.

PEN Y GWRYD

The 1953 British Mount Everest Expedition summited on Friday May 29th, at 11.30am. The popular misconception or common 'myth' about the Pen y Gwryd Hotel is that the members of the

team stayed here during training in Eryri (Snowdonia) prior to setting off for the expedition. The 'reality' is that Pen y Gwryd has been the location for the annual reunions ever since.

Why climb Everest? 'Because it's there' answered George Mallory. Mallory and his climbing companion Andrew 'Sandy' Irvine were lost on the north-east ridge during the first attempt at the summit in 1924. Mallory's body was discovered in 1999 but it remains a mystery whether they made it to the summit. We will probably never know.

It was Edmund Hillary and Tenzing Norgay that first made it to the top in 1953. Their signatures are on the ceiling of the bar / side room along with others who have climbed Everest. This is one of the highlights of visiting Pen y Gwryd Hotel. Straining one's head to read the signatures on the roof. Tenzing Norgay's signature is not much more than a squiggle and not easy to spot. Hillary is easy enough to find.

The other popular story or 'myth' about Pen y Gwryd (which may have an element of truth) is that the four Beatles wanted to sign their autographs on the bar ceiling but were refused because their accomplishment was cultural rather than physical. The 'exception' to the signatories of Everest mountaineers is Dr Roger Bannister who ran the first sub-four minute mile. The Beatles could only manage three-minute pop songs. Bannister looks like he scribbled his name from below.

Old boots, ice axes, pieces of rope and other bits of climbing paraphernalia hang from beams or are displayed in glass cases all around the pub. Wooden panels give the whole place an Alpine feel. You can imagine howling gales and snowstorms outside while the fire rages. Old water pipes clank and make funny random noises. This is a great stop for tea or coffee. Full of atmosphere. Bang in the middle of the mountains.

Pen y Gwryd sits on the junction with Nant Gwynant which drops sharply towards Beddgelert to the south, the wide-open moors of Dyffryn Mymbyr to the east and Bwlch y Gwyddel and the pass over to Llanberis via Pen y Pass to the west. This was always an important pass through Snowdonia. The threat of a German invasion from neutral Ireland during World War II saw the building of four rectangular pillboxes here during 1940-1941. Standing guard on each approach to the pass. Turf-covered, they maintain an air of menace.

Almost two thousand years earlier, around the time of the

Agricolan campaign of 77AD, the Romans built a marching camp here. The half way stage between their forts at Caer Llugwy (Capel Curig) and Segontium (Caernarfon). The road junction and the hotel sit within the banks of the fort. It's geography that dictates here. Following the pass through the mountains the route has changed little over the centuries. This is the only way through.

YR WYDDFA (SNOWDON)

The Snowdon Ranger Path or Llwybr Cwellyn up Snowdon is generally accepted as the earliest path established to the summit and is the route referred to in historical documents as the one used by the early guides of the late eighteenth century. One guide in particular, Ellis Griffiths, who lived at Bron y Fedw near Llyn Cwellyn, is described as having a 'goat-like agility' and appears to have had the honour of guiding a botanical party which included the poet Samuel Taylor Coleridge to the summit during the summer of 1794.

A path runs up from Bron y Fedw, 'The Guide's House', and joins up with the Snowdon Ranger path on reaching the plateau of Cwm Treweunydd. The Snowdon Ranger path itself starts at the Youth Hostel, a former inn near the Cwellyn or Snowdon Ranger Station. The station was built in 1874 as part of the North Wales Narrow Gauge Railway line serving the Moel Tryfan slate quarry and the quarries of Cwm Gwyrfai and Rhyd Ddu. Passenger services ended in 1936 and the track remained dormant until its reopening in 2003 as a heritage line, the Welsh Highland Railway.

Initially zig-zagging its way up the steep slope from Llyn Cwellyn, it's likely that the early guides established the route. Zig-zagging must have been easier for the mules and walkers, than a direct uphill struggle before reaching the relatively flatness of Cwm Treweunydd. It takes about thirty minutes to walk up the zig-zags. Thirty minutes of strenuous uphill walking. With views towards Moel Hebog and Y Gyrn to the south and Mynydd Mawr to the west, this is dramatic scenery.

On a still day the surface of Llyn Cwellyn displays the reflection of Y Gyrn and Mynydd Mawr. Llanrwst poet Gwilym Cowlyd[6] describes 'llun y dydd', (the picture of the day), reflected on the surface of the still lakes of the Conwy Valley in his 1868 awdl

'Mynyddoedd Eryri'. This applies here just as well:

Y llynnau gwyrddion llonydd – a gysgant
Mewn gwasgod o fynydd;
A thynn heulwen ysblennydd
Ar len y dŵr lun y dydd.

*'The calm green lakes are sleeping in the mountain shadows, and on
the water's canvas, bright sunshine paints the picture of the day'*

On a calm day it's a good idea to pause on the zig-zag section of the path. Catch your breath. Enjoy the reflections on the still surface of Llyn Cwellyn. Think Gwilym Cowlyd. Then continue. On other days the waters of Llyn Cwellyn are choppy. Frothy white and no reflection. Llyn Cwellyn actually supplies drinking water for the Caernarfon area and parts of Anglesey. A glacial lake that has been damned at its northern end – it's deep and supports a natural population of Arctic Char.

Dramatically in 2005 an outbreak of cryptosporidium, a parasite that can cause diarrhea, occurred in the waters of Llyn Cwellyn. The resulting press hysteria, panic and indeed valid concern, boosted the sales of bottled water in Gwynedd and Anglesey superstores. New treatment facilities were built by Dŵr Cymru Welsh Water to improve the quality of the water for drinking. 76,000 north Wales residents could drink the waters of Llyn Cwellyn again – safely.

Cwm Treweunydd offers some relief. Another mile or so of flat plateau before arriving at Llyn Ffynnon y Gwas where the climb proper starts. Despite the Snowdon Ranger being a lesser used and lesser known path up Snowdon, the footfall is giving the path a hammering. Gravel is being placed underfoot. Paths are consolidated and conserved by the Snowdonia National Park Authority. Manicured but essential. On my trip I pass a small mechanical digger, high up along Cwm Treweunydd. Silent today, maybe it's tea-break. The newly deposited gravel slowly but surely filling in the ruts caused by thousands of walking boots. This is artificial but essential.

Walking along Cwm Treweunydd the huge stone of *Maen Bras* in unmissable. More than likely a natural boulder or glacial erratic left at the end of the Ice Age by melting glaciers (SH 581550). The stone is discussed on the *Archwilio* website but any archaeological

origin is dismissed. Standing earth-fast to a height of almost ten metres, prominent and positioned almost central in relation to the valley, it's disappointing to learn that this is a natural feature rather than a standing stone in memory of one of Eryri's Bronze Age leaders or mythical giants. Travelling west from Rhyd Ddu on the A4085 back towards Waunfawr, *Maen Bras* is visible on the horizon, a landmark, well placed, but natural.

The summit cairn on Snowdon however is accepted by archaeologists to be a much damaged, altered and rearranged Bronze Age funerary cairn. Sometimes associated with the giant Rhita Gawr, Rhita was a king who fought other kings, killed them off and made a cloak from their beards. I am reliably informed of this fact at the summit café where information boards double up as tables in the café. Rhita was eventually killed by King Arthur according to other stories.

I have decided to tackle the Snowdon Ranger Path on a hot May day (2019). In my younger days I could reach the summit in 1hour 45. At the time of writing, at the grand old age of fifty-six I have set myself a two-hour target. Catching the 9am Beddgelert bus from Caernarfon I arrive at the Snowdon Ranger halt at 9.30 precisely. This is good for calculating the time. Round figure. In the far distance the Snowdon train is audible and the smoke visible.

Just beyond Llyn Ffynnon y Gwas, I'm greeted by my local GP – on the way down already. A ten-minute conversation later I have some catching up to do if I'm to keep to the two-hour target. Shortly I meet two south Walians, they are from Aberdare. It would be rude not to welcome them to north Wales. Another twenty minutes is lost. A couple from London, perched on a boulder enjoying a sandwich just below the railway track are acknowledged but I keep on going.

As I cross the railway track and join with the Llanberis Path I spot a familiar face, or rather a familiar haircut, a dyed blonde feathercut – a local hairdresser and marathon runner from Caernarfon. We push each other on. We chat. We lose breath but we are heading for that summit, no nonsense. Conversations, albeit good conversations, have cost me thirty minutes. Subtract the conversations and in actual walking time I have made it to the top in two hours.

A cup of tea with too much sugar at the Hafod Eryri café is my reward. Recyclable cardboard cup in hand I count the visible lakes through steamy windows: Llyn Nantlle, Llyn y Gadair, Llyn Dywarchen, Cwellyn of course and Ffynnon y Gwas. Just beneath us, partly obscured by the cliffs are Llyn Coch, Llyn Nadroedd (Lake of Snakes) and another smaller lake.

Hafod Eryri replaced Clough Williams-Ellis's earlier building from the 1930s. Dismissed by Prince Charles as the 'highest slum in Wales'. Clough Williams-Ellis has his architectural merits whatever the opinions held by Charles. It's a shame to lose an historic Clough building, slum or not. I would have preferred

'Brutalist' as a description. Twentieth century concrete. Nothing remains. Hafod Eryri is a café fit for Snowdon arrivals in the twenty-first century. Clean. Stone. Glass. Clinical. Busy. A bit like a train station.

An inscription on the outside wall confirms that we are closer to heaven, 'yn nes at y nefoedd'. We are indeed, there is no closer point in Wales or England. Nes at y nefoedd could be a term of endearment in the Welsh language, signifying a special place rather than literally being the highest point. Often used in everyday language – 'nes at y nefoedd' could be anywhere special.

I'm off down once the tea is finished. Buses are less frequent from Rhyd Ddu or Beddgelert. I take the route of least resistance down the mountain. Heading for Llanberis with hundreds of other walkers, no real pleasure in this but at least I'll catch a bus when I get to the village. Two hours of non-stop walking and I'm back on tarmac.

RHYD DDU

Rhyd Ddu, surrounded by mountains, right at the heart of Snowdonia. Landscape nothing short of dramatic. Barren sheep farming land that gives way to rocky crags and jagged peaks. Lakes lie on the valley floor and planted forests occupy the lower slopes. The stuff of picture postcards. Poet Thomas Herbert Parry-Williams was born here, took the train out as a young boy and never really returned. T.H. Parry-Williams is however firmly and forever associated with the village of Rhyd Ddu but in fact lived here only as a child, in the school house. He was gone by the age of eleven.

Initially, as a schoolboy, he took the train out to school at nearby Porthmadog but still walked the first four miles to Beddgelert. Later, career-wise, the train was to take him on to Aberystwyth, Oxford, Freiburg and Paris. Quite a journey, beautifully captured and articulated by Angharad Price in her 2013 *Ffarwél i Freiburg*. Price's book describes the early part of T.H.'s life. Sounds almost like a psychogeographical adventure by train. Too far to walk.

Price covers these early years with clarity and an academic thoroughness which will never translate into a popular bed time reading book. I'd argue that this is research and work of national importance in that this period of T.H.'s life is documented and documented fully and extensively. It's arguably more than you ever really need to know.

Price and myself share a pot of tea at Caffi Ty Mawr in the centre of the village. Owned by a Dutchman, the menu includes *uitsmijter*, a Dutch speciality of fried egg on white bread with cold ham and cheese. Vegetarian option just means leaving out the ham. T.H. Parry-Williams, well-travelled, would have appreciated the internationalism of the menu. He took an interest in the avant-garde, in Cubism, in the city landscape, I'm told by Angharad. I'm left wondering whether there was a disconnect between T.H. and his home village in later life – a form of alienation – he's moved out and moved on.

During the latter half of the nineteenth century the train served the slate quarries and connected Porthmadog with Dinas just outside Caernarfon and eventually Caernarfon itself. Branches connected from Moel Tryfan and the Nantlle slate quarries. In its current form, 'Rheilffordd Eryri' is a heritage narrow gauge railway used almost exclusively by tourists. Swop trains at Porthmadog and continue the journey to Blaenau Ffestiniog making this the longest heritage railway journey in the UK.

Wandering the slopes, treading the sheep paths of Y Garn and Yr Wyddfa he produced wonderful verses. In 1913 his *soned* 'Llyn y Gadair' describes a rather unimpressive lake bounded by two closed quarries. In some ways his descriptions are harsh. Realistic even. He grew up here and had time to consider.

> Dim byd on mawnog a'i boncyffion brau
> Dau glogwyn, a dwy chwarel wedi cau
> (*Only peat and fragile stumps, two cliffs, and two closed quarries*)

On the edge of Llyn y Gadair, Pitt's Rock is a local landmark, featuring on O.S. maps as a natural boulder. Grid Reference SH 575515. Travelling on the A4085 from the west, heading towards Beddgelert, the profile of a face becomes clear as the rock is approached. Elongated round head, prominent temple, eyes set deep, a long curving nose, pouting lips and small chin. Resting on the ground.

Having a perceived likeness to that of William Pitt the Younger, (prime minister from 1783 to 1801 and 1804 to 1806), resulted in the glacial erratic boulder being given an associated name. Appearing for the first time on the 6" 1888 OS map it's likely that

the cultural association would be contemporary with the terms served by Pitt as prime minister. The name has stuck.

'Cerrig Collwyn' is the accepted Welsh name for this rock. I have seen references to Cerrig Hyllion (Ugly Rocks) but I suspect that this is not factually correct. Rather a corruption of the name and in use by locals, according to D.E. Jenkins (1899). Afon Colwyn, the river, flows nearby from its source on the slopes of Snowdon down towards the confluence with the Glaslyn at Beddgelert. But it would appear that Cerrig Collwyn has no commonality in name with the River Colwyn.

'Collwyn' probably refers to Collwyn ab Tango one of the leaders of Early Medieval Gwynedd tribes. This is the stuff of legend and borderline facts relating to genealogies dating to the fifteenth century. These refer to the 'five royal tribes of Wales' and the 'fifteen tribes of Gwynedd'. Centuries after the fact, genealogies were constructed providing the aristocracy of the day with suitable lineage.

Less than a mile along the road towards Beddgelert is another OS marked stone. Lion's Head, not so easy to spot, obscured by a telegraph post, Grid Ref SH 575500. Once again this is a stone where the profile is only apparent from one direction. Heading uphill from Beddgelert the side profile of the lion is glimpsed briefly before being obscured by the telegraph post. Photographing the lion's head is no easy task.

BEDDGELERT

I cried in primary school on hearing the story of Gelert. A tragic story, it probably accounts for my becoming a vegetarian later in life when at university. Gelert was the faithful hound of Llywelyn Fawr (Llywelyn the Great) who was slain by mistake by his master when on returning home believed the hound had killed his infant child. In fact, Gelert had defended the baby from an intruding wolf and the infant's blood-stained bed sheets had covered the dead wolf. Llywelyn believing his baby lay dead under the blood-soaked sheets took out his sword and took out poor Gelert – before hearing the cries of a very much alive baby.

Victorian entrepreneur David Pritchard, realising the potential of the legend as a draw for tourists, promoted the story and built the monument (Gelert's Grave) that stands near the Glaslyn river to this day. Pritchard was the first tenant manager of the Goat Hotel from 1865 and with the coming of the railway and increasing numbers of visitors coming to climb Snowdon he soon realised that a good story would help bring in the tourist dollars.

Pritchard's ghost was said to have wandered between the centre of the village and the Goat Hotel for years after his death. Eventually his onetime servant challenged the ghost and found that Pritchard had hidden money behind the piano in the hotel bar. The servant was rewarded for his troubles and the ghost was never seen again.

Many of the present staff at the Goat seem blissfully unaware of the story of Pritchard's ghost. They are missing a trick (or page) from Pritchard's book. Exploit the legends. Exploit any ghost stories. It all helps to attract visitors.

Meteorites can also make great stories. Crashing through the roof of the Prince Llywelyn Hotel on the night of 21 September 1949 a meteorite was not found until the following morning according to one story. So much beer had been consumed at the hotel bar that no one heard the crashing sound from above. Dogs barked apparently. Others thought that there were Royal Navy manoeuvres out at sea near Porthmadog. Great story for such a quiet village.

DINAS EMRYS

A fragile hillfort, perched on a rock outcrop in the Gwynant Valley. Often shrouded in mist. Ancient moss-covered oak trees protect the approach. Associations with dragons and wizards make this a special site indeed. Dragons may or may not exist in reality, but at Dinas Emrys the case is made more convincing. Here you really could argue: never let the truth get in the way of a good story.

Archaeological excavations by H.N. Savory during the 1950s confirmed post-Roman occupation of the site. Emrys (Ambrosius), according to the legend, is the bastard child brought here for sacrifice in order that Gwrtheyrn (Vortigern) could complete the building of his fortress on the hill top.

Vortigern is discussed more fully during our discussion on Nant Gwrtheyrn (page 128). Fleeing west to avoid the treacherous Saxons, Dinas Emrys is said to be the site of Vortigern's fortress. Building work was constantly thwarted by collapsing walls each evening. Eventually Vortigern's wizards suggested that only by the sprinkling of sacrificial blood of a bastard boy could the walls remain standing.

Emrys was found following a countrywide search and brought up to site. At the point of execution, I'm guessing most victims would use their best endeavours to avoid their fate and come up with an answer. Emrys explained that the walls collapsed because they were built above an underground pool. Within the pool two vessels contained the white dragon and the red dragon. As the dragons fought each evening the walls came tumbling down.

As an analogy of the conflict between the Welsh (red dragon) and the Saxons (white dragon) this is in many ways, the perfect tale. The red dragon of course becomes the national symbol of Wales. The pool is still here. Or rather a medieval cistern built by the princes of Gwynedd. But the princes of Gwynedd could well have built their cistern on the site of Vortigern's pool. At Dinas Emrys it's difficult to dismiss or disprove the legend.

A square tower, built of stone, probably belongs to the princes of Gwynedd. In form it resembles the towers at Dolwyddelan and Carndochan. That would date the tower to the thirteenth century. Llywelyn Fawr built castles of stone from the 1220s onwards. Dinas Emrys is a wonderful example of a multi-period site, beginning life as an Iron Age hillfort and then being re-used during the post-Roman and Medieval periods.

BLAENAU FFESTINIOG

ond gennai lechan yn y gwaed
'Graffiti Cymraeg', Anwlededig.

Too industrial, too many slate tips, not green enough to be included within the Snowdonia National Park, Blaenau Ffestiniog is an island cut off from the rest of the park by slate tips. But there it is, sitting right in the middle, dissected by the A470, with high rainfall and sheep on the streets. No argument; in Blaenau Ffestiniog's case the clichés are visibly true.

Like Bangor, Blaenau Ffestiniog has a long High Street and like Bangor there are slate inscribed inserts in the pavement. At Blaenau bits of poetry are trampled on by busy shoppers. Poetic advice, words of wisdom, cultural signposts – all underfoot. One reads 'diwylliant ymysg diwydiant' – 'Culture amongst industry' – which pretty well sums up Blaenau Ffestiniog. Once an industrial town. Now a post-industrial town. Always a cultural and cultured town.

And not forgetting humour – another reads 'Al Fresco, Hen Foi Iawn!' – 'Al Fresco – good bloke!'. I read another 'Y Cymry Rhydd Cymraeg', 'The Free Welsh Speakers'. Cultured streets indeed.

Anweledig are the most famous rock band from Blaenau, mixing reggae and funk. They are a rural slate town version of what the Happy Mondays would have been like had they been born here rather than in Manchester. It's never fair to compare bands but the analogy with the Happy Mondays is that Anweledig come across as a gang and they have been known to party. But they are nice lads with a political sensibility and a community grounding that makes them important cultural lights on these streets of slate.

Rhys the bassist, now runs Cell B, a café, venue, cinema, community space housed in the old Court / Police Station. Ceri the singer, works for community enterprise Antur Stiniog bringing life and commerce back in to this post-industrial town. Gai Toms the guitarist, has a recording studio in Tanygrisiau and continues to release records under his own name (having been known as Mim Twm Llai).

Anweledig's first gig was at Canolfan yr Urdd, just off the High Street supporting my own band Anhrefn. That was in the latter half of the 1980s. Once a cinema and function hall, I met someone outside while taking a photograph that had met his wife at a 'bop' or dance held in the hall. Faint and weathered remains of a painted sign on slate can be seen on the gable end of the building 'something Hall'. Hard to read. I find out later it read 'Central Hall'.

Our theme of lost venues continues with the Wynnes Arms on the A470 at Manod. Southern end of Blaenau Ffestiniog. Boarded

up for a while now, this pub was never a 'proper' venue but did have
bands playing in the beer garden. In north Wales, anywhere that
puts on bands is welcome – proper venue or not – even if it was a
ramshackle stage in the beer garden.

Queens in central Blaenau was another venue – backroom of a
pub type venue. I'm not sure when Queens last hosted live bands.
During the quarry strike late 1980s benefit gigs were held here for
the striking quarrymen and their families. Gigs are held frequently
at the community run Pengwern Arms at Llanffestiniog. Cell B has
gained a reputation as a venue for touring reggae bands. Blaenau
Ffestiniog – always cultured.

FFESTINIOG RAILWAY

On a misty or drizzly day, when the clouds are low, passengers on
the Ffestiniog Railway can end up seeing very little. Add to this the
steam from the train and any condensation on the carriage windows
and visibility becomes almost zero. I describe these kinds of
journeys as 'atmospheric'. The journey on the train from Blaenau
Ffestiniog down to Porthmadog on the coast, follows the north side
of the Vale of Ffestiniog. Passing through an ancient oak forest
which has been describes as a 'Welsh rainforest'. The landscape is

riddled with streams and waterfalls. Everything about this journey screams, wet, wet, wet.

There are bright sunny days of course in this part of central Snowdonia. The valley floor and the Dwyryd river glisten in the distance below when the sun is out. But the passage through the woods of Coed Maentwrog maintains an otherworldly feel whatever the weather. Expect to see fairies dancing on the abundant mosses, lichens and liverworts that cover the bases of the oaks. This is a real forest, natural, native.

The forest was managed by the Tan-y-Bwlch estate from the Medieval period but in previous centuries, forests like this would have provided wood for building, burning and bark for tanning. Natural Resources Wales maintain the woodland at present and a clear and well-trodden footpath runs from Llyn Mair in the west alongside and just below the railway revetment wall towards Dduallt station.

Nature and the landscape were no obstacle to Victorian engineers. They seemed to relish the challenge. Revetments and bridges were built. The track cuts into the steep hillside high above the valley floor. Oak forest above and below. W.G. Oakley Esq laid the first stone on the 26th February 1833. The Oakleys of Plas Tan-y-Bwlch owned the Oakley Quarry at Blaenau Ffestiniog. Getting the slate to market was always the challenge and the commercial aim. Transporting the slate via railway from Ffestiniog to the harbour at Porthmadog was the preferred solution.

Prior to the construction of the railway by James Spooner, slate was shipped downstream to Porthmadog from Tyddyn Isa Quay on the banks of the Dwyryd on flat bottomed boats. Dating to the eighteenth century this stone build quay just outside Penrhyndeudraeth is a hidden gem. Accessible via footpath off the A487 and visible from the A496 Maentwrog to Llandecwyn road on the south side of the Dwyryd. The quay belongs to a period of quarrying before the boom of the nineteenth century. Before the big landowners took charge. Before Spooner's railway. This is early industrial archaeology indeed.

I took the train from Blaenau Ffestiniog down to Porthmadog while writing this book and the overall sense was one of claustrophobia for the best part of the journey. Tunnels, narrow cut rock sections. Always hugging the hill side. Narrow gauge surrounded by trees. Only brief glimpses of the Vale below.

Stations such as Dduallt, Campbell's Platform, Coed y Bleiddiau, Tan-y-Bwlch and Plas Halt only come into view at the last minute. There is no approaching view of anywhere or any station until the lowland stops of Penrhyn, Minffordd, Boston Lodge and finally crossing the Cob to Porthmadog. Only here could we describe the view as wide-open space as we cross the Glaslyn estuary.

Impressive as the Victorian railway construction may be, the loop at Dduallt where the track does a 360 degree turn over and below itself dates to the 1960s. The building of the pumped-storage power station at Tanygrisiau required a reservoir (Llyn Ystradau), a dam and a re-routing of the original railway track. I'm sure the Victorians would have come up with a similar solution. In order to keep the gradient of the line, the loop was constructed. Passengers hardly notice until they realise that the track is below or above them. Spooner's original railway was horse drawn using gravity to assist in the transportation downhill to Porthmadog.

Plas y Dduallt or manor dates back to the sixteenth century. Stone built, high chimneys, arched doorways. A glimpse of Dduallt is caught from the train but not enough to make sense of the architecture. This is an example of a 'unit system' of a linked dwelling. The rear building is an earlier storied Snowdonia House[7] with hall linked to the 'parlour' at the front by a passageway. At one time these two buildings may have been independent dwellings although the relationship between them remains uncertain. Dduallt is discussed in *Discovering the Historic Houses of Snowdonia* (2014).

Coed-y-Bleiddiau has many claims to fame. Restored by the Landmark Trust, the cottage is only accessible via the train or on foot. The first claim is that this area was home to Wales's last native wolf. They became extinct sometime during the seventeenth century. Another claim to fame is that composer Granville Bantock lived here. Bantock composed operas such as *The Pearl of Iran* (1894) and the Celtic themed *The Seal Woman*.

Not so pleasant are the fascist connections with Coed-y-Bleiddiau. The father of KGB agent Kim Philby, Harry St John Bridger Philby, spent time here. Philby senior was a leading British fascist. And continuing on the fascist theme, a less likely, if not wholly disputed, claim is that William Joyce, 'Lord Haw-Haw', visited his friend Philby at Coed-y-Bleiddiau. Gwynedd Archaeological Trust certainly dispute this claim on *Archwilio* (Barker and Gwyn, 2017) as do the Imperial War Museum, the BBC and various Joyce biographers. It seems that this has become a 'local myth' along with stories that Joyce referred to the area in his wartime broadcasts. Some local stories are not so good.

BWLCH (Y SLATERS), MANOD QUARRY AKA CWT Y BUGAIL

One of the most iconic images of the Second World War in Wales is that of the lorry transporting artworks from the National Gallery up to Manod Quarry for safekeeping. The drama is accentuated by the lorry getting stuck under Cwm Teigl railway bridge (LJT2 103 Hen Capel) whilst carrying Van Dyck's famous equestrian portrait of Charles I. Word has it that air was let out of the lorry tyres in an attempt to reduce the height of the load.

In reality, and in preparation for the transportation of up to two thousand pieces of art from the National Gallery in London during 1940 following the fall of France, the road had been lowered by up to 0.9m under the bridge and concrete reinforcing aprons were built at the base of the bridge. The four mile stretch of narrow mountain road from Llanffestiniog up to the disused Manod Quarry was also improved.

Still, it's a great story and iconic image. They obviously got the picture up there in the end. They probably did let air out of the tyres.

Even today navigating the sharp bend under the 10ft 6" bridge arch is a challenge. Two cars cannot pass at once and care is needed because oncoming traffic is obscured. The four-mile climb along the single-track road up Cwm Teigl is nothing short of breath taking. An adventure for sure. The views on the way down over Trawsfynydd power station are again stunning. Probably a good idea to stop the car, get out and enjoy the views because deep ruts each side of the road mean one mistake and it's time for a tow out by tractor.

'Going Underground' was the first number one hit in the British charts for the punky-mod band The Jam. That was March 1980 and its difficult not to sing the chorus out loud in the car as I approach what is now known as Cwt Y Bugail Quarry, an active quarry or rather re-activated quarry. Quarryman and local town councillor Erwyn Jones is here to meet me. We are indeed 'going underground' into the old Manod Quarry caverns where the artworks were stored in 1940.

Correctly and historically we should be referring to the quarry as Bwlch (Y Slaters) SH 732455. The original Cwt y Bugail quarry SH 734468 lies half a mile or so to the north high up above the town of Blaenau Ffestiniog and Rhiwbach Quarry SH 740462 approached from Cwm Penmachno lies about half a mile east of Manod. Both these quarries can be easily approached via the Rhiwbach tramway from the modern visitor car park at Cwt y Bugail.

Erwyn J. as he is known to all locally is a fourth-generation quarryman. Proud. As we bounce up the dusty quarry track towards the adit in Erwyn's Land Rover I'm told that despite graduating in geography, he made the decision to work as a quarryman. My father's generation, born into quarrymen family in the Nantlle Valley saw education as a way out. My father and two brothers all became teachers. They got out. Erwyn made a decision to get back in.

At the locked and gated entrance to the mine adit, Erwyn tells me that another often repeated 'myth' about Manod is that the Crown Jewels were stored here. Shrouded in mystery and protective boxes, the artworks were transported 'secretly' up to Manod in 1940. But you can't keep secrets from the locals. It's good stuff all this 'local myths and legends'. Facts should not spoil great stories, but I'm an archaeologist and dealing with facts rather than myths is the day job.

Padlock opened. Hard hats donned. Torches switched on. We venture in. Once out of sunlight there's an immediate chill in the air. The drip drip drip sounds of water falling from the roof and the crunching and splashing underfoot is all that we hear. Rubble lies everywhere and the drops of water form little puddles. Each step has to be taken with a degree of care but the sense of adventure is beyond exciting. This is a privilege and a rare opportunity to gain access. The fact that I'm writing *Real Gwynedd* secured the keys to the padlock and Erwyn J. as a guide.

About a hundred yards in and we pass a small room which must have held generators. Another fifty yards and we approach the red brick buildings that once held the artworks. The nature of slate quarrying in the Ffestiniog area is that all the quarries were underground caverns, often several floors o'r levels of them deep below the mountains rather than the open cast quarries that we see at Penrhyn, Dinorwig and Nantlle.

Each cavern was quarried by a combination of blasting and the hard graft of the quarrymen shifting the slate from beneath granite or rhyolite layers. The geology here is of slate in seams, sandwiched between other rock. Erwyn points his torch up to the granites and rhyolites that form the roof to these caverns. Slate was extracted and moved out on trams – the Ffestiniog slate eventually served by the Ffestiniog Railway to Porthmadog for export.

All that remains of the art storage is a series of red brick buildings deep underground. Any fittings and frames for the art are long gone as are the roofs to these structures within the caverns. But the whole area is littered with bits of electrics and surprisingly many rooms still contain the air conditioning and humidity equipment. I wonder why these were not stripped out as scrap in the post war period. Maybe it was too much hassle?

Above us the current quarrying operation or top-slicing is removing huge tracts of granite in order to expose the slate seams below. At the end of one cavern we enter daylight. This is the modern quarrying (open cast) above us reaching down to the caverns for slate that was never removed during the nineteenth and early twentieth centuries. My concern for the archaeology, the 1940s red brick art storage buildings, turns out to be a false alarm. Erwyn reassures me that the direction of work with the present quarrying activities is away from the 1940s site. The World War II archaeology is probably safe for my lifetime.

However, the modern blasting taking place above does result in large chunks of the roof collapsing. I see several red brick walls flattened by huge slabs of slate that have dislodged from the roof. There may be a case after all for the archaeology being threatened. The ever affable and smiling Erwyn reassures me that we are safe on our Friday afternoon visit. The quarry stops work at 1-30pm. No blasting expected. I make sure my hard hat is still firmly in place.

Parts of the railway tracks serving each storage room are visible. Huge chains support the cavern roof. We even stumble across an underground portaloo. A glorified bucket with seat. Left unemptied since God knows when. A bog roll survives, just, but surely readily turned to dust if touched. I notice a powdered milk tin on one shelf – an image that I easily find on a Google images search. Things are left here. Untouched. Preserved in their own little way deep underground.

CRIMEA (BWLCH Y GORDDINAN)

Heading north from Blaenau Ffestiniog the A470 makes its winding way over the Crimea Pass. Climbing gradually past the quarries of Llechwedd and Oakley the slate tips are left behind as open moorland is reached. One strange archaeological anomaly is seen on the roadside just on the Gwynedd / Conwy border. Known as Esgidiau Meirw Boot Dump, this circular patch of dark rusty earth is the site of a World War II boot dump.

All sorts of stories are heard about the 'boot dump' in Blaenau Ffestiniog but there is an explanation and good reason for the existence of this site. During the Second World War damaged boots were brought from the Front to the Market Hall in Blaenau for repairs. The business was set up by a local entrepreneur, a certain Mr Ackett. Both US (brown) and British boots (black) were repaired having been brought up to Blaenau by train.

The remaining pieces of boots deemed unrepairable were then burnt at the 'dump' on the Crimea. Presumably, the burning of leather boots would have been unpleasant and the site, away from town, was offered for this purpose by Martyn Williams-Ellis manager at Llechwedd. Interestingly, Martyn, spelt with a 'y', was the brother of architect Clough Williams-Ellis but more importantly in this context he was the head of the local Home Guard and as manager of Llechwedd was in a position to help the war effort.

Thousands of hobnails boots, heel plates and eyelets remain on the site. Burnt and corroded. Staining the patch of land as a permanent reminder that Blaenau was not unaffected by the war.

Nothing grows here. I was told the story by Peggy Williams who was Ackett's secretary at the Market Hall. It was Peggy who emphasised that Martyn 'was spelt with a 'y' during our conversation. Her memory was good. This account is probably the closest we will ever get to the truth about the 'boot dump'.

Bwlch y Gorddinan is a much more evocative name for the Crimea Pass but it's Crimea' that's most often used. Just over the county border in Conwy was the site of the Crimea Inn. Now a carpark. The road was constructed at the time of the Crimea War, around 1854. There are rumours that some of the walls in the area were built by Russian prisoners of war captured at Inkerman and Balaclava.

According to the *Geiriadur Mawr*, 'Cerddidden' would be the Welsh for a rowan tree while 'Gorddin' is the Welsh for oppression. The Pass of the Rowan Tree seems much more likely that the Pass of Oppression.

PORTMEIRION

My work as a tour guide often takes me to Portmeirion. Over the years I have developed a close working relationship with manager Meurig Jones. Our shared interests in music and Welsh history have created a stronger bond than usual. When faced with guiding elderly American ladies with limited walking capacity I quite often give Meurig a quick ring. "Golf buggy available?". Meurig will pop out, and give us the red-carpet treatment.

Meurig is the font of all knowledge at Portmeirion and an excellent guide. Zooming around the village, with Meurig at the wheel of the golf buggy, invokes scenes from *The Prisoner*. We pass a bust of Patrick McGoohan near the entrance, by-pass the Prisoner Shop and then hurtle down towards the beach and hotel. Visitors look at us with amazement. They also jump out of our way.

My American visitors are highly impressed with their five-star treatment. Meurig I suspect is more than happy at the golf buggy wheel. Any excuse. Whether the 1960s TV series created by Patrick McGoohan, who also played the role of No 6, is appreciated in the same way in the States I'm never quite sure. For many Portmeirion is the Prisoner Village.

The Prisoner has a worldwide following. Prisoner Conventions are held here. Popstars such as Glen Matlock (Sex Pistols), Suggs (Madness), Ian McCulloch (Echo & the Bunnymen) and Paul Weller are members of the Cape Club. Invitation only or as is often the case – invitation following a request made by popstars. Members are inaugurated by Meurig. They also have to don a Prisoner's cape. Photographs taken with Portmeirion as background.

For others it's the architecture of Clough Williams-Ellis that attracts. Clough created his Italianate village on the cliffs bordering the west shore of the Dwyryd river. A lifelong project which started in 1925 and continued until his death in 1973. In actual fact, work continues to this day. Everything at Portmeirion is pleasing to the eye. But everything at Portmeirion is not what it seems. On initial viewing this seems to be a perfectly constructed concept. In reality, this is 'magpie' architecture. Bits of old buildings, columns, busts and railings are recycled. Stored until the opportunity to include these pieces in the right place arise.

Clough's genius and vision was to piece all this stuff together. Windows are sometimes painted on. Paint is deliberately varied to make buildings look older than they are. Perspective is key. Illusion and trickery always present. Towers mask chimneys. Small windows give the impression of a larger wall. A Buddha prop used in the film *The Inn of the Sixth Happiness* (1958) with Ingrid Bergman, which was filmed around Beddgelert, stands proud on the way down to the village. Out of context and yet taking its place perfectly.

Clough's stated aim was that Portmeirion should be a place of 'inspiration for creative people'. The fact that Noël Coward wrote *Blyth Spirit* here is one obvious testament to Clough's vision. Portmeirion attracted movers and shakers. Actors, writers, poets, music moguls and musicians all came here to visit Clough.

An unintended consequence, in a way, was that Clough's village provided a 'safe space' for the gay community during the post war years. The Sexual Offences Act 1967 decriminalised sex between consenting males over the age of twenty-one. There was still some way to go obviously in 1967. Amongst the creative community, sexuality was far less of an issue. Celebrated rather than persecuted.

Beatles manager, Brian Epstein found himself at Portmeirion. Family connections at Harlech had brought him to the area. Epstein was to take on a short term let at Portmeirion. Complaining that there was not enough wardrobe space in his room, Clough was forced to build extra wardrobe capacity. Visitors who stay at the Gatehouse even to this day, hang their clothes in Epstein's double wardrobe.

For Epstein this was a place to impress and entertain guests. An active participant in Clough's dream. The fifth Beatle, producer George Martin, hung out here with Epstein. Lennon was invited alone for the weekend by Epstein but declined. This was at the time of Epstein's sexual infatuation with Lennon. Epstein's rooms at the Gatehouse overlook the spectacular Dwyryd estuary. Golden sands and mountains.

George Harrison was to stay here in 1966 or 1968 and was to return on his fiftieth birthday in 1993. Meurig tells a great tale of Harrison's security insisting that he roomed at the beach side hotel rather than in one of the cliff edge cottages. Just in case the party got out of hand. Harrison's comment on the hotel guest book was "Fab!".

Lennon is known to have holidayed at Tywyn in 1969, sending Ringo a postcard on the 23d June from the Corbett Arms. It's never been confirmed if Lennon visited Portmeirion en route home to Liverpool from Tywyn. Meurig still searches for confirming evidence.

During 2008, I was asked to promote a tour of Wales by a band called The Peth. Featuring actor Rhys Ifans, this all-star cast included members of the Super Furry Animals and Big Leaves as backing musicians. My task was to book them into unusual venues. Established music venues were strictly off limits. Portmeirion as the starting point of the tours seemed to make perfect sense and was the obvious choice.

Meetings were arranged with Meurig and the Hercules Hall (aka the Town Hall) was booked. Meurig and myself had embarked on our own voyage. Portmeirion became a regular gig venue and our friendship blossomed. One memory sticks in my mind about that gig, The morning after, I had checked that everybody was present and correct on the tour bus. Affirmed, I waved the bus on to the next location which was to be Bala Golf Club.

My conditions for undertaking the role of tour manager and promoter was that I would have my own hotel room and that I would travel separately in my own car. The madness of the tour bus was not for me. Ten minutes later, a dishevelled Rhys was to appear from the toilets by the entrance to Portmeirion. The band and the tour bus had left without the lead singer. That summed up the insanity and mayhem on that particular tour.

In recent years Portmeirion has hosted gigs by Simon Townshend (brother of Pete), The Vapours and southern soul, gospel and blues singer Lisa Mills from Alabama.

PENRHYNDEUDRAETH

Penrhyndeudraeth is the nearest village to Portmeirion. And here I come across another Beatles connection. Guitarist Gwilym Phillips was a member of local band The Vikings in the late 1950s early 1960s. When original singer Glyn 'Gwndwn' was replaced by Eurwyn Pierce (aka Dino) the band renamed themselves Dino & the Wildfires. A poster from 5th July 1963, confirms Dino & the Wildfires as a support act for Gerry and the Pacemakers and Billy J. Kramer and the Dakotas. This concert took place at Cricieth Memorial Hall as part of a regular club night called the 'The Tender Twist Trap Club'.

Gwilym had also supported the Beatles, fresh from their return from Hamburg, at the Tower Ballroom, New Brighton. Lead guitarist with the Vikings and Wildfires, Bernard (Bernie) Lee had already met George Harrison and Paul McCartney. During teenage holidays at Harlech 1956, 1957 and 1958, the story goes that the young George and Paul had hung out and jammed with Bernie and friends. These stories abound at Harlech and many are featured in *100 Facts about Harlech* and in my discussions of Harlech in this book.

Bernie was to confirm at the time of writing that George and Paul had guested with the Vikings Skiffle Band at the Queen's Hotel, Harlech over several weekends during August of 1958. Or as

Bernie put it, they were members of the band. Gwilym was to join The Vikings after the Harlech episodes.

Penrhyndeudraeth Memorial Hall, which is still in use, hosted one of the final concerts by Them. Organised by local promoter and DJ, Mici Plwm, this was in 1968, just before Van Morrison went off to the States and recorded his masterpiece *Astral Weeks*. Some have claimed that this was the final concert by Them in the UK. I have been unable to verify this claim. But whatever the facts, it does place Penrhyndeudraeth on the 1960s rock and roll circuit.

Before nightclubs, village halls and certainly many of the memorial halls in Gwynedd must have been exciting places in the 1960s. Gwynedd youth were able to see Them, Gerry and the Pacemakers, Billy J. Kramer and the Dakotas – that's pretty good going. Gwilym had also made the pilgrimage to the Cavern Club in Liverpool along with so many other north Wales youth to watch bands during the early 1960s.

TRAWSFYNYDD

At times it feels like a losing battle. All my friends, colleagues, fellow travellers, Punk Rock associates are Anti-Nuclear. I get that 100%. It's just that 'Atomfa Traws', Trawsfynydd nuclear power station was designed by architect Basil Spence. He of Coventry Cathedral fame. *Phoenix at Coventry, The Building of a Cathedral – by its Architect BASIL SPENCE* is one of the most inspiring books I've ever read. Spence's masterpiece, the twin towers at Trawsfynydd at least deserve architectural recognition. Few agree.

Like many things, we have to separate the politics from the architecture – to see the wood from the trees. Not easy. Not popular. As a sheer Brutalist construction this is surely one of Spence's masterpieces. If it were not a 'Nuke' Station I think there would be more sympathy. I imagine a one-man solitary protest to protect the twin towers of the reactor buildings from eventual destruction (or at least partial demolition and capping by 2040?).

De-commissioned as a power station, but the site is not expected to be fully restored back to its natural state until 2083, a hundred and twenty-four years after the construction started and ninety-two years after its closure as a power station. An archaeological / architectural dilemma. How much of Spence do we preserve? The concrete is deteriorating naturally anyway. Preservation is not an option.

From the east Spence's two huge reactor buildings resemble the twin gate towers of Cricieth Castle, a nod to the princes of Gwynedd perhaps? Imposing. Threatening. No messing. Spence has gone for huge square concrete towers in a definite twentieth century Brutalist style while Cricieth would be D-Shaped or apsidal towers, typical of the build by the thirteenth century princess of Gwynedd. Were the castles of Gwynedd an element of his

inspiration here? It would seem more likely that Spence would mirror Edward I's castles rather than those of the Welsh princes.

From the west, looking at the rear of the power station, the twin blocks more closely resemble Trellick Tower[8] in west London. Less threatening and imposing than the view from the east, this could almost be housing tower blocks with stairwells. A modern cycle path allows visitors to walk or cycle outside the perimeter fence. 'Keep Out' notices are spaced regularly. The path allows good views around the rear of the power station. Through woodlands. Peaceful. Tranquil. Heading further west, and after a few minutes walking through the trees we are back in open fields – a nuclear free zone.

Less than a mile to the north, the Roman fort of Tomen y Mur overlooks the power station and lake. Built around 77AD during the Agricola campaign. This is right on the western frontier of the Roman Empire. Roman roads connect with Segontium (Caernarfon), Caer Llugwy to the east and then Caer Gai near Bala further south.

Tomen y Mur shares a similar historical sequence as Cardiff Castle and Caerwent in that a Norman motte and bailey castle was built on top of an earlier Roman fort or site. Are there other Welsh examples I wonder? Was this common practise by the Normans, the reuse of earlier forts? The church of St Cybi at Holyhead is situated within a Roman fort. Convenient. Ground already levelled and in good or suitable locations.

Trawsfynydd's most famous son Hedd Wyn, was one of around ten million soldiers killed during World War I. Born at Yr Ysgwrn, Hedd Wyn was the bardic name of Ellis Humphrey Evans. Killed on the first day of the Battle of Passchendaele, Hedd Wyn is best remembered as the bard who posthumously won the Chair at the Birkenhead Eisteddfod, 1917. As a soldier his fate was similar to the other ten million. Killed in the trenches.

For the Welsh speaking community, Hedd Wyn's death and his chairing at the Eisteddfod has become a symbol of this monumental waste of life. A symbol of loss, of innocence, of the rural farmer, of the hills around Trawsfynydd. Forever tainted by war. Tragic. If he were not a chaired bard his story would be as common as the ten million other stories. No more or less tragic or sad. His life's story became the subject of the Oscar Nominated Film, *Hedd Wyn* (1992) directed by Paul Turner.

Notes

1. Snowdon Mountain Railway – one of the technical wonders of the Victorian Age climbing 3,100 feet over a distance of just under five miles from Llanberis to the summit of Snowdon. Built 1896. Using a rack and pinion track system.
2. J.M.W. Turner, 'Dolbadarn', exhibited 1800, oil on canvas, Royal Academy of Arts London (03/1383).

3. Saunders Lewis academic, poet and author. *Siwan* (1960) a play based on the life of Joan the illegitimate daughter of King John and wife of Llywelyn Fawr. An English translation was published in 1960 sometimes referred to as *The King of England's Daughter.*
4. Dafydd ap Gwilym (c.1315-1350) one of the great medieval Welsh poets. Probably buried at Strata Florida Abbey although there are advocates for his burial at Talley Abbey, Ceredigion.
5. For Merched Chwarel see: *Merchedchwarel.org*
6. Gwilym Cowlyd, (William John Roberts, 1828-1904). Trefriw born poet, publisher and bookseller who established the open air Arwest Glan Geirionydd in 1865 with fellow Conwy Valley poets and radicals Trebor Mai and Owen Gethin Jones. Colwyd believed that the Eisteddfod should be held in the open air and the Arwest was founded because they believed the National Eisteddfod was too English in its outlook.
7. The Snowdonia House was a vernacular style of architecture specific to Snowdonia with developed during the sixteenth century, evolving from the Hall House. See: Suggett, R, Dunn. M., 2014, *Discovering the Historic Houses of Snowdonia.*
8. Trellick Tower is a Grade II* listed tower block on the Cheltenham Estate in Kensal Green, London. Opened in 1972, it was commissioned by the Greater London Council and designed in the Brutalist style by architect Ernö Goldfinger.

WORKS CONSULTED

Avent, R., 2004, *Dolwyddelan Castle, Dolbadarn Castle, Castell y Bere.* (Cadw)

Barker, E.C., 1976, *Sir William Preece, F.R.S. Victorian Engineer Extraordinary*

Barker, L., Gwyn, D., 2017, *Gwynedd Slate Industry Transport Routes*

Berks, T., Davidson, A., 2007, *Historic Towns Survey of Gwynedd: Bangor.* (GAT Report No 681)

Borrow G., 1862, *Wild Wales*

Carr, H.R.C, Lister, G. A., 1948, *The Mountains of Snowdonia*

Caffell, G., 1983, *The Carved Slates of Dyffryn Ogwen*

Carrazé, A, Oswald, H., 1989, *The Prisoner*

Chamberlain, B., 1987, *Tide-race*

Clayton, P., 2012, *Octavia Hill, Social Reformer and Co-Founder of the National Trust*

Clews, R., 1980, *To Dream of Freedom*

Clowes, C., 2004, *Nant Gwrtheyrn*

Cowlyd, G., 1868, *Y Murmuron*

Cybi., 1923, *Cymeriadau Hynod Sir Gaernarfon*

Daniel, J., 1892, *Archaeologia Lleynensis*

Darwin, C., 1859 *On the Origin of Species*

Davidson, A., 2008, *Coleg Harlech, Harlech, Archaeological Assessment* (GAT Report No 761)

Davidson, A., Roberts, J., 2005, *Ports and Harbours of Gwynedd* GAT Report No 577)

Davidson Cragoe, C., 2008, *How to Read Buildings*

Davies, G., Gerallt., 1976, *Gwilym Cowlyd* 1828-1904

Davies, P., 1984, *Great Little Tin Sheds of Wales*

Driver, T., 2016, *The Hillforts of Cardigan Bay*

Eames, M., 1969, *Y Stafell Ddirgel*

Ebenezer, L., 2006, *Fron-Goch and the Birth of the IRA*

Edwards, David, R., 1992, *Al, Mae'n Urdd Camp*

Edwards, David, R., 2017, *Dave Datblygu's Search in English for the House of Intolerance*

Eifion, A., 1888, *John Ystumllyn neu "Jack Black"*

Emlyn, M., 2019, *Cofiwch Dryweryn, Cymru'n Deffro*

Finch, P., 2002, *Real Cardiff*

Finch, P., 2015, *The Roots of Rock from Cardiff to Mississippi and Back*

Fychan, C., 2006, *Gwlad y Blaidd*

Gruffydd, A., 2004, *Mae Rhywun yn Gwybod*

Gruffydd, E., 2003, Llŷn

Gwyn, D., Davidson, A., 2007, 'Ports and Harbours of Gwynedd: Aberdyfi' (GAT Report No 671.1)

Harlech WI, 2015, *100 Facts about Harlech*

Hoole, J., Simons, M., 2013, *James Dickson Innes 1887-1914*

Hopewell, D., 2013, *Roman Roads in North-West Wales*, (Ymddiriedolaeth Archaeolegol Gwynedd)

Hopewell, D., 2017, *High Status Medieval Sites Castell Carndochan Excavation Report 2016-17*

Humphries, P., 1995, *On the Trail of Turner, In North and South Wales* (Cadw)

Jenkins, D, E., 1899, *Bedd Gelert, Its Facts, Fairies & Folk-lore*

Jones, R, M., 1982, *The North Wales Quarrymen 1874-1922*

Meirion Hughes, T., 2013, *Hanesion Tre'r Cofis*

Hughes, H, North, H. L., 1908, *The Old Cottages of Snowdonia*

Hughes, H, North, H. L., 1924, *The Old Churches of Snowdonia*

Hughes, T.R., 1944, *William Jones*

Johnstone, N., 1999, 'Cae Llys, Rhosyr: A Court of the Princes of Gwynedd, *Studia Celtica* : Vol 33

Johnstone, N., 2000, 'Llys and Maerdref: The Royal Courts of the Princes of Gwynedd. A study of their Location and Selective Trial Excavation', *Studia Celtica*: Vol 34

Jones. D., 2007, *The Botanists and Mountain Guides of Snowdonia*

Kerouac, J., 1957, *On The Road*

Kershaw, A., 2011, *Andy Kershaw, No Off Switch, An Autobiography*

Lloyd-Jones, J., 1928, *Enwau Lleoedd Sir Gaernarfon*

Lord, P., 2000, *Diwylliant Gweledol Cymru: Delweddu'r Genedl*

Lynch, F., 1995, *A Guide to Ancient and Historic Wales, Gwynedd* (Cadw)

Marsden, J., 1991, Revised 2009, *Penrhyn Castle* (National Trust)

Matthews, C., 2019, *Where the Wild Gooks Go*

Meyrick, R., 2012, *Christopher Williams '...an artist and nothing else'*

Middles, M., 1999, *Manic Street Preachers*

Mwyn, R., 2014, *Cam i'r Gorffennol, Safleoedd archaeolegol yng ngogledd Cymru*

Mwyn, R., 2016, *Cam Arall i'r Gorffennol, Safleoedd archaeolegol yng ngogledd-ddwyrain Cymru a'r gororau*

Mwyn, R., 2019, *Cam i'r Deheubarth, Safleoedd archaeolegol yn ne-orllewin Cymru*

National Museum of Wales., 1998, *St Fagans National History Museum, Visitor Guide*

Owens, D., 2000, *Cerys, CATATONIA and the Rise of Welsh Pop*

Owen, H.D., 2015, *Sesiwn yng Nghymru, Cymru, Cwrw a Chân*

Parker, M., 2007, *Neighbours From Hell? English Attitudes to the Welsh*

Parker, M., 2011, *Real Powys*

Parry-Williams, T.H., 1940, *Hen Benillion*

Parry-Williams, T.H., 2011, *Cerddi rhigymau a sonedau*

Pennant, T. 1778, *Pennant's Tours in Wales Vol II* (Humphreys Caernarvon) Edited: Rhys, J.M.A., 1883

Price, A., 2013, *Ffarwél i Freiburg, Crwydriadau cynnar T.H. Parry-Williams*

Pritchard, P., 1961, *Un Nos Ola Leuad* (also translation *One Moonlit Night*)

Rawlins, R., 2015, *The Rise of the Super Furry Animals*

RCAHM, 1956, *An Inventory of the Ancient Monuments in Caernarvonshire Volume I East*

Redknap, M., 2011, *Discovered in Time, Treasures From Early Wales*

Rice, M., 2009, *Rice's Architectural Primer*

Richards, A.J., 1991, *A Gazetteer of the Welsh Slate Industry*

Roberts, T., 2016, 2017etc, *Barmouth Sailors Institute Newsletter*

Rogers, B., 2006, *The Man Who Went Into the West, The Life of R.S. Thomas*

Rowland, W., 1953, *Gwŷr Eifionydd*

Rowlands, E, W., 2001, *Y Llew Oedd Ar Y Llwyfan*

Savage, J., 1991, *England's Dreaming*

Spence, B., 1962, *Phoenix at Coventry, The Building of a Cathedral – by its Architect BASIL SPENCE*

Steele, P., Williams, R., 2006, *Môn Mam Cymru, The Guide to Anglesey*, (Magma)

Suggett, R., Dunn. M., 2014, *Discovering the Historic Houses of Snowdonia*

Thirsk, S., 2010, *Not Quite White*

Thomas, W., 2019, *John Jenkins, The Reluctant Revolutionary?*

Tomos, D., 1980, *Llechi Lleu*

Tudur, G., 1989, *Wyt Ti'n Cofio? Chwarter Canrif o Frwydr Yr Iaith*

Turner, K., 2005, *The Way to the Stars – The Story of the Snowdon Mountain Railway*

Voelcker, A., 2011, *Herbert Luck North, Arts and Crafts Architecture for Wales* (RCAHMW)

Williams, G. A., 2015, *Dyddiau Olaf Owain* Glyndŵr

Williams-Ellis, C., 1971, *Architect Errant, The Autobiography of Clough Williams-Ellis*

Williams, J. Ll., 2019, 'Tafarndai Dyffryn Ogwen', *Hanesdyffryn ogwen.wordpress.com*

Williams, 'Maffia', N., 2012, *O'r Ochr Arall*

Williams, O., 2016, *Tryweryn: A Nation Awakes. The Story of a Welsh Freedom Fighter*

Williams, S. J., 1958, *Y Geiriadur Mawr*

Woods, R., 2010, *Rheilffordd Ffestiniog Railway*

The Lady Lever Art Gallery (2004, National Museums Liverpool)

Penrhyn Castle, Bangor Caernarvonshire (National Trust)

Web Sites:
Archwilio.org.uk
Cat.org.uk
Merchedchwarel.org
Nationaltrust.org

Recordings:
Harry Parry's Radio Rhythm Club Sextet, *Crazy Rhythm*

THE PHOTOGRAPHS

Arrow Stone, Cwm Anafon	21
Bwthyn	25
Streic Fawr Penrhyn Memorial	26
The Victoria, Bethesda	27
Slate Bed, Castell Penrhyn	30
Harry Parry plaque, Caellepa	33
Eva Stone, Bangor Cathedral	36
Caban, Joseph van Lieshout	39
Jazz Room Poster, Alan Holmes	41
George Stephenson Lion, Britannia Bridge	44
Penscoins incline, Y Felinheli	46
1969 Investiture slate platform, Caernarfon Castle	49
Plaque commemorating Caernarfon Pavilion	52
Ed Povey Helter Skelter Mural, Caernarfon	53
Llew Llwyfo gravestone, Llanbeblig cemetery	55
Petrol pumps, Groeslon Marc, Llanrug	57
Peace March plaque, Penygroes Memorial Hall	59
Plas Wernfawr, Harlech	63
Coleg Harlech accommodation block	64
Alvin Langdon Coburn plaque, Harlech	66
'Roman Steps', Cwm Bychan	68
Interior Salem, Cefncymerau	70
Ty Cwrn, Bermo	75
World War II 'Dragon's Teeth' coastal defence, Fairbourne	76
St Cadfan's Church, Tywyn	78
'Cadfan Stone', Tywyn	79
Bwlch y Groes	85
St Tydecho, Llanymawddwy	86
Whale bones above south porch, St Tydecho, Mallwyd	89

St Mark's Church, Brithdir, exterior 93

St Mark's Church, Brithdir, interior 94

Pont Dolgefeiliau, Coed y Brenin 96

Tin shed, Llanycil, Arenig 102

Frongoch memorial 105

Thomas Charles statue, Capel Tegid, Bala 197

Tomen y Bala 108

Neuadd Buddug, Bala 109

Bala Lake Railway 110

Owen and Ifan Edwards statue, Llanuwchllyn 113

Llyn Tegid, canoe 114

Llyn Celyn notice 116

Gwynedd Archaeological Trust excavation at Carndochan 118

Gwynedd boundary, Y Berwyn 120

Sheep Dog Trails 1873, memorial, Y Berwyn 121

Nant Gwrtheyrn 127

Tre'r Ceiri, view from summit cairn 132

Rupert Davies gravestone, Pistyll 134

St Beuno, Pistyll, interior 136

Tŵr Nefyn 138

Norman arch, St Hywyn, Aberdaron 140

Anelog Stones, St Hywyn, Aberdaron 14?

Coron Enlli, Storiel 143

The boat to Enlli 144

Plas yn Rhiw 145

Outside double toilet Plas yn Rhiw 146

The harbour, Abersoch 147

St Gwninin, Llandegwning 149

Polish village, Penyberth 153

Capel Salem, Pwllheli 154

Hafan y Môr, Pwllheli 156

David Lloyd George graffiti, Llanystumdwy bridge   157

Cofiwch Dryweryn, Cricieth   159

John Ystumllyn   161

Lawrence of Arabia plaque, Tremadog   162

Gothic arch, St Mary's, Tremadog   166

R.S. Thomas grave plaque, Porthmadog   168

R.S. Thomas shrine, Llanfaelrhys   169

Y Lôn Goed   171

Old school bell, Bwlch Derwin   174

Icorix Stone, Llystyn Gwyn, Bryncir   175

The Llanberis sword created by blacksmith Gerallt Evans   179

Castell Dolbadarn   180

Pete's Eats cafe, Llanberis   181

Craig yr Undeb   184

Pen y Gwryd Hotel   185

Maintaining the Snowdon Ranger path   189

Hafod Eryri, Yr Wyddfa   191

Pitt's Head, Rhyd Ddu   193

Gelert's Grave, Beddgelert   194

Cell B, Blaenau Ffestiniog   197

Wynnes Arms, Blaenau Ffestiniog   198

Ffestiniog Railway   200

Cwm Teigl railway bridge   202

Bwlch (Y Slaters) adit   203

Crimea Pass   206

Portmeirion   207

Carving of Clough Williams-Ellis head, Portmeirion   208

Gwilym Phillips, The Vikings   211

Penrhyndeudraeth Memorial Hall   211

Trawsfynydd Power Station   213

Tomen y Mur   214

ACKNOWLEDGEMENTS

From the outset of this project, Series Editor Peter Finch's continual positive encouragement provided inspiration, focus and signposts for my road trips along the gravel roads of Gwynedd. I also wish to thank Mick Felton and Sarah Johnson at Seren for their support.

Many have been on call to confirm facts, provide further information or to help with various questions. There are too many to mention fully but some went that extra mile. Erwyn J took me underground to visit the World War II Art Stores at Bwlch (Slaters) Quarry. To gain access to this site was amongst the highlights of the whole writing period. Colin on the boat trips over to Enlli both inspired and informed. A more opinionated guide would be difficult to find.

Dr Angharad Price set me on the route to become an archaeology author several years ago and she set me on the trail of T.H. Parry-Williams for this book. Dr Rhian Parry and Hywel Wyn Owen of Cymdeithas Enwau Lleoedd Cymru have been a constant port of call for various place names. Dafydd Whiteside Thomas was another historian who was always at hand to confirm and double check information.

Alwyn Gruffydd provided the facts as opposed to the 'Myths' about Meibion Glyndŵr. Not that I set out to destroy the myths entirely but Alwyn has researched this episode of Welsh history fully. Peggy Williams of Tanygrisiau provided more truths about the Crimea Boot Dump.

Andrew Davidson, David Hopewell, Jane Kenney, Jade Owen and Dan Amor of Gwynedd Archaeological Trust have been a constant source of information and continued discussions about the archaeology of Gwynedd.

Music information has come from Owen 'Cob' Hughes, Alan Holmes, Meurig Jones at Portmeirion and Gwilym Phillips of The Vikings. Another book shouts out to be written here on the history of Gwynedd Music. I am also grateful for the continued support of Gareth Iwan Jones and Dylan 'Dyl' Wyn at BBC Radio Cymru, Bangor.

From a distance, the multifaceted Cerys Matthews was another source of inspiration. Sunday mornings were mostly spent planning the next road trip while listening to Cerys's show on BBC 6Music.

Fellow travellers physically and / or spiritually include Jeb Loy Nichols, Iwan Gwyn Parry, Meirion Ginsberg. Luned Rhys Parri, Catrin Williams, Sion Maffia, White Ether, Lleuwen, Llio Rhydderch, Manon Steffan Ros, Mike Parker, Sian James, Angharad Penrhyn, Claire Holmes (Snowdonia Society), Patrick Jones, Gwyn Awen Meirion, Iwan Cwrw Llŷn, Gwyn Jones Plas Glyn-y-Weddw, Steffan Caffi Ceunant, Y Dyniadon Ynfyd Hirfelyn Tesog.

The following artists were amongst my music soundtrack: Geraint Jarman, Betty Davis, Blodau Papur, both albums by MR, The Cane Toads, Merched y Chwyldro, Huw V Williams, Gruff Rhys, Ani Glass, Adwaith, Los Blancos, Libertino Records, Aleighcia Scott, Carwyn Ellis & Rio 18, John Langford's Men of Gwent, Rufus Mufasa, Stuart Moxham, She's Got Spies, Steve Eaves, 9Bach, Gwenno.

For his words, R.S. Thomas.

Closer to home, Nêst my soul mate, partner, friend and wife was always there to reassure, support and inspire. My teenage sons, Aron and Ilan were too busy listening to great music and hanging out with their mates in the Republic of Cofiland to take any interest in my writing activities and rightly so!

THE AUTHOR

Rhys Mwyn is a musician, archaeologist, writer and broadcaster. Montgomeryshire born, now living in Caernarfon.

As a music manager, agent, publicist, record label owner and promoter, Rhys has worked with acts as varied as Catatonia, Big Leaves, The Rich Kids, Viv Albertine (The Slits), Jeb Loy Nichols, Gwenno, Amy Wadge, Patrick Jones, 9Bach, Larry Jon Wilson, Y Cyrff and Datblygu.

He previously played bass guitar in the Welsh Punk band, Anhrefn. He established the record label Recordiau Anhrefn in 1983 with his brother Siôn in order to release his band's music and to release records by up and coming Welsh acts.

A regular contributor to *Yr Herald Gymraeg* and *Llafar Gwlad*, Rhys has published his autobiography *Cam i'r Tywyllch* (Y Lolfa) and has written three Welsh language books on Welsh Archaeology (Carreg Gwalch).

Rhys currently presents the Monday evening show on BBC Radio Cymru and is a qualified Wales Blue Badge Guide.

INDEX

100 Facts About Harlech 67, 210

A470 8, 15, 69, 84, 92, 94-97, 165, 196, 197
A5 15, 101, 119, 120, 164

Aber 22-23
Aber Cegin (*q.v.* Porth Penrhyn) 34, 46
Abercywarch 85
Aberdaron 14, 125, 135, 139-42, 168; Pont Fawr 142; Porth Meudwy 143; St Hywyn's church 140-42
Aberdesach 124
Aberdyfi 15, 82, 150
Abererch 156
Aberfan 115
Aberffraw 131
Abergwyngregyn 19-23
Abergynolwyn 106
Abersoch 134, 137, 138, 146-50; Glan Soch 149; Zinc Café 147
Aberystwyth and Welsh Coast Railway 72
Ac Eraill 129, 130
River Adda 34, 42
Afon Wen 50, 59, 124, 171
Albin, Tim 37
Alcock, Leslie 140
Altan 170
Llyn Anafon 20, 21
Anafon Valley 19
Andrews, Solomon 150, 153
Anglesey (q.v. Ynys Môn) 18, 131
Anhrefn 23, 24, 25, 41, 65, 81, 95, 100, 197
Anorac 146-47
Antur Stiniog 197
Anweledig 197-98
Aran Benllyn 114
Aran Mawddwy 114
Archwilio 19, 68, 87, 104, 188, 201
Ardudwy 62
Arenig 100-04
Arenig fawr 100
Llyn Arenig 103, 108
Arfon 56, 124
Arfon Council 51
Arrow Stone 20-21
Arthog 75, 150
King Arthur 142, 178-79, 189
Assheton Smith family, of Vaenol 182, 183
Hugh of Avranches 22

Bae Ceredigion 145, 150

Baker, Robert 64-65
Bala 100, 101, 102, 106-09, 113; Arenig Street 107; Awen Meirion 109; Bala Backpackers 106; Capel Tegid 106; Cowbois 109; Heol y Domen 107; Heol Tegid 106; High Street 107, 108; Neuadd Buddug 108; Rhiwlas 105; Theatr Derec Williams 38, 108; Tomen y Bala 107; Ysgol y Berwyn 108
Bala Lake Railway 109-10
Bangor 9, 15, 16, 31-43; Bangor City FC 33, 43; Belle Vue 43; BBC Bryn Meirion 33; Caellepa 33; Cathedral 32, 35-36, 37; Clwb Blewyn Glas 43; Cob Records 34; Crossville Club 43; Dean Street 32, 42; Deiniol Road 34, 40; Garth Pier 33; Garth Road 34; Glanrafon 42; Glanrafon Hill 40; High Street 31-34, 42, 43; Hirael 43; Jazz Room 40-42, 43; Library 33; Lon Las Ogwen 35; Maesgeirchen 33; Y Menai 43; Mount Street 32; Museum 33; Normandie 43; Octagon 42; Old Glan 42; Parc Gegin 32; Penrhyn Arms 34; Pontio 38-40, 42; Railway Institute 43; Rascals 42, 43; Satz 42; The Skerries 43; Storiel 36-38, 142, 151; Stryd y Ffynnon 31; Students' Union 38, 40; swimming pool 33; Tan y Coed 34; Theatr Bryn Terfyl 42; Three Crowns pub 31; Trax 42; University 31, 33, 34, 37, 43; Upper Bangor 34, 42
Bangor Mountain 32, 33
Bannister, Roger 186
Bantock, Granville 201
Bardsey Island (*q.v.* Ynys Enlli) 78, 125, 142
Barmouth (*q.v.* Y Bermo) 71, 76
Barmouth Junction and Arthog Tramway 150
Beaumaris (*q.v.* Biwmares) 18; castle 29
Becket, Thomas 35
Beddgelert 16, 128, 186, 191, 193, 194-95, 208; Gelert's Grave 194; Goat Hotel 194-95; Prince Llywelyn Hotel 195
Bergman, Ingrid 208
Y Bermo (*q.v.* Barmouth) 71-74; Dinas Oleu 72-74; 'Frenchman's Grave' 73-74; High Street 72, St John's church 72; Milk Bar 72; Sailor's Institute 74; Theatr y Ddraig 72, 81; Ty Crwn 74
Berwyn mountains 16, 109, 120-21
Bethesda 15, 24-28, 37, 38, 183; Adwy'r Nant 24; Bwthyn 24-25; High Street 24, 25,

27-28; Neuadd Ogwen 25-26, 81; pubs
27-28
Betws y Coed 102; Royal Oak 102
Big Leaves 209
Billy J. Kramer and the Dakotas 210, 211
Biwmares (*q.v.* Beaumaris) 16
Black, Jack (*q.v.* John Ystumllyn) 160-61
Black Rock Sands 169
Blaen-y-Cae studio 135
Blaenau Ffestiniog 94, 196-98, 202;
Canolfan yr Urdd 197; Cell B 197; High
Street 196, 197; Manod 197; Market Hall
205; Oakley quarry 199, 205; Queens 198;
Wynne Arms 197-98
Bob Delyn 65
Borth-y-Gest 164
Boston Lodge 200
Botwnnog 149
Bowen, Dewi 114
Boyce, Max 8
Brierley, John 67
Britannia Bridge 43-45
Brithdir 92-94; Roman fort 92; St Mark's
church 92-94
British and Foreign Bible Society 106
Bron Heulog 146
Bronaber 94, 96
Bron y Fedw 187
Bryn Cader Faner 82, 100
Bryn Derwen Studio 15
Bryn Derwin 174
Bryn Mawr 91
Bryncir 79, 174, 175-76
Butlin, Billy 156
Bwlch quarry (Y Slaters) 202
Bwlch Derwin 174
Bwlch y Gorddinam 206
Bwlch y Groes 84-87
Bwlch y Gwddel 186
Bwlch Mawr 174
Bwlch yr Oerddrws 88
Bwlch Tyddiad 68-69

Cader Idris 72
Saint Cadfan 77-78, 144
River Cadnant 47
Caer Gai 213
Caer Llugwy 187, 213
Caernarfon 9, 13-14, 16, 31, 47-56, 59,
192; Allt Pafiliwn 51; Bangor Street 51, 53;
Beddgelert Road 55; Capel Pendref 52;
castle 22, 29, 47-48, 55; Cei Llechi 48, 50;
Celtic Royal Hotel 52; Coed Helen tunnel
50; Cwrt Pafiliwn 51; Ffordd Pafiliwn 51; Y

Foryd 14; Galeri 38; Institute 51, 52, 54;
Library 51-52; Y Maes 53; Maes Barcer 50;
Majestic nightclub 52, 55; North Penrallt
51; Pavilion 51-52, 152; Twthill 14, 54;
Roman fort 47; Tanybont 55; Theatr Seilo
51
Caffell, Gwenno: *The Carved Slates of
Dyffryn Ogwen* 38
Cale, John 11, 62
Camelod Fflat 65
Campbell's Platform 200
Canolfan Felin Uchaf 139
Cantre'r Gwaelod 77, 139
Capel Celyn 110, 111, 116
Capel Salem 69-71
Capel Uchaf 125
Carndochan 116-18, 196
Carmel 14, 58
Carndochan
Carn Fadryn 12, 125, 131, 147, 149
Carnedd y Filiast 101
Carneddau Mountains 18
Castell Odo 140
Castell Penrhyn 28-30
Castell y Bere 116-17
Catatonia 14, 41, 65, 170
Cawr Mawddwy 87
Cefn Amlwch 149
Cefncymerau 69
River Cegin 34, 35
Cegin Viaduct 34
Llyn Celyn 110, 115-16
Cenfaes Estate 28
Central Slate 40
Centre for Alternative Technology 83
Cerrig Collwyn 193
Cerrig Hyllion 193
Chamberlain, Brenda 144
Chapman, Sir Thomas 162
Prince Charles 49-50
Charles, Thomas 106
Chester & Holyhead Railway 33
St Christopher 135
Churchill, Winston 157
Ciaran, Cian 126
Cilgwyn 14
Clews, Roy: *To Dream of Freedom* 110
Clowes, Carl: *Nant Gwrtheyrn* 129
Clynnog Fawr 124, 125, 135, 139
Coburn, Alvin Langdon 65-66
Llyn Coch 190
Coed y Bleiddiau 200, 201
Coed y Brenin Forest Park 95-96
Coed Maentwrog 199

Coleg Menai 101
Coleridge, Samuel Taylor 187
Collins, Michael 105
Afon Colwyn 193
Collwyn ab Tango 193
Conwy 16; castle 29
Côr Meibion Y Penrhyn 25
Corbett, John 80
Corris 83-84
Coslett, Dennis 111
Coward, Noël: *Blyth Spirit* 208
Cowbois Rhos Bottwnnog 11-12, 146
Cox, David 102
Craig Rhiwarth 121
Craig yr Undeb 183-85
Crawcwellt 96
Crew, Peter 96
Cricieth 124, 125, 158-59; castle 159;
Memorial Hall 210
Crimea Pass 94, 205-06; Crimea Inn 206;
Esgidiau Meirw Boot Dump 205-06
Crogan Estate 119
Cunnington, Ceri 197
Cut Tunes 40
Llyn Cwellyn 187, 188, 190
Cwm Bychan 11, 68, 103
Cwm Ceunant 101
Cwm Coch 101
Cwm Cynfal 104
Cwm Gwyrfai 187
Cwm Idwal 101
Cwm Maethlon 11, 81-82
Cwm Nantcol 69
Cwm Penmachno 203
Cwm Pennant 156
Cwm Perfedd 101
Cwm Teigl 201-02
Cwm Treweunydd 187, 188
Cwrt 81
Cwt y Bugail quarry 202-05
Cybi: *Cymeriadau Hynod Sir Caernarfon* 170
Cyfanedd quarry 75
Cymer Abbey 97
Cymru'r Plant 112
Cynan (Albert Evans-Jones) 154-55
Y Cyrff 25, 41, 65
River Cywarch 85, 86

Chwilog 124

ap Dafydd, Myrddin 8
Dafydd, Fflur 95
Dafydd ap Gruffudd 174
Dafydd ap Gwilym 180

Daily Post 19, 39
Darby, Abraham 91
River Daron 142
Darwin, Charles 101; *On the Origin of
Species* 101
Datblygu 42, 65, 111
Davidson & Roberts: *Ports and Harbours of
Gwynedd* 50
Davidson, Andrew: *Anarchists and Artists*
62-63
Davies, Hoagie 135
Davies, Dr John 90
Davies, Pete 102
Davies, Rupert 134-35
Davison, George 63, 65-66
Deane, Henry 37
River Dee 113, 119-20
Dee Valley 107, 117
Deganwy Castle 16
St Deiniol 32
Derec Brown a'r Racaracwyr 84
Dewhurst, Antonia 102
Dewi Sant 78
Dewi Wyn o Eifion (David Owen) 170
Dinas 192
Dinas Dinlle 124
Dinas Emrys 128, 195-96
Dinas Mawddwy 84, 88, 94; Y Llew Goch
84; Village Hall 84
Dino and the Wildfires 210
Dinorwic quarry 46, 56, 182, 183, 204
Dinorwic Railway 46
Dolbadarn castle 116, 174, 179-180
Dolgellau 85, 88, 90-91, 94, 161; Cottage
Hospital 94; Eldon Square 91; Siamas 81
Dolgun 91
Dolwyddelan castle 116-17, 196
Dorothea 38; quarry 59
Driver, Toby: *The Hillforts of Cardigan Bay*
132-33
Llyn Du 69
Dugoed 88
Dunn & Suggett: *Discovering the Historic
Houses of Snowdonia* 201
Dŵr Cymru 188
Afon Dwyfach 172
River Dwyfor 9, 156
Afon Dwyryd 164, 199, 208, 209
Afon Dyffryn Gwyn 80
Dyffryn Mymbyr 186
Dyffryn Nantlle (*q.v.* Nantlle Valley) 14
Dyffryn Ogwen 37-38
Afon Dyfi 82, 86, 87
Y Dynion Ynfyd Hirfelyn Tesog 158

Llyn Dywarchen 190

Dduallt 199, 200; Plas y Dduallt 200-01

Eames, Marion: *Y Stafell Ddirgel* 90-91
Eaves, Steve 65, 95
Eben Fardd (Ebenezer Thomas) 170
Ectogram 40
Afon Eden 95, 96
Edern 151
Ednyfed Fechan 30
Edward I 16, 18, 22, 29, 47-49, 174, 180
Edward VII 49
Edwards, David R. aka Dave Datblygu
111-13
Edwards, Ellen 56
Edwards, Ifan ap Owen 112-13
Edwards, O.M. 112-13
Edwards, Phil 130
Eglwys y Gwyddelod 81 82
St Egryn 79
Eifionydd 124, 125, 159, 170-73
Eifion, Alltud: *John Ystumllyn Neu "Jack Black"* 160-61
Yr Eifl 127
Einion Frenin 148
Eldridge, Elsie 168
Elfyn Presli 65, 170
Ellesmere Canal 115
Ellis, Rowland 91
Emlyn, Endaf 124
Emrys aka Merlin 128, 195-96
Enlli (q.v. Bardsey Island) 78, 125, 135,
136, 139, 141, 142-46; John Williams I 142;
John Williams II 142; Love Pritchard 143;
Plas Bach 144; St Mary's Abbey 144, 148;
Swnt Enlli 78, 143
Epstein, Brian 209
Afon Erch 124
Eryri (q.v. Snowdonia) 11, 15, 31, 186
Eternus 151
Eva Stone 36
Evans, Cayo 111
Evans, Colin 143-44
Evans, Gerallt 178-79
Evans, John 43-44

Fairbourne 72, 75-77; Beach Road 75; St
Cynon's church 75; Heol Rowen 76
Fairbourne Railway 77
Fay Ray 15
Felinheli (q.v. Port Dinorwic) 45-47, 174;
Halfway pub 46; marina 46-47; Penscoins
Incline 46

Finch, Peter: *The Roots of Rock* 42
Y Foel 175
Foel Goch 101
Free Wales Army 50, 110-11
Y Friog 72, 75
Frongoch 102, 104-06; internment camp
105-06
Llyn Ffynnon y Gwas 189, 190

Vale of Ffestiniog 164, 198
Ffestiniog Railway 161, 198-201, 204
The Fflaps 40, 41

Llyn y Gadair 190, 912
Ganllwyd 94, 96
Garlick, Iestyn 130
Y Garn 192
Garn Boduan 125, 131, 138, 147
Garndolbenmaen 135
Y Garreg Wen 161
Garth Celyn (q.v. Pen y Bryn House) 23
Gelert 127, 194
George V 97
George, W.R.P. 158
Geraint Lovgreen a'r Enw Daw 95
Gerry and the Pacemakers 210, 211
Get Wet 119
Glan-Llyn 111-13
Glanrafon 119
Afon Glaslyn 164, 193, 194, 200
Glassblobbery 119
Glyderau 19
Glynrhonwy 182-83; quarry 182
Goddard, Stuart 24
Goleuwen quarry 75
Gomer-Lewis, Ethel 135
Gorky's Zygotic Mynci 15, 40, 108
Graves, Alfred Percival 67
Graves, Robert 67
Great Strike (q.v. Streic Fawr) 26, 28, 29
Greaves family, of Caernarfon 161
Griffith, Moses 66
Griffiths, Ellis 187
Grove, Arthur 93
Gruffudd ap Cynan 22, 35
Gruffydd, Margaret 160-61
Gruffydd ap Llewelyn 158-59
Guyard, Auguste 73-74
Gwanas, Bethan 8
Gwenno 115
Gwilym Cowlyd (William John Roberts)
187-88
Gwrtheyrn aka Vortigern 65, 128, 195
Gŵyl Arall 53

Gŵyl y Gwyniaid 108-09
Gŵyl Pen Draw'r Byd 125
Gwylliad Cochion Mawddwy 88
Gwyn, John 15
Gwynant Valley 195
Gwynedd Archaeological Trust 22, 38, 117, 133, 201
Gwynedd County Council 37, 77, 108, 158
Gwynhoedl 151
Y Gyrn 187

Hafod y Gelyn 19-20, 21-22
Hanes Dyffryn Ogwen 28
Harlech 16, 62-67, 100, 209; Bryn Bugeilydd 65; Cae Besi 66; castle 29, 62, 164; Coleg Harlech 63-65, 67; Ffordd Isaf 65; Ffordd Newydd 66; Ffordd Uchaf 66; golf course 65; Morfa Harlech 164; Plas Amherst 63; Plas Wernfawr 63, 66; Queens Hotel 67, 210; St David's Hotel 65, 66; Stryd Fawr 65; Theatr Harlech 66
Harpwood, Cleif 130
Harrison, George 67, 209, 210
Hedd Wyn (Ellis Humphrey Evans) 213-14
Hell's Mouth (q.v. Porth Neigl) 149
Hen Capel
Henddol quarry 75
Hendre Cennin 171
Herald Gymraeg 19, 24
Hergest 84
Hillary, Edmund 186
Holmes, Alan 40-42
Hopewell, David 22-23, 117, 133; Roman Roads in North-West Wales 69
Hopper, Thomas 28, 29
River Horon 149
Hughes, J. Elwyn 24
Hughes, Owen 'Cob' 34
Hughes, T. Rowland 180-81; William Jones 181
Hughes & North: The Old Churches of Snowdonia 20
Huws, Ifan 11
Huws, Iwan 146-47
Hwfa Mon (Rowland Williams) 54

Icorix 175
Ieuan, Dafydd 129
Ifan, Tecwyn 50, 130
Ifans, Rhys 209-10
St Illtud 78
The Inn of Sixth Happiness 208
Innes, J.D. 54, 100-04, 108
Investiture (1911) 49

Investiture (1969) 37, 48, 49-50, 51, 53, 90, 111
Iolo Morgannwg 142, 154
Iovenalis 151
Irvine, Andrew 186
Iwan, Dafydd 8, 49-50

James of St George 48
James, Constance 70
Jecsyn 5 26
Jenkins, John 49, 111
Joan aka Siwan 180
King John 180
John, Augustus 54, 100-04, 107
John Ystumllyn (q.v. Jack Black) 160-61
Johnstone, Neil 22, 23
Jones, Carwyn 44
Jones, Eric 163
Jones, Erwyn 202-04
Jones, Huw 115
Jones, Jack 184
Jones, Col. John 69
Jones, Jonah 113, 142
Jones, Meurig 206-07, 209
Jones, Paul 65
Jones, R. Merfyn: The North Wales Quarrymen 1874-1922 184
Jones, T. James 135
Jones, Thomas 63
Joyce, William 201
Junner, Sarah 162

Keating, Eileen 145, 146, 168
Keating, Honora 145, 146, 168
Keating, Lorna 145, 146, 168
Kennedy, Henry 139
Kershaw, Andy 80-81

Landmark Trust 201
Lavan Sands 18
Lawrence, John 15
Lawrence, T.E. 162-64; Seven Pillars of Wisdom 163
Lee, Bernard 67, 170, 210
Lennon, John 129, 209
Lord Leverhulme (William Lever) 70
Lewis ap Owen 88
Lewis, Robyn 151
Lewis, Saunders 53, 152
Lhuyd, Edward 103
van Lieshout, Joseph 38-39; 'Caban' 39-40
Lion's Head 193
Liverpool 110-11, 115, 116, 127
Y Lôn Goed 171-73

Los Blancos 42
Love Hope Strength 27
Love Jones Parry family, of Madryn 150
Lovgreen, Geraint 125
Lynch, Frances 36, 78, 80; *Gwynedd* 141

Llanaelhaearn 124, 125, 131
Llanbeblig Church 55-56
Llanbedr 69
Llanbedrog 150-51
Llanberis 56, 178-82, 185, 186, 191;
Goodman Street 180-81; High Street 178,
182; quarries 56; Pete's East 180
Llandecwyn 100
Llandegai 32
Llandegwning 149
Llandderfel 119; Llandderfel Horse 119; St
David's church 119
Llanddwyn 131
Llanegryn 79
Llanelltyd 94, 97
Llanengan 148; St Engan's church 139,
148-49
Llanfaelrhys 14; St Maelrhys church 168
Llanfair 66
Llanfairfechan 18
Llanfihangel-y-pennant 106
Llanfrothen, Plas Brondanw 151
Llanffestiniog 94, 104, 201; Pengwern Arms
198
Llangadfan 78
Llangian 148; St Cian's church 148
Llangower 113
Llangwnnadl 135, 139; St Gwynhoedl
church 139, 149
Llanllyfni 56
Llannor 138; Pemprys farm 151
Llanrug 56-57; garej Milwyn 57
Llanrhystud 115
Llanuwchllyn 56, 85, 87, 113, 117
Llanycil 100
Llanymawddwy 85-86, 87, 89; Highgate
cottage 157; Lloyd George Museum 9, 156,
158; Y Plu 158; St Tydecho's church 85-66
Llanystumdwy 9-10, 156-58
Llechwedd quarry 161, 205
Llidardau 102
Llithfaen 124, 131
Lloyd, Richard 156
Lloyd George, David 9, 49, 52, 53, 54,
156-58
Lloyd Price, John 105
Lloyd Price, Richard 105
Llwyfo, Llew 54, 55

Llwyngwril 75
Llyn Llydaw 178
Llŷn 10, 15, 124-25
Llys Rhosyr 22
Llystyn Gwyn 79, 175
Llywelyn Fawr (*q.v.* Llywelyn ab Iorwerth)
22, 108, 117, 118, 127, 196
Llywelyn Fawr o Fawddwy 86-87
Llywelyn ap Gruffudd 18, 48, 90, 117, 118,
174, 179
Llywelyn ab Iorwerth (*q.v.* Llywelyn Fawr)
8, 18, 22, 23, 30, 159, 179, 180, 194

M.A.C. (Mudiad Amddiffyn Cymru) 49,
50, 111
Machynlleth 82, 85
Madocks, William 164-66, 167, 170
Maelgwn Gwynedd 15-16
Maentwrog 94
Maes y Garnedd 69, 71
Maes Gwyn 172
Maffia Mr Huws 24-25
Llyn Mair 199
Mallory, George 186
Mallwyd 8, 16, 84, 85, 88-90, 94; Brigand's
Inn 90; St Tydecho's church 88-89
Manod Quarry 201-05
Martin, George 209
Matlock, Glen 170, 207
Matthews, Cerys 14, 41
River Mawddach 71-72, 76, 96, 97
McCartney, Paul 67, 210
McCulloch, Ian 207
McDougall, Arthur 75-76
McGoohan, Patrick 207
McLaren, Malcolm 100
Megane, Leila 155
Meibion Glyndŵr 136, 137
Meillionydd 140
Meirion, Rhys 163
Meirionnydd 94
Melus 148
Menai Strait 18, 23, 31, 34, 43-45, 47, 57,
133
Merched Chwarel 185
Migneint 100, 103, 104
Mills, Lisa 210
Mim Twm Llai 197
Minffordd 200
Moel Hebog 187
Moel Tryfan quarry 187, 192
Morfa Bychan 161, 169
Morfa Henddol 76
Morgan, William 90

Morris, Jan 10
Morris, William 30, 35
Morris-Jones, Sir John 78-79
Morrison, Van 211
Morys, Twm 10, 65
Mostyn, Sir Thomas 171
Mountain That Had To Be Painted, The 100, 103
Mudiad Adfer 130
Mwyn, Rhys: *Cam i'r Gorffennol* 100, 175
Mynydd Anelog 141
Mynydd Cennin 174
Mynydd Cilgwyn 58
Mynydd Gwylwyr 137
Mynydd Mawr 187
Mynydd Nefyn 136, 137
Mynydd Perfedd 101
Mynydd Ystym 140

Llyn Nadroedd 190
Nant Ffrancon 101
Nant Gwrtheyrn 11, 125-30, 131, 195; Café Meinir 127; National Welsh Language and Heritage Centre 126, 129; Porth yn Nant 127; New Atlantis Commune 128-29; Seilo 127
Nant Gwynant 186
Nant Peris 185
National Gallery 201-05
Llyn Nantlle 190
Nantlle quarry 59, 181, 192, 204
Nantlle Tramway 50, 59
Nantlle Valley (*q.v.* Dyffryn Nantlle) 14, 29, 38, 48, 59, 203
National Trust 28, 29, 45, 72, 142, 145
Natural Resources Wales 199
Nefyn 135, 136-39; Bryn Cynan pub 137; Carreg Lefain 137; Cwrw Llŷn 138-39; Dwyfor Coffee Co. 139; Watch Tower 138
Nelson, Horatio 45
Newborough Estate 142, 182, 183
Nicander (Morris Williams) 170
North, Herbert Luck 92-94
North Wales Highland Railway 48, 161
North Wales Narrow Gauge Railway 187
North Wales Quarrymen's Union 183

Oakley family, of Tan-y-Bwlch 199
Oakley, W.G. 199
Old Grey Whistle Test 81
Offspring 24
Ogof Owain 16
River Ogwen 26, 28
Ordovices 15

Owain Glyndwr 16, 137
Owain Goch ap Gruffudd 174
Owain Gwynedd 22, 35
Owen, Dafydd 161
Owen, Ellis 170
Owen, Huw Wyn 68
Owen, Siân 70-71

Llyn Padarn 57, 178-79, 182, 183
Padarn Railway 46
Paget, Clarence 45
Paget, Henry (first Marquess of Anglesey) 48
Pant Glas 14, 172, 173-75; Lon Eifion 173
Papur Wal 42
Parker, Mike: *Neighbours from Hell* 83
Parry, Harry 33-34
Parry, Iwan Gwyn 100-04
Parry-Jones J. 57
Parry-Jones, Milwyn 57
Parry-Williams, T.H. 191-92
Pearce, Vernon 54
Pedr Fardd (Peter Jones) 170
Peel, John 41, 65, 170
Pen y Bryn House (*q.v.* Garth Celyn) 23
Pen y Bryn Quarry 38
Pen y Gwryd 185-87; Pen y Gwryd Hotel 185-86
Pen y Pass 186
Pen yr Orsedd 14; quarry 59
Penrhyndeudraeth 164
Penllech 135
Penllyn 108, 124-25
Pennant, Douglas 28, 183, 184
Pennant, Richard 28
Pennant, Thomas: *A Tour in Wales* 131
Penrhyn 200
Penrhyn Estate 28
Penrhyn Quarry 26-27, 28-29, 35, 204
Penrhyn Quarry Railway 34
Penrhyndeudraeth 199, 210-11; Memorial Hall 210
Pentrefelin 160-61; St Cynhaearn's church 160, 161
Penyberth 151-53; RAF Penrhos 152; Wakestock 152
Penygroes 58-59; Memorial Hall 58; Victoria Hotel 58
Pep le Pew 135
Llyn Peris 182
Peters, Mike 27
The Peth 209
Philby, Harry St John Bridger 201
Philby, Kim 201

Phillips, Gwilym 210-11
Pierce, Eurwyn 210
Pistyll 125, 134-36; Cae Hosbis 135; St
Beuno's church 134-36
Pitt, William, the Younger 192-93
Pitt's Rock 192-93
Plaid Cymru 152
Plant Bach Ofnus 65
Plas Glyn y Weddw 150-51
Plas Halt 200
Plas Newydd 45
Plas yn Rhiw 14, 145-46, 149
Plas Talhenbont 171
Plwm, Mici 210
Polish Village 152-53
Pont Borth 45
Pont Dolgefeiliau 96
Pont Tai-hirion 103
Pont yr Afon Gam 104
Port Dinorwic (q.v. Felinheli) 45-47
Portmeirion 165, 206-10
Porth Dinllaen 164
Porth Neigl (q.v. Hell's Mouth) 145, 149
Porth Penrhyn (q.v. Abercegin) 33, 34, 46
Pont Rhyd y Porthmyn 103
Pont Rhythallt 57
Pont Saint 57
Pontllyfni 124
Porthaethwy 45
Porthmadog 10, 14, 161, 165, 167-70, 191,
192, 195, 198, 199, 200, 204; Cob 10, 164,
170, 200; Cob Records 10, 34, 170; Y
Ganolfan 170; Queen's Hotel 170; St John's
church 167; Ship & Castle 170; Toll House
165
Potentinus 175
Potter, Gareth 169-70
Povey, Ed 53
Preece, William Henry 56
Prenteg 170; Glaslyn pub 170
Price, Angharad: Ffarwél i Freiburg 191-92
Price, Moses 154, 172
Price, Rhian 68
The Prisoner 207
Pritchard, Caradog 37
Pritchard, David 194-95
Proffwyd 26
Punk, Mickey 24
Pwllheli 72, 124, 125, 153-55; Yr Ala 155;
Cardiff Road 153; Church Place 154; Hafan
y Mor 155-56; marina 152; Neuadd Dwyfor
38, Penlan Street 154; Police Station 152,
155; Promenade 150; Salem 154; Town Hall
155; West End Hotel 150

Pwllheli and Llanbedrog Tramway 150

Quennell, Charles 93

Rawle, Sid 129
Reid, Jamie 101, 129
Robert ap Gwilym Ddu (Robert Williams)
170
Robert of Rhuddlan 22, 47, 48
Roberts, Gorwel 65
Roberts, John 22-23
Roberts, Kate 184-85
Roberts, Mark 65
Roberts, Rhys 197
Roberts, R. Silyn 58
Robeson, Paul 51-52
Rogers, Byron: The Man Who Went Into the
West 169
Roman Steps 11, 68-69, 103
Rowlands, William: Gwyr Eifionydd 170
Ruth, Georgia 15

Rheilffordd Eryri 192
Rhen Eglwys 19-20
Rhinog Fawr 68-69
Rhita Gawr 178, 189
Rhiw 14
Rhiwbach quarry 202-03
Rhiwlas Estate 121
Rhosgadfan 184
Rhoshirwaun 139
Rhyd Ddu 187, 189, 191-93; Caffi Ty mawr
192
Rhyd Uchaf 102
Rhys, Gruff 15, 25
Rhys, Gwilym Bowen 125
Rhys, John 131
River Rhythallt 57

Afon Saint 47, 48, 57
Sarn Mellteyrn 149
Savory, H.N. 195
Scorsese, Martin: Living in the Material
World 67
Sedgwick, Adam 101
Segontium 47, 55, 133, 134, 187, 213
Seithenyn 139
Senacus 141
Sex Pistols 100, 153, 167, 169-70
Shelley, Mary: Frankenstein 162, 166
Shelley, Percy Bysshe 162, 166; Queen Mab
166
Shrewsbury 107
Silyn, Mary 58

Sion, Owen 71
Skevington, Thomas 37
Smith, Patti 91
Lord Snowdon (Anthony Armstrong-Jones) 49
Snowdon 69, 178, 194; Hafod Eryri 190; Llanberis Path 11, 178, 190; Rhyd Ddu Path; Snowdon Ranger Path 187-88, 189
Snowdon Mountain Railway 178
Snowdonia 69, 117
Snowdonia National Park 96, 163, 188, 196
River Soch 12, 147-50
South Caernarfon Creameries 124
Spooner, James 161, 199
Stephens, Huw 147
Stephenson, George 59
Stephenson, Robert 18, 43-45, 59
Stevens, Meic 115
Streic Fawr (q.v. Great Strike) 28
Suggs 207
Super Furry Animals 15, 25, 126, 129, 170, 209
Swn-y-Mor 136

Tabor 91
Tai Cochion 133
Taihirion 104
Afon Taihirion 103
Talsarnau 82
Talysarn quarry 59
Tanygrisiau 197
Tan-y-Bwlch Estate 199
Llyn Tegid 108, 109, 112, 113-15, 117
'Teggie' 114
Telford, Thomas 18, 44-45, 101, 115, 119, 164
Tenzing Norgay 186
Terfel, Bryn 174
Theatr Gwynedd 38, 40, 42
Them 210, 211
Third Spain 40
Thomas, Aneurin 67
Thomas, Dafydd 181
Thomas, Dylan 111, 167
Thomas, Gwydion 168
Thomas, Ifor 9
Thomas, John 43
Thomas, R.S. 10, 14, 111, 145, 151, 167, 172
Toms, Gai 197
Tomos, Rhiannon 15
ap Tomos, Dafydd 150
ap Tomos, Gwyneth 150
Thompson, Richard 35-36

Townshend, Simon 210
Traddodiad Ofnus 169
Traeth Mawr 164
Trawsfynydd 94, 212-14; nuclear power station 202, 212-13; Tomen y Mur 213
Llyn Trawsfynydd 96, 213
Tre'r Ceiri 125, 131-34,
Treborth 43, 45
Trefor 124
Tregarnedd 149; Pwllcoed 149
Tregarth 15
Tremadog 162-67; Tan-yr-Allt 166; Church Street 163, 165; Dublin Road 165; Gorphwysfa 162-63, 164; London Road 165; St Mary's church 165-66; Snowdon Lodge 163, 164; Town Hall 164, 166
Tryweryn 37, 58, 110, 115-16
Afon Tryweryn 105
Turner, J.M.W. 179
Ty Newydd 138
Ty Newydd Writing Centre 9, 10
Ty'n-y-fawnog 71
Ty'n y Mwd 22, 23
Tyddyn y Garreg 91
Tyddyn Gwêr 136-37, 138
Tyddyn Isa Quay 199
Tynal Tywyll 41
Tywyn 77-81, 209; St Cadfan's church 77; Corbett Arms 209; Golden Sands 80; High Street 80; Magic Lantern 80-81; Pier Road 80; Promenade 80; Salt Marsh Kitchen 81; Tywyn Cinema 80

Urdd Gobaith Cymru 112
Uwchmynydd 142

Valentine, Rev Lewis 53, 152
The Vapours 210
Veracius 141
Queen Victoria 30
The Vikings 67, 210, 211
Vosper, Sidney Curnow 69; 'Salem' 69-71
Voteporix 175-76
Lake Vyrnwy 85

Wadge, Amy 15
Walton, George 63
Waunfawr 189
Weller, Paul 207
Duke of Wellington (Arthur Wellesley) 48
Welsh Highland Railway 187
'Welsh Not' 37
Welsh Whisky Distillery Co Ltd 104-05
Whaite, Clarence 102

William, Eurwyn: *Discovered in Time, Treasures From Early Wales* 176
Williams, Bedwyr 39-40
Williams, Catrin 26
Williams, Christopher 54-55
Williams, D.J. 53, 152
Williams, Glyn 'Gwndwn' 67, 210
Williams, Sir Ifor 78-79
Williams, John Llywelyn 28
Williams, Laura 71
Williams, Peggy 206
Williams, Robert 71
Williams-Ellis, Clough 105, 165, 190, 206, 207-09
Williams-Ellis, Martyn 205-06
Williams Parry, Robert 172, 173
Wilson, Henry 92-93
River Wnion 91
Women's Peace Pilgrimage 58-59
Wordsworth, William 72
Workers Education Authority 59, 63-64
Wrench, David 15
Yr Wyddfa 178, 192
Wyn, Dylan 33
Wynne, Ellis 160-61
Wynne family, of Glynllifon 142-43, 182
Wynne family, or Ystumllyn 160-61

Ynys-y-Bugail 76
Ynys Gwylan Bach 142
Ynys Gwylan Fawr 142
Ynys Mon (*q.v.* Anglesey) 18
Ysbyty Ifan 103
Llyn Ystradau 200

Zip World 27